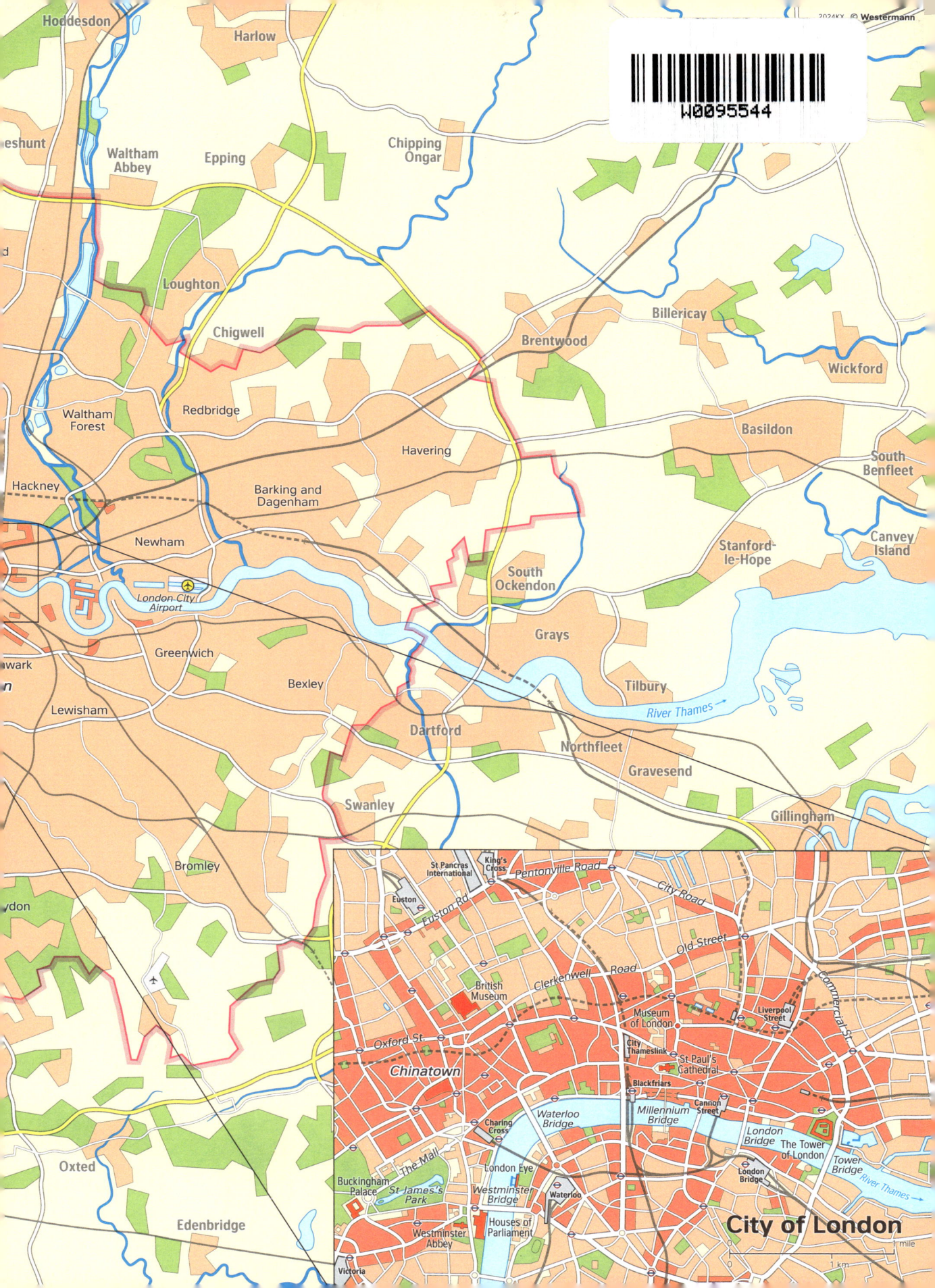

westermann

NOTTING HILL GATE

Textbook 7
Basis-Ausgabe

Erarbeitet von:
Hanna Hoof (Schacht-Audorf), Gabriele Linke (Marburg),
Sascha Mohr (Wiesbaden), Penelope Pedder (Köln),
Maike Pegler (Sarstedt/Gödringen)

sowie Denise Arrandale (Neumünster), Michael Biermann (Hamburg),
Hannelore Debus (Mörfelden-Walldorf), Phil Mothershaw-Rogalla
(Volkmarsen-Külte), Susanne Quandt (Bremen)

Fachliche Beratung:
Martina Pods-Sievers (Ahrensburg), Martin Weber (Wiesbaden)

Story „Jamie and Lucy" von Lisa Fast

Notting Hill Gate 7
Basis-Ausgabe
Textbook

Zusatzmaterialien zu Notting Hill Gate 7

Für Lehrkräfte:
· Textbook für Lehrkräfte 7 (ISBN 978-3-14-128290-0)
· Materialien für Lehrkräfte 7 (ISBN 978-3-14-128296-2)
· Lernerfolgskontrollen 7 (ISBN 978-3-14-128322-8)
· CD für Lehrkräfte 7 (ISBN 978-3-14-128310-5)
· DVD für Lehrkräfte 7 (ISBN 978-3-14-128316-7)
· Online-Diagnose zu Notting Hill Gate 7
  www.onlinediagnose.de

Für Schülerinnen und Schüler:
· Workbook 7 (inkl. Audios) (ISBN 978-3-14-128216-0)
· Interaktive Übungen 7 (WEB-14-128226)
· Arbeitsbuch Inklusion 7 (inkl. Audios)
  (ISBN 978-3-14-128232-0)
· Klassenarbeitstrainer 7 (ISBN 978-3-14-128248-1)
· Grammatiktrainer 7 (ISBN 978-3-14-128388-4)
· Wortschatztrainer 7 (ISBN 978-3-14-128242-9)

Das digitale Schulbuch und digitale Unterrichtsmaterialien für Schülerinnen und Schüler und
für Lehrkräfte finden Sie in der BiBox – dem digitalen Unterrichtssystem passend zum Lehrwerk.
Mehr Informationen über aktuelle Lizenzen finden Sie auf www.bibox.schule.

www.westermann.de/nhg

 DIGITAL+

Alle digitalen Ergänzungen zum Buch erkennen Sie an dem Symbol DIGITAL+.
Dazu zählen Audiotracks, Videoclips, Arbeitsblätter zur Medienbildung, zusätzliche Übungen zu
den Practise-Seiten und Zusatzmaterialien zum Buch. Gehen Sie auf www.westermann.de/webcode
und geben Sie den Webcode WES-128206-001 ein. Sie können auch den QR-Code scannen.

© 2024 Westermann Bildungsmedien Verlag GmbH, Georg-Westermann-Allee 66, 38104 Braunschweig
www.westermann.de

Druck A[1] / Jahr 2024
Alle Drucke der Serie A sind im Unterricht parallel verwendbar.

Redaktion: Doris Bos sowie Lisa Fast und Dr. Katja Nandorf
Vokabelanhang: Doris Bos
Illustrationen: Mario Ellert, Bremen
Umschlaggestaltung: LIO Design GmbH, Braunschweig
Layout: LIO Design GmbH, Braunschweig
Druck und Bindung: Westermann Druck GmbH, Georg-Westermann-Allee 66, 38104 Braunschweig

ISBN 978-3-14-**128206**-1

So arbeitest du mit dem Buch

Im Buch findest du folgende Verweise:

1 audio — Hier gibt es einen Audiotrack, den du auch online abrufen kannst.

2 video — Hier gibt es einen Videoclip, den du auch online abrufen kannst.

3 workbook — Hier siehst du, auf welcher Seite im Workbook es weitere Übungen gibt.

4 wordbank — In den Wordbanks findest du Wörter nach Wortfeldern geordnet.

5 skill — Auf den Skills-Seiten findest du Tipps und Strategien fürs Lernen.

6 grammar — Zu dieser Aufgabe gibt es Erklärungen und Beispiele im Grammatik-Teil.

7 media worksheet — Dieser Hinweis kennzeichnet Aufgaben, in denen du Medienkompetenz aufbaust und trainierst. Zu diesen Aufgaben gibt es Arbeitsblätter, die du über den Webcode oder den QR-Code auf Seite 2 abrufen kannst.

DIGITAL+ practise more — Dieser Hinweis zeigt, dass es zusätzliches Material auf der Webseite gibt.

In den Units gibt es verschiedene Arten von Aufgaben:

8 CHOOSE YOUR LEVEL — Bei diesen Aufgaben gibt es drei unterschiedliche Schwierigkeitsgrade:
I leicht **II** mittel **III** schwierig

9 GET TOGETHER — Hier arbeitest du mit einem Partner oder einer Partnerin zusammen. Entscheidet, wer Partner A und wer Partner B ist und wählt jeweils einen Schwierigkeitsgrad. Geht dann zur entsprechenden Seite und bearbeitet die Aufgabe.

Partner A	Partner B
I Go to page 128.	I Go to page 137.
II Go to page 131.	II Go to page 140.
III Go to page 134.	III Go to page 143.

10 CHOOSE YOUR TASK — Hier gibt es drei Aufgaben, von denen du dir eine aussuchen kannst. Du kannst mit einem Partner oder einer Partnerin oder in einer Gruppe arbeiten.

TARGET TASK — In der Target Task (Zielaufgabe) wendest du an, was du gelernt hast. Du erarbeitest ein kleines Produkt, das du in der Klasse vorstellen und in deinem Portfolio aufbewahren kannst.

Ein ausführliches Inhaltsverzeichnis befindet sich auf den Seiten 248 bis 253.

Lily and Harry Norris

- 13 years old (twins)
- live with their mums, Olivia and Sarah
- used to live in Brighton
- their grandparents live in Bristol
- have got two rabbits, Double and Trouble
- like playing board games
- Lily's hobby is upcycling
- Harry plays the guitar in the school band

Ava Kogan

- 13 years old
- lives with her mum, her dad and her two brothers: Joshua (8) and Noah (14)
- has got a dog, Ollie
- likes skateboarding
- wants to be an engineer when she grows up
- her grandma Edyta lives in Poland

Tarek Adil

- 14 years old
- lives with his dad
- has got an uncle, Sami
- his family is originally from Egypt
- plays hockey in a team
- likes science fiction books and cooking

1. What can you see in the pictures?
2. Which of the foods in the pictures do you like?
3. Have you ever cooked a meal? What was it?

Food

Part A Delicious dishes

· Du unterhältst dich über Essen aus aller Welt.
· Du hörst dir einen Podcast an.
· Deine Klasse stellt ein internationales Kochbuch zusammen.

Part B At a restaurant

· Du liest etwas über einen Restaurantbesuch.
· Du sprichst über Speisekarten.
· Ihr präsentiert in einem Rollenspiel eine Szene in einem Restaurant.

Favourite food

1 workbook p. 4 / 1-2

What do you like to eat? Collect the names of your favourite dishes in class and talk about them.

You can say:

My favourite dish is …

I really like … It's yummy.

spaghetti · pizza · curry · chips ·
pasta with tomato sauce ·
mashed potatoes with sausages · …

Different dishes

2a

Look at the pictures on this double page and talk about them.

You can say:

There is … / There are …

In the first / second / third / fourth picture, I can see …

2b

Read the four texts on this double page. Where are the dishes from?

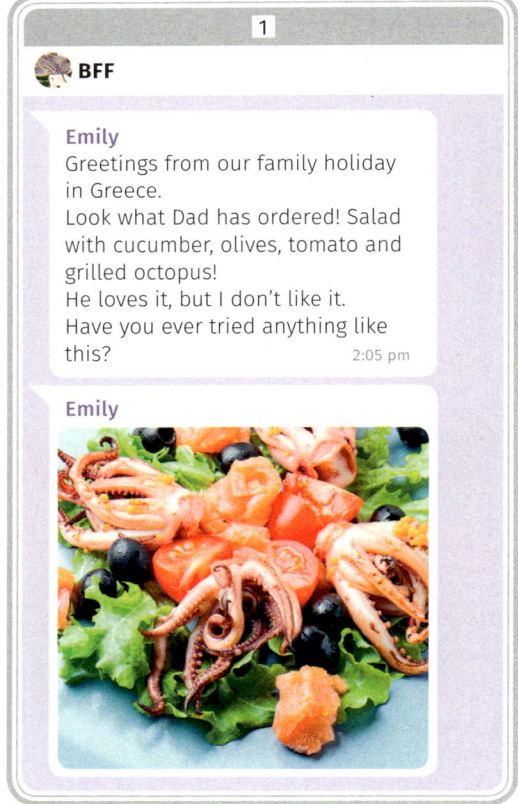

1

BFF

Emily
Greetings from our family holiday in Greece.
Look what Dad has ordered! Salad with cucumber, olives, tomato and grilled octopus!
He loves it, but I don't like it.
Have you ever tried anything like this?   2:05 pm

Emily

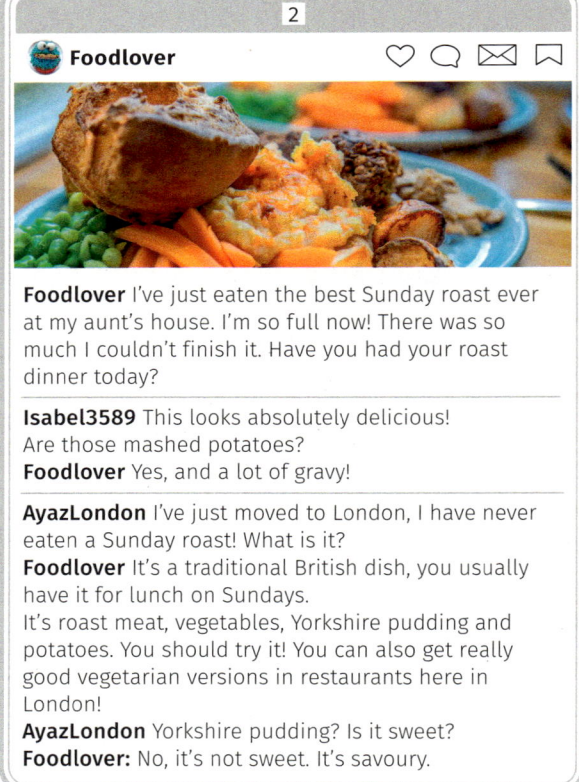

2

Foodlover

Foodlover I've just eaten the best Sunday roast ever at my aunt's house. I'm so full now! There was so much I couldn't finish it. Have you had your roast dinner today?

Isabel3589 This looks absolutely delicious! Are those mashed potatoes?
Foodlover Yes, and a lot of gravy!

AyazLondon I've just moved to London, I have never eaten a Sunday roast! What is it?
Foodlover It's a traditional British dish, you usually have it for lunch on Sundays.
It's roast meat, vegetables, Yorkshire pudding and potatoes. You should try it! You can also get really good vegetarian versions in restaurants here in London!
AyazLondon Yorkshire pudding? Is it sweet?
Foodlover: No, it's not sweet. It's savoury.

ACTIVATE PRACTISE DEVELOP PRACTISE APPLY

3 https://www.katie.co.uk/Berlin-streetfood × –

Berlin street food

KATIE'S BLOG

I spent a week in Berlin in the summer – since then my comfort food has been Lahmacun. I first tried it in Berlin and it was so good! Lahmacun is a thin rolled flatbread filled with minced meat, onions and tomato. It's very spicy. It's a dish from Turkey, but there are similar dishes in many other countries, like Lebanon or Egypt. I've found some places in London where you get good Lahmacun, too!

There's also a German speciality you must try when you are in Berlin: currywurst. You sometimes get currywurst in London, too – but it's not as good as it is in Berlin!

4 https://www.worldfoodfestival/streetfood × –

Fantastic street food at the World Food Festival ∗ ∗ ∗ *by Jason and Laura* ∗ ∗ ∗

Shakshuka

Our number one street food is very popular in Israel and North Africa: Shakshuka. It's a savoury, healthy and vegetarian dish served with flatbread. The tomatoes were really good, the eggs were fresh and there was just a little bit of garlic. All in all: perfect.

2c CHOOSE YOUR LEVEL skill: reading p. 154

I **Unscramble the sentences and write them down.**

1 in Greece. – You can eat – grilled octopus –

2 British dish. – is a traditional – The Sunday roast

3 is – Yorkshire pudding – savoury.

4 Currywurst – German speciality. – is a

II **Match the sentence parts. Write down the sentences.**

1 In Greece
2 The Sunday roast
3 Yorkshire pudding
4 Lahmacun

A is not sweet.
B is a dish from Turkey.
C you can eat grilled octopus.
D is a traditional British dish.

III **True or false? Correct the false statements and write down all the sentences.**

1 In the holiday, Emily's dad had a salad with grilled octopus.

2 You can't get a vegetarian Sunday roast in London.

3 Lahmacun is filled with minced meat, cheese and olives.

4 In Lebanon or Egypt you can find dishes that are similar to Lahmacun.

5 Katie thinks that the currywurst in London is better than the currywurst in Berlin.

2d skill: talking with people p. 152, workbook p. 5/3

Walk around the classroom. Talk to your classmates.

You can ask:

Have you ever tried …?

Have you ever eaten …?

Did you like it?

What was it like?

You can answer:

Yes, I have. / No, I haven't.

Yes, I have. / No, I haven't.

Yes, I did. / No, I didn't.

It was delicious / yummy / disgusting / …

GRAMMAR HELP   the present perfect (R) p. 172-173

Schau dir die Beispielsätze an. Kannst du erklären, wann man das *present perfect* benutzt? Achte besonders auf die Signalwörter *never*, *just*, *not yet* und *already*.

I have never tried a vegetarian roast.	Ich habe noch nie einen vegetarischen Braten probiert.
Dad has just eaten lots of salad. Now he is full.	Papa hat gerade viel Salat gegessen. Jetzt ist er satt.
Mum hasn't finished her salad yet.	Mama hat ihren Salat noch nicht fertig gegessen.
We have already made lunch. It's ready now.	Wir haben schon Mittagessen gemacht. Es ist jetzt fertig.

Auf den Seiten 172 und 173 findest du ausführliche Erklärungen und weitere Beispiele zum *present perfect*. Eine Liste mit unregelmäßigen Verben gibt es auf den Seiten 245-247.

What have they done?

3   grammar: present perfect (R) p. 172, workbook p. 5/4

Unscramble the sentences and write about Ollie and the children.

1 yet. – Ava – hasn't finished – her breakfast
2 yet. – hasn't tidied – the kitchen – Tarek
3 already – eaten – Ollie has – all his food.
4 Harry and Lily – yet. – haven't done – their homework

You can write:
1. *Ava hasn't finished her breakfast yet.*
...

Have you tried Lahmacun?

4   grammar: present perfect (R) p. 172, wordbank: eating and eating out p. 160, workbook p. 5/5

Write about three or more dishes that you have tried.

You can write:
I have tried … and I liked it. It was good. / …
I have tried … and I didn't like it. It was …
It's a savoury / sweet …

Food words

5a   wordbank: eating and eating out p. 160, skill: working with words p. 150

Make a list of English food words that are similar to food words in German or in other languages.

You can write:

English	German	???
tomato	Tomate	…
…	…	…

5b

Work with a partner. Compare your lists and add words from your partner's list.

DIGITAL+ practise more 1-3
ACTIVATE **PRACTISE** DEVELOP PRACTISE APPLY

International week

6a

Look at the web page. What is it about?

https://www.worldfoodfestival/streetfood

Holland Park School Cafeteria
International week
**Next week it's international week at the school cafeteria.
Come and enjoy dishes from around the world!**

MONDAY	TUESDAY	WEDNESDAY	THURSDAY	FRIDAY
Currywurst	Fried noodles	Chicken tikka masala	Vegetarian sushi	Spaghetti bolognese
 *Germany*	 *China*	 *India*	 *Japan*	 *Italy*

6b 🔊 audio 1/1

**Listen to Lily, Harry, Ava and Tarek. What is Lily and Harry's problem?
What do they all decide to do? Take notes.**

6c CHOOSE YOUR LEVEL   skill: listening p. 151

I **Listen again and answer the questions.**

1 Is Harry OK? What is his problem?
2 Who do Lily and Harry meet?
3 What are they talking about?

You can write:

1. Harry is …
2. Lily and Harry meet …
3. They are talking about …

II **Listen again and answer the questions.**

1 What did Harry have for lunch?
2 What did Harry eat for breakfast?
3 What did Lily have for lunch?
4 What is Harry looking forward to?

III **Listen again and answer the questions.**

1 Why is Harry annoyed?
2 Why didn't Harry eat in the cafeteria?
3 Why is Harry looking forward to next week?
4 What does Tarek miss on the menu?

6d workbook p. 6/6-7

Do you have a cafeteria at your school? What is your favourite dish there?

Home cooking

7a 🔊 audio 1/4

Listen and read along. What are the children talking about?

The children are in the kitchen at Tarek's house.

Harry: What could we cook? Have you got any ideas?

Ava: We could make one-pot pasta!

Tarek: What's that?

Ava: You cook everything together in one pot – it's quick and easy and you only have to wash one pot! Noah and I sometimes make it for dinner.

Harry: Quick and easy sounds good – I'm still starving!

Tarek: What do we need? I don't think we have any meat.

Ava: We need pasta, veggies, tomatoes, herbs and spices. Let's see what you've got!

Tarek: All the spices are in the drawer over there. Lily, could you check what there is in the fridge? And could you please get the pasta from the cupboard, Ava?

Lily: There aren't many onions. But there are a lot of carrots and peppers and there's some cabbage. And there isn't much cheese.

Tarek: Ava, do we need any cheese?

Ava: We could add some cheese if you like. Oh, here are cans of chickpeas and tomatoes. But there is not much pasta left … Hm, there's a big jar with small yellow crumbs. What is it?

Tarek: It's couscous.

Ava: What is it like?

Tarek: It's really good, and it's super easy to cook. You just bring water to the boil, add the couscous and some salt, cover it and let it stand for five minutes. We often have it.

Harry: Cool! Can't we cook a dish from Egypt then, Tarek? What do you think?

Tarek: Couscous is NOT from Egypt, but we can try to cook a meal with it.
But I'm not sure how to put it all together and what spices we need.

Ava: Can't we search for a recipe online?

Lily: Sure, wait a second … Ah, here, I've found something. It's a dish from Morocco. And here is a cook-along video. Look, it says we need couscous, veggies, an onion, garlic, chickpeas and a lot of spices.

7b

What is the children's first idea? What do the children decide to cook in the end?

7c CHOOSE YOUR LEVEL skill: reading p. 154, workbook p. 7/8

I Read the dialogue again. Choose the correct words and phrases from the brackets and write down the sentences.

1 One-pot pasta is (quick and difficult / quick and easy).
2 We need (pasta and couscous / pasta and veggies).
3 All the spices (are in the drawer over there / are in the cupboard).
4 There aren't many (tomatoes / onions) and there isn't much (cheese and pasta / fruit and water).

II Read the dialogue again. Complete the sentences and write them down.

1 One-pot pasta is quick and easy and …
2 All the spices are …
3 There aren't many …
4 There isn't much …
5 There are cans of …

III Read the dialogue again. Correct the sentences and write them down.

1 "Noah and I sometimes make it for lunch."
2 "We need pasta, veggies, tomatoes, ketchup and spices."
3 "There aren't many carrots."
4 "Do we need any meat?"
5 "Can't we cook a dish from China then?"

A cook-along video

8a video 1, skill: watching a video clip p. 156

Watch the video clip. What do you have to do after you have put the couscous in the pot?

8b

Copy the following verbs:
chop, cut, heat, slice, cook, enjoy, cover, stir in
Then watch the video clip again and put the verbs in the correct order.

International food

9 **CHOOSE YOUR TASK**   wordbank: eating and eating out p. 160, skill: writing p. 153, C: media worksheet 13

A   Draw your favourite dish and label it.
B   Write and design your dream menu for an international week at your school cafeteria.
C   Write a text message to a friend and describe a dish that you know and like.

Vegan Steven

10a   ▣ audio 1/5

Listen to the limerick. What is it about?

10b

What do you know about vegan and vegetarian food? Collect words.

10c   workbook p. 8/9

Learn the limerick by heart and present it.

> There was a young vegan called Steven,
>
> Who just would not kill for no reason,
>
> This kid would not eat
>
> No cheese or no meat
>
> And he hated the foxhunting season.
>
> *Benjamin Zephaniah*

LAND & LEUTE 1 ▣ video 2

Essen in Großbritannien

Traditionelle britische Gerichte sind *fish and chips* (Fisch mit Pommes frites) und *Sunday roast* (Sonntagsbraten) mit *Yorkshire pudding. Yorkshire pudding* wird aus den gleichen Zutaten wie Pfannkuchen gemacht, man backt ihn aber im Ofen und isst ihn als Beilage zu herzhaften Gerichten.
Das englische Wort *pudding* bedeutet sonst allgemein „Nachtisch".
Einige britische Gerichte haben ungewöhnliche Namen, wie zum Beispiel *toad in the hole* (wörtlich: Kröte im Loch) – Würstchen in einem großen *Yorkshire pudding.*
Bangers and mash (wörtlich: Knaller und Brei) sind Würstchen mit Kartoffelpüree, und *bubble and squeak* (wörtlich: Blase und Quieken) ist gebratenes Kartoffelpüree mit Kohl oder anderem Gemüse.

chicken tikka masala

Neben traditionellem britischen Essen kann man in Großbritannien auch Essen aus aller Welt bekommen. Besonders indisches Essen ist sehr beliebt. Eines der beliebtesten Gerichte ist *chicken tikka masala* – manche Menschen sagen sogar, dass es das Nationalgericht Nummer eins der Briten ist. Es ist ein ursprünglich indisches Gericht, dem eine Soße aus Joghurt, Kokosmilch und einer Mixtur aus verschiedenen Gewürzen *(masala)* hinzugefügt wird.

Hast du schon einmal ein traditionelles britisches Gericht gegessen oder kennst du ähnliche Gerichte?

ACTIVATE   PRACTISE   **DEVELOP**   PRACTISE   APPLY

Dishes with funny names

11a video 3, skill: watching a video clip p.156

Watch the video clip.
Which name do you like best?

11b

Watch the video clip again.
Make a list of the dishes that really exist.
Which dish would you like to try?

11c workbook p.9/10-11

Do you know any dishes with funny names in other languages? Try to translate the names into English. Describe the dishes to the class.

You can say:

In Germany, there is "Arme Ritter".
That's "poor knights" in English.
It is white bread fried with milk and egg.

Foods invented by accident

12a audio 1/8, skill: listening p.151

What do you think "by accident" means? Guess.
Then listen to the first part of the podcast and find out. Were you right?

12b audio 1/9

Listen to the podcast. What foods do the people talk about? Take notes.

12c CHOOSE YOUR LEVEL skill: mediation p.155, workbook p.10/12

A German friend has some questions about the podcast. Read the questions first.
Then listen again and answer your friend's questions in German.

I 1 Wer hat denn das Sandwich erfunden?
　　2 Wer hat das Eis am Stiel erfunden?

II 1 Warum wurde das Sandwich erfunden?
　　2 Wie wurde das Eis am Stiel erfunden?

III 1 Wer hat denn das Sandwich erfunden und warum?
　　2 Wer hat das Eis am Stiel erfunden und wie kam es dazu?
　　3 Was war eigentlich auf dem ersten Sandwich?

Much or many?

13   grammar: quantifiers (R) p.174

Choose the correct word and write down the sentences.

1   I need **much/many** tomatoes for the sauce.
2   Have you got **much/many** favourite dishes?
3   How **much/many** ice cream have you eaten this week?
4   I'd like to go to a restaurant, but I haven't got **much/many** money.

Cookbook language

14a

Complete the sentences with the correct verbs and write them down.

bring · add · cook · wash

1   ??? the water to the boil.
2   ??? the veggies before you cut them.

3   ??? the pasta for ten minutes.
4   ??? some salt.

14b   workbook p.10/13

Read the recipe. Then tell a friend in English how to cook spaghetti.

SPAGHETTI
Nimm pro Person 100-125 g Spaghetti. Koche Wasser mit etwas Salz. Wenn das Wasser kocht, gib die Spaghetti in den Topf. Nach ca. 8 Minuten sind die Spaghetti fertig.

Odd one out

15

Find the odd one out. Make more "odd one outs" with food words for a partner.

1   pot – fork – knife – spoon
2   carrot – potato – banana – onion

3   spices – chickpeas – tomatoes – carrots
4   potatoes – chickpeas – rice – milk

Cooking

16   **CHOOSE YOUR LEVEL**   wordbank: eating and eating out p.160

Copy the word web.

▌   Add two or more words to every branch.

▌▌   Add three or more words to every branch. You can add another category.

▌▌▌   Add four or more words to every branch. Add other categories.

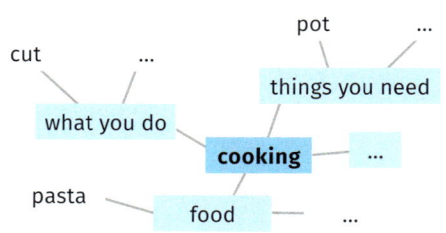

cut   ...   pot   ...
what you do   things you need
cooking   ...
pasta   food   ...

DIGITAL+ practise more 4-5

ACTIVATE   PRACTISE   DEVELOP   **PRACTISE**   APPLY

Our international cookbook TARGET TASK

17 workbook p. 11/14, wordbank: eating and eating out p. 160, media worksheet 1

Your task is to make an international cookbook in your class.
Before you start, look at these steps:

STEP 1

In class, decide what kind of cookbook you want to create: a book, a digital cookbook, …

STEP 2

Work with a partner or in small groups. Think of dishes from different countries.
Then choose a dish, for example:
- a family recipe
- something you have tried in a restaurant
- something you have eaten on holiday
- …

STEP 3

Find an English name for the dish or write down the original name.
Then find a recipe for the dish.

STEP 4

Make a list of ingredients. Write down how to prepare your dish.
You can add a photo for each step or even make a tutorial.

STEP 5

Put all the recipes together in your cookbook.
If you like, sort the recipes in your cookbook: starters, main courses, desserts.
Try them out! You can organize a class party and serve your dishes!

COUSCOUS for two people

Ingredients:
- *olive oil*
- *1 red onion*
- *3 red or yellow peppers*
- *1 carrot*
- *garlic*
- *1 can of chickpeas*
- *½ teaspoon of: paprika, coriander, cumin, cinnamon*
- *cayenne pepper, salt and pepper*
- *1½ cups of vegetable stock*
- *1 cup of couscous*

Wash the vegetables and cut them.
Chop the onion and slice the garlic.
Heat the olive oil and cook the vegetables.
Add the spices and the vegetable stock.
Cook until the vegetables are soft.
Add the couscous.
Take the pot from the cooker, cover it and let it stand for five minutes.
Enjoy!

Restaurants in your area

1   workbook p. 12/1

What kinds of restaurants are there in your area? Talk about them.

You can say:

There is an Italian restaurant in my area.
You can eat … there.
… is the best …

Italian · Greek · Turkish · Vietnamese · Thai · …

fast food restaurant · takeaway · …

Restaurant reviews

2a

Look at the pictures. Which restaurant would you like to go to? Which restaurant would you not like to go to? Why?

You can say:

I would like to go to … because I like …
I wouldn't like to go to … because I don't like …

2b   skill: reading p. 154

Now skim the reviews. Which restaurant would you like to go to now? Say why.

Sushi Blue

It's not cheap, but the food is very good!
The fish is the freshest that I've ever tasted.
The service is very quick and friendly. It is
more expensive than other sushi restaurants
in the area, but you get better quality.

I would go again.

Pizza Extra Notting Hill

Stay away from this restaurant!
I had the worst pizza I've ever had in my life.
It was burnt, the vegetables were disgusting and
the service was terrible! I waited over an hour
for the most disappointing pizza I've ever had.
My friend's pizza was as bad as mine.

We will never go back.

    × −

The Taj Mahal

This place has the hottest curry you can find in London!

The vindaloo curry was so spicy that I could not finish it.

Even the vegetable korma was a bit too hot for my children. We had to add lots of yoghurt to finish our food. But the rice was perfect and the naan bread was yummy.

Only go there if you like *really* hot food!

    × −

The Black Horse

Very nice atmosphere, food OK, but not as good as the food we ate at The King's Head in North London the day before.

My fish was a bit overcooked, but the chips were delicious. My wife had a very juicy veggie burger with a side of chips.

The large choice of desserts was great.

The pub is cosy – we stayed for two hours and could have stayed longer!

The pub also has a beautiful garden where children can play.

2c   CHOOSE YOUR LEVEL

I   **Read the first two reviews and take notes. What did people like at Sushi Blue and Pizza Extra? What did they not like?**

II   **Read the first three reviews and take notes. What did people like at Sushi Blue, Pizza Extra and The Taj Mahal? What did they not like?**

III   **Read the four reviews and take notes. What did people like at these restaurants? What did they not like? Which restaurant do you think is the best and which is the worst? Why?**

2d   skill: talking with people p. 152

What does a good restaurant need? Collect ideas. Talk to a partner.

You can say:

I think a good restaurant must offer …

In my opinion, a good restaurant should …

… is important to me.

GRAMMAR HELP the comparison of adjectives (R) p. 175

Erinnerst du dich noch daran, wie man im Englischen Dinge oder Personen miteinander vergleichen kann? Schau dir die Beispiele an und erkläre, wie die Formen gebildet und verwendet werden.

The food at Sushi Blue is fresher and more expensive than the food at Pizza Extra.	Das Essen bei Sushi Blue ist frischer und teurer als das Essen bei Pizza Extra.
The fish is the freshest that I've ever tasted. Sushi Blue is the most expensive sushi restaurant in the area.	Der Fisch ist der frischeste, den ich je probiert habe. Sushi Blue ist das teuerste Sushi-Restaurant in der Gegend.
My friend's pizza was as bad as mine.	Die Pizza meines Freundes war so schlecht wie meine.

Auf Seite 175 findest du weitere Beispiele und Erklärungen zur Steigerung von Adjektiven.

Tasty food

3a   grammar: comparison of adjectives (R) p. 175

Compare different kinds of food. Write three or more comparisons with 'than' or 'as … as'. You can look at the box for help.

> as tasty as · tastier than · as good as ·
> better than · as fresh as · fresher than ·
> as delicious as · more delicious than ·
> healthier than · spicier than · …

You can write:
Hot dogs are as tasty as …
… are tastier than …
…

hot dog	chicken curry	salad	vegetable soup	???

3b   grammar: comparison of adjectives (R) p. 175, wordbank: eating and eating out p. 160, workbook p. 12/2-4

Write three or more statements about your favourite food or restaurant. Look at the box for help.

> the tastiest · the best · the freshest ·
> the most delicious · the healthiest ·
> the spiciest · the cheapest · …

You can write:
The pizza at … is …
It's … restaurant I know.
The restaurant has … food in our area.

Where is the stress?

4a 🔊 audio 1/11

Listen to the words and repeat them.

> perfect · dessert · vegetable · disgusting ·
> expensive · restaurant · beautiful · delicious

4b

Is the stress on the first or the second syllable? Make two lists.

first syllable	second syllable
perfect	*dessert*
…	…

🔲 **DIGITAL+** practise more 6-7

ACTIVATE   **PRACTISE**   DEVELOP   PRACTISE   APPLY

Making plans

5a  audio 1/12

**Listen to Ava's mum Fiona talking to
Grandmother Edyta.
What are they talking about?**

5b CHOOSE YOUR LEVEL   skill: listening p. 151

I **Listen again. Then match the sentence parts and write the sentences in your exercise book.**

1 The family is planning to
2 Grandma Edyta wants to
3 They don't want to go to
4 They decide to go to

A an Indian restaurant.
B a Chinese restaurant.
C go to a restaurant.
D try something different.

II **Listen again. Are the statements true or false? Take notes. Then copy the true statements
into your exercise book.**

1 The family is planning to go to a
   restaurant on Wednesday evening.
2 Grandma Edyta is allergic to raw fish.
3 Sushi is Grandma Edyta's favourite food.
4 Joshua loves Turkish food.

5 There is a Chinese restaurant on
   Portobello Road.
6 Edyta likes the Indian restaurant
   near the station.

III **Listen again and take notes. Then correct these statements.**

1 The family is planning to go to a
   restaurant on Tuesday evening.
2 Fiona is allergic to raw fish.
3 Grandma Edyta would like to go to a sushi
   restaurant.

4 Joshua loves Turkish food.
5 Fiona suggests a Vietnamese restaurant
   on Portobello Road.
6 The Indian restaurant doesn't have many
   vegetarian dishes.

5c   wordbank: eating and eating out p. 160, workbook p. 14/5

**Is there a restaurant you and your family
go to on special occasions?
Or do you prepare something special to eat?
Tell your class about it.**

You can say:
We always go to ... on my dad's birthday.
My mum always cooks ... when ...
...

ACTIVATE   PRACTISE   **DEVELOP**   PRACTISE   APPLY

At The Palace of India – part one

6a   wordbank: talking about pictures p. 166, grammar: present progressive (R) p. 176

Look at the picture. What are the people doing?

You can say:

The waiter / Ava / … is …

The guests / The Kogans are …

arriving · smiling · looking at ·
eating · drinking · showing · …

6b   audio 1/13

Listen to the dialogue and read along. What food does everybody order?

Waiter: Good evening and welcome to The Palace of India. Have you got a reservation?

Mrs Kogan: Hello, yes, the name is Kogan – a table for six.

Waiter: Certainly. Let me show you to your table. Please come this way. Take a seat.

***

Waiter: Here are your menus. Today I can recommend a tikka masala with salmon and home-made mango ice cream for dessert. Can I bring you some drinks to start with?

Mr Kogan: We'd like to look at the menu first, but can we please have a bottle of water for the table?

Waiter: Of course. I'll be back in a minute with your water and I'll take your order.

***

Waiter: So, have you decided what you would like to eat?

Mrs Kogan: Yes, two vegetable kormas for the boys and a chicken tikka masala for me, please. What are you having, Edyta?

Edyta: I'd like the tikka masala with salmon please, with rice on the side.

Waiter: What about the others?

Ava: I'm starving! I'll have the butter chicken with rice *and* some naan bread, please.

Waiter: Of course. And for you, sir?

Mr Kogan: I'll have the lamb vindaloo, please.

Waiter: Just to warn you, our vindaloo is extremely spicy.

Mr Kogan: I love hot food! I'll be OK.

Waiter: OK, great.

6c   workbook p. 14/6-7

These sentences are not very polite. Rewrite them in a more polite way. Look at the text for help.

1   Your table is over there. Sit down.

2   Do you want a drink?

3   We want a bottle of water.

4   What do you want to eat?

The menu

7a

Read the menu of The Palace of India. What do they serve with all main courses?

```
┌─────────────────────────────────────────────────────────────────────┐
│                                                                       │
│  DRINKS                                                               │
│  Lemonade, cola, mineral water ............................... £2.20  │
│  Mango lassi (a cool yoghurt drink) .......................... £3.00  │
│                                                                       │
│  STARTERS                                                             │
│  Poppadoms (fried chickpea crackers) with a selection of dips £1.85   │
│  Onion bhaji (golden fried onions) ........................... £2.30  │
│  Vegetable samosa (fried pastry filled with potatoes and vegetables) £3.95 │
│                                                                       │
│  MAIN COURSES  *** We serve all main courses with rice or naan bread. *** │
│  Butter chicken (chicken cooked in a mild sauce with garlic, tomato and coriander) £10.95 │
│  Korma (a mild curry with coconut cream)                              │
│  Choose from vegetable, lamb or chicken. ..................... £13.95 │
│  Tikka Masala (a curry with ginger, tomato, coriander and chilli)     │
│  Choose from vegetable, lamb, chicken or fish. ............... £13.95 │
│  Vindaloo (our hottest curry with lots of chilli)                     │
│  Choose from vegetable, lamb or chicken. ..................... £9.95   │
│  Palak paneer (soft cheese in a spinach curry) ............... £7.95  │
│  Mixed kebab plate (grilled lamb, chicken and beef with salad) £11.95 │
│                                                                       │
└─────────────────────────────────────────────────────────────────────┘
```

7b   CHOOSE YOUR LEVEL   skill: mediation p. 155

I You are at The Palace of India with your grandmother. Answer three of her questions in German.

II You are at The Palace of India with your grandmother. Answer five of her questions in German.

III You are at The Palace of India with your grandmother. Answer her questions in German.

1 Was ist ein *mango lassi*?
2 Was gibt es denn alles als Vorspeise? Ist da etwas ohne Zwiebeln dabei?
3 Bekommt man auch was zum Hauptgericht dazu, Kartoffeln oder so?

4 Welche Vorspeise ist vegetarisch?
5 Was genau ist ein *vegetable samosa*?
6 Was ist eigentlich *butter chicken*? Ist da wirklich nur Butter in der Soße?
7 Gibt es ein besonders scharfes Gericht?

7c

You have £20 to spend. What would you order? Make notes and talk to a partner.

At The Palace of India – part two

8a audio 1/14

Listen to the rest of the dialogue and read along. Who has not finished his or her food? Why?

Waiter: Is everything OK with your food? Can I get you any more drinks?
Noah: Really yummy, thank you.
Mrs Kogan: Yes, it's really good.
Mr Kogan: I'll have another mango lassi, please!
Waiter: Of course.
Mrs Kogan: How is the vindaloo?
Mr Kogan: It is really spicy!
Edyta: Are you OK?
Mr Kogan: Yes, yes, very good!

* * *

Noah: I can't eat anymore. I'm full already! I'll have to leave the rest. Do you think I can take it home?
Edyta: I'm sure that will be OK. Sebastian, you haven't finished either! Was it too spicy for you?
Mr Kogan: Umm, no, err … I just … I'm getting full. But I think I'll have just one more mango lassi …

* * *

Waiter: Would you like to see the dessert menu? We also have teas and coffee.
Mrs Kogan: No, thank you very much. We've all eaten too much already.

Mr Kogan: Can we get the bill, please?
Waiter: Of course. I'll be back in a minute. Would you like to pay with cash or card?
Mr Kogan: Card, please.
Waiter: OK. Just a minute. I'll bring the card machine over.

***

Edyta: What a great meal, thank you!
Mrs Kogan: I'm happy you enjoyed it!
Mr Kogan: And the mango lassi is really excellent.
Mrs Kogan: We can take some home if you need some more …

8b wordbank: eating and eating out p. 160, skill: writing p. 153, workbook p. 16/8-10

After the trip to the restaurant, Ava texts her friends. Write down three or more sentences.

You can write:
Hi guys, I'm just back from The Palace of India.
The food was …
I had …
Dad had …

ACTIVATE PRACTISE **DEVELOP** PRACTISE APPLY

Ordering food

9 **GET TOGETHER**   workbook p.17/11

Get together with a partner.
Decide what you would like to order.

Partner A
| Go to page 128.
|| Go to page 131.
||| Go to page 134.

Partner B
| Go to page 137.
|| Go to page 140.
||| Go to page 143.

Eating out

10 **CHOOSE YOUR TASK**   wordbank: eating and eating out p.160, C: skill: writing p.153, media worksheet 9, workbook p.17/12

A Write a menu for your dream restaurant.
B Collect useful phrases that you need when you are at a restaurant.
C Write about a good or a bad restaurant experience. It can be a real experience or you can make one up. You can look at 2b on pages 18 and 19 for help.

A

STARTER
small muffins and chocolate soup

MAIN COURSE
chocolate cake with strawberries

DESSERT
ice cream with chocolate sauce

B

Eating out

Could I have a ..., please?

I would like the ..., please.

What is ...?

Can I have chips with my burger?

A difficult customer

11a   video 4, skill: watching a video clip p.156

Watch the video clip. What is happening?

11b

What do you think the lady is going to eat in the end? Collect ideas.

11c   skill: writing p.153, workbook p.18/13

Later that evening the waiter and the lady both send text messages to a friend.
Choose one of them and write his or her text message.

You can write:
Guess what happened to me today. I ...
Can you believe what ...? I ... Then ...

What is going on?

12   CHOOSE YOUR LEVEL

I   Look at the pictures and read the texts. Are the people happy or not?

You can say:

I think, the … in picture … is …

II   Look at the pictures and read the texts. Then match the captions to the pictures.

You can say:

Picture … matches caption …

| A A disgusting experience | B Waiting for my lunch | C Sitting next to a famous person |

III   Look at the pictures and read the texts. Then choose one picture and think about what could happen next. Make notes.

Sorry, will be late. I'm still sitting here waiting for my lunch.

OMG! I can't believe that I'm having dinner at the same restaurant as Preppy Rappy!

So disgusting! I found a spider in my soup!!! But I'm getting a free dessert now.

At the restaurant

13a   skill: mediation p. 155

You are at a restaurant with your family. Two English-speaking tourists at the table next to you ask you for help with the German menu. Can you help them?

Tourist: We would like soup, one vegetarian main course and one with meat. We'd also like a dessert!

You: Then you could order …

13b   skill: performing a scene p. 159, workbook p. 18/14

Take notes and act out the conversation with a partner. Remember to be polite.

Ratsstübl

Vorspeisen und Suppen
Kleiner bunter Salat
Kartoffelsuppe
Tomatensuppe

❦

Hauptgerichte
Schnitzel mit Bratkartoffeln
Backfisch mit Salzkartoffeln
Spaghetti Bolognese
Bratwurst und Kartoffelpüree mit Salat
Gemüselasagne
Grillgemüse mit Käse überbacken

❦

Nachtisch
Erdbeerkuchen
Vanilleeis mit heißen Früchten

 DIGITAL+ practise more 8

ACTIVATE   PRACTISE   DEVELOP   **PRACTISE**   APPLY

Our restaurant role play TARGET TASK

14 workbook p. 19/15, wordbank: eating and eating out p. 160, skill: performing a scene p. 159, media worksheet 2

Your task is to present a scene at a restaurant. Before you start, look at these steps:

STEP 1
Get together in small groups and plan your role play. Decide:

- What type of restaurant is it?
  (A fast food restaurant, a very expensive restaurant, a takeaway, …?)
- What can you eat there?
- Who are your characters? What are they like?
- …

STEP 2
What is going to happen in your scene? Will it be a good or a bad experience?
Think of an unusual event, for example:

- someone finds something disgusting in their food
- someone famous visits the restaurant
- something funny happens
- …

STEP 3
Decide who will play which part.

STEP 4
Make notes for your role play. Collect words and phrases you will need.
You can write cue cards for each character.

STEP 5
Practise your role play. You can use props or costumes if you like.

STEP 6
Perform your scene. If you like, you can film your scene and show it to the rest of the class.

Check out

Kannst du einen Blogeintrag zum Thema Essen verstehen?	Workbook, p. 20
Kannst du ein Gespräch zum Thema Kochen verstehen?	Workbook, p. 20
Kannst du über Gerichte sprechen, die du schon einmal probiert hast?	Workbook, p. 20
Kannst du wichtige Redewendungen, die man bei einem Restaurantbesuch braucht?	Workbook, p. 21
Kannst du jemandem sprachlich aushelfen, der eine Speisekarte nicht versteht?	Workbook, p. 21
Kannst du einen kurzen Text über ein Restaurant schreiben?	Workbook, p. 21

Delicious disaster

1 Hi, I'm Jamie and this is my sister Lucy. We live with our mum and dad.

Well, he's not our *real* dad, but he behaves like one and we like him a lot.
5 Our mum met him when I was three and Lucy was one.

Mum's a hairdresser. She works in the city centre and she's really good. Dad sells fridges.

10 Last week, Dad's sister Sally came to our place for dinner. We like her very much, she's really cool.

That morning Mum said, "Tonight is going to be very busy. I've got a lot to do at work today, and Dad won't be home before seven. You'll have to let Sally in and then we'll order some pizza
15 as soon as I'm home." Both my parents are quite bad at cooking so we order in a lot. Or get takeaways. But we're all really good at making sandwiches.

When I came home from school that day, no one was there and I went to the kitchen to get a snack. While I was looking for some snacks, I found this really fancy cookbook Mum has: *French kitchen: 300 traditional recipes.* I looked through it and there were lots of pictures of really yummy-looking
20 food. The last part of the book was *Suggestions for menus.* There were ideas for three-, four- and even twelve-course menus!!!

Just at that moment Lucy came home and found me staring at the cookbook.
"What are you doing?" she asked and looked at
25 the cookbook. "Oh, that looks yummy. Why do we never have anything like that?" At that moment I had an idea. "Lucy," I said. "Why don't we cook our dinner for tonight? "But we can't cook," Lucy said.
30 "Well, that's what cookbooks are for," I said. "You have to start somewhere – look at that four-course meal with chicken. It doesn't look too difficult. Mum makes chicken nuggets all the time."
35 "OK, let's try it," Lucy said. "What do we do first?"

disaster = *Katastrophe;* fancy = *nobel;* course = *Gang;* four-course-meal = *Vier-Gänge-Mahlzeit*

I looked at the cookbook. "I think we'll have to go shopping first," I said. "Let's take the pizza money." So we went shopping. To our great surprise, salad for the first course, some cheese and tomatoes for the second course, a chicken, potatoes and vegetables for the main course and fruit and cream for the dessert were cheaper than our usual pizza dinner.

40 "Right, let's do this," I said when we got home. "You could start peeling the potatoes. I'll prepare the chicken." "Alright," Lucy said and started to peel the potatoes.

About half an hour later the kitchen looked like a battlefield.

There was not much left of the potatoes, but we had lots of peels. I was still trying to cut the chicken, but it didn't look right. On the pictures in the cookbook there was a lot less blood and mess.

"Maybe you could start whipping the cream for the dessert," I told Lucy. "OK," she said and took out the mixer.
Big mistake! Lucy was as bad at whipping cream as she was at peeling potatoes. The cream went everywhere!
When Sally arrived at half past six, we hadn't even started with the first two courses yet … There was food everywhere, and I was still holding the knife. Sally laughed so hard she almost cried.

We explained our plan to her and she said: "Oh, that's a lovely idea. But I don't think we have
60 enough time for that now. Why don't we do that another day? We can quickly make some pancakes for tonight. And maybe we should clean the kitchen first?"
She started laughing again.
So we cleaned the kitchen and Sally showed us how to make pancakes. With her help it was quite easy and we managed not to make any more mess.

65 When Mum and Dad came home, the kitchen was clean and there were lots of pancakes on the table. Mum and Dad were so surprised!
We all sat down and had a lovely pancake dinner. I ate five, Lucy ate three and Dad ate twelve!!!
"That was sooooo good. Thank you guys," Mum said.
"Maybe you can do the cooking from now on. Then we wouldn't always have to eat takeaways or
70 sandwiches."
"That's a brilliant idea, dear," Dad said and licked his fingers. "They could learn to prepare some more dishes. Something with chicken maybe. Chicken's not too difficult."

surprise = *Überraschung*; peel = *schälen, Schale*; battlefield = *Schlachtfeld*; mess = *Unordnung*; whip cream = *Sahne schlagen*; hadn't even started = *hatten noch nicht einmal angefangen*; manage = *es schaffen*; lick = *ablecken*

Curious about curry?

Curry is a traditional dish in many countries such as India, Pakistan and Bangladesh. The word 'curry' comes from the word 'kari' meaning 'sauce' in Tamil – a language spoken in South India and other parts of Asia.

There are many types of curries. They can be very spicy or mild, but they all use a combination of spices.
In most curries you find chillies, coriander, cumin and turmeric. Many curries also include ginger, cardamom and garlic. A mix of some of these spices also goes into curry powder, a spice mix very popular in the Western world.

So why is curry – and Indian food in general – so popular in the UK today? In the 17th century, Britain and India started trading goods like spices and tea.
At that time in Britain, Indian spices were very expensive, and only rich people could buy them.

In the 18th and 19th centuries, British influence in India grew, and the British East India Company, which controlled large parts of trade in India, became more and more powerful.

In 1858, India officially became a British colony until it became independent in 1947. Many people from India have moved to Britain and brought their culture and eating habits with them.
Today there are thousands of Indian restaurants all over the country.

curry powder

curry

a spice and tea stall
at a market in India

United Kingdom

India

Find out more about an Indian dish or spice and report your findings to the class.

1. Look at the pictures. What are the people doing?
2. What is important for a healthy lifestyle?
3. What sports do you like?

Healthy living

Part A Keeping fit

- Du unterhältst dich über verschiedene Sportarten.
- Du hörst dir ein Interview an.
- Du sammelst und präsentierst Tipps für einen gesunden Lebensstil.

Part B At the doctor's

- Du sprichst über Gesundheitsthemen.
- Du siehst dir ein Video darüber an, wie man jemanden aufheitert, der krank ist.
- Du stellst ein Rollenspiel vor.

What's the right sport for you?

1a

Answer the questions to find out: what could be a good sport for you?

1 Do you like playing games?

    A Yes, I do.
    B No, I don't.

2 Do you like ball sports?

    A Yes, I do.
    B No, I don't.

3 Where do you prefer to be?

    A Indoors.
    B Outdoors.

4 Do you like water sports?

    A Yes, I do.
    B No, I don't.

5 Are you a good loser?

    A Yes, I am. I don't care if I win or lose.
    B No, I'm not. I get really angry.
    C I'm not, but I try not to show it.

6 Do you prefer doing sports in a team or do you prefer being on your own?

    A I prefer doing sports in a team.
    B I prefer being on my own.

Different sports:

Water sports:	swimming · diving · rowing · …
Team sports:	football · hockey · basketball · American football · …
Sports you can do on your own:	marathon · darts · yoga · running · weight training · climbing · …

1b workbook p. 22/1–3

Work with a partner. Talk about what you think could be a good sport for you. Take turns.

You can say:

I like … I think … could be a good sport for me.
I prefer … so I think … is a good idea.
I don't like … but I think …
…

Finding the right sport

2a skill: reading p.154

Scan the profiles and find out:

1 Who loves being in nature?
2 Who likes maths?
3 Who does not like being alone?

Hi, I'm Kristin. I love being active. I'm not good at sitting still. I like spending time outside with my friends – that makes me really happy. I don't like being alone. Having people around me is very important to me.

Hi, I'm Ben. I like to choose when and where I train. I don't really like team sports because I like being on my own.
I love spending time in nature. It feels great to reach a goal just by using my own skills and strengths. Living a healthy life is important to me so I try to eat healthy food in order to stay fit.

Hi, I'm Amira. I don't like big groups of people. I prefer being indoors – on my own or with my best friend.
I'm not much of an outdoor person.
My favourite subject at school is maths. I'm good at logical thinking and solving puzzles. I'm not a very good loser. It makes me really angry when I'm not the best at something.

2b CHOOSE YOUR LEVEL   wordbank: keeping fit p.162

I **Read Kristin's profile. What does she like? What does she not like? Take notes. Look at 1a again. What could be a good sport for her?**

You can write:
Kristin likes being …
Kristin doesn't like being …
… could be a good sport for her.

II **Read Ben's profile. Take notes on what he likes and what he does not like. Write down what could be a good sport for him.**

You can write:
Ben likes being … He doesn't like …
I think … could be a good sport for Ben
    because he likes …

III **Read Amira's profile. Take notes on what she likes and does not like. What is she good at? Think of a good sport for her and write her a short message.**

You can write:
Hi Amira, you say that you like …
… could be a good sport for you because …
You don't like … so maybe …
…

GRAMMAR HELP   the gerund p. 177

Die *ing*-Form von Verben hast du schon beim *present progressive* kennengelernt, wie etwa in diesem Satz: *The children are playing football.* Schau dir nun folgende Sätze an. Wie werden die *ing*-Formen hier benutzt?

Swimming keeps you fit.   (Das) Schwimmen hält dich fit.
Do you like diving?   Magst du Tauchen? (= Tauchst du gerne?)
I'm good at climbing.   Ich bin gut im Klettern.

In diesen Fällen nennt man die Formen *gerund*. Auf Seite 177 findest du weitere Beispiele und Erklärungen.

A sport for Matilda

3   grammar: gerund p. 177, workbook p. 23/4

Read what Matilda said and copy it.
Complete it with the words from the box.

swimming · playing ·
sitting · going ·
spending · running

I don't like ??? at home. I want to find a sport that I really like. I've tried ???, but I stopped ??? to the pool after a few weeks.
Maybe a team sport is better for me. I'm really good at ??? fast and I prefer ??? time outside. How about ??? rugby? Do you think it's a cool sport?

Doing sports

4   grammar: gerund p. 177, workbook p. 23/5

What do you think about different sports and activities? Write four or more sentences.
You can use words from the boxes.

You can write:
I think swimming is …
Doing karate is not …
I think … can be …
…

swimming · doing karate · running · cycling ·
playing football · playing basketball · …

fun · exciting · boring · easy ·
difficult · exhausting · …

What are you good at?

5   grammar: gerund p. 177, wordbank: keeping fit p. 162, workbook p. 24/6

What sports and activities are you good at?
Write three or more sentences.

You can write:
I'm good at playing …
I'm good at …
…

ACTIVATE   **PRACTISE**   DEVELOP   PRACTISE   APPLY

An interview

6a skill: working with words p. 150, media worksheet 3

Match the definitions to the words. Look up the words you do not know.

1 They tell you how to play a game.
2 A … is what you need in order to do something well.
3 A series of games where the best team or player wins a prize at the end.
4 When you focus on something, you …
5 Training is a …

A skill
B physical activity
C rules
D concentrate
E tournament

6b audio 1/20, skill: listening p. 151

You are going to hear the words from 6a in an interview. What do you think the interview is about? Collect ideas in class. Then listen to the interview. Were you right?

6c CHOOSE YOUR LEVEL

▌ **Listen again and choose the right word to complete the statements. Write down the statements.**

1 Chess is a ??? (new / very old) game.
2 You need a lot of ??? (training and practice / lessons) to be good.
3 Being fit can help you ??? (win / concentrate) when you play for hours.

▌▌ **Listen again and take notes. Copy the true statements and correct the false statements.**

1 Chess is sometimes called "the game of kings".
2 You can't play chess online.
3 Anna likes chess because it is relaxing.
4 There are four elements that make a sport a sport.

▌▌▌ **Listen again and take notes. Copy the true statements and correct the false statements.**

1 Chess is probably 150 years old.
2 In Anna's opinion, chess is a game.
3 You have to learn different strategies.
4 Being fit does not help you in a game of chess.
5 Chess is very competitive.

6d wordbank: expressing opinions p. 165, media worksheet 15, workbook p. 24/7-9

What do you think? Is chess a sport?

You can say:

I think chess is a sport because …
I don't think chess is a sport because …

Feeling good

7a skill: reading p. 154

Scan the posts and write down what sports the teenagers do.

www.nothing-but-place.xx   × –

ELLIE, 13

I love dancing and I'm in a dance group. It's so much fun moving to the music and practising together as a team. You exercise and have a great workout without even noticing it. After the training I'm really exhausted, but I always feel great. At school I really hate PE lessons. Our teacher thinks it's the most important subject ever, but I am not very good at running, jumping and playing football, so the sports that we usually do are not for me. Why can't we do something like dancing?

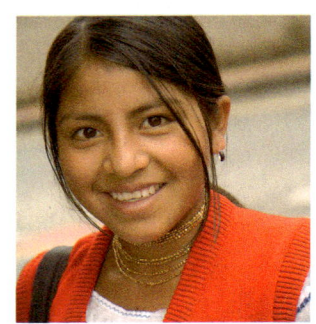

RYAN, 15

I love playing wheelchair basketball. Playing in a team with your friends is great fun. I go to practice twice a week, and we play matches against other teams at the weekends.
My dream is to play for the national team some day.
In the summer holidays we always go to a special practice camp for a week. There we also learn about things like looking after ourselves – how to get enough sleep and what to eat and how not to stress too much. This is also important to be good at your sport.

ALEX, 16

I don't like the fact that most sports are about competing against others and winning. But I know that doing something for my body is important.
So I tried running and cycling – but I didn't like that very much. I wanted to find an indoor activity.
One day I went to yoga class with my mum and I really liked it! I do yoga regularly now and I love it.
Yoga not only keeps me fit and flexible, it also helps me to learn about myself. I now know how to relax when feeling stressed.
Even my marks at school are better now. So, if you have the chance – try it out!

ACTIVATE PRACTISE **DEVELOP** PRACTISE APPLY

MIRA, 14

I've always been quite sporty – but last year I broke my leg
and was in hospital for some time. I spent a lot of time watching
TV or playing computer games. I also ate a lot of sweets.
When my leg got better, the rest of me wasn't feeling too well.
I felt tired and sad most of the time.
My mum had the idea that I should start swimming again and eat
less chocolate. It was really hard, but after about three weeks I felt
a lot better. The swimming helped my leg, and I can ride my bike
to school again. Of course I still eat sweets, but not as many as
before, and I eat a lot more fruit and vegetables because I can really
feel that that's better for me.

7b CHOOSE YOUR LEVEL

I **Read two or more of the posts and answer the questions about them.**
II **Read three or more of the posts and answer the questions about them.**
III **Read all of the posts and answer the questions.**

Questions on Ellie's post:
1 What does Ellie think about PE at school?
2 What does she like about dancing?

Questions on Ryan's post:
1 What does Ryan like about playing wheelchair basketball?
2 What does Ryan learn in the summer holidays?

Questions on Alex's post:
1 What kinds of sports does Alex not like?
2 Why does yoga make him feel good?

Questions on Mira's post:
1 What happened when Mira had to stop doing sports?
2 What made her feel better?

7c workbook p. 25/10-11

What makes you feel good? Make notes and talk to a partner about it.

You can write: You can say:

- doing sports   ... makes me feel good.

- being with my friends   I love ...

- listening to music   ... is what I'm good at. It makes me ...

...   ...

LAND & LEUTE 2 video 5

Schulsport im Vereinigten Königreich

Viele Schulen im Vereinigten Königreich haben drinnen und draußen Bereiche für alle möglichen Sportarten. Die Schülerinnen und Schüler üben während des Schuljahres verschiedene Sportarten aus, sowohl Teamsportarten wie Fußball und Hockey als auch Individualsportarten wie Badminton und Geländelauf. Damit jeder sehen kann, für welche Schule sie bei Wettkämpfen antreten, tragen sie auch beim Sport eine Schuluniform, normalerweise ein T-Shirt, Shorts und Strümpfe in den Schulfarben.
Im Sommer gibt es an den meisten Schulen ein Sportfest. Die Schülerinnen und Schüler messen sich in verschiedenen Aktivitäten.

Beim Sportfest kann man wie auch bei anderen Aktivitäten im Schuljahr für sein Haus Punkte gewinnen. Die meisten Schulen sind in vier oder fünf verschiedene Häuser unterteilt. Am Ende des Jahres gewinnt das Haus mit den meisten Punkten einen Pokal.

Vergleicht Schulsport im Vereinigten Königreich mit dem an eurer Schule oder an Schulen anderer Länder, über die ihr etwas wisst. Was ist gleich? Was ist anders?

Martin's favourite sport

8a video 6, skill: watching a video clip p. 156, workbook p. 26/12

Watch the video clip.
What is Martin's favourite sport?

8b **CHOOSE YOUR LEVEL** skill: mediation p. 155

A friend wants to know what Martin is talking about. Read his or her questions.
Then watch the video clip again.

▌ Take notes and answer two or more of the questions in German.
▌ Take notes and answer three or more of the questions in German.
▌ Take notes and answer four or more of the questions in German.

1 Wie lange macht Martin seinen Sport schon?
2 Wie oft ist er schon getaucht?
3 Warum braucht er manchmal einen „dry suit"?
4 Wieso hat er eine so große Uhr?
5 Was sind das für Fotos, die er zeigt?
6 Was ist ein „buddy check"?

ACTIVATE   PRACTISE   **DEVELOP**   PRACTISE   APPLY

Sports

9   **CHOOSE YOUR TASK** wordbank: keeping fit p. 162, C: media worksheet 10, workbook p. 27/13

A **Find a picture of your favourite sport or draw one and label it.**
B **Create a poster, a flyer or an advert for your favourite sport.**
C **Write a post about a sport you like doing or watching.**
   You can look at the posts on pages 36 and 37 again.

Sports poems

10a   audio 1/23-25

Listen to the poems and read along.

Choose your sports

Let's turn off our video games,
and run outside.
From so many sports,
we may choose and decide.
Baseball, soccer,
and basketball are fun.
Let's grab some friends,
and play in the sun.
(...)
Whatever sports,
you decide to play,
enjoy them with friends,
each and every day.

SKATEBOARDING

Knee pads, elbow pads,
start the show.
Grab your helmet;
Come on, let's go!

Margo L. Dill

What
Can You
Do With a
Football
?

Well…

You can
kick it - you can catch
it - you can bounce it - all
around. **YOU CAN GRAB IT** you can
pat it you can roll it - on the ground.
You can throw it *you can head it*
you can hit it - with a bat. You can
biff it you can boot it you can spin
it **you can shoot it.** You can
drop it you can stop it. Just
like that!

James Carter

10b

Which of the words in the first two poems are rhyming words? Collect them on the board.

10c

Look at the two boxes and find the rhyming pairs. Write them down. You can add more.

fun · trick · match · dream · ball · throw   go · team · catch · run · all · kick

10d   wordbank: keeping fit p. 162, workbook p. 28/14

Be a poet. Write a sports poem. You can use one of the poems in 10a to help you.

10e

Work with a partner or in small groups. Choose a poem and learn it by heart.

Word families

11 skill: working with words p. 150

How many words that belong to
each word family can you find?
Write them down.
You can use a dictionary to help you.

run · play ·
swim · dance ·
train

You can write:
run: runner, running, …
play: playground, …
…

A sports idol

12a audio 1/26

Listen to the interview with Jada.
What does she say about Tony Hawk
and his "Skatepark Project"?

12b **CHOOSE YOUR LEVEL** skill: listening p. 151, workbook p. 28/15

I **Listen again. Choose the right words from the box and write down the sentences.**

1 Jada started ??? when she was six.
2 Skateboarding is a great sport for ??? fit.
3 Tony Hawk ??? the Skatepark Project.

started · keeping · skating

II **Listen again and match the sentence parts. Write down the sentences.**

1 Jada started competing
2 Looking out for each other is
3 Skateboarding is a great sport
4 Jada's idol is

A Tony Hawk.
B for keeping fit.
C when she was ten.
D important for skateboarders.

III **Listen again and complete the sentences. Write them down.**

1 Jada started ??? when she was six years old.
2 Jada loves being able to do a new trick after hours of ???.
3 Tony Hawk is her ???.
4 Tony Hawk was really good at ??? new tricks.
5 Jada started ??? yoga because it helps her to ???.

12c wordbank: keeping fit p. 162, workbook p. 28/16

Who is your sports idol? Write four or more sentences about him or her.
You can make one up if you do not have a sports idol.

You can write:
My idol is … He / She is …
He / She was born in …

He / She is a …
I like him / her because he / she is …

DIGITAL+ practise more 10

ACTIVATE PRACTISE DEVELOP **PRACTISE** APPLY

Tips for a healthy lifestyle TARGET TASK

13 workbook p. 29/17, wordbank: keeping fit p. 162, presenting something p. 168, skill: presentations p. 158

Your task is to collect and present tips for keeping fit and healthy.
Before you start, look at these steps:

STEP 1

In class: think about how you would like to present the tips.
You could make:

- leaflets
- posters
- slides for a slide show
- a short video clip
- …

STEP 2

Get together with a partner or in a small group and collect information.
You can look at the unit again and / or search the Internet.
Make notes.
Think about the following:

- How much sleep do you need?
- What should you do before you go to sleep? What should you not do?
  (switch off your mobile phone, switch off the TV, read a good book, …)
- What should you eat? What should you not eat?
- What kind of sport do you like?
- What is good for you?
- How often should you do sports?
- What else could you do to keep fit and to relax? (yoga, pilates, …)
- …

STEP 3

Create your poster, leaflet, slide show, short video clip, …
Edit it with a partner or in a small group.

Tips for a healthy lifestyle

STEP 4

Present your work, for example in a gallery walk.
Which tips do you think are the most important ones?

1. Get enough sleep
Make sure to …
Switch off your …
Don't …

STEP 5

Give each other feedback. Remember to be polite.

2. Eat healthy food
Eat at least

What's the matter?

1a

Look at the pictures on this double page. What is the matter with the people?

You can say:
Matthew / Sarah / Linda / Tom / Demir has …

a toothache · a swollen wrist · a bad cold · a stomach ache · a wound

1b audio 1/27

Listen to the dialogues and read along. What is each patient's problem?

Matthew: Ow, my shoulder and my wrist hurt so much! And look, my wrist is swollen.
John: I know.
Matthew: What if my wrist is broken?
John: Don't worry too much. They'll probably take an X-ray, and if it is broken, you will get a cast.
Matthew: But if I have a cast, I'll miss the match next week! Ow – it really hurts!

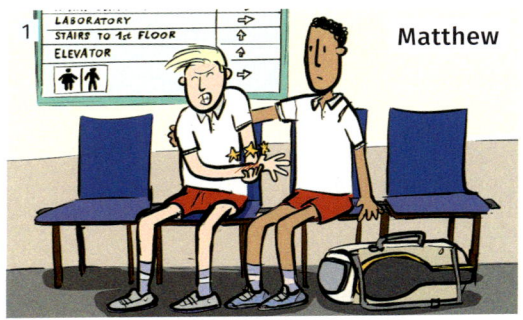

Sarah: My tooth hurts so much!
Mum: Then I'll make an appointment at the dentist's for you.
Sarah: Oh no!
Mum: If it hurts so much, you'll have to go to the dentist. The toothache will only get worse if you don't go.
Sarah: I know. But I really hate going to the dentist.

Receptionist: Good morning, Dr Hill's practice. This is Jemima speaking. How can I help you?
Linda: Hello, this is Linda Miller. I think I've caught a cold. I have a headache and a sore throat, and my nose just won't stop running. I also have a fever and a cough.
Receptionist: Oh yes, you don't sound too good. Let me see … If you come in at twelve o'clock, the doctor can see you just before his lunch break.
Linda: That sounds good. Thanks.

ACTIVATE   PRACTISE   DEVELOP   PRACTISE   APPLY

Mum: Oh dear. What's happened?
Tom: I fell on my knee and it really hurts.
Mum: Let me have a look at it. Oh, it's bleeding. We have to clean the wound. If we don't do that, you will get an infection. Then I'll put a plaster on it. If it doesn't get better soon, we'll go and see a doctor.

Nurse: Good morning, Demir. How are you feeling today?
Demir: My stomach still hurts.
Nurse: Well, it's only been two days since your operation, but you can have some toast today.
Demir: Oh, great. I'm so hungry.
Nurse: Yes, I know. But please eat slowly. It'll be quite painful if you eat too fast. And here is your medicine for today.

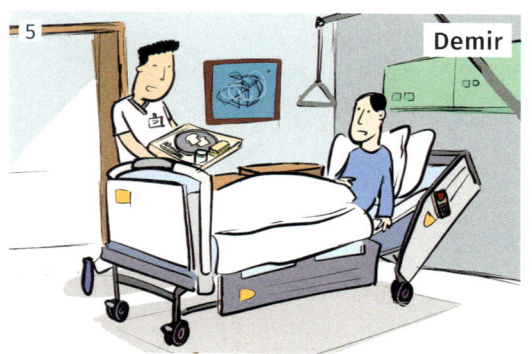

1c   CHOOSE YOUR LEVEL   skill: reading p. 154

▌ **Read the first three dialogues again. What health problems do the people have?**

You can write:
Matthew: shoulder hurts, wrist is swollen
Sarah:
Linda:

▐▐ **Read the first three dialogues again.**
Collect words for body parts and words for health problems.

You can write:

body part:	problem:
shoulder, wrist, …	hurt, …

▐▐▐ **Read all the dialogues again. Collect words for body parts and words for health problems.**

1d   skill: performing a scene p. 159, media worksheet, 2, 5, workbook p. 30/1-2

Work with a partner. Try to imagine how the people are feeling in each situation and do a dramatic reading of one of the dialogues. You can record it if you like.

GRAMMAR HELP conditional clauses 1 p. 178

Wenn du sagen möchtest, was unter bestimmten Bedingungen geschehen wird, benutzt du Bedingungssätze. Diese Sätze bestehen aus zwei Teilen. Sieh dir die Beispiele an. Was fällt dir auf?

If you have a broken wrist, you will miss the tennis match.
Wenn / Falls du ein gebrochenes Handgelenk hast, wirst du das Tennisspiel verpassen.

The toothache will only get worse if you don't go to the dentist.
Die Zahnschmerzen werden nur schlimmer werden, wenn / falls du nicht zum Zahnarzt / zur Zahnärztin gehst.

If you come in at twelve o'clock, the doctor can see you just before his lunch break.
Wenn / Falls du um 12 Uhr kommst, kann der Arzt dich direkt vor seiner Mittagspause drannehmen.

Auf Seite 178 findest du weitere Erklärungen zur Bildung und Verwendung von Bedingungssätzen.

If you …

2   grammar: conditional 1 p. 178

Match the sentence parts. Write the sentences in your exercise book.

1	If you don't see a doctor,	A	if you don't wear a warm jacket.
2	If you break your leg,	B	it will get worse.
3	If you stay in bed,	C	your stomach will hurt.
4	If you don't eat slowly,	D	you take your medicine.
5	You'll feel a lot better soon if	E	you'll get well soon.
6	You will catch a cold	F	you will get a cast.

What if …?

3a   grammar: conditional 1 p. 178

Write sentences. There can be more than one solution.

If you have a really bad cold, you ??? (will / must) stay at home.
If you stay at home, you ??? (will / can) play lots of video games.
If you play lots of video games, you ??? (will / can) become really good at playing video games.

3b   grammar: conditional 1 p. 178, workbook p. 31/3

Choose one of the sentence beginnings below and write about a chain of events like in 3a. Write three or more sentences starting with "If …".

A If the weather is nice tomorrow, I'll go to the park. If I go to the park, I'll …
B If it's rainy tomorrow, I will / I won't …
C If my mum / dad goes to …, she / he will … If she / he ….
D If …

Tarek's accident

4a

Look at the picture. What can you see?
What do you think is going to happen next?

4b  audio 1/28

Listen to the dialogue and read along.
Who is Tarek's coach going to call?

Tarek: Ow! I banged my head really hard.
Coach: Tarek, are you alright? Can you get up? Let me help you!
Tarek: Ow, I don't think I can! I can't move my foot, it hurts too much. I'm feeling dizzy, too.
Coach: OK, stay down then. I'll call an ambulance. Could somebody call Tarek's dad, please?
Chris: I can call Mr Adil.
Coach: Thanks, Chris. Tell him that I'll let him know which hospital we're at as soon as I know.

4c audio 1/29, skill: listening p. 151

Listen to Tarek's coach calling the emergency services. What is going to happen next?

4d CHOOSE YOUR LEVEL workbook p. 32/4-5

I Listen again. Choose the right words and write down what Tarek's coach explains to the operator.

There was ??? (a match / an accident) on the playing field. One of my players is hurt. He is able to ??? (talk / see). He can't stand on his ??? (left foot / right foot) and he is feeling ??? (sad / dizzy).

II Listen again. Choose the right words and write down what Tarek's coach explains to the operator.

There was an accident ??? (on the playing field / on the playground). During a hockey match, ??? (three / two) players ran ??? (into a wall / into each other). One of them can't stand on his ??? (right / left) foot and is feeling ??? (dizzy / cold). His head ??? (is bleeding / hurts).

III Listen again. Imagine you are Tarek's coach. Answer the operator's questions.

1 What is your emergency?
2 How many people are hurt?
3 Is the person able to talk?
4 What exactly is wrong with him?
5 How old is he?
6 Where are you exactly?

At the hospital

5a skill: working with words p. 150, media worksheet 3

Look up the words and phrases in a dictionary. Write them down and add the German meanings.

injury · examine · sprained ·
put on a bandage · X-ray

5b audio 1/32

Listen and read along. What do you find out about Tarek's injuries?

In the waiting room
Coach: Ah Tarek, there's your dad.
Hello Mr Adil.
Dad: Tarek! Are you OK? Does it hurt?
Have you seen a doctor yet?
Tarek: Calm down, Dad. It's not that bad.
Coach: Yes, we've already seen a doctor.
She's examined his head, there is nothing
wrong with it.
Dad: Phew.
Coach: But the doctor wants to take an X-ray
of his foot. We were just waiting for you,
there are a few papers to sign.
Dad: Oh yes, of course.
Coach: Is it OK if I go back to the team?
Dad: Yes sure, thanks for taking care of him.
Tarek, I'll just go and sign those papers.
Tarek: OK, Dad.

***

In the doctor's practice
Dr Weston: Well, hello Mr Adil. I'm Doctor
Weston. I've met your son already.
Dad: Hello.
Dr Weston: So, Tarek. How are you feeling
now?
Tarek: My head is a lot better.
But my foot still hurts really badly.
Dr Weston: Yes, I can imagine. But the good
news is that it's not broken. You've got a

sprained ankle. It's very important that you
rest your ankle for the next few days. We'll
put a bandage on it and you must keep it up
as much as possible.
Dad: What about school?
Dr Weston: He should stay at home for the
next two days. And no sports for at least
three weeks.
Tarek: No sports? That'll be so boring. And
I won't be able to play in our next hockey
match.
Dad: I promise that I'll play that hockey
video game with you if it gets too boring.
And I'm sure your friends will visit you.
Thanks a lot, Doctor Weston.
Dr Weston: No problem. Please make an
appointment for a check-up in about a week.
Bye, Tarek.
Tarek: Bye. And thank you.

ACTIVATE   PRACTISE   **DEVELOP**   PRACTISE   APPLY

5c CHOOSE YOUR LEVEL skill: reading p. 154

I Read the dialogues again. Unscramble the words in brackets and copy the sentences.

1 Tarek's dad arrives at the ??? (s-t-l-p-**h**-o-i-a).
2 He has to sign a few ??? (r-**p**-p-s-a-e).
3 Tarek's ??? (l-k-**a**-n-e) is sprained.
4 He has to ??? (e-t-**r**-s) it for the next few days.

II Read the dialogues again and write down the sentences in the correct order.

1 Tarek's coach goes back to the team.
2 Tarek's coach says that the doctor wants to take an X-ray.
3 Tarek's ankle is only sprained.
4 Tarek's dad arrives at the hospital.

III Read the dialogues again. Are the sentences true or false? Correct the false sentences.

1 Tarek's dad cannot come to the hospital.
2 Tarek's coach has gone back to the team before Tarek's dad arrives.
3 No one has examined Tarek's head yet.
4 Tarek's dad has to sign a few papers.
5 Tarek's ankle is broken.
6 Tarek should stay at home for two days.

5d skill: performing a scene p. 159, workbook p. 33/6-7

Work in groups of three. Practise reading out one or both of the two scenes.

What now?

6 grammar: modal verbs (R) p. 179, workbook p. 34/8-11

Copy the sentences and fill in the gaps with the words from the box.

> will be able to · will be able to · will be able to ·
> will have to · won't be able to

1 Tarek's dad has arrived at the hospital. – Now he ??? find out what happened.
2 Tarek has a sprained ankle. – Now he ??? do sports for the next three weeks.
3 Tarek can't walk properly. – Now he ??? stay at home for two days.
4 Tarek can't do sport for three weeks. – But he ??? play video games with his dad.
5 Tarek has to rest his ankle for a few days. – Then he ??? walk properly again soon.

Cheering Tarek up

7a

Read the text message.
What do you think: who is Ava writing to?

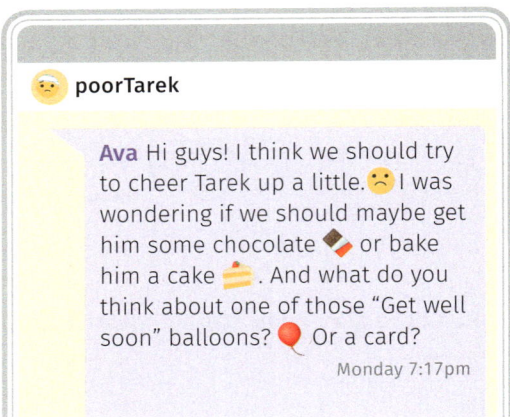

poorTarek

Ava Hi guys! I think we should try to cheer Tarek up a little. 😔 I was wondering if we should maybe get him some chocolate 🍫 or bake him a cake 🍰. And what do you think about one of those "Get well soon" balloons? 🎈 Or a card?

Monday 7:17pm

7b

What are Ava's ideas for cheering Tarek up?

You can say:
Ava's ideas are to get him chocolate, …

7c   wordbank: health p. 163

Work with a partner and collect more ideas for cheering up someone who is ill.

7d

Talk about your ideas in class.
What are the three best ideas?

You can say:
I think … is the best idea.
In my opinion, … is a very good idea.

Poor Ellie

8a   video 7, skill: watching a video clip p. 156

Watch the video clip.
What is wrong with Ellie?

You can say:
Ellie is …
She feels …

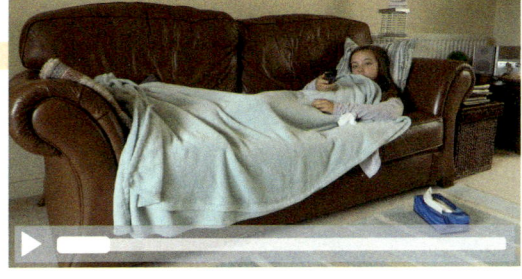

8b   workbook p. 35/12-13

Watch the video clip again. What do Ellie's family and friends do to cheer her up?
Take notes and talk about it.

What do they miss?

9   GET TOGETHER   audio 1/34

Get together with a partner.
Listen to Ben and Jacob in hospital and find out what they are talking about.

Partner A	Partner B
I Go to page 129.	I Go to page 138.
II Go to page 132.	II Go to page 141.
III Go to page 135.	III Go to page 144.

ACTIVATE   PRACTISE   **DEVELOP**   PRACTISE   APPLY

Helping out at the doctor's

10a audio 1/35, skill: listening p. 151

An exchange student called Sophie is staying with you. She does not speak much German. One day she must go to the doctor. Listen to Sophie. What is wrong with her? Take notes.

10b skill: mediation p. 155, workbook p. 36/14

You have to take Sophie to the doctor.
Explain what is wrong to the German doctor.

You can say:
Sophie hat … Sie kann …

What's wrong?

11 wordbank: health p. 163

Work in small groups. Mime an injury or an illness. The others have to guess what it is and tell you what to do to get better. Take turns.

toothache · fever · cold ·
stomach ache · sprained ankle ·
broken leg · wound · …

You can say:
Have you got a …?
You should …
…

Being ill and getting well

12 **CHOOSE YOUR TASK** wordbank: health p. 163, C: skill: writing p. 153

A Design or draw a "Get well soon" card.
B Look at the meme. Make your own meme.
C Have you ever been ill or to hospital? Write a short text about it.

A

B

Doctor, my back hurts when I wake up in the morning.

Wake up in the afternoon then.

C

Last year I had to go to hospital.

I was a bit nervous because it

was my first time in a hospital.

After the operation I didn't feel

well, but the girl in my room

was really nice. We talked and

played lots of different games.

Who's asking?

13 CHOOSE YOUR LEVEL workbook p.36/15

I Complete the questions from an emergency call with words from the box.

How many · What · Where · What

1 ??? is your emergency?
2 ??? exactly happened?
3 ??? people are hurt?
4 ??? exactly are you?

II Read the questions. Which ones does a doctor ask and which ones a patient? Make two lists.

1 Where does it hurt?
2 How much chocolate have you eaten?
3 Will I have to stay at home for a week?
4 How exactly did it happen?
5 Will I be able to walk again soon?
6 How are you feeling?

III Unscramble the questions. Which ones does a doctor ask and which ones does a patient ask? Make two lists.

1 got – as well – have you – a fever
2 move – like this – can you – your fingers
3 hit you – the ball – did – where exactly
4 how long – in bed for – stay – will I have to
5 how long – a headache for – have you – had
6 will I – when – do sport – again – be able to

Can you hear the *r* ?

14a audio 1/36

Listen to the sentences. In which of the marked words can you hear the "r"? Can you guess why?

1 There are some papers to sign.
2 The waiting room is over there.
3 My shoulder and my wrist hurt.
4 Where does your shoulder hurt?
5 The doctor is in the doctor's practice.
6 You can see the doctor now.
7 I'll put a plaster on your knee.
8 Don't remove the plaster too soon.

14b

Listen again and repeat the sentences.

Odd one out

15

Find the odd one out. Why is it the odd one out?

1 doctor – examine – dentist – nurse
2 leg – tooth – stomach ache – ankle
3 hospital – swollen – broken – sprained
4 medicine – chocolate – cake – toast

DIGITAL+ practise more 12-13

ACTIVATE PRACTISE DEVELOP **PRACTISE** APPLY

A medical problem   TARGET TASK

16 [icons] workbook p.37/16, wordbank: health p.163, skill: performing a scene p.159, media worksheet 2

Your task is to do a role play about a medical problem.
Before you start, look at these steps:

STEP 1

Get together with a partner or in a small group and plan your role play.
Decide the following:

- What is wrong with the patient? What happened?

   - *I fell off a horse / my bike / my skateboard / … and hurt my shoulder / arm / knee / …*
   - *My shoulder / wrist / arm / leg / stomach / knee / … is swollen / is broken / hurts.*
   - *I have a toothache / stomach ache / headache / sore throat / fever / cough / …*

- Where are you? (At the doctor's? At the hospital? At home? On the phone?)
- Who are the characters in your scene?
- What do the characters say? How do they feel?

   - *Good morning! How can I help you?*
   - *This is … / I have a … I would like to see the doctor.*
   - *The doctor can see you at …*
   - *Thanks. See you later.*

STEP 2

Collect ideas for your scene and make notes. You can also write cue cards.
Make sure each character has something to say.

STEP 3

Decide who will play which part and practise your role play.
You can use props or costumes if you like.

STEP 4

Act out your scene. If you like, you can film your scene and show it to the rest of the class.

Check out

Kannst du verstehen, wenn jemand darüber spricht, welchen Sport er oder sie mag?	Workbook, p. 38
Kannst du deine Meinung zu einer Sportart ausdrücken?	Workbook, p. 38
Kannst du Reimwörter finden und eigene Reime schreiben?	Workbook, p. 38
Kannst du darüber schreiben, was unter bestimmten Bedingungen passieren wird?	Workbook, p. 39
Kannst du wichtige Wörter und Redewendungen zum Thema Krankheit und Arztbesuch?	Workbook, p. 39
Kannst du jemandem beim Arzt sprachlich aushelfen?	Workbook, p. 39

Sports day

1   We finally had our sports day yesterday. I was so excited that I almost couldn't sleep the night before. This year I was going for the top!

5   My training programme had been really good, and I had signed up for as many events as I could.

I began the day with a healthy breakfast: a banana milkshake, fried eggs and porridge.

10   "Don't you think they meant you should have ONE of these for breakfast?" asked Dad, who was reading the newspaper at the kitchen table.

"Well, since I've signed up for ten events, this should be OK," I told him.

"You signed up for ten events? What were you thinking?" my brother Jamie asked. "We only have to take part in one. I only have the football match at eleven, and the rest of the day is free."

15   "I'm sorry we won't be there to cheer you on, darling," Mum said. "I have to work and Dad has this really important customer to visit."

If you ask me, no one in my family was very interested, as usual.

Our school looked brilliant that day. There were flags and streamers in our school colours everywhere, the sun was shining, and everyone was happy. Well, almost everyone.

20   "I hate sports day. All that running and sweating," my best friend Makena said.

"I'm off to my chess game. I'm so glad chess is one of the disciplines today. See you later."

Since my day was about to get busy, I hurried to get to my first event – the mini javelin. I could not wait for my javelin to land because I had to be on time for my

25   second event, the 1500-metre race. During the run I didn't look left or right. I just ran, ran, ran. When I crossed the finishing line, I just kept running to get to the long jump on time so I didn't hear who won. But since I didn't see anyone else near me,

30   I was pretty sure I was first.

300-metre hurdles

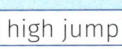

high jump

mini javelin

1500-metre race

long jump

At the long jump I did my three jumps, and then I ran to the next event, the 300-metre hurdles.

35   I didn't knock over any of the hurdles because of my technique.

had been = *war gewesen*; had signed up = *hatte angemeldet*; flag = *Fahne*; streamer = *Wimpel*; discipline = *Disziplin, Teilgebiet im Sport*

Luckily, the high jump was right next to the track for the 300-metre hurdles so I could walk over immediately after crossing the finishing line.

40 Once again, I left before they **announced** the winner. Next was the lunch break, and I wanted to be the first at the cafeteria. Super athletes need lots of **carbohydrates** and I still had five more events to do.

I felt quite full after lunch so it was good that the next two disciplines were throwing rather than running: discus and softball throw. Once again, I did well – the other students' discuses and
45 softballs landed nowhere near mine.

After the throwing events I was in great form again. I did the triple jump, and then I had to hurry to get to the relay in time. I was the first runner on my team, which was good because I could run over to my last event for the day as soon as I was finished.

discus

softball throw

triple jump

relay

walking

The last event was easy – walking. I can walk with my eyes closed,
50 and that is what I did. Once again, there was no one at the finishing line when I crossed it – probably because I was so fast that everyone else was way behind me.

I was really happy with myself. Now, the last thing to take part in was the **award ceremony** so I walked back to the
55 main playing field, where there was a small stage.

"Well done, Lucy," said Ms Fisher, my PE teacher, and handed me a large trophy. "You're the only student who managed to compete in ten disciplines. That's a new school record, and I'm
60 very pleased to present you with this *School Champion of the Hearts* trophy."
I was so happy! I heard Jamie and Makena and my house cheer really loudly for me. What a **success**!

"Yes, very well done, Lucy," added Mr Dunkerley,
65 our headteacher. "You came last in every single event, but you showed great **spirit**! We're really proud of you."

announce = *bekannt geben*; carbohydrate = *Kohlenhydrat*; award ceremony = *Preisverleihung*; success = *Erfolg*; spirit = *hier: Kampfgeist*

Paralympics

Every four years thousands of athletes from all around the world come together and compete in the Paralympics. The Paralympics always take place in the same year as the Olympics and usually in the same place. There are summer and winter games.

In the Paralympics, athletes with a disability compete against each other. The first official Paralympic Games took place in Rome in 1960 with 400 athletes from 23 countries.

In the Tokyo 2020 Summer Paralympics, more than 4,000 athletes from over 160 countries competed in 22 different sports.

Paralympic sports include athletics, football 5-a-side (blind football), paratriathlon, sitting volleyball and wheelchair rugby.

Sitting volleyball

In sitting volleyball the players sit on the floor – so the net is much lower. The rules are similar to volleyball, for example there are also six players on a team.

Paratriathlon

A triathlon is made up of three sports – swimming, cycling and running. At the Paralympics it consists of 750m swimming, 20km cycling and a 5km wheelchair or running race.

Football 5-a-side

Football 5-a-side – or blind football – is a kind of football for athletes who can't see much or who are blind.

The field is smaller, and there are boards along the field to keep the ball inside. There are five players in a team, including the goalkeeper. Teams are allowed to have sighted goalkeepers and sighted guides. The guide can help the team by directing the players from outside the field. The ball has bells inside so the players can hear where it is.

Find out more about a Paralympic athlete or sport and present your findings to the class.

1. Look at the pictures. What do you think: where are the people?
2. What are the people doing?
3. Have you ever been to events like these? What was it like?

What's on?

Part A At the car boot sale

- Du sprichst über Wochenendaktivitäten.
- Du findest etwas über *Kofferraum-Flohmärkte* heraus.
- Du machst ein Rollenspiel über das Kaufen und Verkaufen von gebrauchten Dingen.

Part B Festivals

- Du findest etwas über Festivals im Vereinigten Königreich heraus.
- Du liest einen Artikel darüber, wie Festivals umweltfreundlicher werden können.
- Du machst ein Poster über ein Festival.

Weekend activities

1

Talk to a partner about weekend activities.
Think about where you can go, what you
can do there, what the activities cost, …

You can say:

At the weekend, I sometimes go to …
I like to …
… is free. / … is not expensive. / … costs …
…

What's on in London?

2a   skill: reading p. 154

Read these tips for events in London at the weekend.
What can you do if you do not want to spend much money?

LONDON WEEKEND TIPS
your guide to fun events in London

PORTOBELLO ROAD MARKET | Notting Hill   Saturday and Sunday 9am – 7pm
Find anything from clothes to arts & crafts at hundreds of shops and stalls.
There are some stalls which are only open on Saturdays, so come early to
find the best things and to avoid the crowds.

CHARITY RUN | Finsbury Park   Saturday 11am
Run 5km for charity – this charity run is perfect for people who
like running and doing something good at the same time.
All money goes to charity. Registration fee: children £10, adults £14.99.

FAMILY FILM CLUB | The Barbican Cinema   Saturday 11am
Watch a family film at the Barbican Cinema.
Adults can only come if they bring a child, and children can
only come with an adult. Tickets cost £3.50.

CAR BOOT SALE | Notting Hill   Sunday 10am – 6pm
Visit the biggest car boot sale in Notting Hill and look for
second-hand items that you can't find anywhere else.
The entrance fee is only £1.50 and goes to charity.

THE LION KING | Lyceum Theatre   Sunday 2:30pm
A great show for people who love musicals. See the
famous musical now and remember it forever. Tickets from £23.50.

2b   wordbank: what's on? p. 164, workbook p. 40/1-2

Work with a partner and talk about the events.
Where would you like to go?
What would you like to do?

You can say:

I would like to go to … because I love …
I would love to do … / watch … / … because …

What to do?

3a 🔊 audio 2/2

Listen and read along. What are the friends talking about? What do they decide in the end?

Ava: Hi guys, finally Friday! What are you up to this weekend? Would you like to do something together?

Tarek: I have no plans so far.

Lily: Me neither. Any ideas?

Ava: We could go to the cinema. We haven't been there for ages.

Harry: That's too expensive, I haven't got enough pocket money left.

Ava: We could go to the Family Film Club at the Barbican. The tickets are just £3.50.

Tarek: But you have to take an adult with you! I don't want that! Can we please find something else?
What about the charity run on Saturday? Or a game of football?

Ava: Oh, Tarek. You always want to do sports. I'd rather do something else. Actually, I really need a new hoodie. We could go shopping together.

Harry: Shopping would be OK. I'm sure I could get some money from our mums for new clothes. They keep telling me to get a new pair of jeans.

Lily: But you don't have to buy new things. I could help you with upcycling second-hand hoodies and jeans. We could go to a flea market! I need to get some ideas for my next upcycling project anyway.

Ava: Should we go to Portobello Road Market then?

Harry: OK with me. Maybe that guy who sells those really funny T-shirts is still there.

Tarek: I only remember the funny guy that sells old cameras that nobody needs …
But Portobello Road Market is always so crowded at the weekend.
And there are so many shops which are pretty expensive.

Lily: Hm, there's a car boot sale on Sunday. Shall we go there then?

Harry: Why not? And it's even for charity – I'll definitely get money for that.

Ava: That's a cool idea. Do you want to meet at 10:30 on Sunday?

Tarek: Sounds great.

Harry: Yeah.

Ava: Great! See you on Sunday then!

3b CHOOSE YOUR LEVEL skill: reading p.154

I Read again. Which activities do Ava and Harry suggest? Take notes.
II Read again. Which events do the children talk about? Take notes.
III Read again. Who suggests what? Take notes for each person.

3c workbook p.41/3-4

Which of the weekend tips from number 2a is your favourite?
Write a short text message in which you suggest the event to a friend.

GRAMMAR HELP   relative clauses p. 180

Wenn du Personen oder Dinge genauer beschreiben willst, kannst du Relativsätze benutzen. Meist beginnt ein Relativsatz mit einem der Relativpronomen *who, which* oder *that*. Sieh dir die Beispielsätze an. Wann verwendest du welches Relativpronomen? Auf welches Wort bezieht es sich jeweils?

There are some stalls which are only open on Saturdays.	Es gibt ein paar Stände, die nur samstags offen sind.
Maybe that guy who sells those really funny T-shirts is still there.	Vielleicht ist der Typ noch da, der diese lustigen T-Shirts verkauft.
Look for stalls that you can't find anywhere else.	Suche nach Ständen, die du sonst nirgendwo finden kannst.
There is a funny guy that sells old cameras.	Es gibt einen lustigen Typen, der alte Kameras verkauft.

Auf Seite 180 findest du weitere Erklärungen und Beispiele, auch zur Verwendung des Relativpronomens *that*.

Tips for the weekend

4   grammar: relative clauses p. 180, workbook p. 42/5

Write sentences.

There is a **car boot sale**		takes place in Notting Hill.
At the car boot sale there are **people**		are especially interesting for children.
There is a **cinema**	who	like running.
You can see **films** there	which	has a Family Film Club.
At the theatre you can see a **musical**		sell second-hand clothes.
On Saturday, there is a **charity run** for people		is very famous.

Making plans

5   grammar: relative clauses p. 180

Complete the sentences. Use 'who', 'which' or 'that'.

1   The friends are talking about **activities** ??? they can do at the weekend.
2   Tarek suggests **activities** ??? have to do with sports.
3   Harry would like to see if the **guy** ??? sells funny T-shirts is still at Portobello Road Market.
4   The **car boot sale** ??? takes place on Saturday is the biggest in Notting Hill.

It's a person who …

6   grammar: relative clauses p. 180

Write four or more sentences for a partner.
He or she has to find out who or what it is.

You can write:

It's a person who acts in films.

actor / actress · camera · book · teacher · …

It's a thing which you can use to take pictures.

It's a … that …

DIGITAL+ practise more 14

ACTIVATE   **PRACTISE**   DEVELOP   PRACTISE   APPLY

LAND & LEUTE 3 ▪ video 8

Secondhand-Shopping im Vereinigten Königreich

Secondhand-Shopping wird immer beliebter, nicht nur, weil es billiger ist, gebrauchte Dinge zu kaufen, sondern auch, weil es besser für die Umwelt ist.
Man kann Secondhand-Ware auch zum Upcyceln verwenden und so aus gebrauchten Dingen neue machen.
Im Vereinigten Königreich gibt es viele Flohmärkte, aber auch Wohltätigkeitsläden. Dort kann man Dinge wie Bücher, Kleidung, Schmuck oder sogar Möbel kaufen, die gespendet wurden. In diesen Läden arbeiten hauptsächlich Ehrenamtliche, die kein Geld für ihre Arbeit bekommen.

At a car boot sale

Es lassen sich günstig gute Sachen finden und manchmal sogar interessante Schätze entdecken. Das Geld, das eingenommen wird, wird für einen guten Zweck verwendet.

Gibt es bei euch in der Gegend solche Läden? Habt ihr schon einmal auf einem Flohmarkt Dinge gekauft oder verkauft? Sprecht in der Klasse darüber.

Look at that!

7a ▪ audio 2/5

Listen to Ava, Lily, Harry and Tarek. Where are they?

7b **CHOOSE YOUR LEVEL** skill: listening p. 151, workbook p. 42/6-8

a hockey stick · a fish · a hoodie

I Listen again. What does Ava want to buy? Write it down.

II Listen again. Which of these things do the children talk about? Write them down.

books

telephones

bicycle bells

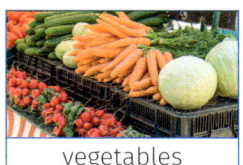

vegetables

a singing fish

paintings

toys

clothes

III Listen again. Who wants to buy what at the car boot sale? Take notes.

You can write:

Ava: …

Lily: …

Looking for bargains

8a 🔊 audio 2/6, skill: reading p. 154

Look at the pictures and the heading above. What do you think the dialogues are about? Then listen and read along. Were you right?

Dialogue 1

Harry: Look, there's a jeans stall. This pair looks OK, doesn't it?

Tarek: Yes, it does.

Seller: Hi guys. Good taste – those are original jeans from the 1950s, and I can sell them to you for just £249.

Harry: Oh, I thought second-hand clothes are cheaper than new ones.

Seller: Well, why don't you look at the jeans over there then? They're all good quality. They start from £5.

Harry: Great. Thanks.

Tarek: What do you think about these ones?

Harry: I like them. Excuse me, could I try these on?

Seller: Sure, just go behind that curtain.

Harry: What do you say, Tarek?

Tarek: They look good on you.

Seller: Do they fit?

Harry: Yes, they do. I think I'll take them. How much are they?

Seller: This pair is £7.

Harry: Great. Here you are.

Seller: £10, thanks. And here's £3 change.

Harry: Thank you. Bye.

Seller: Have a nice day! Bye.

Dialogue 2

Seller: Hello, can I help you?

Lily: We're just looking. But thank you.

Seller: OK.

Lily: I really like this old flowerpot. It's only 50p and it would make a great lamp.

Tarek: Why don't you just buy a lamp? There's a nice one.

Lily: But that's not as much fun as making your own lamp. I also like this coffee grinder. Excuse me, how much is this? There's no price tag.

Seller: Oh, I got that from a man who lives in his grandparents' old house and keeps finding interesting things. His grandparents brought that back with them from a holiday in Italy because they liked Italian coffee so much. It's really old. There's also a coffee pot that came with it. See?

Lily: Oh, it's great. How much for both and this flowerpot?

Seller: I can give you the flowerpot for free if you take the other two things for £12, well, let's say £10.

Lily: That's a fair price. Here you are. Thank you! – Hey guys, I think I've just found a bargain!

ACTIVATE   PRACTISE   **DEVELOP**   PRACTISE   APPLY

Dialogue 3

Lily: OK, that was a very successful day. I found lots of good things for my next lamp. Did you find anything, Tarek?

Tarek: Yes, I got five new science fiction books for only £2.50. They're in my rucksack.

Ava: Is there any more room on your shelves for new books?

Tarek: No, I have to get rid of some old ones.

Ava: If you want to get rid of old stuff, you could take it to a charity shop. There is a small one on Portobello Road.

Harry: I've got an idea! Why don't we sell some of our old things at a flea market?

Lily: I like Harry's idea. I think selling things at a flea market would be fun.

Harry: Yes! We have so many old board games that we don't play anymore. And Double and Trouble's old cage and …

Lily: Oh no, not the old cage. I've got an idea for that …

8b CHOOSE YOUR LEVEL

I Read dialogue 1 again. Complete the sentences and write them in your exercise book.

1 Harry and Tarek look at a jeans ???.
2 Harry tries on a pair of jeans behind a ???.
3 He thinks he'll ???.
4 The jeans cost ???.

II Read dialogues 1 and 2 again. Complete the sentences and write them in your exercise book.

1 Harry and Tarek are at a ???.
2 Harry buys ???.
3 He spends ???.
4 Lily buys ???.
5 She spends ???.

III Read the dialogues again and answer the questions.

1 How much are the cheapest jeans at the jeans stall?
2 How much are the jeans that Harry buys?
3 What does Lily buy?
4 How much does Lily pay?
5 What kind of books has Tarek bought?
6 How much did he pay for them?

8c   wordbank: expressing opinions p.165, media worksheet 15, workbook p.43/9

Lily says that buying a lamp is not as much fun as making your own lamp. What do you think?

How much is it?

9a wordbank: buying and selling p. 164

Look at the prices. Ask and answer questions with a partner. Take turns.

You can ask:
How much is the ...?
How much are the ...?

You can answer:
It's ...
They are ...

1 £1.50

2 80p

3 £3.90

4 £5.25

5 £7

9b skill: searching the internet p. 157, workbook p. 44/10

How much do the items cost in euros?
You can find out on the Internet.

You can say:
One pound fifty is one euro ... cents.
...

Tom's day out

10a video 9, skill: watching a video clip p. 156

Watch the video clip. Where is Tom?
What is he doing?

10b CHOOSE YOUR LEVEL

Watch the video clip again.

I Answer the questions. You can find help in the box.
  1 Which animal does Tom buy?
  2 What kind of book does he buy?

a children's book · a giraffe ·
an elephant · a guitar · a travel guide · ...

II Answer the questions.
  1 What day is it?
  2 What does Tom buy at the first stall?
  3 How much does he pay for it?

III Answer the questions.
  1 What does Tom buy at the first stall?
  2 At the second stall Tom buys several things. Why does he buy them?
  3 What does Tom buy at the third stall?
  4 How much does the woman want for it and how much does Tom pay for it in the end?

ACTIVATE PRACTISE **DEVELOP** PRACTISE APPLY

At the market

11 skill: mediation p. 155

You are at a market in England with a friend who does not speak English very well.
Help him or her. Write down what you say.

Your friend: Oh, schau mal da an dem Stand, da gibt es Marmelade und – Chutney? Könntest du mal fragen, was das ist?
(1) You: *Gern.*
Excuse me, what is …?

Seller: Chutney is really popular in the UK, especially mango chutney. It's a kind of sauce. It's originally from India. This one contains tomatoes and onions. You can eat it with vegetables, fish or meat.
(2) You: *Das ist … Man kann es …*

Your friend: Das hört sich gut an. Das könnte ich meinen Eltern mitbringen. Wie teuer ist denn ein Glas?
(3) You: …

Seller: £3.50. We've also got other kinds. This one contains pumpkin and carrots for example.
(4) You: …

Your friend: Super, mein Vater liebt Kürbis. Ich nehme beide. Dann habe ich zwei tolle Geschenke für meine Eltern.
(5) You: …

Seller: Great. That's £7 then.

Out and about

12 **CHOOSE YOUR TASK** B: wordbank: events p. 165, C: buying and selling p. 164

A Think of an object you could upcycle. Find a photo or draw a design and write a caption.
B Create an event calendar for your dream weekend.
C Imagine you want to sell something really odd. Advertise it!

Old pair of jeans makes cool new bag

C
Do you like fish?
Do you like music?
Then this is the _perfect item_ **for you!**
This decorative fish sings one of 20 songs for you whenever you walk past it. It looks great in any room! So, what are you waiting for? Come and get your singing fish today for _only £35!_

I'd like the blue one

13   grammar: prop words one and ones p. 181, workbook p. 44/11-12

Complete the sentences with 'one' or 'ones' and write them in your exercise book.

1 Which **T-shirt** do you like better? The red ??? or the green ????
2 I don't like these **socks**. The blue ??? are nicer.
3 This **ring** is too small for me. Have you got a bigger ????
4 Have you got another **book** like this ????
5 Which **shoes** are cheaper? The brown ??? or the black ????
6 This **cup** is broken. Have you got another ????

Buying and selling

14   **CHOOSE YOUR LEVEL**   workbook p. 46/13-16

I   **Match the English and the German phrases and write them down.**

Excuse me, how much is this?	Das kostet £6.
It's £6.	Und hier ist Ihr Wechselgeld.
I'll take it. Here you are.	Entschuldigung, wie viel kostet das?
And here's your change.	Ich nehme es. Hier, bitte.

II   **Read the phrases. What does the customer say? What does the seller say? Make a table.**

Excuse me, how much is this? · It's £6. · You can have it for £4.50. · Have you got another one of these? ·
I'll take it. · Here's your change. · Can I help you? · That's too much. I only have £4.

You can write:

seller	customer
It's …	Excuse me, …
…	…

III Match the sentence parts. Then sort the sentences into two lists: one for the seller, one for the customer.

1 Excuse me, can
2 Hi there, are you
3 Do you need
4 This cap is quite expensive,
5 Thank you, we're just

A how much is that one?
B looking.
C looking for anything special?
D anything else?
E I try these on?

Second-hand shopping TARGET TASK

15 workbook p. 47/17, wordbank: buying and selling p. 164, skill: performing a scene p. 159, media worksheet 2

Your task is to do a role play of a second-hand shopping situation.
Before you start, look at the following steps:

STEP 1

Get together in small groups and plan your role play.
Think about:
· Where does your role play take place?
  At a car boot sale, a flea market, …?
· How many people do you need?
  Who are they? What are they like?

STEP 2

What is going to happen in your shopping situation?
Collect ideas.
· What can you buy? What can you sell?
· How much are the items?
· Make up an interesting story behind one or
  more of the objects.

STEP 3

Decide who will play which part.

STEP 4

Make notes for your role play.
Collect words and phrases you will need.
Write cue cards for each character.

STEP 5

Practise your role play.
You can use your cue cards.

Remember to be friendly and polite!

STEP 6

Present your role play.
Make a video recording or act it out in class.

Good morning. / Hello.
Excuse me, could you …?
…, please.
Thank you.
You're welcome!
Have a nice day.
Thanks. Bye.

A festival

1a

Look at the poster. What festival is it about? Where and when does it take place? What can visitors expect?

1b

What do you know about the Vikings? Collect information in class.

You can say:
I think they lived …
The Vikings were …
…

THE JORVIK VIKING FESTIVAL

Join us in York for the largest Viking festival in Europe!

26th - 28th February
with an exciting programme of events

The Jorvik Viking festival

2a   wordbank: talking about pictures p. 166

Describe the pictures in 2b.
What are the people doing?

You can say:
In picture number …, the people are …

2b

Andy is a student in York. He likes travelling around the UK and writes a travel blog as *Adventuring Andy*. Read his post about the Jorvik Viking Festival.

1 March

Hey guys,

It's me, Adventuring Andy. Last weekend the *Jorvik Viking Festival* took place here in York. York has an interesting Viking past. The Vikings conquered York in 866. They lived here in the 9th and 10th centuries and had a big influence on everyday life.

What can I say? The festival was amazing. On my first day I checked out a show fight at the festival combat arena. When I arrived, two Viking warriors in armour were fighting each other while hundreds of people were watching.

After that I was really hungry. When I walked into the dining room, lots of people were already eating delicious Viking food.

ACTIVATE   PRACTISE   DEVELOP   PRACTISE   APPLY

The next day, I watched the *Best Beard Competition*. That's a competition where men, women, children and even dogs – really anyone – present their beards. The beards don't have to be real. Although it was raining, everyone there had such a great time!

Then I went to the *Birds of Prey Show* at Barley Hall. While I was watching the birds, I listened to the bird trainer. He told us a lot about the role of birds in old Viking stories.

My personal highlight was the *Battle Spectacular* in which two Viking hordes fought against each other. Then there was a breathtaking firework display. Throughout the festival, you could tell that all the visitors were really enjoying this trip to the Viking world.

Follow me for more interesting festival content. Coming soon: *Highland Games* and the *Notting Hill Carnival*.

2c CHOOSE YOUR LEVEL skill: reading p.154

I **Read the post in 2b again.**
Write captions for the pictures in the post.

You can write:
Picture 1: A show …   Picture 2: Delicious …
Picture 3: …   Picture 4: …

II **Read the post again. Put these pictures in the correct order and write captions for them.**

III **Read the post again. List all the events and activities that Andy mentions.**
What can you say about the activities?

2d wordbank: events, expressing opinions p.165

Which part of the Jorvik Viking festival do you find the most interesting?
What do you find the least interesting?
Say why.

You can say:
I find the … the most interesting because …
I find … the least interesting because …
…

2e workbook p.48/1

Do you know any events like this? Talk about them in class.

GRAMMAR HELP the past progressive p. 182-183

Du benutzt das *past progressive* um zu beschreiben, was zu einem bestimmten Zeitpunkt in der Vergangenheit gerade passierte.
Sieh dir die Beispiele an. Was fällt dir auf?

At 3 o'clock, two Viking warriors were fighting each other.	Um drei Uhr kämpften gerade zwei Wikingerkrieger gegeneinander.
Although it was raining, everyone there had such a great time!	Obwohl es gerade regnete, hatte jeder solchen Spaß!
Throughout the festival, the visitors were enjoying this trip to the Viking world.	Während des Festivals genossen die Besucher diesen Ausflug in die Welt der Wikinger.

Auf den Seiten 182 und 183 findest du weitere Erklärungen, auch zu verneinten Sätzen und Fragen.

Preparing for the competition

3   grammar: past progressive p. 182

Joe is taking part in the Best Beard Competition. Write about what he was doing in the morning.

1 At 6:30, Joe ??? (have) breakfast.
2 At 7:00, he ??? (wash) his beard.

3 At 7:45, he ??? (style) his beard.
4 At 8:00, he ??? (put on) his costume.

What were they doing?

4a   grammar: past progressive p. 182

Look at the pictures. What was happening? Write sentences in your exercise book.

5pm, two Vikings / fight

7pm, Andy / eat

10am, men, women, children and dogs / take part in competition

2pm, Andy / watch

9pm, visitors / watch

You can write:
At 5pm, two Vikings were …
At 7pm, Andy was …
…

4b   grammar: past progressive p. 182-183, workbook p. 49/2

What were you doing yesterday at 6pm, last Saturday at 10am, this morning at 7am, …?
Work with a partner. Ask and answer questions. Take turns.

You can ask:
What were you doing yesterday at 6pm?
What were you doing last Saturday at …?

You can answer:
I was talking to my dad. / I was …

◼ **DIGITAL+** practise more 16-17

ACTIVATE   **PRACTISE**   DEVELOP   PRACTISE   APPLY

Opinions

5a 🔲 audio 2/8

Listen to the three statements. Who is a fan of the Jorvik Viking Festival and who is not?

Chris

Cathy

Edward

5b CHOOSE YOUR LEVEL skill: listening p.151

▍ Listen to the first two statements again and complete the sentences.

1 The Viking Lodge is a hotel in …
2 Over the year they have …
3 Cathy absolutely loves …
4 She always has …

all kinds of guests · the Jorvik Viking Festival ·
the centre of York · the time of her life

▍▍ Listen to the three statements again. Complete three or more of the sentences.

Statement 1 (Chris)   1 Chris Cooper runs a ??? in York.
                      2 ??? is the best month of the year for the hotel.

Statement 2 (Cathy)   3 Cathy made her ??? from an old teddy bear.
                      4 She made a lot of new ??? from all over the world.

Statement 3 (Edward) 5 Edward has lived in York all his ???.
                      6 Last year, pickpockets stole Edward's ??? out of his pocket.

▍▍▍ Listen to the three statements again. Answer the questions.

1 What is the "Viking Lodge"?
2 Who stays there?
3 What is the best month of the year for the Viking Lodge?
4 What does Cathy say about her shoes?
5 What kind of competition does Cathy take part in every year?
6 How long has Edward lived in York?
7 Why is February not Edward's favourite month?

5c wordbank: events p.165, workbook p.49/3-4

In class, collect positive and negative aspects of having a big festival in your area. Take notes.

You can write:

positive: many tourists, …

negative: too many people, …

You can say:

I think … / In my opinion …

On the one hand, … / … is a positive aspect.

On the other hand, … / … is a negative aspect.

More festivals

6a

Andy checked out three more festivals. Look at the photos. What can you see?

6b   skill: reading p. 154

Read Andy's blog posts. Which festival do you find interesting?

29 June

Hey festival lovers,
Today I'm going to tell you about one of the biggest open-air music festivals in the world: the Glastonbury Festival in south-west England. It started in the 1970s and got bigger every year. At the Glastonbury Festival you sleep in tents, and when it rains everything is muddy at the end of the festival. But this isn't a problem for anyone. Every year, there are thousands of tents but it is not just a huge camping site, of course. At the festival itself there is so much to see. At Glastonbury there are always world-famous musicians, and you can listen to really good live music. A lot of people bring their children with them, and there's even an area with activities just for children.
I definitely recommend going there. The atmosphere is really special – it's like diving into another world.

4 August

Hey guys,
It's me again. This time I checked out the Notting Hill Carnival. It was impressive, loud and colourful! People from all over the world celebrate it in London every year in August. The carnival is a happy and cheerful event, but its beginnings in 1959 were quite serious. The organizers wanted to draw attention to the difficult situation of Caribbean immigrants.

ACTIVATE   PRACTISE   **DEVELOP**   PRACTISE   APPLY

If you like multicultural events, steel drums, colourful costumes and impressive parades, this is the right event for you. You can also taste a lot of different Caribbean dishes and drinks.
I had a really great time. I loved the final parade on Monday the most. Over 60 bands in fantastic costumes – where else can you see such a spectacle?

29 August
Hi there, lads and lasses!
Can you guess where I am? That's right, I'm in Scotland, in Braemar! I came here to see the world-famous Highland Games. They take place every summer in lots of different places.
Well, let me tell you this: the Highland Games are really worth a visit. You'll hear a lot of bagpipes and see men in kilts. There are many events to watch, for example Highland dancing, throwing the hammer or the most popular sport of all: tossing the caber. Here, you have to lift a big log and toss it so that it turns over and lands on the other end. Amazing!

6c CHOOSE YOUR LEVEL workbook p. 50/5-6

I Read the post about the Glastonbury Festival again. Copy the sentences and complete them.

1 The Glastonbury Festival started in the 1970s and ??? every year.
2 At the Glastonbury Festival, you sleep in ???.
3 You can listen to ??? musicians and ??? live music.
4 The ??? is really special.

II Write down four or more questions about the Glastonbury Festival. Then work with a partner and ask and answer the questions. Take turns.

You can write:
What is the Glastonbury Festival?
What can you …?
Where do / is …?
When does / is …?
How many …?

III Write down five or more questions about the Glastonbury Festival, the Notting Hill Carnival or the Highland Games. Then work with a partner and ask and answer the questions. Take turns.

Andy's picture show

7a   wordbank: talking about pictures p. 166

**Andy took a lot of pictures on his trips. Look at these four. What can you see?
Where do you think Andy took them?**

7b   video 10, skill: watching a video clip p. 156, workbook p. 51/7

**Andy is showing his pictures to a friend.
Watch the video clip. What was new to you?
What did you find the most surprising?**

You can say:

... was new to me.

I found ... the most surprising.

Party!

8   **CHOOSE YOUR TASK**   C: wordbank: events, expressing opinions p. 165, media worksheet 5, workbook p. 52/8

A   Create your own look! How would you dress
if you went to a festival or a carnival?
Draw your costume and label it.

B   Look at the pictures of the festivals on pages
70-72 again and write slogans for one or
more of the festivals.

C   What do you think people who live in
Glastonbury think about the festival?
Write down what someone who lives there
might say. Record it.

B

FOR MUD AND MUSIC LOVERS

*Get the full experience
at the Glastonbury
Music Festival!*

ACTIVATE   PRACTISE   **DEVELOP**   PRACTISE   APPLY

Help the environment!

9a skill: reading p. 154

Read the newspaper article. What problem does it describe?

How to clear up Britain's biggest events

Over three million people attend UK festivals each year and produce 23,500 tons of waste, which means 2.8kg of waste per person, per day. It is the UK's plan to be plastic-free by 2042, and festivals must become greener.

What's the plan?

In 2018, the British government published a plan on how to reduce waste over the next 25 years. Part of that plan was to get rid of plastic bags, food packaging and plastic straws. These and other products made of plastic have been in use a lot at festivals across the country. For example, in the past visitors threw away more than one million plastic bottles at each Glastonbury Festival, and it cost organizers almost £800,000 to get rid of the waste every year. Since 2019, visitors are no longer allowed to bring plastic bottles in order to help protect the environment. Another problem at the festival is the large number of tents that people leave at the festival site.

Do green festivals exist?

At 'No Planet B', the UK's first 'zero waste' festival, there was a list of 'zero waste rules'. For example, festival guests had to bring their own bottles, and the organizers asked them to use digital tickets and not paper.

9b skill: mediation p. 155, workbook p. 53/9

Your sister has some questions. Read the article again and answer them in German.

1 Wieso ist denn da ein Bild von so vielen Zelten?
2 Was steht da über das Jahr 2042?
3 Was steht da mit 800.000?
4 Was steht in dem Artikel darüber, wie man Festivals umweltfreundlicher macht?

Which festival?

10 GET TOGETHER

Get together with a partner.
Read and talk about different festivals.

Partner A	Partner B
I Go to page 129.	**I** Go to page 138.
II Go to page 132.	**II** Go to page 141.
III Go to page 135.	**III** Go to page 144.

Check your spelling

11   grammar: past progressive p. 182

Look at the verbs in the box. What are their –ing forms?
Sort them into three lists in your exercise book.

run · have · watch ·
happen · put · talk ·
listen · make · sit ·
dance · drive · swim ·
play · stop · get

You can write:

run – running	have – having	watch – watching
…		

When it started to rain

12   **CHOOSE YOUR LEVEL**   grammar: past progressive p. 182, workbook p. 53/10-11

What were the people at the festival doing when it started to rain?

▌ **Choose three or more of the pictures and write sentences.**

▌▌ **Choose four or more of the pictures and write sentences.**

▌▌▌ **Write sentences about the pictures.**

You can write:

Picture A: Jill and Suzy were setting up their tent when it started to rain.
Picture B: Becky was eating … when …
…

A — Jill and Suzy / set up tent

B — Becky / eat

C — Levi / listen to

D — Sheree / talk on the phone

E — Juan / sleep

F — the people / dance

Writing about a festival

13   workbook p. 54/12-14

Match the sentence parts.

1 The atmosphere
2 I listened
3 I can definitely
4 I had a

A to a lot of cool music.
B really great time.
C is really special.
D recommend going there.

A blog post TARGET TASK

14 workbook p. 55/15, wordbank: events p. 165, skill: writing p. 153, media worksheet 1, 10

Your task is to write a blog post about a festival or an event.
Before you start, look at these steps:

STEP 1

What do you want to write about?
A carnival, a music festival, a street party, …?
It can be a festival or event you have been to.
You can also make something up.

STEP 2

Collect ideas. Think about the following:
· Where did the event or festival take place?
· When did it take place? For how long?
· How much was it? Or was it free?
· What could you see or do there?
· Who was it for?
· What was special about it?
· What did you like about it?
· …

3 March

Hi everyone,

It's me, …, again.
Last weekend, I was at …

Look forward to next week's
blog – I'll write about …

Your …

STEP 3

Plan your post.

STEP 4

Write a first version of your post.
You can ask a classmate or your teacher to give you feedback.

STEP 5

Edit your post and write the final version.

Check out

Medieval mischief

1 You can't imagine how glad I am to be back home! This weekend Mum forced us all to go to the *Medieval Weekend at Arundel Castle*. We had to sleep in a tent and wear funny
5 costumes and I almost got killed.
But let me start at the beginning.
Two weeks ago, one of Mum's customers told her about this "really great event" which was "so much fun".
10 Mum said "we never do things together" and "I'm sure it'll be good for us as a family". My plan had been to spend the weekend at my best friend Joe's house. He's got a really good console and he has loads of games.
15 I was looking forward to finally improving my score. But no.
On Friday I found myself in the car, stuck between Lucy on one side and a **spinning wheel** and a sword on the
20 other. Mum had **borrowed** those from her friend "to make it more authentic". The boot of the car was completely full of **camping gear** and costumes and tins of baked beans.

25 Lucy was really excited because there were going to be horses, and she had always wanted to go horse riding.
When we arrived, a guy dressed like a knight showed us where to park the car and where to put up the tent. There were people dressed in medieval clothing everywhere.

The next morning, Mum woke us up and served porridge in wooden bowls. Except she called it
30 "**gruel**". More authentic, you know. After breakfast, Lucy wanted to go and see the horses.
"But first, let's get dressed," Mum said and handed me something that looked like a brown curtain.
"What's that?" I asked. "It's a **tunic**. Just put it on. You'll look just like a medieval teenager," Mum said happily. Then she handed Lucy another curtain (beige) and grabbed the spinning wheel.
"Why are you taking the spinning wheel with you?" Lucy asked.
35 "It's for the mother-daughter living **picture competition** I've registered us for," Mum replied.
"You've done WHAT?" Lucy asked. "I thought we were going horse riding and then I could go back to the tent and read my book." "Oh no, dear," Mum said. "And now let's go and make some beautiful memories."

medieval = *mittelalterlich*; mischief = *Unfug*; force = *zwingen*; spinning wheel = *Spinnrad*; sword = *Schwert*; had borrowed = *hatte geliehen*; camping gear = *Campingausrüstung*; gruel = *Grütze*; tunic = *Tunika*; living picture competition = *Wettbewerb der lebendigen Bilder*

"That's a great idea," Dad said and looked like he was trying really hard not to laugh. But Mum
40 didn't notice. She just smiled at him. "It is, isn't it?" she said.
So we all followed Mum to the stage in the middle of the festival ground. She set herself and Lucy
and the spinning wheel up, and a jury came by and looked at all the mothers and daughters
spinning and baking and doing all that other stuff women did in the Middle Ages. Then the jury
went off to decide who had created the best living picture.
45 "OK," Lucy said, "that's it. I'm off to find the horses now." And she was gone.

Since there were posters all over the place advertising a show fight in the combat arena somewhere
near our tent, I thought it might be a good idea to offer to take the spinning wheel back to the tent
and check out the arena. Mum was happy with that, too.
I was nearly at our tent when someone behind me suddenly shouted: "Careful! Get out of the way
50 everyone!!!" I turned around and saw the biggest horse I'd ever seen galloping towards me. On its
back was my sister, barely hanging on. "Lucy!" I shouted.
"Help!" Lucy shouted.

I jumped out of the way and fell on my
left knee. It really hurt, but I saved the
55 spinning wheel!
Meanwhile, the horse with Lucy on its
back was galloping away.
But another horse was already on its
way. Someone who was a lot better at
60 riding than my little sister was trying to
help her.
Behind him came Mum and Dad,
running and out of breath and clearly
panicking.

65 Dad panicked even more when the knight's sword almost cut my ear off. That was the moment
when I decided I liked the 21st century very much. Not so many swords and less gruel, much safer.

I don't know how, but the knight managed to bring Lucy and the horse back. Lucy was fine and she
wanted to get back on her horse and try again, but my knee hurt so much that they had to take me
to the emergency tent first.

70 When we came back, Mum said, "Alright, that was a bit too authentic. Even for me. I'm so glad they
invented modern medicine. I think I'm ready to go home, order some pizza and watch TV on the
couch in our living room."

Just at that moment, Mum and Lucy were called back to the stage and the jury announced that
they had won the mother-daughter living picture competition. They got the first prize: a week at
75 a Middle Ages Camp in the Cotswolds for the whole family.

the Middle Ages = *das Mittelalter*; I'd ever seen = *ich je gesehen hatte*; gallop = *galoppieren*; meanwhile = *inzwischen*

The legend of King Arthur

Glastonbury is not only famous for its music festival, it is also connected with the legend of King Arthur. It is said that King Arthur was buried in Glastonbury at the ruins of Glastonbury Abbey.
Another place connected with King Arthur is Glastonbury Tor, a tall hill with a tower. Some people say that it is the mythical island of Avalon.

There are different versions of the legend of King Arthur, and it is not clear if King Arthur really existed. However, there are many stories about King Arthur and also about the wizard Merlin, Arthur's loyal friend and counsellor. A well-known part of the legend is the story about the sword in the stone and how Arthur became king.

Once upon a time, when King Uther Pendragon of Britain had died, there was no new king. For years, many men fought to get to the throne, but no one won and still there was no new king.

In one corner of the kingdom lived a young man, Arthur. He lived in the castle of Sir Ector and his son, Sir Kay. They had taken in Arthur when he was a baby and had raised him. Now Arthur was sixteen years old.

One morning, a great stone with a sword appeared in the middle of the town. On the stone there were these words:

"He who pulls this sword from its stone shall be the rightful King of Britain."

The town was full of talk of this stone. Who had put it there? Where did it come from? Who would be the next king? For days, people tried to pull the sword from the stone, but it did not move. When Sir Ector, Sir Kay and Arthur walked past, Sir Kay also tried to pull the sword from the stone, but Arthur paid little attention.

Later, Kay was preparing for a tournament and couldn't find his sword. He asked Arthur to look for it.
Some time later, Arthur came back with a sword. "That ... that's not Kay's sword! Wh-where did you find this?" stuttered Sir Ector, who already recognized the sword. Arthur explained that he had taken the sword out of the stone because he couldn't find Kay's sword. "You are our new king! My brother is king!" cried Sir Kay.

Later, the great wizard Merlin appeared, and he explained everything to Arthur. "Your real father was the great King Uther, but he could not raise you and I gave you to Ector to raise you like his own child. But now your time has come to rule Britain."
And so Arthur ruled Britain, kindly and bravely, and the people were finally happy.

Do you know any stories, books or films about the legend of King Arthur? Search the Internet for more information and talk about it in class.

1. Describe the photos.
2. What do you think? How are the people feeling?
3. Choose one photo. What could be the story behind it? Collect ideas.

You are not alone

Part A Exploring roots

- Du erfährst etwas über die Wurzeln und Lebensgeschichten verschiedener Menschen.
- Du sprichst darüber, was an deinem Wohnort besonders für dich ist.
- Du stellst eine Lebensgeschichte vor.

Part B Giving a helping hand

- Du übst, Gefühle und Situationen zu beschreiben.
- Du lernst, wie man um Rat fragt und Ratschläge gibt.
- Du stellst eine Szene darüber vor, wie man jemandem helfen kann.

The place where you live

1   workbook p. 58/1

**What do you like about the city or village where you live? What is special about it?
Make notes and share your thoughts in class.**

a halfpipe · restaurants ·
friendly people · kebab stalls · …

You can say:

There is /are … in …

I like … because …

… is my favourite place in …

Living in London

2a

**Read what four people from London posted on this website.
Why did they come to London? Where in London do they live now? Take notes.**

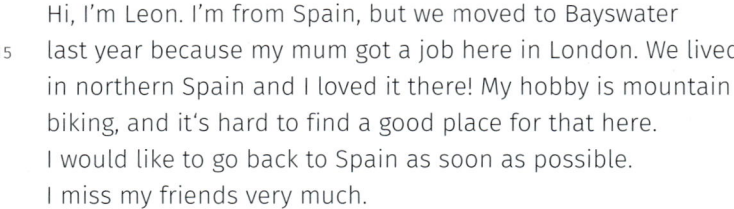

✴ **LIVING IN LONDON** ✴ ✴ ✴ ✴ ✴ ✴ ✴ ✴ ✴ ✴ ✴ ✴ ✴ ✴ ✴ ✴ ✴ ✴ ✴

1   My name is Jenna, and I am 16 years old. I was born in Korea,
but my parents moved to London when I was four because they
found better jobs here.
I have one brother. We live in south-west London, in Merton.

5   There's a Korean church in our neighbourhood and we go there
every Sunday. I like going to church because I always meet my
friends there.
My first memory of London was when I went on the London Eye.
It was lots of fun, and the view was amazing! The riverside near

10   the London Eye is my favourite place in London.
My grandparents still live in Korea. We fly to Korea every two
years to visit my grandparents.
We speak Korean and English at home. I like Korea, but I feel at home in London.

Jenna

Hi, I'm Leon. I'm from Spain, but we moved to Bayswater

15   last year because my mum got a job here in London. We lived
in northern Spain and I loved it there! My hobby is mountain
biking, and it's hard to find a good place for that here.
I would like to go back to Spain as soon as possible.
I miss my friends very much.

20   I also don't like my school here. When I first came here, I didn't
understand much of what people said and sometimes people
thought I was stupid just because of my accent.
The only thing I like about London is that there are a lot of parks
here – Hyde Park is my favourite.

Leon

ACTIVATE   PRACTISE   DEVELOP   PRACTISE   APPLY

25 My name is Sam. My family has always lived in London. I grew up
    in Battersea and now I live in Hammersmith. I went to university
    in Bristol, but I didn't like it very much because I missed London
    so much.
    There are so many things to do here. You can go shopping, visit
30 museums, go to parks or lots of concerts and shows …
    My favourite place in London is the Science Museum. There are
    always new exhibitions and I often go there. I love London.
    I don't want to live anywhere else!

Sam

Hello, I'm Erika. I'm from Sweden, and I came to London in 2006
35 to go to university here. I met my husband here. He's from Ghana
    and we both liked the lively atmosphere in London so much that
    we decided to stay here. We got married in 2014 and moved to
    Elephant & Castle in 2016. What I like most about this part of
    London are the people. I often meet someone I know in the street!
40 There is a very strong community here.
    My husband and I have a son and a daughter and we talk to them
    a lot about our family roots – both the West African side and the
    Swedish side. We all like cooking and we often cook dishes that
    are a mixture of West African, Swedish and British food.

Erika

2b CHOOSE YOUR LEVEL skill: reading p. 154

I **Read the first two texts again.**
What do Jenna and Leon like about London?
Take notes. In which lines did you find the
information?

You can write:

Jenna likes going to church.
In lines 6 and 7 she says: "I like …"

II **Read the first three texts again. What do the people like about London? Take notes.**
In which lines did you find the information?

III **Read the texts again. What do the people like about London? Take notes.**
In which lines did you find the information?

2c skill: talking to people p. 152, workbook p. 58/2-3

If you could live anywhere in the world, where would you like to live? Why?
Work in small groups and talk about your dream places to live.

| in the country | in a big city | in a small village | in London | … |

You can say:

I would like to live … because there are …
I would like to live … because I could have …

many shops · many animals ·
many things to do · not so many cars ·
a garden · a horse · …

GRAMMAR HELP the simple past (R) p. 184–185

Die Zeitform *simple past* kennst du schon. Du benutzt sie, wenn du über etwas sprechen möchtest, das in der Vergangenheit liegt und abgeschlossen ist. Sieh dir die Beispielsätze an. Erinnerst du dich? Wie bildest du die Formen? Worauf musst du bei der Verneinung und bei Fragen im *simple past* besonders achten?

My parents moved to London when I was four. They found better jobs here.	Meine Eltern zogen nach London, als ich vier war. Sie fanden dort bessere Jobs.
I didn't like Bristol very much. Why did the people come to London?	Ich mochte Bristol nicht sehr. Warum kamen die Leute nach London?

Auf den Seiten 184 und 185 sind die wichtigsten Punkte zum *simple past* noch einmal zusammengefasst.

Writing about the past

3a   grammar: simple past (R) p. 184

Write down the simple past forms of these verbs and use them to write three or more true or false statements about the people from pages 80 and 81.

1 move   2 live   3 be   4 like

5 grow up   6 meet   7 go

You can write:

Jenna's parents moved to Korea from London.
Leon …

3b   grammar: simple past (R) p. 184, workbook p. 59/4

Work with a partner. Your partner has to correct the false statements. Take turns.

Who, what, when, where?

4a   grammar: simple past (R) p. 185

Unscramble the questions and write them down.

1 move to – where – Jenna's parents – did
2 in London – was born – who
3 Sam – did – to university – go – where
4 to study – went – who – to London
5 when – move to Elephant & Castle – did – Erika's family

4b   grammar: simple past (R) p. 184

Look at pages 80 and 81 again and write down the answers to the questions from 4a.

4c   grammar: simple past (R) p. 184, wordbank: family history p. 166, workbook p. 60/5

Write three or more statements about yourself and your family.

You can write:

I was born in …
My great-grandmother came from …
…

DIGITAL+ practise more 19

London neighbourhoods

5a 🔊 audio 2/14

Listen to the podcast. Match the neighbourhoods with the pictures.

A Golders Green   B Southall
C Chinatown   D Brixton

5b CHOOSE YOUR LEVEL skill: listening p.151, workbook p.60/6-8

I Listen to the podcast again and take notes. Complete the sentences and write them down.

1 There are more than 80 different Chinese restaurants in ???.
2 ??? is sometimes called "Little India".
3 You will find a lot of Caribbean restaurants and reggae music shops in ???.

Brixton ·
Southall ·
Chinatown

II Listen to the podcast again and take notes. Complete the sentences and write them down.

1 Many tourists visit ???.
2 In ??? you can try dishes from many South Asian countries.
3 Many people in ??? have an African or Caribbean background.
4 The largest Jewish community in London lives in ???.

III Listen to the podcast again. Choose the correct information and write it down.

1 A Chinese immigrants have lived in Chinatown for more than 200 years.
   B There is a parade for Chinese New Year in Chinatown in December.
2 A Southall is in South London.
   B Many people who live in Southall have an Indian background.
3 A You can hear more than 130 different languages in Brixton.
   B Over 50% of the population in Brixton has an African or Caribbean background.
4 A Only Jewish people live in Golders Green.
   B Many of the people who live in Golders Green have German or Polish roots.

LAND & LEUTE 4  video 11

Multikulturelles London

Großbritannien ist schon immer multi-kulturell gewesen. Nach dem Zweiten Weltkrieg sind viele Menschen aus ehemaligen britischen Kolonien nach Großbritannien gekommen, zum Beispiel aus Indien, Pakistan, Hongkong und einigen afrikanischen Ländern. Viele sind vor allem nach London gekommen, weil sie dort auf bessere Jobs hofften.

Die Einwanderer haben ihre Kultur und ihre Sprachen mitgebracht. London ist der Schmelztiegel dieser Kulturen. In London werden mehr als dreihundert verschiedene Sprachen gesprochen.

In einigen Stadtteilen kann man einen starken Einfluss der verschiedenen Gruppen sehen. Beispielsweise leben viele Menschen aus Bangladesch im Osten Londons. Die bekannteste Gegend dort ist die *Brick Lane,* in der man sogar Straßenschilder auf Bengali sehen kann, einer Sprache, die hauptsächlich in Bangladesch und Indien gesprochen wird.

Es gibt auch viele Menschen in London, die Polnisch, Türkisch, Gujarati, Panjabi oder Urdu sprechen.

Welche Sprachen sprechen deine Mitschüler und Mitschülerinnen? Macht eine Umfrage.

The Grandparent Project

6a

What do you think: what is "The Grandparent Project"?

6b   skill: mediation p. 155

Your grandparents have found this website. Tell them in German what it is about.

Connecting children & grandparents all over the world

This programme helps children all over the world to write their grandparents' stories and learn about their family history.

→ Interview your grandparents and listen to their story.
→ Write your grandparents' story. If you like, you can put it into a digital format, make a drawing or create a multimedia series.
→ Learn creative storytelling skills.

6c

What questions would you ask in an interview for the Grandparent Project? Collect ideas in class.

You can ask:
What did you do in your free time?
Where did you meet Grandma / Grandpa?
Tell me about your parents. Were they …? …

Edyta's life story – part one

7a 🔊 audio 2/17

Ava has decided to take part in the Grandparent Project and talks to her grandmother Edyta in Poland on the phone. Listen and read along. Who do they talk about?

Ava: Hi Grandma. Thanks for helping me with this project.

Edyta: Of course. I'm looking forward to talking to you about our family history. Where would you like to start?

Ava: Maybe with your parents? I know that my great-grandfather left Poland and came to England. Can you tell me more about it?

Edyta: Of course. My father, your great-grandfather Radek, was a pilot. When World War II began in 1939, he and many other Polish pilots went to England and joined the Royal Air Force to help fight the Nazis.

Ava: And what happened after the war?

Edyta: He decided to stay in Britain.

Ava: And how did he meet your mother?

Edyta: Oh, he knew her already. She was from the same town in Poland as he was. In 1946 my mother – your great-grandmother Agata – left Poland and emigrated to Great Britain to marry him and start a new life in London.

Ava: How did she feel about it? Was it hard for her to move to a foreign country?

Edyta: It wasn't easy at first. She didn't speak any English and she was homesick. But they lived in a neighbourhood with a lot of Polish people, so it was OK. She learnt to speak English, and after a while she felt at home. And then my oldest brother, Pavel, was born in 1951.

Ava: When was your brother Jan born?

Edyta: Jan was born in 1955 and then I was born in 1958 …

7b **CHOOSE YOUR LEVEL** skill: reading p.154, workbook p.61/9-10

I **Read the dialogue again. What do you learn about Edyta and her brothers? Take notes.**

II **Read the dialogue again. What do you learn about Edyta's mother Agata? Take notes.**

III **Read the dialogue again. What do you learn about Edyta's father Radek? Take notes.**

Edyta's life story – part two

8a   wordbank: talking about pictures p. 166

Look at the pictures. What do you think happened in Edyta's life?

8b   audio 2/18, skill: reading p. 154

Listen to the dialogue and read along. What does Edyta say about speaking Polish?

Ava: You looked so cute when you were a baby. I remember the old photo of you in your funny baby dress …

Edyta: Ha, ha. That was the latest fashion for babies then! But I had a wonderful childhood. We lived in a nice house and I loved playing in our garden.

Ava: You speak English and Polish. How did you learn to speak both languages?

Edyta: Well, at school I always spoke English, and at home we mostly spoke Polish. It was very important to my parents that my brothers and I were able to speak Polish with our family in Poland.

Ava: It's a shame that I don't speak Polish that well. Did you have Polish lessons at school?

Edyta: No, I didn't. But I went to a Polish theatre group once a week. That's where I met your grandad Filip.

Ava: He was Polish too, wasn't he?

Edyta: Actually, we were both British. We just came from Polish families.

Ava: Oh. Right. But you still spoke Polish at home. That's why Dad can speak Polish a lot better than Noah, Joshua and me.

Edyta: Yes, we did. And we often spent the summer holidays in Poland when your father was little.

Ava: Yes, he told us about that. He really liked it there. But back to you. What about your job? Did you like it?

Edyta: Yes, I did. I liked working as a nurse and, when your father was old enough, I went back to my job.

Ava: Grandpa Filip died when Dad was still quite young, didn't he?

Edyta: Oh, that was a very sad time for

ACTIVATE   PRACTISE   **DEVELOP**   PRACTISE   APPLY

all of us. Your father was at university in Manchester and I felt a bit lonely at that time, but then I began to visit my family in Poland more often.

Ava: And how did you get the idea to move to Poland?

Edyta: My cousin had the idea and I liked it.

Ava: Do you miss anything about London?

Edyta: Sure. I miss you. That's why I come to visit as often as I can. But Poland feels as much like home as London. I feel like I have two homes.

Ava: "Two homes". That's a good title for my story for the Grandparent Project. I think I have a lot to write about now.

Edyta: I really enjoyed talking to you. Just let me know if you want to know anything else about our family.

Ava: Thanks for answering all my questions.

Edyta: You're welcome, darling.

8c CHOOSE YOUR LEVEL skill: writing p. 153, media worksheet 11

I Choose three or more of the pictures from 8a and write captions for them.

You can write:

Picture 1: Edyta in her funny baby dress

Picture …

II Choose three or more of the pictures from 8a and write speech or thought bubbles for Edyta.

You can write:

Picture 1: "I …"

…

III Choose two or more of the pictures from 8a and write Edyta's diary entries or letters for those days.

You can write:

Dear diary,

Today was a great day. I …

…

London, 24 March 1982

Dear Janina,

Today, I …

Love,
Edyta

8d wordbank: family history p. 166, workbook p. 63/11-13

What does 'home' mean to you? Is it a place? A feeling? People? Collect ideas in class.

You can write:

To me, 'home' means …

Home is …

Tell us more

9 CHOOSE YOUR TASK A+B: wordbank: family history p. 166, C: skill: searching the internet p. 157, media worksheet 6

A **Create a picture or collage about what 'home' means to you and label it.**

B **What were important events in your own life? Make a timeline.**

C **Find a map of London on the Internet. Choose a neighbourhood that looks interesting to you. Find out more about it. Then write a fact file.**

Interviewing grandparents

10 **CHOOSE YOUR LEVEL** grammar: simple past (R) p. 185, workbook p. 64/14-15

Read the following answers to interview questions. Write questions to the answers.

I 1 I was born in 1959.
2 My grandmother had three children.
3 I went to school in Bristol.

You can write:
When were you …?
How many … did your …?
Where did you …?

II 1 My father was from Italy.
2 My mother had two brothers.
3 My parents got married in 1952.
4 I went to school in Exeter.

You can write:
Where was your …?
How many … did …?
When did …?
Where …?

III 1 My mother was born in Egypt.
2 My father had two brothers and a sister.
3 My parents moved to Liverpool in 1955.
4 Yes, I did. I liked going to school a lot.

Adjectives and nouns

11

Match all the adjectives to the nouns. There can be more than one solution.

better · foreign · happy ·
good · sad · wonderful

job · place · time · language · roots ·
family · childhood · life · people

How to pronounce the letter *s*

12a audio 2/20

Listen and repeat.

parks · roots · things · brothers ·
towns · accents · groups · friends

12b

Make two lists in your exercise book and listen again. Write the words in your lists.

/s/	/z/
parks	*things*
…	…

12c audio 2/21

Listen and check your lists.

 **DIGITAL+** practise more 20

ACTIVATE   PRACTISE   DEVELOP   **PRACTISE**   APPLY

A life story TARGET TASK

13 workbook p. 65/16, wordbank: family history p. 166, media worksheet 1

Your task is to present someone's life story.
Before you start, look at these steps:

STEP 1

Who do you want to present? You could choose:
· yourself
· someone from your family
· a famous person
· someone from a book or film
· ...

born in 1926

four sisters

married 1951

worked in family business

two children 1951 and 1953

STEP 2

Think of questions you would like to ask the person
and decide how you want to present his or her life story.
You could:
· create a poster
· create a photo story with speech and thought bubbles
· create a collage with labels
· create a timeline with photos
· write a text about the person's life
· ...

STEP 3

Find out as much as you can about the person's life story.
Think about:
· the family (parents, grandparents, ...)
· the places where the person lived
· important people in the person's life
· the person's school, university, job, ...
· ...

first grandchild 1979

husband died 1983

STEP 4

Create your work.

first great-grandchild when she was 87 years old

died when she was 96 years old

STEP 5

Present your work.

How are you today?

1   skill: talking with people p. 152, wordbank: feelings p. 167, workbook p. 66/1

Work in small groups.
How are you feeling today?
Talk to each other.

happy · sad · angry ·
bored · worried · nervous · …

You can say:
I'm happy / sad because …
I feel OK. How about you?

What's up?

2a   wordbank: talking about pictures p. 166

Look at the pictures. Describe the situations. What do you think: how are the people feeling?

You can say:
In picture A, there are …
They are …
The boy looks …
I think the girl on the left is feeling …
…

2b   audio 3/1, skill: listening p. 151

Listen to the dialogues. Which picture from 2a goes with which dialogue?

You can say:
I think picture … goes with dialogue …

2c

Read the three dialogues. What are the problems?

Dialogue 1

Louise: Hi Emily! What's wrong? You look sad.
Emily: Hi Louise. Oh, it's about Chloe. We had an argument.
Louise: Why, what happened?
Emily: She wanted to copy my French homework. But I said no and that she should do her homework herself because our French teacher always notices and is very strict. Now Chloe is so angry with me that she won't talk to me anymore.
Louise: Should I try to talk to her?
Emily: Thanks, Louise – that would be great!

ACTIVATE   PRACTISE   DEVELOP   PRACTISE   APPLY

Dialogue 2

Toby: Hi guys. Anyone up for hanging out at my place this afternoon?

Jack: I'm in!

Paul: I have maths tuition on Tuesdays.

Toby: Why don't you ask your mum if you can skip the lesson?

Paul: I don't think that she will let me. She's not happy with my marks. Just because I got a D in my last test …

Jack: And what does your dad say?

Paul: Oh, no chance, he is even stricter! It's really annoying. What if I join you guys later?

Toby: Yeah, good idea. We'll save some snacks for you!

Paul: That would be great. Thanks, guys.

Dialogue 3

Faisal: Guys, have you heard about James and Delia? Delia invited James to her party, but she says that he won't come.

Linda: Why not? What happened?

Faisal: She says that he says that her party will be lame – because she didn't invite his rugby friends.

Matt: But Delia doesn't even know his rugby friends!

Faisal: Exactly. Why should she invite people that she doesn't know? Now James is angry and says that he doesn't even want to go to Delia's party. He's telling everybody that he'll have his own party on that day!

Linda: That's so silly. Delia must be really upset. I'll go and talk to her.

2d CHOOSE YOUR LEVEL skill: reading p. 154

I **Complete the sentences with words from the box and write them in your exercise book.**

1 Emily looks ???.
2 Chloe is ??? with Emily.
3 Paul's mum is not ??? with his marks.

strict · sad · angry · happy · afraid

II **Match the sentence parts. Write the sentences in your exercise book.**

1 Emily tells Louise that	A he has to go to maths tuition before he can join them.
2 Louise thinks that	B James won't come to her party.
3 Paul explains to his friends that	C Chloe is wrong.
4 Delia says that	D she is sad because she had an argument with Chloe.

III **Are the sentences true or false? Copy the true sentences and correct the false sentences.**

1 Emily tells Louise that she is sad because she got a bad mark in maths.
2 Louise thinks that Chloe is right.
3 Paul has to go to maths tuition on Fridays.
4 Paul says that his mum is even stricter than his dad.
5 Delia wants to invite James's rugby friends to her party.

2e workbook p. 66/2

Choose one of the situations from 2c.
What do you think will happen next? Collect ideas.

You can say:
I think … will …

ACTIVATE PRACTISE DEVELOP PRACTISE APPLY

GRAMMAR HELP reported speech 1 p. 186

Wenn du wiedergeben möchtest, was jemand anderes sagt, benutzt du indirekte Rede *(reported speech)*. Schau dir die Sätze an und achte dabei vor allem auf die Pronomen und die Verbformen. Was fällt dir auf?

Direkte Rede:	**Indirekte Rede:**
Louise: "You look sad."	Louise tells Emily <u>that</u> she looks sad.
Louise: „Du siehst traurig aus."	Louise sagt Emily, <u>dass</u> sie traurig aussehe.
Emily: "We had an argument."	Emily says <u>that</u> they had an argument.
Emily: „Wir hatten einen Streit."	Emily sagt, <u>dass</u> sie einen Streit gehabt hätten.

Auf Seite 186 findest du weitere Beispiele und Erklärungen zur indirekten Rede.

Text messages

3   grammar: reported speech 1 p. 186, workbook p. 66/3-4

What do the people say in their text messages? Write at least one sentence for each text message.

James

Hi everyone, my party will be at my house this Saturday. We start at four! James

Matt

Hi James, I'm really sorry. I can't come. I've already said yes to Delia's party. Matt

Faisal

Hi guys, I can get the present for Delia. You can give me the money on Monday.

Phil

Hi James, I'll be there and I'll bring my friends from the football team. Phil

You can write:

James says that his party …
Matt says that he is …
Faisal says that he can …
Phil says that …

Feelings

4a   wordbank: feelings p. 167

How do you think the people are feeling? Make notes.

OK · sad · proud · stressed · lonely · happy · …

Mia

Eric

Michelle

Oliver

4b    audio 3/2, skill: listening p. 151, grammar: reported speech 1 p. 186

Listen to the statements and take notes.
Compare with your notes in 4a.
Then write about the people.

You can write:

Mia says that she is …
Eric says that his …
…

DIGITAL+ practise more 21

ACTIVATE **PRACTISE** DEVELOP PRACTISE APPLY

Lily's problem

5a

Read the text messages. Why does Lily want to talk to Noah?

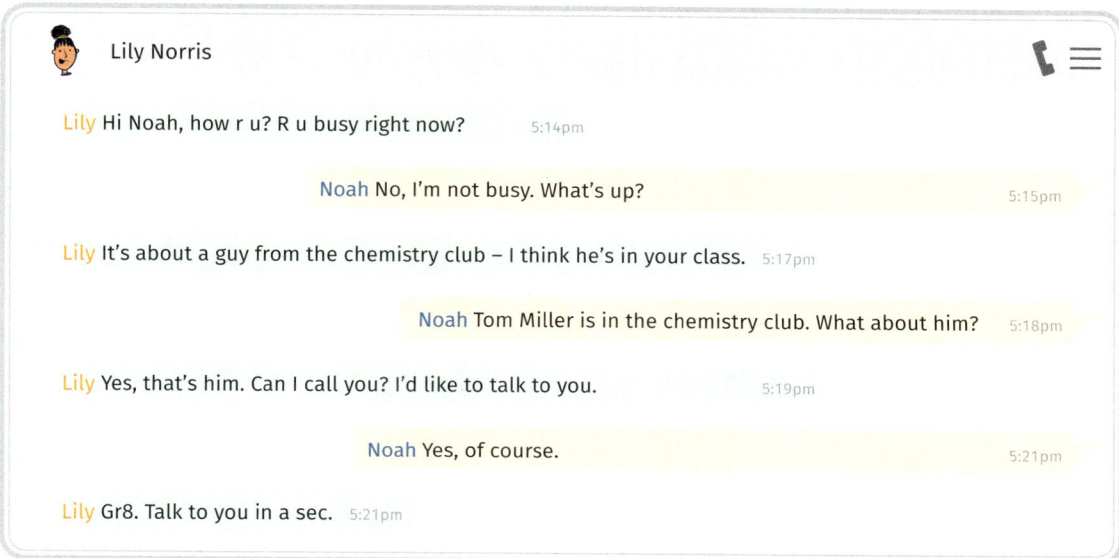

Lily Norris

Lily Hi Noah, how r u? R u busy right now? 5:14pm

Noah No, I'm not busy. What's up? 5:15pm

Lily It's about a guy from the chemistry club – I think he's in your class. 5:17pm

Noah Tom Miller is in the chemistry club. What about him? 5:18pm

Lily Yes, that's him. Can I call you? I'd like to talk to you. 5:19pm

Noah Yes, of course. 5:21pm

Lily Gr8. Talk to you in a sec. 5:21pm

5b audio 3/3

Listen to Lily talking to Noah on the phone. What is Lily's problem?

5c CHOOSE YOUR LEVEL skill: listening p. 151

I Listen again. What does Noah say? Take notes.

You can write:
Tom: no right to …

II Listen again. Then write down Noah's ideas.

You can write:
Noah says that he could …
He says that Lily could …

III Listen again and answer the questions.

1 Why did Lily tell Tom to delete the photo?
2 What was Tom's reaction when Lily asked him to delete the photo?
3 What do Lily's mums always say about the Internet?
4 What does Noah say Lily could do now?

5d skill: talking with people p. 152, workbook p. 68/5

What can you do if you have a problem?
Who could you talk to? Talk about it with a partner.

You can say:
We could …

Seeking advice

6b skill: reading p. 154

6a
Look at the headline of the website.
What kind of content do you expect?

6b skill: reading p. 154
Read the texts. Who is writing?
Who is the website for?

× −

* *

LONDON TEEN HELP – ASK OUR EXPERTS ONLINE

* *

1   **School, parents, friends – there's a lot that teenagers can have problems with.
If you need advice, we're here to help. Send your questions to our team of
experts. We'll answer every question and post some of them anonymously with
our answers on this website.**

5   Q Dear expert,
I have a problem with a boy. He took a silly photo of me with his phone after
school. I told him to delete it, but he said no. He says that the photo is his and
that he can keep it and do whatever he wants with it – even put it on the Internet.
I really don't want that and I tried to talk to him about it, but he only laughs at me.
10 Now I don't know what I can do to stop him. Can you help me?
Thanks a lot,
Sunnyday

A *Dear Sunnyday,
I'm sorry to hear about your situation, but I'm sure there's a solution to your
15 problem. That boy has no right to keep or publish that photo. You did not agree
to anything so he must delete it if you say so. I think that he does not know that he is
doing something wrong. I suggest that you talk to him as soon as possible to make that
really clear to him. I would also suggest that you ask a parent or a teacher to help you.
All the best and good luck!*
20 *Your expert*

Q Dear expert,
I am 13 years old and I have a problem with my parents. They are very strict
when it comes to online time. I am not allowed to be online more than one
hour per day. That's just enough time to do some work for school, check my messages
25 and answer them. All my friends are online all day. They chat and play online video
games. I am completely left out unless I go to a friend's house and go online with
them. My parents worry about my marks. They think I won't do my homework if I spend
more time online and they don't listen to my arguments. Help! What can I do?
Lonelygirl

30 **A** *Hi Lonelygirl,*
I know how important it can be to be online. Teenagers today live in a very digital world – you use laptops or tablets at school and at home. Have you explained to your parents that you're not only online for fun but that you also communicate with your classmates about school matters, do research and so on? Maybe you could keep a
35 *diary to show your parents how much time you need for your online school work alone? You could also ask them to let you have more time online so that you can prove that your marks won't get worse. There are also official websites that give parents an idea of how much screen time is OK for children and teenagers. I wish you good luck!*
Your expert

40 **Q** Dear expert,
I am 14 and I have a problem that I can't solve. There is this girl in the chemistry club at my school and I really like her – but I am too shy to tell her. Last week, after school, we walked home together and we took funny pictures of each other with our phones. She did not like one of the photos that I took of her – but I think she looks cute
45 in it, so I didn't want to delete it when she asked me to. I thought it was really funny and told her that I might put the photo on the Internet. She got so angry with me that she doesn't look at me or talk to me anymore. What can I do now? I really want her to like me again. Can you help me?
Anonymous

50 **A** *Dear Anonymous,*
Why don't you talk to her again and apologize? You are definitely not allowed to keep that photo or put it on the Internet if she doesn't want you to do so. And don't you think she might be happy if you tell her the real reason for keeping the picture? Teasing her is definitely the wrong way! Just tell her that you like her. Good luck!
55 *Your expert*

6c **CHOOSE YOUR LEVEL** skill: writing p. 153

I In your own words, describe Sunnyday's problem. Write two or more sentences. Can you guess who Sunnyday is?

You can write:
Sunnyday has problems with …
She doesn't want that …

II In your own words, describe Sunnyday and Lonelygirl's problems. Write three or more sentences for each person. Can you guess who Sunnyday is?

III In your own words, describe the people's problems. Write three or more sentences for each person. Can you guess who Sunnyday and Anonymous are?

6d wordbank: expressing opinions p. 165, skill: talking with people p. 152, workbook p. 68/6-9

Work in small groups. What do you think about the answers on the website? Are they helpful? Have you got any other ideas?

Solving the problem

7 skill: writing p. 153, workbook p. 70/10-11

Work with a partner. Write a dialogue between Tom and Lily in which they try to solve the problem.

You can write:

Tom: I wanted to talk to you about …
Please listen to me and …
I'm sorry that …
I didn't mean to …
…

Lily: But you …
It's important to me that …
…

Tom/Lily: Why don't we …?
Let's …
…

A person to talk to

8a video 12, skill: watching a video clip p. 156

Watch the video clip.
Where does the woman work?

8b workbook p. 71/12

Watch the video clip again.
What does the woman talk about?

You can say:

The woman talks about …
She says that …

8c wordbank: expressing opinions p. 165

Would you talk to a school counsellor about your problems? Why or why not? Work with a partner. You can talk in German.

Sheree's problems

9 GET TOGETHER audio 3/5

Get together with a partner.
Listen to Sheree's call to the teen helpline.

Partner A
I Go to page 130.
II Go to page 133.
III Go to page 136.

Partner B
I Go to page 139.
II Go to page 142.
III Go to page 145.

ACTIVATE PRACTISE **DEVELOP** PRACTISE APPLY

Dealing with feelings

10 CHOOSE YOUR TASK A, C: wordbank: feelings p. 167, B: skill: performing a scene p. 159, media worksheet 2, 5

A **Draw at least eight emojis and label them.**
B **Work in groups or pairs and read out one of the dialogues from pages 90/91. You can record your reading.**
C **Make a word search for a partner with words for feelings.**

Helping out

11 skill: mediation p. 155, workbook p. 71/13

**Bob is an exchange student at your school. He does not speak much German.
He is upset because he has lost his rucksack. Help him to get it back.**

Bob: I can't find my rucksack! I think I left it on the bus yesterday when we were on the school trip. Could we call the bus company and ask if they have found my rucksack?
(1) You: *Yes, sure. I'll call their office. (…) Guten Tag, …*

Office manager: Wie spät war das? Und wo hat er denn gesessen? Welche Farbe hat der Rucksack?
(2) You: *What time …? And …? What …?*

Bob: It was about three in the afternoon and I was sitting in the middle of the bus on the left. It's a red rucksack.
(3) You: …

Office manager: Alles klar. Da muss ich mal eben mit einem Kollegen sprechen, einen Moment bitte. (…) Ich habe eine gute Nachricht! Sie haben einen Rucksack gefunden. Das muss seiner sein. Ihr könntet ihn heute Nachmittag abholen.
(4) You: *She says …*

Bob: Oh great, thank you very much. Where can we pick it up?
(5) You: …

Office manager: In der Husarenstraße 10. Direkt beim Busbahnhof.
(6) You: …

Your problem or mine?

12 workbook p. 72/14-15

Copy the sentences and fill in the correct words from the brackets.

1 Your brother is wrong: it's not your problem, it's ???. (he / his)
2 The photo belongs to me, it's ??? and I can do whatever I want with it. (mine / my)
3 She took my cap and now she says that it's ???. (her / hers)
4 Who left the dirty T-shirt in the living room? Is it ???? (your / yours)
5 The TV belongs to all of us, it's ???. (ours / our)
6 Do you think the ball in our garden belongs to our neighbours? - Yes, I think it's ???. (theirs / their)

Linking parts

13 CHOOSE YOUR LEVEL

I **Choose the correct word and write down the sentences.**

1 I feel worried **because / but** my dog is sick.
2 **So / When** I have too much to do, I feel stressed.
3 I wanted to go the party **when / but** now I can't.

II **Match the sentence parts and write down the sentences.**

1 I feel stressed
2 My parents are really strict
3 I'm angry with my brother
4 I'm really sad

A and don't allow me to stay up late.
B when I have too much homework.
C because I can't go to my friend's party.
D but he only laughs at me.

III **Choose the correct linking word and write down the sentences.**

1 I always feel sad when / but my parents have an argument.
2 My friend is angry because / and I forgot her birthday.
3 I got a very rude message from a classmate when / and I definitely won't answer it.
4 My sister can stay up late because / but I have to be in bed by nine.

How to pronounce the letters *th*

14 audio 3/10

Listen to the words and repeat them. Then sort them into two lists:
words with /ð/ as in "this" and words with /θ/ as in "thanks".

this · thanks · that · think · thought · then · through · there · they

DIGITAL+ practise more 21

ACTIVATE   PRACTISE   DEVELOP   **PRACTISE**   APPLY

Giving a helping hand   TARGET TASK

15 　　 workbook p.73/16, wordbank: seeking and giving advice p.167, skill: performing a scene p.159, media worksheet 2

Your task is to prepare a scene about helping somebody.
Before you start, look at these steps:

STEP 1

Work in small groups. Choose a situation in which you can give advice or help, for example:

· A friend always panics before tests.

· A classmate tells you that his or her best friend says bad things behind his or her back.

· The new pupil in your class looks very sad and lonely.

· …

STEP 2

Make notes for your scene. You can look at the box for help. You do not have to write the complete script but you can write cue cards for each character.

Think about what you can do.	You can sit next to him or her. · You can spend time with him or her. · You can try to talk to … · …
Think about what you can say.	You are not alone. · It's not your fault. · Maybe you could … · Maybe it would help to … · …
Ask questions to find out more.	What exactly is the problem? · Why …? · Do you think …? · Are you afraid of …? · …
Talk about your experience.	When I had this problem, I … · I've tried … · I know someone who … · He / She … · …
Think about who else could help.	Could you talk to your parents? · Could you ask a teacher for advice? · …

STEP 3

Decide who will play which part and practise your scene.

STEP 4

Perform your scene. If you like, you can film your scene and show it to the rest of the class.

Check out

Kannst du einem Blogeintrag Informationen entnehmen?	**Workbook, p. 74**
Kannst du über vergangene Ereignisse schreiben?	**Workbook, p. 74**
Kannst du einen Podcast über Stadtteile in London verstehen?	**Workbook, p. 74**
Kannst du verstehen, worum es geht, wenn jemand über ein Problem spricht?	**Workbook, p. 75**
Kannst du wiedergeben, was jemand sagt?	**Workbook, p. 75**
Kannst du deine Meinung zu einem Problem äußern?	**Workbook, p. 75**

Wrong impressions

1   A couple of months ago, my English teacher,
Mr Rogers, asked me after class if I could help
a student from another class with her work for
English Literature because she didn't like to
5   read and wasn't doing well in her exams.
I wasn't happy about that, especially when he
said, "It's Marianne Hamilton from your year."
Until that day I had talked to Marianne exactly
three times.

10   The first time was in the queue at lunch break. She said, "Oh, could you pass me a fork, please?
I forgot to take one," and I said, "Yeah sure. Here you are." The second time was during the music
project all the students in our year did together. She said, "Could you move your chair, please?"
and I said, "Yeah sure. Sorry."

The third time was in our school library. I was there with my friends
15   having fun when she said, "Could you please be quiet? I am trying
to work here," and I said, "Yeah sure."

Well, anyway, I had always been a bit shy around Marianne.
I thought that she was probably quite boring and one of those
students who are good at everything and always on time and
20   always do their homework and always study before exams.

I don't like studying too much. I'm good at English by accident. I just like reading and writing about
what I've read. That helps a lot.
"If you help Marianne for about one hour every week, I can let that count as your group project for
this year," Mr Rogers went on. At my school we have to do one group project in English every year.
25   I hate doing group projects. I wasn't sure what was worse, but then I thought I may as well give it
a try so I said, "Yeah, OK, I'll help her."

"Brilliant!" Mr Rogers said and seemed very happy. He told me to come back to his room at the end
of the school day. Marianne was there, too, and we worked out a plan together. She didn't seem to
be too excited about Mr Rogers' idea, either. All she said was, "Yes. OK. Yes, Saturday is fine. We can
30   meet at my house. Just give me your phone number and I'll text you my address." Which she did.
On Saturday, Marianne's mum let me in. The house was really nice. Marianne's mum seemed nice,
too. She gave us a plate of biscuits and some lemonade and told us to have fun. I wasn't sure I'd
have much fun in the next hour but at least there were biscuits. Really good chocolate biscuits.
We went upstairs and Marianne opened the door to her room. It was full of books!

---

impression = *Eindruck*; exam = *Prüfung*; queue = *Schlange*; by accident = *zufällig, aus Versehen*; count = *zählen*; give a try = *ausprobieren*

35 Really, there were books EVERYWHERE.
"Whoa," I said, "I thought you didn't like reading?"

"I LOVE reading" she said, "It's just that I didn't
like the first book we had to read in Year 7. I hated
it. I don't like books with animals as the main
40 characters. I think they're silly. I think we should
read books about real people. So I wrote what
I thought was bad about the book. But it is Mr
Rogers' favourite book and now he thinks that
I'm not good with books.
45 I can say and write and do whatever I want –
he has this image of me and I can't change it."

"That's not fair of him," I said, "I liked the book
but maybe only because my dad read it to my
sister and me when we were younger. I'm not sure
50 I would like it as much otherwise. But now Mr
Rogers seems to like me and I get good marks."

"See?" Marianne said, "He's got this opinion and it's really hard to change it. I really like the book
we're reading now, but I'm sure he won't give me anything better than a C. So, why bother? –
What are you reading at the moment?"
55 "*Noah can't even*," I said, "It's about a boy who's …"
"Oh, I've read it," Marianne interrupted me, "I loved it. Have you ever read this one?" and she
pulled a book from the pile next to her bed.

We spent the next three hours discussing books, and Marianne let me borrow five of her books that
I hadn't read yet. I didn't help her with her homework at all, but we had a good time and set a date
60 for Marianne to come to my place so that she could borrow some of my books.
From then on, we spent all our "lessons" talking about books and reading. When Mr Rogers asked
how it was going, we always smiled and told him that we were working hard and that Marianne
was doing very well.
The day before her next exam, we studied a little
65 but not too much. Then we went out for ice cream.

Three days later Marianne got her very first A in
an English exam. She told me that Mr Rogers had
smiled at her when he returned her exam paper
and said: "That was very well done. I'm happy
70 that my plan worked out so well."

bother = *sich Mühe geben*; interrupt = *unterbrechen*; pull = *ziehen*; pile = *Stapel, Haufen*; set a date = *sich verabreden*;
A = *etwa: 1, sehr gut*; paper = *hier: Klassenarbeit, Klausur*; work out = *hier: aufgehen*

On the Move Again

You know
You gotta go.
No time to grieve
You just gotta leave.

Get away from the pain
On the move again.

Take the train.
Catch a plane.

Make the trip
In a ship.

Take a hike
Ride a bike.

Go by car.
Going far.

Use your feet
On the street.

Get stuck
In a truck.

Then you arrive
And you're alive.

What you leave behind
Won't leave your mind.

But home is where you find it.
Home is where you find it.
Home is where you find it.
Home is where you find it.

Michael Rosen

1. Look at the pictures. What can you see?
2. What can you do with the objects?
3. Which of the objects do you use? Which of them would you like to use?

Everyday science

Part A Inventions

· Du liest etwas über verschiedene Erfindungen.
· Du lernst, wie man über Erfindungen, Erfinder und Erfinderinnen schreibt.
· Du stellst deine Ideen für eine neue Erfindung vor.

Part B Communication

· Du liest über eine Projektwoche an der Holland Park School.
· Du siehst dir eine Präsentation an.
· Du hältst einen dreiminütigen Vortrag über einen Aspekt der Geschichte der Kommunikation.

Everyday objects

1a

What objects from your everyday life could you not live without? Talk about them in class.

mobile phone · fridge · tablet · book · TV · toothbrush · pen · …

You can say:
I couldn't live without a …
I really need my …

1b

Look at these pictures.
Match them to the definitions.

You can say:
Picture number … goes with definition …

1
2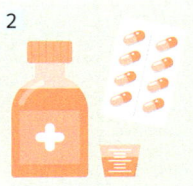
3
4
5

6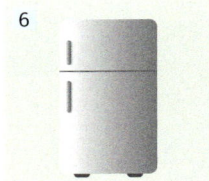

A   A telephone that has lots of apps.
B   A type of transport which has two wheels and needs muscle power to move.
C   Lots of pages with text that was written by an author.
D   A small computer that you can take with you.
E   An electric cupboard which you use to keep your food cool.
F   Something that helps you to get better when you are ill.

1c   skill: talking with people p. 152, workbook p. 76/1

Which of the objects from 1b do you find most important? Why?
Share your thoughts with a partner.

You can say:
I think the … is most important because …
What do you think?

British inventions

2a

Look at the pictures. Which invention came first?
Which one came last? Work with a partner.

You can say:
I think the … came first, then the …

telephone

toothbrush

TV

steam locomotive

ACTIVATE   PRACTISE   DEVELOP   PRACTISE   APPLY

2b

Read the article. Did you put the inventions in the correct order?

British inventions

British inventors are very creative. Let's have a look at some of their inventions.

The toothbrush

People have always cleaned their teeth, but toothbrushes as we know them today were invented in 1780 by a man named William Addis. His toothbrush was made of horsehair and cow bone. The basic design of the toothbrush has not changed much, but today other materials are used.

The steam locomotive

In 1802, the first high-pressure steam engine for locomotives was invented by Richard Trevithick. Some years later, Robert and George Stephenson built a steam locomotive that could pull passenger trains. Soon this invention was used all over the world. Today, most trains are pulled by locomotives with electric or diesel engines.

The telephone

The telephone was invented in 1875. It was patented by Alexander Graham Bell from Scotland, but the American Thomas Watson helped him with his invention. The first phone call was made between Bell and Watson in the same building. Soon long-distance phone calls were possible as well, but they were extremely expensive. In 1927, the first three minutes of the first transatlantic telephone call cost $75 – half the price of a car at that time.

The television

The first working television was presented in London in 1927 by John Logie Baird.

2c CHOOSE YOUR LEVEL skill: reading p.154, workbook p.76/2

▌ Choose the correct words to complete the sentences and write them down.

1 Toothbrushes were made of **wood / horsehair and cow bone** in 1780.
2 Today, most **trains / ships** are pulled by locomotives with electric or diesel engines.

▌▌ Match the sentence parts and write down the sentences.

1 William Addis invented a toothbrush that	A	could pull passenger trains.
2 Steam locomotives	B	were extremely expensive.
3 The first telephone calls	C	was made of horsehair and cow bone.

▌▌▌ Copy the sentences and complete them.

1 The basic design of the ??? has not changed much.
2 Steam locomotives were used all over the ???.
3 The first ??? was made between Bell and Watson in the same building.
4 The first working ??? was presented in London in 1927.

GRAMMAR HELP

the passive p. 187

Aktivsätze stellen den oder die Handelnden in den Vordergrund. Bei Passivsätzen dagegen ist es nebensächlich oder nicht bekannt, wer oder was handelt. Die Handlung selbst steht im Vordergrund. Sieh dir die Beispielsätze an. Was fällt dir auf?

An author wrote lots of pages. Ein/e Autor/in schrieb viele Seiten.	Lots of pages were written by an author. Viele Seiten wurden von einem Autor/einer Autorin geschrieben.
Many people used this invention. Viele Menschen verwendeten diese Erfindung.	This invention was used by many people. Diese Erfindung wurde von vielen Menschen verwendet.
Today, electric engines pull many trains. Heutzutage ziehen Elektromotoren viele Züge.	Today, many trains are pulled by electric engines. Heutzutage werden viele Züge von Elektromotoren gezogen.

Weitere Erklärungen findest du auf Seite 187.
Die Liste mit den unregelmäßigen Verbformen findest du auf den Seiten 245 bis 247.

Inventions

3a   grammar: passive p. 187

Unscramble the sentences and write them down.

1   were invented – a lot of things – by British inventors
2   by William Addis – the first toothbrush – was invented
3   the first steam locomotive – in Britain – was built
4   in Scotland – of the telephone – was born – the inventor

3b   grammar: passive p. 187, workbook p. 76/3

Copy the sentences and complete them with words from the box.

1   The fridge ??? to keep your food cool.
2   A laptop is a small computer that ??? anywhere.
3   The telephone ??? in 1875.
4   Steam locomotives ??? by railway companies.

was invented · were used ·
can be taken · is used

Important inventions

4   grammar: passive p. 187, workbook p. 77/4-5

Rewrite the sentences in the passive.

1   Doctors give medicine to sick people.
2   A British inventor invented the telescope.
3   William Addis made the modern toothbrush.
4   In the 1820s, steam locomotives pulled trains.
5   Thomas Watson helped Alexander Graham Bell.

You can write:

Medicine is given to sick people by …
The telescope was …
The toothbrush was …
Trains were …
Alexander …

DIGITAL+ practise more 22

ACTIVATE   **PRACTISE**   DEVELOP   PRACTISE   APPLY

A day out

5a

Look at Ava's computer screen.
What is on at the London Science Museum?

You can say:

There is a section on …
There is an exhibition about …

5b  audio 3/12

Listen to Ava, Lily and Harry. What are they talking about?

5c CHOOSE YOUR LEVEL skill: listening p. 151

I Listen again and choose the correct sentence ending.

1 Ava is looking at the website of **the London Science Museum / the Museum of London**.
2 They have a section on **animals / science and medicine**.
3 Ava wants **Harry and Lily / Tarek, Harry and Lily** to come, too.

II Listen again and choose the correct answer.

1 Which section of the London Science Museum ist Ava excited about?
  A science and medicine   B everyday technology   C clock design

2 Who was Stephen Hawking?
  A Ava's neighbour   B an inventor   C a scientist

3 What is the everyday technology section about?
  A inventions that have changed our lives   B the history of computers   C space travel

III Listen again. Match the sentence parts and write down the sentences.

1 Ava's mum is going to take Ava and her brothers   A on different topics or people.
2 Ava is really excited   B inventions that have changed our lives.
3 There are always special exhibitions   C to the London Science Museum.
4 The everyday technology section is about   D about the everyday technology section.

5d skill: searching the Internet p. 157, media worksheet 6, workbook p. 78/6

What would you like to see at the London Science Museum?

Find out more on the Internet and tell your class.

You can say:

I would like to see …

Visiting the London Science Museum

6   skill: mediation p. 155

You are at the London Science Museum. A German family does not understand the visitor information. Help them and answer their questions in German.

TICKETS
The museum is free to visit.
We recommend you book a free ticket
online in advance.

OPENING TIMES
The museum is open from Wednesday to
Sunday from 10am to 6pm.
Exhibition areas start to close 30 minutes
before the museum closes.

FOOD AND DRINK
1. There are several cafés in the museum.
2. You can bring your own food and drink,
   which can be eaten in the picnic area
   outside.
3. Eating in the exhibition rooms is not allowed.

GETTING HERE
The museum is located on Exhibition Road
in South Kensington. The nearest tube
station is South Kensington.

PLEASE NOTE
We are renovating some of our exhibitions.
To find out which exhibitions are closed,
please see our home page.

1 Was muss man zum Thema Tickets wissen?
2 Wie sieht es mit den Öffnungszeiten aus?
3 Wo im Museum kann man etwas essen?

4 Wie kommt man zum Museum?
5 Was muss man sonst noch beachten?

Everyday technology

7a

**Read the info texts that Ava and her friends saw at the London Science Museum.
What objects did they look at?**

1 Everyday technology that ... **_saves time_**

Zip

When you look around you – how many zips can you count?
They are everywhere! On trousers, jackets, bags, rucksacks, ...
Just imagine how long it would take to button all these things.
But that's what people did until zips were first used for clothes.
Although early versions of the zip appeared from the 1870s
onwards, the clothes industry only discovered in the 1930s
how useful zips can be.

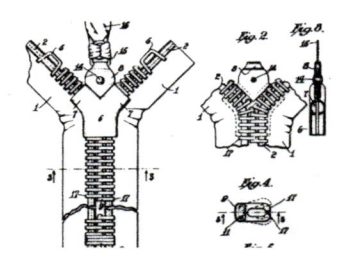

*construction drawing for one of
the first zips*

2 Everyday technology that ... *saves lives*

Seat belts

Early seat belts were simple straps of leather that you fastened in front of you like a belt. They kept you in your seat but did not really prevent injuries. But in the 1950s, Swedish engineer Nils Bohlin invented the kind of seat belt that looks like the letter Y. It is a lot more comfortable and safer and it is still used in cars today.

Nils Bohlin with his invention in 1958

3 Everyday technology that ... *keeps food fresh*

Tins and tin openers

For centuries, people looked for ways to keep food fresh, especially meat and fish. Peter Durand had an idea in 1810. If you put food inside tins, close them and then heat them, the food inside the tins can be stored for a long time and the food inside can still be eaten years later.

The tin opener was only invented in 1870. Until then, people had to use other tools to open their tins.

an early tin

4 Everyday technology that ... *was invented by accident*

Penicillin

Until 1942, a small wound could actually kill you if it became infected with bacteria. But in 1928, Alexander Fleming accidentally discovered penicillin, the first antibiotic. He was tidying up some Petri dishes with different bacteria in his lab when he noticed something unusual on one dish – there were bacteria all over the dish except for one area where some mould was growing. It looked like the mould was killing the bacteria. This discovery was the beginning of modern antibiotics. It is estimated that penicillin has saved at least 200 million lives since its first use as a medicine in 1942.

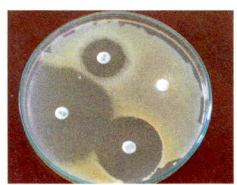

antibiotic mould killing bacteria

7b CHOOSE YOUR LEVEL skill: reading p. 154, workbook p. 78/7

❙ Read the info texts 1 and 2 again and complete the sentences with the words from the box.

1 The clothes industry discovered in the 1930s how useful ??? can be.
2 Early ??? were simple straps of leather.
3 A Swedish engineer invented the ??? seat belt that looks like the letter Y.

kind of · zips · seat belts

❙❙ Read the info texts 1 to 3 again and match the sentence parts.

1 First versions of a zip
2 Until the 1930s,
3 The first seat belts
4 The tin opener

A did not prevent injuries.
B was only invented in 1870.
C zips were not used on clothes.
D appeared from the 1870s onwards.

❙❙❙ Read the info texts 1 to 4 again and complete the sentences.

1 The clothes industry discovered very late how ???.
2 Early ??? were simple straps of ???.

3 For centuries, people looked ???.
4 The beginning of modern antibiotics was when Fleming discovered ???.

LAND & LEUTE 5 ▣ video 13

Die Industrielle Revolution

Die sogenannte „Industrielle Revolution" nahm vor ungefähr 300 Jahren im Vereinigten Königreich ihren Anfang. Seit den 1730er Jahren veränderten viele Erfindungen auf Gebieten wie der Landwirtschaft, dem Verkehr und der Industrie das Alltagsleben dramatisch. Diese Erfindungen wurden bald überall auf der Welt übernommen. Eine der wichtigsten Erfindungen war vermutlich die Dampfmaschine, die 1765 von James Watt

verbessert wurde. Sie machte Produktionsprozesse schneller und billiger. Diese Erfindungen hatten sowohl positive als auch negative Auswirkungen auf das Leben der Menschen, aber ohne sie wäre unser Alltag heute nicht vorstellbar.

Welche positiven und negativen Aspekte der Industriellen Revolution fallen dir ein? Tauscht euch in der Klasse aus.

Useful inventions?

8a ▣ video 14, skill: watching a video clip p. 156

Watch the video clip. What is George watching on TV and why? What inventions are presented? You can take notes in German.

8b   wordbank: inventions p. 168, workbook p. 79/8-9

How useful are the inventions to you? Rate each one from 1 (not useful) to 10 (very useful). Compare your ratings with a partner.

You can say:

I think the … is very useful. I would give it a 9.
I think the … is not so useful. I would …

Writing about inventions

9   CHOOSE YOUR TASK   A + B: wordbank: inventions p. 168, C: skill: writing p. 153, workbook p. 80/10

A **Look at 2b on page 105 again. Draw one of the inventions and write about it.**

B **Write quiz cards for a partner. Describe an invention. Your partner has to guess what it is. Take turns.**

You can write:

You use it to see when it is dark.
You can use it when there is no electricity.

C **Imagine there was no electricity last Tuesday. Write about your day.**

In the morning, I got up really late because my mobile didn't work. I couldn't listen to music while I had breakfast and … Then …

Visiting a German museum

10 skill: mediation p.155, media worksheet 2, 5

You want to take a British friend to the Technik Museum in Speyer. Look at the brochure and work with a partner. He or she plays the role of your friend and asks you two or more questions in English about the museum. Take turns. You can record your dialogues.

TECHNIK MUSEUM SPEYER

Im Technik Museum in Speyer erwarten Sie mehr als 3000 Ausstellungsstücke: Flugzeuge, klassische Automobile, Lokomotiven, U-Boote, Schiffe und viele andere technische Meisterleistungen. Zu den größten Attraktionen zählen eine Boeing 747, die russische Raumfähre BURAN und das voll zugängliche U-Boot U9.

Wir haben **365 Tage im Jahr geöffnet**.
Montag bis Freitag: 9–18 Uhr
Samstag, Sonntag, Feiertage: 9–19 Uhr

+ + + + + + + + + + + + + + + + + +

Unser **Restaurant** bietet jeweils von 9 bis 18 Uhr eine Auswahl an kalten und warmen Speisen.

+ + + + + + + + + + + + + + + + + +

Die **Buslinien 564 und 565** bringen Sie direkt vom Bahnhof zum Museum.

Eintrittspreise
Kinder 5 – 14 J.   15,00 €
Erwachsene   19,00 €

Funny inventions

11a

Look at the pictures and guess what you can do with the inventions.

11b

Match the descriptions to the pictures. Were you right in 11a?

Emma: "My invention is a good idea for birthday parties. All I do is watch my biscuit baker."

Leona: "My invention is practical. With my cleaning skates I can clean the floor and have fun at the same time."

Chris and Claire: "With our invention we always know the answers to the homework. We can read the teacher's book with our X-ray glasses."

11c   skill: writing p.153, media worksheet 13, workbook p.81/11-13

I **Choose one of the inventions from the box and write about it.**
II **Choose two of the inventions from the box and write about them.**
III **Write about the inventions from the box.**

close-your-eyes lamp ·
singing toilet roll ·
homework butler

More inventions

12   **CHOOSE YOUR LEVEL**   grammar: passive p. 187

I   **Unscramble the sentences and write them down.**

1   in 1860. – invented – Dog biscuits – were
2   by Levi Strauss. – Blue jeans – designed – were
3   made – The first – cornflakes – in 1894. – were
4   teddy bear – The first – made – in 1902. – was

II   **Unscramble the two texts about dog biscuits and cornflakes. Copy one of them into your exercise book.**

III   **Unscramble the two texts and copy them into your exercise book. Find headings for them.**

For a long time, dogs were given almost exactly the same food as their owners ate: meat, vegetables and bread. Cornflakes were first made in 1894 by John Harvey Kellogg. They were originally created as a healthy food for the patients at the hospital where he worked. In 1860, James Spratt had the idea to produce special biscuits for dogs. Although there was no sugar in the first recipe, they soon became very popular as a breakfast food. They were made of flour, vegetables and a little meat and became very popular with rich dog owners.

Nouns and verbs

13a

Copy the verbs from the box. Add the nouns. You can find help in a dictionary.

begin · collect · invent · spell ·
build · meet · celebrate · end

You can write:
begin — beginning
collect — ...

13b   workbook p. 82/14-15

Look at the endings of the nouns. What do you notice? Sort them into two lists. Add more nouns.

Where is the stress?

14a   📢 audio 3/18

Listen to the words and repeat them.

vegetarian · invention · television ·
toothbrush · information · smartphone ·
communicate · inventor · understand

14b

Where is the stress? On the first, second or third syllable? Make three lists.

first syllable	second syllable	third syllable
television	*invention*	*vegetarian*
...	...	...

📱 **DIGITAL+** practise more 22

ACTIVATE   PRACTISE   DEVELOP   **PRACTISE**   APPLY

Ideas for a new invention TARGET TASK

15 🔲 🔲 workbook p.83/16, skill: giving a presentation p.158, wordbank: inventions, presenting something p.168, media worksheet 13

Your task is to present your ideas for a new invention.
Before you start, look at these steps:

STEP 1

Work with a partner or in a small group.

STEP 2

Think of objects that should be invented or objects that you would like to improve.
You can think of something from the following categories:
· food
· school
· tasks at home
· free time and holidays
· medicine
· travel
· ...

STEP 3

Agree on one object and be creative: what should the object be able to do?
How could it help people? Which problem should it solve?
Make notes and make a draft.

STEP 4

Decide how you would like to present your idea. You can:
· make a collage and label it
· draw a picture and label it
· write a text
· ...

STEP 5

Create your collage, picture, text, ...
Check it.

STEP 6

Present your ideas in class.

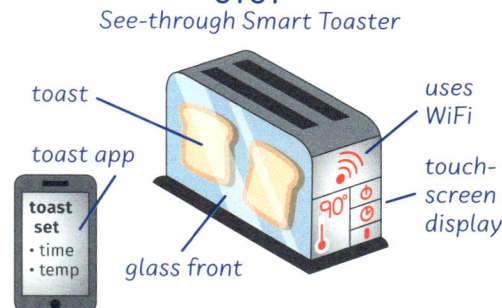

STST
See-through Smart Toaster

toast

uses WiFi

toast app

touch-screen display

toast set
· time
· temp

glass front

Communication

1 workbook p. 84/1

How do people communicate with each other? Collect ideas in class.

You can say:

Many people use … to communicate.
Some people use …

Project week at Holland Park School

2a skill: reading p. 154

Scan the noticeboard. What is the topic of the project week? What workshops are there?

PROJECT WEEK – COMMUNICATION IN THE PAST AND PRESENT

Workshop 1: **Written communication – from hieroglyphs to emojis**
From hieroglyphs in ancient Egypt to then writing postcards and letters on paper to sending texts with your smartphone – in this workshop we are going to look at the development of writing and the history of written communication. For the presentation we are going to learn different ways to do a digital presentation.

Workshop 2: **The history of the telephone**
From the beginnings to your smartphone – in this workshop we are going to focus on the development of the telephone. We are going to build models of low-tech telephones that work without electricity. At the end of the workshop we are going to present our results on different posters.

Workshop 3: **Radio and TV**
No streaming, no video on demand, no podcasts – can you imagine life in the early days of radio and TV? In this workshop we are going to look at the history of radio and TV and record our own radio or TV show to present our findings.

GENERAL INFORMATION

All groups have to do research at the library.

At the end of the week all students are going to show their results and give short presentations on their topic.

All groups have to write handouts for the other students.

2b CHOOSE YOUR LEVEL workbook p. 84/2

I   Read the texts on the noticeboard and correct the statements.

1 In workshop 1, students are going to learn how to do a poster presentation.
2 The students in workshop 2 are going to focus on the development of radios.
3 In workshop 3, students are going to look at the history of writing.

II Are the statements true or false?
Read the texts on the noticeboard and correct the false statements.

1 Students can explore the future of written communication in workshop 1.
2 In workshop 1, students are going to make paper.
3 In workshop 2, students are going to look at the beginnings of the telephone.
4 They are going to build models of high-tech telephones in workshop 2.
5 In workshop 3, students are going to create posters about their findings.

III Read the texts on the noticeboard and answer the questions.

1 What kind of presentation are the students in workshop 1 going to do?
2 How are the students going to present the results of workshop 2?
3 What are the newer developments in the area of radio and TV?
4 Where do all students have to do research?
5 What do all groups have to prepare for the other students?

Talking about the workshops

3a 🖭 audio 3/19, skill: listening p. 151

Listen to Ava, Lily, Harry and Tarek. Who is going to take part in which workshop?

You can write:

Ava is going to take part in workshop …
Lily is going to …
…

3b skill: talking with people p. 152, workbook p. 84/3

Which workshop would you be interested in? Talk to a partner.

You can say:

I would be interested in the workshop on …
I would choose … because …

GRAMMAR HELP

the going to-future (R) p. 188-189

Wenn du sagen möchtest, was jemand für die Zukunft plant oder beabsichtigt, benutzt du das *going to-future*. Du benutzt es auch, wenn du ausdrücken möchtest, dass etwas mit großer Wahrscheinlichkeit passieren wird. Schau dir die Beispiele an. Was fällt dir auf?

Harry thinks the workshop is going to be a bit boring.	Harry denkt, dass der Workshop ein bisschen langweilig sein wird.
We are going to produce our own show.	Wir werden unsere eigene Show produzieren.
I am not going to choose the workshop on the history of the telephone.	Ich werde den Workshop über die Geschichte des Telefons nicht auswählen.

Auf den Seiten 188 und 189 findest du weitere Erklärungen und Beispiele zum *going to-future*.

They are going to …

4   grammar: going to-future p. 188, workbook p. 85/4

Write down what is going to happen.

Anna: get dirty	Tim and Bob: miss bus	Suzy: fall off horse	Dan: wake up soon

You can write:

Anna is going to get dirty.
Tim and Bob are …

Plans

5a   grammar: going to-future p. 188

Read Lily's planner.
What is she going to do next week?
What is she not going to do? Write it down.

You can write:

Next Monday afternoon, Lily is going to …
Next Tuesday, Lily is not going to …

Monday afternoon: *meet Ava*
Tuesday: ~~*do yoga with Olivia*~~
Wednesday: *hand in English homework*
Thursday: *do research*
Friday afternoon: ~~*do some upcycling*~~, *go skateboarding (park)*

5b   grammar: going to-future p. 188-189, workbook p. 85/5

Work with a partner. Ask and answer questions about his or her plans for next week.

You can ask:

Are you going to … next Monday afternoon?
Are you going to …?

You can answer:

Yes, I am.
No, I'm not. I'm going to …

DIGITAL+ practise more 23

At the library

6a  audio 3/20

**Listen to the dialogue and read along.
Why are the friends at the library?**

Tarek: Lily, why did you bring your tablet?
I thought we came here for the books.
Lily: Yes, we did. But I'm going to take notes on my tablet.
Harry: Cool. You're connected to the school network and the Internet, aren't you? Can I use your tablet when you're done with it, Lily?
Lily: Sure. I'm going to have a look at the books first, so you can use the tablet now. I hope they have some useful books on ancient Egypt.
Ava: Hey guys, look. I've found all these books on the history of TV and radio. Harry, come on!

You're in my workshop, too.
Harry: No, thanks, Ava. I'm going to use modern methods and research online.
Tarek: But Mr Patel told us to use books.
Harry: No, he didn't. He told us to go to the library to do research. And where are we now? Right. I'm going to find all the information I need on the Internet.

6b audio 3/21

Listen to the rest of the dialogue. What are the friends talking about?

6c CHOOSE YOUR LEVEL skill: listening p. 151

I Listen again. Choose the correct word or phrase and write down the sentences.
1 Harry used a **search engine / dictionary** and has 59 pages of information now.
2 Mr Patel said it was **not important / important** that the students really understand the texts.
3 Harry **has named / has not named** his sources.

II Listen again. Complete the sentences.
1 Harry copied all the ??? into his document.
2 He has no idea what is ??? and what is not.
3 Lily says that he has to ??? his sources and save the ??? to the pages where he found his information.
4 Ava gives Harry a ??? and Tarek suggests that he should make a poster about his findings.

III Listen again. Copy the true sentences and correct the false sentences.
1 Harry used a search engine and has 59 pages of information now.
2 Harry understands all the texts and knows exactly what is important.
3 Lily says that they have to name their sources.
4 Harry has saved the links of the pages where he found his information.

6d workbook p. 86/6-7

Listen to the rest of the dialogue again and take notes on what is important when doing research online. Use your notes and write down tips in German.

The history of communication

7a skill: reading p.154

Lily found some information for her project. Skim the texts. Match the headings to the texts.

| The invention of paper | Modern communication | Rock art | First letters |

You can say:

Text number … matches the heading …

1. The beginning of writing can be seen in rock art – pictures that people painted on stone.

Some of these pictures are more than 28,000 years old. There are different theories on why people created them. Maybe they wanted to remember special events or tell a story or maybe the pictures had a religious function.

2. Already in 9,000 BC, people used pictures and signs on stone tablets to make notes. The first letters, the hieroglyphs, were invented by people in ancient Egypt about 3,000 BC. With hieroglyphs, people could tell longer stories in writing. People in ancient Egypt also invented papyrus, which made writing a lot easier.

3. Before papyrus and paper were invented, people used stone or clay tablets to write on. Paper was first used by the Chinese around 105 AD. From then on paper was used in communication for letters and – perhaps even more important – books.

With the invention of the modern printing press in the 15th century, information could travel faster and wider than ever before.

ACTIVATE   PRACTISE   **DEVELOP**   PRACTISE   APPLY

4. The invention of the computer changed the way we communicate once more. 😃
The first email was sent in 1971 by computer engineer Raymond Tomlinson. The rise of the Internet began in the 1990s and smartphones appeared in the 2000s. 😉
Texting, messaging and emojis 😮 have made it even easier and quicker to keep in touch with each other, and many people like a simple and uncomplicated 'thumbs up'. 👍

7b CHOOSE YOUR LEVEL

I Choose one of the texts and read it. Take notes on the most important facts.

II Choose two of the texts and read them. Take notes on the most important facts.

III Choose three of the texts and read them. Take notes on the most important facts.

7c workbook p. 87/8-9

Share your findings in class. Organize them in a table.

What?	When?	Where?	Who?	Other information
pictures on stone	...	...	...	...
...	...	...	...	...

An interview

8 skill: talking with people p. 152, wordbank: communication p. 169, workbook p. 87/10

Work with a partner. Interview each other about your communication habits.

You can ask:

How often do you text someone?

Do you write letters or postcards?

How do you contact your grandparents?

Have you ever made a video call?

What's your favourite way to communicate?

...

You can answer:

I often / sometimes / never text ...

Yes, I do. / No, I don't. I ...

I write / text / phone ...

Yes, I have. / No, I haven't. I ...

My favourite way to communicate is ...

...

A challenge

9a 📹 video 15

Watch the video clip. What is Zara's challenge?

You can say:

Zara's challenge is to …

…

9b skill: watching a video clip p. 156, workbook p. 88/11

Watch the video clip again and take notes. What are difficult situations for Zara? How does she solve her problems?

You can say:

Difficult situations for Zara are …

She solves her problems by …

…

Modern technology

10 **CHOOSE YOUR TASK** C: wordbank: inventions p. 168, media worksheet 13

A **Design at least one new emoji and explain what it stands for.**

B **Imagine a day without your phone, your tablet and your console. Describe the situations in which you would miss them. How do you help yourself?**

On a day without my phone,

I wouldn't be able to …

I could …

My friends would …

C **Design an app that solves one of your everyday problems. Write down what problem you want to solve and how the app can help.**

Two inventions

11 **GET TOGETHER**   workbook p. 88/12-14

Get together with a partner.
Read and talk about two different inventions.

Partner A
| Go to page 130.
|| Go to page 133.
||| Go to page 136.

Partner B
| Go to page 139.
|| Go to page 142.
||| Go to page 145.

ACTIVATE PRACTISE **DEVELOP** PRACTISE APPLY

Being online

12a

What are "dos and don'ts"? Share your ideas in class.

12b skill: mediation p. 155

Read this list from a British magazine. Tell a partner in German what the rules say.

SIX DOS AND DON'TS FOR USING THE INTERNET

(1) Only give your password to your parents, not to anyone else!

(2) Don't post personal information like your name, address, phone number etc.

(3) Be careful what you download. Check links before clicking on them and don't trust just anybody.

(4) Don't befriend people online that you don't know in real life.

(5) If someone bullies you on the Internet, don't react! Show their messages to your parents or a teacher.

(6) Always treat other people on the Internet in the way you would like to be treated. Use respectful language.

12c wordbank: going online p. 169, media worksheet 7, workbook p. 89/15

Work with a partner. Can you think of any more dos and don'ts for using the Internet?
Collect as many as you can and share your ideas in class. You can collect your ideas in German.

A presentation

13a video 16

Watch Jason's presentation.
What is it about?

13b skill: watching a video clip p. 156

Go to www.westermann.de/webcode and enter the webcode WES-128206-001 to find the feedback sheet. Watch the presentation again and fill it in.

13c wordbank: presenting something p. 168, workbook p. 90/16

Give some written feedback. Do not forget to mention the positive aspects.

You can write:
At the beginning, you spoke loudly and clearly. That was good.
The pictures were very helpful.
Your summary was …
was …

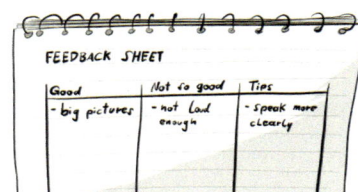

Mr Patel's feedback

14 🔊 audio 3/25, skill: listening p. 151, workbook p. 90/17

**Listen to Mr Patel. He is giving feedback on another presentation.
Is he happy with the student? Say why or why not.**

You can say:

*I think Mr Patel is happy / not happy with the
student because he says …*

Giving feedback

15   **CHOOSE YOUR LEVEL**

I   Match the German and the English sentences. Write them down.

1 Das hast du gut gemacht!
2 Deine Informationen waren richtig.
3 Du hast alle Quellen genannt.
4 Die Bilder hatten die richtige Größe.

A You named all your sources.
B You did a great job!
C The pictures were the right size.
D Your information was correct.

II   Match the German and the English sentences. Write them down.

1 Deine Präsentation war sehr interessant.
2 Du hast etwas zu schnell gesprochen.
3 Ich konnte einige der Bilder nicht richtig
   sehen, weil sie zu klein waren.
4 Du hast frei vorgetragen.

A You spoke a bit too fast.
B You spoke freely.
C Your presentation was very interesting.
D I couldn't see some of the pictures
   because they were too small.

III   Match the sentence parts. Write down the sentences.

1 It was good that you spoke
2 I liked your
3 Why don't you use
4 You could
5 You were very well

A add some more pictures.
B prepared. You could answer all the
   questions.
C loudly and clearly.
D introduction. It gave me an idea about
   what to expect.
E words like "because" the next time?

🔲 **DIGITAL+** practise more 24

ACTIVATE   PRACTISE   DEVELOP   **PRACTISE**   APPLY

A three-minute talk TARGET TASK

16 workbook p. 91/18, skill: searching the Internet p. 157, presentations p. 158, media worksheet 4, 6

Your task is to give a three-minute talk.
Before you start, look at these steps:

STEP 1

Decide what you would like to talk about. Think about:
· an invention you find interesting or useful
· one aspect of the history of communication
· …

STEP 2

Do your research.
· Do some research on your topic. Use books or the Internet.
· Find some good pictures. Do not forget to list your sources.
· Choose texts which are easy to understand.
· Write down the most important facts in your own words.

STEP 3

Prepare your presentation.
· Read through your findings.
· Organize the information. What is important? What is not?
· In which order do you want to present the facts?
· You can make a digital presentation or a poster.
· Write the most important facts of your presentation on cue cards.

STEP 4

Practise your presentation with a partner.
· Use your cue cards.
· Give each other feedback.

In my presentation, I'm going to talk about …
This is a picture of …
Now I'd like to talk about …
If you look at this …, you'll see …
My next point is …
Finally, …

STEP 5

Give your presentation.

Check out

1. Kannst du über Erfindungen sprechen?	Workbook, p. 92
2. Kannst du einem Gespräch Informationen entnehmen?	Workbook, p. 92
3. Kannst du Informationen aus einem deutschen Museumsflyer auf Englisch wiedergeben?	Workbook, p. 92
4. Kannst du einem Aushang die wichtigsten Inhalte entnehmen?	Workbook, p. 93
5. Kannst du über Zukünftiges schreiben?	Workbook, p. 93
6. Kannst du Feedback formulieren?	Workbook, p. 93

A field trip

1 Last Tuesday, all the students at my school in years 8 to 10 went to the Science and Industry Museum in Manchester.
I love science, so I was quite excited to go.
5 Jamie wasn't that excited, but he said it would be better than a day at school.

We went to Manchester by train, but I didn't see Jamie at all because there were so many of us.
10 My group almost lost Daniel Thomas from my class twice before we even got to the museum.

The first time was at the station in Manchester. Ms Barlow, one of the teachers who was with us, counted us to make sure no one was missing. "40, 41, 42," Ms Barlow went. "42, 42, wait, where's
15 43? There should be 43 of us. MS KERSHAAAAAAW!"
Ms Kershaw is the other teacher who went with us because 43 students were about 42 too many for Ms Barlow, who is always a bit nervous. Also, Ms Barlow doesn't teach our class so she didn't know Daniel Thomas. She didn't know that he always gets lost. Sometimes he gets lost at school on his way to class …
20 But anyway, Ms Barlow was getting really nervous: "Ms Kershaw! There's one student missing. WHO IS MISSING? WHO IS …?"
Suddenly, Daniel Thomas said, "I'm here. Everything is OK."
"Oh," Ms Barlow said. "Yeah, alright. Let's go then."

The museum was not too far from the station so we walked there because Ms Barlow and Ms
25 Kershaw thought it would be good for us to get some exercise. But maybe that wasn't such a good idea because we lost Daniel Thomas for the second time. On the way he met this very nice little old lady who asked him where Manchester Cathedral was. Daniel Thomas told her that he didn't know because he was from London, and then the lady told him that she liked London a lot, and then

they talked about London for a bit. Ms Kershaw, who counted
30 us at the entrance of the museum, didn't get as nervous as Ms Barlow at the station, but when Daniel Thomas appeared, she wasn't very friendly to him.

35 When we were finally ready and could go inside, there were sooooo many cool things. We started with a guided tour of the exhibition.
"Hi, I'm Ben," the guide said. "I'll show you around our Science of the Future exhibition today.
This way please, we'll begin with the section on drones."

field trip = *Exkursion*; be missing = *fehlen*; get lost = *verloren gehen*; guided tour = *Führung*; section = *Abteilung*; drone = *Drohne*

Ben was really nice, and he told us about how science and technology and inventions might
develop in the future. We were allowed to try things out, and he asked me to control a robot just by
moving my eyeballs. The robot followed my eyeballs, and I could give it simple orders by opening
and closing my eyes. That was brilliant.

Daniel Thomas almost got lost again at the station with the VR glasses. He put on a pair and then just walked around. We found him when he crashed into one of the tables at the back of the exhibition hall.

Ben continued to be friendly, but he seemed to become a bit nervous, too. He did the rest of the tour a lot faster than the first bit. But that was good, because after the tour we were allowed to walk around the museum by ourselves. "But remember to be back at the meeting point near the main entrance at two o'clock for our lunch break. Don't break anything and stay inside the exhibition area. Don't leave the museum and don't go anywhere you're not allowed to go. Is that clear?" Ms Kershaw asked.
"Yes, Ms Kershaw," we all said.

I wandered around and met Jamie at the Textiles Gallery. Jamie is always reading books about the past so this part of the museum was exactly right for him.
There was a lot about Manchester's past as the centre of the cotton industry. There was a real
Spinning Jenny, and one of the people working at the museum showed us how it worked. She even let us try it. I wasn't very good at spinning, but Jamie was really talented. The next time Mum takes us to anything medieval, HE gets the spinning wheel!

Just when we wanted to leave the Textiles Gallery, I saw Daniel Thomas walking through
a door with a sign on it that said "NO ENTRY!"
"Oh no," I thought. "Not again."
I knew exactly what was going to happen: Ms Kershaw would count at the meeting point, Daniel Thomas would be missing,
Ms Barlow would be first nervous and then hysterical, we might even have to miss lunch and maybe our train, then someone would call the police … but I would not let that happen!
"Come on, Jamie," I said and pulled him with me through the door. "Hey! What …?" Jamie said, "Lucy, we can't just go there. We're not allowed here. There might be … Wow!"

develop = *sich entwickeln*; eyeball = *Augapfel*; order = *Befehl*; meeting point = *Treffpunkt*; spinning wheel = *Spinnrad*; entry = *Zutritt*

"Wow!" was about right. We were standing in a huge hall with shelves everywhere. On the shelves
80 were collections of everything you can imagine. There were old machines, furniture, books and
paintings.

Then I saw Daniel Thomas. He was looking at a huge machine which had a wheel and something
that looked like a hammer.

"That's an early steam engine," Jamie said.

85 "And over there is a time travelling machine. Unfortunately it's broken so we now have visitors from
the future in Manchester. But they don't show themselves.", Daniel Thomas replied.

"But that's a …" Jamie began.

"Oh, and there's a telescope that lets
you see the people who live on Mars,"
90 Daniel Thomas went on.

"No, that's a …" Jamie tried to say again.
But then he seemed to get it – that this was
the best part of the museum because there
was no one there to tell us what everything
95 was. We could make up our own stories!

"Oh yes," he said and pointed at something
that looked like a collage of newspapers,
umbrellas and shoes, "that's a piece of art
from a group of people who live on the
100 underground in London. They travel on the
Tube all the time and collect the things that
people forget.

They take everything to a secret tunnel, which they call "the place where it happens", and they
create art." Daniel Thomas was looking at Jamie as if he thought Jamie was the cleverest person he
105 had ever met. "Whoa, you're really good at this. Let's go on," he said.

We had so much fun! We found a calculator for numbers that haven't been invented yet, the last egg
of the last British dragon, and a lot of other interesting things. Sometimes you find the best places
when you are lost!

110

115

Luckily, at quarter to two, we found a clock that was still
working and showed the correct time.
We were on time for the lunch break so Ms Barlow didn't have to
get nervous again.

On the way back to the station, I made sure that I could always
see Daniel Thomas.
But when we were finally safely on the train, I relaxed a little.
At the station in Stoke-on-Trent Ms Barlow counted us again.
"40, 41, 42," she went. "42, 42, WHERE IS 43?"

steam engine = *Dampfmaschine*; time travelling = *Zeitreisen*; secret = *geheim*; had met = *hatte getroffen*; be lost = *sich verirrt haben*

Inventions inspired by nature

burdock plant

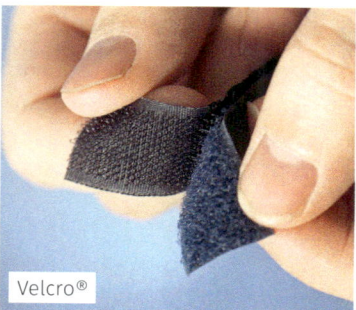

Velcro®

Did you know that the hook-and-loop fastener, or Velcro®, was inspired by the burdock plant?
The seeds of the plant stick to clothes because they have lots of little hooks.

bat

walking stick for the blind

Bats can fly in complete darkness because they give off sounds that echo back. Scientists invented a walking stick for the blind that was inspired by bats. Like a bat, the walking stick can send and receive sound waves. The stick 'sees' objects on the ground and warns the user.

kingfisher

The first Japanese high-speed train could travel over 200 km/h. But going that fast caused a loud noise when the train left a tunnel. Engineers turned to nature to solve the problem. The high-speed train was inspired by the kingfisher.
Their beaks hardly make a ripple when they hit the water to catch fish. Today, Japan's high-speed trains have long, beak-like noses and leave tunnels quietly.

high-speed train

Find out more about one of the inventions or find out about another invention that was inspired by nature. Report your findings to the class.

Ordering food

9a UNIT 1, p. 25 PARTNER A

You and your partner would like to order some food. You are looking at two different menus. Tell your partner about your restaurant and agree on one menu.

Paolo's Pizza Palace – Italian restaurant

SPECIAL OFFER FOR 2
- 2 Pizzas
- 2 Drinks   *for just £29.99*
- 2 Desserts

DRINKS

Water, lemonade, cola £2.20

Orange or apple juice £2.50

STARTERS

Mixed salad £6.30

Tomato soup £5.95
  with bread

PIZZAS

Margherita £10.95
tomatoes, cheese

Fresh from the sea £13.95
tomato sauce, octopus

Farmhouse £13.95
tomato sauce, bacon, mushrooms, onions

Spinach £11.95
mozzarella, spinach, garlic

DESSERTS

Tiramisu £3.95

Ice cream £2.95

You can say:

I've got a menu from an Italian restaurant.

They have …

I really like …

I don't like …

Let's order …

…

You can ask:

What menu have you got?

Have they got … ?

Do you like …?

How much is …?

What about …?

…

9b UNIT 1 p. 25 PARTNER A

Look at the menu you agreed on. Write down what you would like to order.

9c UNIT 1 p. 25 PARTNER A

Do a role play – you call the restaurant and order your food.
Your partner answers the phone.
You can record your dialogue if you like.

You can say:

I would like to order …

How much is it?

How long will it take?

Thank you very much.

What do they miss?

9a UNIT 2, p. 48   PARTNER A, audio 1/34, skill: listening p. 151

Copy the table. Then listen to Jacob and Ben in hospital. What does Ben miss?
Complete the table for Ben.

Ben			meeting friends at school	ice hockey practice	sleeping in
Jacob			inline skating	going swimming	playing the guitar with his band

9b UNIT 2, p. 48   PARTNER A

Work with your partner. Find out what Jacob is missing. Ask and answer questions and
complete the table for Jacob. What activity do both of the boys miss?

Which festival?

10a UNIT 3, p. 73   PARTNER A

Read the table. Then ask and answer questions with your partner and write down the
information for the gaps.

You can ask:

Which festival is ...?

Where is the ...?

You can answer:

The ... is in ...

It's in / on ...

It costs ... pounds (and ... pence).

Which festival?	Where?	When?	How much?	Other information
1	2	usually in February	different fees for different events	three days with Viking events all around York
The Garlic Festival	Isle of Wight	third weekend in August	one day for adults: £12.50, for children: £7.50	garlic lovers from around the world come to the Isle of Wight
The Children's Festival	Edinburgh	27 May to 4 June	adult or child as part of family: £9.00	12 events at different places, lots of activities
The Big Feastival	the Cotswolds	August	weekend for adults: £187.95, weekend for children: £41.80	a family-friendly festival with great music, great food and lots of activities for children

10b UNIT 3, p. 73   PARTNER A, wordbank: what's on? p. 164

Which festival would you like to go to?
Why? Tell your partner.

You can say:

I would like to go to the ... because I like ...

...

Sheree's problems

9a UNIT 4, p. 96 PARTNER A, audio 3/5, skill: listening p. 151

▌ **Listen to Sheree's call to the teen helpline. Which of these problems does Sheree have? Write down the correct sentences.**

1 Her parents are very strict.
2 She is not allowed to play video games.
3 She is really bad at school.

4 She has to do too many chores.
5 Her sister never has to help.

9b UNIT 4, p. 96 PARTNER A

▌▌ **Tell your partner about Sheree's problems. Then listen to your partner. What advice does Gemma from the teen helpline offer? Take notes.**

9c UNIT 4, p. 96 PARTNER A

▌▌ **Work with your partner and match Gemma's tips to Sheree's problems.**

You can say:
When Sheree says …, Gemma suggests …
…

Two inventions

11a UNIT 5, p. 120 PARTNER A, skill: reading p. 154

▌ **Read the text about the hippo roller. Take notes about the most important facts.**

The hippo roller

The problem: many people have to walk very far to get clean water. Then they must carry the water on their head. That means that they cannot transport a lot of water.
The idea: the hippo roller. You fill it with water and roll it, so you do not have to carry the water. Getting water is a lot easier when you use the hippo roller because you can transport more water in one go.

11b UNIT 5, p. 120 PARTNER A

▌ **Use your notes and tell your partner about the hippo roller.**

You can say:
Many people have to …
That means that…
When you use the hippo roller you can …
…

Ordering food

9a UNIT 1, p. 25 PARTNER A

▌ You and your partner would like to order some food. You are looking at menus from two different restaurants. Tell your partner about your restaurant and agree on one menu.

Paolo's Pizza Palace – Italian restaurant

SPECIAL OFFER FOR 2
- 2 Pizzas
- 2 Drinks   *for just £29.99*
- 2 Desserts

DRINKS

Water, lemonade, cola	£2.20
Juice (orange, apple)	£2.50

STARTERS

Garlic bread	£1.85
Fresh bread with garlic	
Mixed salad	£6.30
Salad with our special dressing	
Tomato soup	£5.95
Home-made tomato soup with freshly-baked bread	

PIZZAS

Margherita	£10.95
tomatoes, cheese, basil	
Fresh from the sea	£13.95
tomato sauce, octopus	
Farmhouse	£13.95
tomato sauce, bacon, mushrooms, onions	
Spinach	£11.95
mozzarella, spinach, garlic	
Ham-ster	£11.95
tomato sauce, ham, onions	

DESSERTS

Tiramisu	£3.95
Ice cream	£2.95
Sorbet	£2.95

You can say:

I've got a menu from an Italian restaurant.
They have …
I really like …
I don't like …
Let's order …
…

You can ask:

What menu have you got?
Have they got … at your place?
Do you like …?
How much is …?
What about …?
…

9b UNIT 1 p. 25 PARTNER A

▌ Look at the menu you agreed on. Write down what you would like to order.

9c UNIT 1 p. 25 PARTNER A

▌ Do a role play – you call the restaurant and order your food.
Your partner answers the phone.
You can record your dialogue if you like.

You can say:

I would like to order …
How much is it? How long will it take?
Thank you very much.

What do they miss?

9a UNIT 2, p. 48   PARTNER A, audio 1/34, skill: listening p. 151

‖ **Copy the table. Then listen to Jacob and Ben in hospital. What does Ben miss? Complete the table for Ben.**

Ben				ice hockey practice	sleeping in
Jacob				going swimming	playing the guitar with his band

9b UNIT 2, p. 48   PARTNER A

‖ **Work with your partner. Find out what Jacob is missing. Ask and answer questions and complete the table for Jacob. What activity do both of the boys miss?**

Which festival?

10a UNIT 3, p. 73   PARTNER A

‖ **Read the table. Then ask and answer questions with your partner and write down the information for the gaps.**

You can ask:

Which festival is …?

Where is the …?

When is the …?

You can answer:

The … is in …

It's in / on …

It costs … pounds (and … pence).

Which festival?	Where?	When?	How much?	Other information
1	2	usually in February	different fees for different events	three days packed with Viking events all around York
The Garlic Festival	Isle of Wight	third weekend in August	one day for adults: £12.50 for children: £7.50	garlic lovers from around the world come to the Isle of Wight to get a taste
The Children's Festival	Edinburgh	27 May to 4 June	adult or child as part of family: £9.00	12 performances at different places, lots of additional activities
The Big Feastival	the Cotswolds	3	weekend for adults: £187.95, weekend for children: £41.80	a family-friendly festival with great music, great food and lots of activities for children

10b UNIT 3, p. 73   PARTNER A, wordbank: what's on? p. 164

‖ **Which festival would you like to go to? Why? Tell your partner.**

You can say:

I would like to go to the … because I like …

Sheree's problems

9a UNIT 4, p. 96   PARTNER A, audio 3/5, skill: listening p. 151

❚❚ Listen to Sheree's call to the teen helpline. What are her problems? Take notes.

You can write:

Her parents …

She is not allowed to …

She has to …

9b UNIT 4, p. 96   PARTNER A

❚❚ Tell your partner about Sheree's problems. Then listen to your partner. What advice does Gemma from the teen helpline offer? Take notes.

9c UNIT 4, p. 96   PARTNER A

❚❚ Work with your partner and match Gemma's tips to Sheree's problems.

You can say:

When Sheree says …, Gemma suggests …

…

Two inventions

11a UNIT 5, p. 120   PARTNER A, skill: reading p. 154

❚❚ Read the text about the hippo roller. Take notes about the most important facts.

The hippo roller

The problem: many people have to walk very far to get clean water. The traditional way is to carry the water on your head. That means that one person cannot transport a lot of water.

The idea: the hippo roller. You fill it with water and pull or push it, so you do not have to carry all the weight. Getting water is a lot easier because you can transport more water in one go, which saves a lot of time and energy.

11b UNIT 5, p. 120   PARTNER A

❚❚ Use your notes and tell your partner about the hippo roller.

You can say:

Many people have to …

The traditional way is to …

That means that…

When you use the hippo roller you can …

…

Ordering food

9a UNIT 1, p. 25 PARTNER A

||| You and your partner would like to order some food. You are looking at menus from two different restaurants. Tell your partner about your restaurant and agree on where to order.

Paolo's Pizza Palace – Italian restaurant

SPECIAL OFFER FOR 2
- 2 Pizzas
- 2 Drinks   *for just £29.99*
- 2 Desserts

DRINKS
Water, lemonade, cola £2.20
Juice (orange, apple) £2.50

STARTERS
Garlic bread £1.85
Fresh bread with olive oil and garlic
Mixed salad £6.30
Salad with fresh tomatos and our special dressing
Tomato soup £5.95
Home-made tomato soup with freshly-baked bread

PIZZAS
Margherita £10.95
tomatoes, cheese, basil
Fresh from the sea £13.95
tomato sauce, octopus
Farmhouse £13.95
tomato sauce, bacon, mushrooms, onions
Cheer for cheese £12.95
tomato sauce, four different kinds of cheese
Spinach £11.95
mozzarella, spinach, garlic
Ham-ster £11.95
tomato sauce, ham, onions

DESSERTS
Tiramisu £3.95
Ice cream £2.95
Sorbet £2.95

9b UNIT 1 p. 25 PARTNER A

||| Look at the menu you agreed on. Write down what you would like to order.

You can say:
I've got a menu from an Italian restaurant.
They have …
I really like …
I don't like …
Let's order …
…

You can ask:
What menu have you got?
Have they got … at your place?
Do you like …?
How much is …?
What about …?
…

9c UNIT 1 p. 25 PARTNER A

||| Do a role play – you call the restaurant and order your food.
Your partner answers the phone.
You can record your dialogue if you like.

You can say:
I would like to order …
How much is it?
Thank you very much.
…

What do they miss?

9a UNIT 2, p. 48 PARTNER A, audio 1/34, skill: listening p. 151

▌▌▌ Copy the table. Then listen to Jacob and Ben in hospital. What does Ben miss? Complete the table for Ben.

Ben				sleeping in
Jacob				playing the guitar with his band

9b UNIT 2, p. 48 PARTNER A

▌▌▌ Work with your partner. Find out what Jacob is missing. Ask and answer questions and complete the table for Jacob. What activity do both of the boys miss?

Which festival?

10a UNIT 3, p. 73 PARTNER A

▌▌▌ Read the table. Then ask and answer questions with your partner and write down the information for the gaps.

You can ask:
Which festival is in / on ...?
Have you got any other information on ...?
...

You can answer:
It's ...
Yes, there is / are ...
...

Which festival?	Where?	When?	How much?	Other information
1	2	usually in February	3	three days packed with Viking events all around York
The Garlic Festival	Isle of Wight	third weekend in August	one day for adults: £12.50, for children: £7.50	garlic lovers from around the world come to the Isle of Wight to get a taste
The Children's Festival	Edinburgh	27 May to 4 June	4	12 performances at different places, lots of additional activities
The Big Feastival	the Cotswolds	5	weekend for adults: £187.95, weekend for children: £41.80	a family-friendly festival with great music, great food and lots of activities for children

10b UNIT 3, p. 73 PARTNER A, wordbank: what's on? p. 164

▌▌▌ Which festival would you like to go to? Why? Tell your partner.

Sheree's problems

9a UNIT 4, p. 96 ◼ PARTNER A, audio 3/5, skill: listening p. 151

▮▮▮ Listen to Sheree's call to the teen helpline. What are her problems? Take notes.

9b UNIT 4, p. 96 PARTNER A

▮▮▮ Tell your partner about Sheree's problems. Then listen to your partner.
What advice does Gemma from the teen helpline offer? Take notes.

9c UNIT 4, p. 96 PARTNER A

▮▮▮ Work with your partner and match Gemma's tips to Sheree's problems.

Two inventions

11a UNIT 5, p. 120 PARTNER A, skill: reading p. 154

▮▮▮ Read the text about the hippo roller. Take notes about the most important facts.

The hippo roller

The problem: in a lot of African countries, people
have to walk long distances to get clean water. The
traditional way is to carry the water on your head.
But that means that one person cannot transport
a lot of water. Often children have to do this chore.
This chore takes up a lot of their time, so they
cannot go to school.

The idea: the hippo roller. You fill it with water and
push or pull it, so you do not have to carry all the
weight. Getting water is a lot easier when you use
it because you can transport more water in one go,
which saves a lot of time and energy. Unfortunately,
it does not solve the problem that there is not
enough clean water for everyone.

11b UNIT 5, p. 120 PARTNER A

▮▮▮ Use your notes and tell your partner about the hippo roller.

Ordering food

9a UNIT 1, p. 25 PARTNER B

You and your partner would like to order some food. You are looking at two different menus. Tell your partner about your restaurant and agree on one menu.

The Wonton Wok – the best Chinese restaurant in town

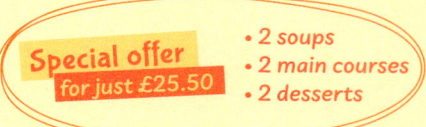

Special offer for just £25.50
- 2 soups
- 2 main courses
- 2 desserts

DRINKS

Water, lemonade, cola	£2.20
Green tea	£1.95

SOUPS

Chicken soup £5.40
Delicious hot soup

Spring soup £2.30
Vegetable soup

MAIN COURSES

Spring rolls £9.95
Five large spring rolls with meat

Vegetarian spring rolls £7.95
Five large spring rolls with vegetables

Mango chilli chicken £11.95
Chicken cooked with mango and chilli

Dim Sum £11.95
A selection of traditional Chinese food

DESSERTS

Baked banana with honey £3.95

Ice cream £2.95

You can say:

I've got a menu from a Chinese restaurant.

They have …

I really like …

I don't like …

Let's order …

…

You can ask:

What menu have you got?

Have they got …?

Do you like …?

How much is …?

What about …?

…

9b UNIT 1 p. 25 PARTNER B

Look at the menu you agreed on. Write down what you would like to order.

9c UNIT 1 p. 25 PARTNER B

Do a role play – your partner calls the restaurant and orders your food.
You answer the phone.
You can record your dialogue if you like.

You can say:

Hello, this is the Wonton Wok.

What can I do for you?

It's … pounds …

It will take … minutes.

…

What do they miss?

9a UNIT 2, p.48 PARTNER B audio 1/34, skill: listening p.151

Copy the table. Then listen to Jacob and Ben in hospital. What does Jacob miss?
Complete the table for Jacob.

Jacob			inline skating	going swimming	playing the guitar with his band
Ben			meeting friends at school	ice hockey practice	sleeping in

9b UNIT 2, p.48 PARTNER B

Work with your partner. Find out what Ben is missing. Ask and answer questions and
complete the table for Ben. What activity do both of the boys miss?

Which festival?

10a UNIT 3, p.73 PARTNER B

Read the table. Then ask and answer questions with your partner and write down the
information for the gaps.

You can ask:

Which festival is ...?

Where is the ...?

You can answer:

The ... is in ...

It's in / on ...

It costs ... pounds (and ... pence).

Which festival?	Where?	When?	How much?	Other information
The Viking Festival	York	usually in February	different fees for different events	three days with Viking events all around York
The Garlic Festival	Isle of Wight	third weekend in August	one day for adults: £12.50, for children: £7.50	garlic lovers from around the world come to the Isle of Wight
1	Edinburgh	27 May to 4 June	adult or child as part of family: £9.00	12 performances at different places, lots of activities
The Big Feastival	2	August	weekend for adults: £187.95, weekend for children: £41.80	a family-friendly festival with great music, great food and lots of activities for children

10b UNIT 3, p.73 PARTNER B, wordbank: what's on? p.164

Which festival would you like to go to?
Why? Tell your partner.

You can say:

I would like to go to the ... because I like ...

...

Sheree's problems

9a UNIT 4, p. 96 PARTNER B, audio 3/5, skill: listening p. 151

Listen to Sheree's call to the teen helpline. Which of these solutions does Gemma from the teen helpline suggest? Write down the correct sentences.

1 Talk to her parents.
2 Ask her parents to look at an official website about screen time for teenagers.

3 Do everything her parents say.
4 Have a family meeting.
5 Move out.

9b UNIT 4, p. 96 PARTNER B

Tell your partner about Sheree's problems. Then listen to your partner. What advice does Gemma from the teen helpline offer? Take notes.

9c UNIT 4, p. 96 PARTNER B

Work with your partner and match Gemma's tips to Sheree's problems.

You can say:
When Sheree says …, Gemma suggests …
…

Two inventions

11a UNIT 5, p. 120 PARTNER B, skill: reading p. 154

Read the text about the pot-in-pot fridge. Take notes about the most important facts.

The pot-in-pot fridge

The problem: in many countries, some people have no electricity. That means they have no fridges to keep their food fresh.
The idea: you take two pots, sand and water to build a simple fridge. You put the smaller pot inside the bigger pot and fill the gap between the pots with wet sand. You put your food inside the smaller pot. When the water in the sand evaporates[1], the smaller pot becomes cooler, and fresh vegetables stay fresh for three to four weeks.

1 (to) evaporate = verdunsten

11b UNIT 5, p. 120 PARTNER B

Use your notes and tell your partner about the pot-in-pot fridge.

You can say:
Many people don't have …
So they cannot …
But you only need … to build …
…

Ordering food

9a UNIT 1, p. 25 PARTNER B

ll You and your partner would like to order some food. You are looking at menus from two different restaurants. Tell your partner about your restaurant and agree on one menu.

The Wonton Wok – the best Chinese restaurant in town

Special offer for just £25.50
- 2 soups
- 2 main courses
- 2 desserts

DRINKS

Water, lemonade, cola	£2.20
Juice (lychee, apple)	£2.50
Green tea	£1.95

SOUPS

Chicken soup	£5.40
Delicious hot soup	
Spring soup	£2.30
Vegetable soup	
Fish and tofu soup	£3.95
Fresh fish, tofu and vegetables	

MAIN COURSES

Sweet and sour pork	£13.95
Pork in a sweet and sour sauce	
Spring rolls	£9.95
Five large spring rolls with meat	
Vegetarian spring rolls	£7.95
Five large spring rolls with vegetables	
Mango chilli chicken	£11.95
Chicken cooked with mango and chilli	
Dim Sum	£11.95
A selection of traditional Chinese food	

DESSERTS

Baked banana with honey	£3.95
Lychees	£4.95
Ice cream	£2.95

You can say:

I've got a menu from a Chinese restaurant.

They have …

I really like …

I don't like …

Let's order …

…

You can ask:

What menu have you got?

Have they got … at your place?

Do you like …?

How much is …?

What about …?

…

9b UNIT 1 p. 25 PARTNER B

ll Look at the menu you agreed on. Write down what you would like to order.

9c UNIT 1 p. 25 PARTNER B

ll Do a role play – your partner calls the restaurant and orders your food.
You answer the phone.
You can record your dialogue if you like.

You can say:

Hello, this is the Wonton Wok.

What can I do for you?

It's … pounds …

It will take … minutes.

…

What do they miss?

9a UNIT 2, p. 48 PARTNER B, audio 1/34, skill: listening p. 151

Copy the table. Then listen to Jacob and Ben in hospital. What does Jacob miss? Complete the table for Jacob.

Jacob				going swimming	playing the guitar with his band
Ben				ice hockey practice	sleeping in

9b UNIT 2, p. 48 PARTNER B

Work with your partner. Find out what Ben is missing. Ask and answer questions and complete the table for Ben. What activity do both of the boys miss?

Which festival?

10a UNIT 3, p. 73 PARTNER B

Read the table. Then ask and answer questions with your partner and write down the information for the gaps.

You can ask:
When is the …?
Which festival is …?
Where is the …?

You can answer:
The … is in …
It's in / on …
It costs … pounds (and … pence).

Which festival?	Where?	When?	How much?	Other information
The Viking Festival	York	usually in February	different fees for different events	three days packed with Viking events all around York
The Garlic Festival	Isle of Wight	1	one day for adults: £12.50, for children: £7.50	garlic lovers from around the world come to the Isle of Wight to get a taste
2	Edinburgh	27 May to 4 June	adult or child as part of family: £9.00	12 performances at different places, lots of additional activities
The Big Feastival	3	August	weekend for adults: £187.95, weekend for children: £41.80	a family-friendly festival with great music, great food and lots of activities for children

10b UNIT 3, p. 73 PARTNER B, wordbank: what's on? p. 164

Which festival would you like to go to? Why? Tell your partner.

You can say:
I would like to go to the … because I like …
…

Sheree's problems

9a UNIT 4, p.96 PARTNER B, audio 3/5, skill: listening p.151

‖ Listen to Sheree's call to the teen helpline. What solutions does Gemma from the teen helpline suggest? Take notes.

You can write:
Gemma suggests that Sheree should …
She says that Sheree could try …
…

9b UNIT 4, p.96 PARTNER B

‖ Listen to your partner. What are Sheree's problems? Take notes. Then tell your partner what Gemma suggests.

9c UNIT 4, p.96 PARTNER B

‖ Work with your partner and match Gemma's tips to Sheree's problems.

You can say:
When Sheree says …, Gemma suggests …
…

Two inventions

11a UNIT 5, p.120 PARTNER B, skill: reading p.154

‖ Read the text about the pot-in-pot fridge. Take notes about the most important facts.

The pot-in-pot fridge

The problem: in many places people in the country have no electricity. That means they cannot use electrical fridges to keep their food fresh.
The idea: you only need two pots, sand and a little water to build a fridge that works without electricity. You put the smaller pot inside the bigger pot and fill the gap between the pots with wet sand. You put your food inside the smaller pot. When the water in the sand evaporates[1], the smaller pot becomes cooler, and fresh vegetables stay fresh for three to four weeks.

1 (to) evaporate = verdunsten

11b UNIT 5, p.120 PARTNER B

‖ Use your notes and tell your partner about the pot-in-pot fridge.

You can say:
Many people don't have …
So they cannot …
But you only need … to build …
…

Ordering food

9a UNIT 1, p. 25 PARTNER B

‖ You and your partner would like to order some food. You are looking at menus from two different restaurants. Tell your partner about your restaurant and agree on where to order.

The Wonton Wok – the best Chinese restaurant in town

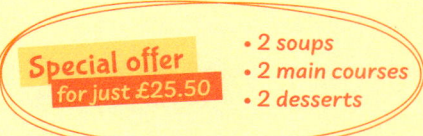

Special offer for just £25.50
- 2 soups
- 2 main courses
- 2 desserts

DRINKS
Water, lemonade, cola	£2.20
Juice (lychee, apple)	£2.50
Green tea	£1.95

SOUPS
Chicken soup £5.40
Delicious hot soup with chicken and noodles

Spring soup £2.30
Vegetable soup

Fish and tofu soup £3.95
Fresh fish, tofu and different vegetables

MAIN COURSES
Sweet and sour pork £13.95
Pork in a sweet and sour sauce

Spring rolls £9.95
Five large spring rolls with different vegetables and meat

Vegetarian spring rolls £7.95
Five large spring rolls with different vegetables

Garlic soy beef £11.95
Tender beef cooked in a soy sauce with garlic

Mango chilli chicken £11.95
Chicken cooked with mango and just enough chilli

Dim Sum £11.95
A selection of traditional Chinese food

DESSERTS
Baked banana with honey	£3.95
Lychees	£4.95
Ice cream	£2.95

You can say:
I've got a menu from a Chinese restaurant.
They have …
I really like …
I don't like …
Let's order …
…

You can ask:
What menu have you got?
Have they got … at your place?
Do you like …?
How much is …?
What about …?
…

9b UNIT 1 p. 25 PARTNER B

‖ Look at the menu you agreed on. Write down what you would like to order.

9c UNIT 1 p. 25 PARTNER B

‖ Do a role play – your partner calls the restaurant and orders your food.
You answer the phone.
You can record your dialogue if you like.

You can say:
Hello, this is the Wonton Wok.
What can I do for you?
Would you like anything else?
It's … pounds …
It will take forty minutes.
…

What do they miss?

9a   UNIT 2, p. 48   ◻ PARTNER B, audio 1/34, skill: listening p. 151

▌▌▌ Copy the table. Then listen to Jacob and Ben in hospital. What does Jacob miss?
Complete the table for Jacob.

Jacob					*playing the guitar with his band*
Ben					*sleeping in*

9b   UNIT 2, p. 48   PARTNER B

▌▌▌ Work with your partner. Find out what Ben is missing. Ask and answer questions and
complete the table for Ben. What activity do both of the boys miss?

Which festival?

10a   UNIT 3, p. 73   PARTNER B

▌▌▌ Read the table. Then ask and answer questions with your partner and write down the
information for the gaps.

You can ask:

Which festival is in … / on …?
How much is the …?
…

You can answer:

It's …
There is … / are …
…

Which festival?	Where?	When?	How much?	Other information
The Viking Festival	*York*	*usually in February*	*different fees for different events*	*three days packed with Viking events all around York*
1	*Isle of Wight*	2	3	*garlic lovers from around the world come to the Isle of Wight to get a taste*
4	*Edinburgh*	*27 May to 4 June*	*adult or child as part of family: £9.00*	*12 performances at different places, lots of additional activities*
The Big Feastival	5	*August*	6	*a family-friendly festival with great music, great food and lots of activities for children*

10b   UNIT 3, p. 73   PARTNER B, wordbank: what's on? p. 164

▌▌▌ Which festival would you like to go to? Why? Tell your partner.

Sheree's problems

9a UNIT 4, p. 96  PARTNER B, audio 3/5, skill: listening p. 151

▌▌▌ Listen to Sheree's call to the teen helpline. What solutions does Gemma from the teen helpline suggest? Take notes.

9b UNIT 4, p. 96 PARTNER B

▌▌▌ Listen to your partner. What are Sheree's problems? Take notes. Then tell your partner what Gemma suggests.

9c UNIT 4, p. 96 PARTNER B

▌▌▌ Work with your partner and match Gemma's tips to Sheree's problems.

Two inventions

11a UNIT 5, p. 120 PARTNER B, skill: reading p. 154

▌▌▌ Read the text about the pot-in-pot fridge. Take notes about the most important facts.

The pot-in-pot fridge

The problem: in many countries people in rural areas have no electricity. That means they cannot use electrical fridges to keep their food fresh.
The idea: you only need two clay pots, sand and a little water to build a fridge that works without electricity. You put the smaller pot inside the bigger pot and fill the gap between the pots with wet sand. You put your food inside the smaller pot. When the water in the sand evaporates[1], the smaller pot becomes cooler. Fresh vegetables stay fresh for three to four weeks in the smaller pot – and people do not have to spend money on electricity!

1 (to) evaporate = verdunsten

11b UNIT 5, p. 120 PARTNER B

▌▌▌ Use your notes and tell your partner about the pot-in-pot fridge.

A country profile: India  ✜ DIGITAL+

Introduction

India is one of the biggest countries in the world. What do you already know about India and what else would you like to know?

These are some questions you may find interesting:

· What famous sights and places are there?
· What sports are popular in India?
· What animals live in India?
· What languages are spoken in India?
· What is the historical connection with the UK?

Find answers to these and other interesting questions in a project about India!

Plan it

1 **In class, collect ideas for topics you could work on. You can make notes in a word web. Here is an example:**

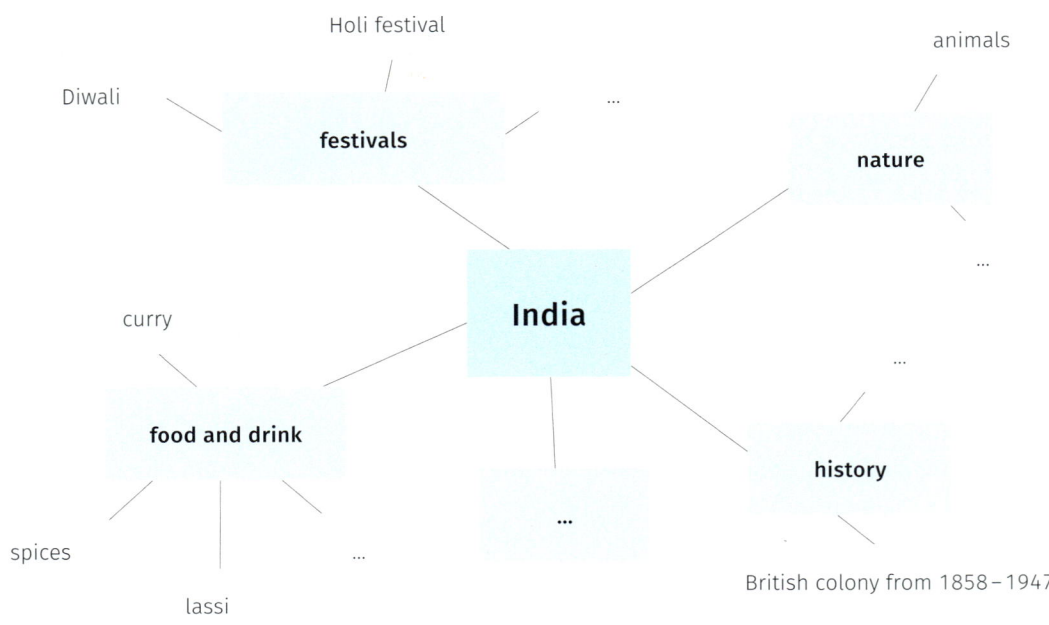

2 **Now collect ideas about what you could create. For example:**

- ▶ fact files
- ▶ posters
- ▶ pages for a computer presentation
- ▶ podcasts
- ▶ ...

Tip

You can make a class product, for example a brochure: every group creates one page and you put everything together in the end.

India
- capital: New Delhi
- population: about 1.4 billion
- languages: English, Hindi, ...
- ...

3 **Now get together in small groups and make a plan. Write down:**

- ▶ what information you need
- ▶ how you can find information
- ▶ how you want to present your work
- ▶ what material you need for your project work (for example: computer, paper, glue, ...)
- ▶ who does what and when

Tip

When you as a group have a plan about what to do and how to present your work, you can ask your classmates from other groups for feedback on your plan.

Do it ▨ ▣ skill: searching the Internet p. 157, media worksheet 4, 6

And ... action! Do research, collect pictures, write texts, ... and create an interesting fact file, poster, computer presentation, ...

Check it

Check everything. Are there any spelling or grammar mistakes? Are the pictures big enough?
Is everything easy to understand? If you want to give a presentation, practise it before you give it.

Present it skill: presentations p. 158

Present your work. You can ask your classmates for feedback after the presentation.

Music  ⬛ DIGITAL+

Introduction

Music plays an important role in many
people's lives. What about you?
What does music mean to you?
What bands or singers do you like?
Do you play an instrument?

Think about the role of music in your life and
explore the world of music in a project.

Plan it

1 **In class, think about what you would like to do in your project.
You can collect ideas in a list, for example:**

▸ Prepare a presentation or a podcast on a band or singer.
▸ Present a song you like and give some background information on it.
▸ Write about a concert you have been to.
▸ Create a poster for a concert or music festival.
▸ Interview classmates about what music they like or what instruments they play.
▸ Collect quotations about music and present them in a creative way.
▸ …

2 Now collect ideas about what you could create. For example:

- ▸ fact files
- ▸ posters
- ▸ pages for a computer presentation
- ▸ podcasts
- ▸ ...

Tip

You can make a class product, for example a music magazine: every group creates one page and you put everything together in the end.

Billie Eilish
- Birthday: 18 December 2001
- Birthplace: Los Angeles, USA
- Famous songs: Bad guy, ...
- ...

3 Now get together in small groups and make a plan. Write down:

- ▸ what information you need
- ▸ how you can get the information
- ▸ how you want to present your work
- ▸ what material you need for your project work (for example: computer, paper, glue, ...)
- ▸ who does what and when

Tip

When you as a group have a plan about what to do and how to present your work, you can ask your classmates from other groups for feedback on your plan.

Do it 🔲🔲 skill: searching the Internet p. 157, media worksheet 4, 6

And ... action! Do research, collect pictures, write texts, ... and create an interesting fact file, poster, computer presentation, ...

Check it

Check everything. Are there any spelling or grammar mistakes? Are the pictures big enough? Is everything easy to understand? If you want to give a presentation, practise it before you give it.

Present it skill: presentations p. 158

Present your work. You can ask your classmates for feedback after the presentation.

1 WORKING WITH WORDS
Wortschatzarbeit

Im *Dictionary* ab Seite 213 kannst du die Wörter aus diesem Buch und die Lernwörter aus den vorigen Bänden nachschlagen. Wenn du ein Wort suchst, das dort nicht steht, kannst du ein Wörterbuch benutzen.

1. Wörterbücher

▷ Die Wörter sind alphabetisch geordnet. Du darfst nicht nur auf den ersten Buchstaben achten, sondern musst auch die folgenden Buchstaben angucken: *face* steht beispielsweise vor *false*.

▷ Hinter den Einträgen stehen Lautschrift und Wortart. Dann folgen in einsprachigen Wörterbüchern eine Definition oder Erklärung des Wortes, in zweisprachigen Wörterbüchern die Übersetzung und Beispiele zur Verwendung des Wortes.

2. Die richtige Übersetzung finden

▷ Wenn du zum Beispiel ein Rezept liest und dort das Wort *season* findest, schlag im Wörterbuch unter „s", dann „se" / „sea" usw. nach, bis du das Wort findest.

Method:
1. Cut the chicken into slices. Then season the chicken with salt, pepper and curry powder.

Betonungszeichen — **Lautschrift**
Wortart (hier Verb) — **Wortart (hier Substantiv/Nomen)**

sea•son /'siːzn/ I *s.* **1.** (Jahres)Zeit *f.*; **2.** (Reife- *etc.*)Zeit *f.*, rechte Zeit *(für et.)*; **3.** Saison *f.*; II *v/t* **4.** *Speisen* würzen; III *v/i* **5.** reifen; **6.** ablagern

▷ *season* als Nomen mit der Bedeutung „Jahreszeit" oder „Saison" ergibt hier keinen Sinn. Weiter unten findest du das Verb *season*. Dort steht unter anderem der Eintrag „würzen" – das passt hier gut als Übersetzung.

▷ Du musst immer alle Einträge durchlesen. Dann entscheidest du, welche Übersetzung am besten passt.

🎞️🟩 Tipp: Nutze elektronische Hilfsmittel! (media worksheet 3)

· Im Internet gibt es viele Seiten, auf denen du Wörter nachschlagen und dir die richtige Aussprache anhören kannst. Oft gibt es Erklärungen zu den unterschiedlichen Bedeutungen in verschiedenen Zusammenhängen.

2 LISTENING
Hören

Folgende Strategien für Hörübungen können dir helfen, Hörtexte besser zu verstehen:

1. Vor dem Hören

▷ Gibt es eine Höraufgabe im Buch? Lies sie dir genau durch. Was sollst du herausfinden?

▷ Wie lautet die Überschrift des Hörtextes? Welche Hinweise gibt sie dir?

▷ Gibt es Bilder? Was ist darauf zu sehen?

▷ Überlege: Worum könnte es gehen? Was weißt du schon über das Thema?

2. Während des Hörens

▷ Höre dir den Hörtext einmal ganz an. Wer spricht? Was passiert? Du musst nicht jedes einzelne Wort verstehen. Versuche erst einmal herauszufinden, worum es ganz allgemein geht *(listening for gist)*.

▷ Achte auch auf die Stimmen der Sprechenden und auf Hintergrundgeräusche. Sie können dir helfen zu verstehen, worum es geht.

▷ Sieh dir noch einmal die Aufgabe an. Dann höre wieder zu.
Achte diesmal auf Details *(listening for detail)* und mache dir Notizen.

Who?	Where?	When?	What?
Wer spricht? Um wen geht es?	Wo findet das Gespräch / die Geschichte statt?	Wann findet das Gespräch / die Geschichte statt?	Was wird besprochen? Was passiert?

3. Nach dem Hören

▷ Vergleicht eure Ergebnisse. Was habt ihr herausgefunden?

🔲 Tipp: Nutze jede Gelegenheit, um Englisch zu hören!

· Alle Hörtexte zum Buch findest du, wenn du auf www.westermann.de/webcode den Webcode WES-128206-001 eingibst oder den QR-Code scannst, den du auf Seite 2 findest.
· Es gibt verschiedene Möglichkeiten, sich Texte in verschiedenen Geschwindigkeiten vorlesen zu lassen. Du kannst probieren, das Tempo nach und nach zu erhöhen.

3 Mit anderen sprechen

TALKING WITH PEOPLE

Sprich so viel Englisch wie möglich mit deinen Mitschülerinnen und Mitschülern.

1. Versuche, so viel wie möglich auf Englisch auszudrücken

▸ Lerne Ausdrücke auswendig, die du im Gespräch verwenden kannst, z.B. „*There is … / There are … / What about …? / Thank you. / You're welcome.*"
Auch in den *wordbanks* ab Seite 160 findest du nützliche Ausdrücke.

▸ Wenn dir ein Wort, z.B. „*spoon*", nicht einfällt, kannst du es umschreiben:
„*Excuse me, could you pass me the … erm … it's not a fork or a knife. You can eat soup with it.*"

2. Merke dir Redewendungen und Sätze

▸ Es gibt eine Reihe von Redewendungen und Sätzen, die du im Englischunterricht häufig verwenden kannst. Viele davon findest du bei den *classroom phrases* auf den Seiten 170-171.

3. Wenn du Interviews durchführst

▸ Schreibe deine Fragen auf.
▸ Stelle Fragen, auf die man nicht nur mit „ja" oder „nein" antworten kann: Verwende Fragewörter wie *what, when, where, who, how* oder *why*.
▸ Wenn du etwas nicht richtig verstanden hast, bitte um Wiederholung:
„*Can you say that again, please?*" oder: „*Can you repeat that, please?*"

4. Sprich so oft Englisch, wie du kannst

▸ Höre dir die Hörtexte aus deinem Englischbuch an und lies die Texte laut mit. Versuche, die Aussprache der Sprecherinnen und Sprecher nachzuahmen.
▸ Singe englischsprachige Lieder mit.
▸ Unterhalte dich auf Englisch mit jemandem, der ebenfalls Englisch sprechen kann.

Tipp: Nimm dich auf! (media worksheet 5)

· Lies einen Text aus dem Buch laut vor oder sprich Englisch und nimm dich auf. Dann kannst du dich selbst anhören und überprüfen, wie dein Englisch klingt.
· Wenn ihr zu zweit zusammenarbeitet, könnt ihr Dialoge und Interviews aufnehmen und gemeinsam prüfen, ob es noch etwas zu verbessern gibt.

4 WRITING Schreiben

Es ist wichtig, dass du deinen Text planst und nach dem Schreiben überarbeitest.

1. Planen

▷ Auf www.westermann.de/webcode kannst du den Webcode WES-128206-001 eingeben und dort Anleitungen zu verschiedenen Textsorten, z.B. Brief, E-Mail oder Blogeintrag, finden.

▷ Wenn du eine Geschichte schreiben willst, kannst du mithilfe von *who, what, where, when* und *why* Ideen sammeln und die Geschichte planen.

▷ Du kannst in einem *word web* oder in einer Liste passende Wörter sammeln. Sieh in den *wordbank*s ab Seite 160 nach, wenn du Hilfe brauchst.

▷ Überlege: Was sollte am Anfang stehen? Was folgt darauf? Wie könnte das Ende sein? Wie kannst du den Text interessant machen? Wenn du einen Artikel oder Bericht schreibst, solltest du dir vorher überlegen, wie du ihn gliedern möchtest.

2. Schreiben und überarbeiten

▷ Schreibe zuerst einen Entwurf *(draft)*.
▷ Überlege dir eine passende Überschrift.
▷ Wenn du Bilder einfügen möchtest, vergiss nicht, anzugeben, wo du sie gefunden hast.
▷ Überarbeite und verbessere *(edit)* dann deinen Text. Du kannst auch andere um Hilfe bitten.
▷ Schreibe dann deinen Text ins Reine. Das kannst du handschriftlich oder mithilfe eines Textverarbeitungsprogramms am Computer machen.

3. Veröffentlichen

▷ Zeige deinen fertigen Text deiner Lehrkraft, einem Mitschüler, einer Mitschülerin oder der Klasse.
▷ Du kannst deinen Text in deinem (digitalen) Portfolio aufbewahren.

Tipp: Texte digital erstellen und veröffentlichen (media worksheet 1, 9-15)

· Wenn du einen Text am Computer schreibst, kannst du zunächst Ideen und nützliche Wörter in einem Dokument sammeln und speichern. Du kannst deine Ideen und deinen Text jederzeit ändern und ergänzen.
· Ihr könnt eure Texte auch zu einem Klassenprodukt zusammenfügen. Vielleicht gibt es die Möglichkeit, dieses Produkt auf der Schul- oder Klassenwebseite zu veröffentlichen.

5 **Lesen**
READING

Folgende Strategien können dir helfen, einen englischen Text
zu verstehen:

1. Skimming
Beim *skimming* überfliegst du den Text erst einmal. Du verschaffst dir schnell einen Überblick:
Worum geht es? Was passiert? Wer ist dabei? Du musst nicht jedes Wort verstehen.

2. Reading for detail
Du liest den Text gründlich, um möglichst viele Details herauszufinden. Mache dir Notizen.
Auf Kopien oder in deinen eigenen Büchern kannst du auch wichtige Textstellen markieren.
Die *wh*-Fragen können dir helfen: Who? Where? When? What?

SWIMMING IS HIS LIFE

This young man is going to make it to the top. Leroy Haffner
will soon be one of Britain's best swimmers! Leroy was born
in Bristol, UK. Swimming has always been his greatest love.
He started swimming at the age of four. Three years later he
had already won medals for his local club. He took part in

one national competition after another. Then last year, Leroy had an injury and couldn't swim
for nearly two months. But Leroy didn't give up. He started swimming again – and with great
success. Next week, Leroy will participate in the National Championships. His coach, Ted Henley,
knows that "Leroy will do really, really well".

---

3. Scanning
Beim *scanning* suchst du einen Text gezielt nach ganz bestimmten Informationen ab.
Wenn es wichtige Wörter gibt, die du nicht kennst, probiere Folgendes aus:
▶ Kennst du einzelne Teile eines langen Wortes oder ähnliche Wörter aus dem Deutschen oder aus
   einer anderen Sprache? Versuche, dir den Sinn des Wortes herzuleiten.
▶ Kannst du dir die Bedeutung eines unbekannten Wortes aus dem Textzusammenhang herleiten?
Erst, wenn das nicht funktioniert, solltest du das Wort in einem Wörterbuch nachschlagen.

Tipp: Suche dir englische Texte zu Themen, die dich interessieren!

· Du kannst im Internet und in Büchereien nach interessanten Texten auf Englisch suchen.
· Lies so viel du kannst. Am Ende jeder Unit in diesem Buch findest du eine Kurzgeschichte
  und einen Sachtext oder ein Gedicht.

6 MEDIATION
Sprachmittlung

Manchmal gibt es Situationen, in denen du jemandem helfen musst, der deine Muttersprache oder eine Fremdsprache nicht so gut kann wie du.

1. Gib den Sinn wieder
Übersetze nicht alles Wort für Wort. Wichtiger ist es, den Sinn wiederzugeben.

2. Fasse dich kurz
Bilde einfache, kurze Sätze. Unwichtige Einzelheiten kannst du weglassen.

Was gibt es heute Besonderes?

Our special recommendation today is fresh fish. Our chef was able to get some fresh trout that was caught this morning. We serve it with a lemon cream sauce, a side dish of rice and a light salad.

Es gibt frischen Fisch in Zitronensauce mit Reis und Salat.

Was steht denn da?

**Science Museum –
New section open now**
Don't miss our brand new exhibition section on the history of the computer. From a model of Konrad Zuse's Z3, the first working computer in the world, to the latest tablets, there's a lot to see, learn and try out.

Sie haben eine neue Abteilung zur Geschichte des Computers eröffnet.

Tipp: Keine Angst vor Fehlern!

· Wenn dir ein wichtiges Wort nicht einfällt, kannst du es umschreiben.
· Versuche, dich an Redewendungen zu erinnern. Zum Beispiel kannst du mit „*What about …?*" Vorschläge machen oder mit „*There is … / There are …*" etwas beschreiben.

7 WATCHING A VIDEO CLIP
Videoclips verstehen

Englischsprachige Videoclips anzuschauen macht Spaß und ist auch eine tolle Möglichkeit, die Sprache besser zu lernen. Dabei solltest du einige Dinge beachten:

1. Bevor es losgeht
▷ Gibt es Bilder aus dem Videoclip? Was ist zu sehen?
▷ Lies den Titel des Videoclips. Welche Hinweise gibt er auf den Inhalt?
▷ Worum könnte es gehen? Stelle Vermutungen an.

2. Währenddessen
▷ Schaue dir den Videoclip in Ruhe an. Was ist dein erster Eindruck? Mache dir Notizen.
Who? Wer ist zu sehen? Um wen geht es?
Where? Wo findet das Geschehen statt?
When? Wann findet das Geschehen statt?
What? Worum geht es? Was passiert?

▷ Es ist nicht schlimm, wenn du nicht alles verstehst. Achte auf die Stimmen, Körpersprache und Gesichtsausdrücke der Personen im Videoclip.

▷ Gibt es eine Aufgabe zu dem Videoclip? Behalte sie im Kopf, während du ein zweites Mal zuschaust. Konzentriere dich stärker auf das, was du hörst. Gibt es Wörter, die immer wieder vorkommen? Notiere sie dir.

▷ Versuche, gleich danach die Frage zu beantworten. Wenn nötig, schaue dir dann den Clip ein weiteres Mal an. Überprüfe dabei deine Antworten.

3. Hinterher
▷ Tausche dich mit deinen Mitschülerinnen und Mitschülern aus.

Tipp: Schaue dir Videoclips und Filme auf Englisch an (media worksheet 8)
· Alle Videoclips zum Buch findest du, wenn du auf www.westermann.de/webcode den Webcode WES-128206-001 eingibst oder den QR-Code scannst, den du auf Seite 2 findest.
· Sieh dir Filme, Serien oder Berichte zu Themen, die dich interessieren, auf Englisch an.
· Auf DVDs oder bei Streaming-Diensten kannst du fast immer den englischen Ton und englische Untertitel einschalten. Nach und nach lernst du besser zu verstehen, was gesagt wird.

8 SEARCHING THE INTERNET
SEARCHING THE INTERNET
Im Internet recherchieren

Hier erfährst du, wie du im Internet zu einem Thema recherchieren kannst.

1. Benutze eine Suchmaschine

▸ Gute Suchbegriffe erleichtern dir die Suche im Internet. Versuche, auf Englisch möglichst genau zu formulieren, wonach du suchst.

▸ Gib die Suchbegriffe in eine Suchmaschine ein. Bei vielen Suchmaschinen kannst du Englisch als Sprache wählen. Dann steht dir der nötige Wortschatz gleich zur Verfügung.

▸ Es kann sein, dass die Suchmaschine sehr viele Treffer anzeigt. Oft genügt es, sich die ersten 10 bis 20 Suchergebnisse anzuschauen.

▸ Es gibt Webseiten, auf denen du Informationen in einfacherem Englisch finden kannst. Deine Lehrkraft kann dir helfen, sie zu finden.

2. Halte nützliche Informationen fest

▸ Überfliege erst einmal die Seiten, die dir interessant erscheinen. Du brauchst nicht jedes Wort zu verstehen.

▸ Dann kannst du dir Notizen zu den Inhalten machen.

▸ Denke daran, dir das Datum deiner Recherche aufzuschreiben und die Quelle abzuspeichern.

▸ Wenn du Textausschnitte unverändert aus dem Internet übernimmst, musst du zeigen, dass es Zitate sind. Setze sie in deinem Text in Anführungszeichen und gib die Quelle und das Datum an, an dem du sie gefunden hast.

3. Sei kritisch

▸ Informationen, die du im Internet findest, sind nicht immer richtig.

▸ Sei deshalb kritisch und überprüfe die Informationen noch einmal auf anderen Seiten oder in einem Lexikon.

Tipp: Nutze digitale Tools (media worksheet 6, 7)

· Es gibt viele sinnvolle Tools im Internet. Du kannst zum Beispiel Währungen und Maßeinheiten umrechnen oder dir Entfernungen anzeigen lassen.

· Viele englischsprachige Einrichtungen, vor allem Museen, bieten virtuelle Rundgänge an. Du kannst auch virtuell durch britische Städte spazieren.

9 PRESENTATIONS
Präsentationen halten

Hier findest du einige Tipps und Tricks für gelungene Präsentationen.

1. Bevor du etwas präsentierst

▸ Überlege: Was möchtest du zu deinem Thema sagen?
   Wie viel Zeit hast du?
▸ Gliedere deinen Vortrag: Überlege, in welcher Reihenfolge
   du was sagen und wie du anfangen möchtest.
▸ Fertige ein Poster oder eine Computerpräsentation an,
   um deinen Vortrag anschaulich zu machen. Wenn du
   Bilder oder Texte aus dem Internet oder aus einem Buch
   kopiert hast, dann schreibe immer dazu, wo und wann
   du sie gefunden hast.
▸ Notiere Stichpunkte zu dem, was du sagen möchtest,
   auf Karteikarten.
▸ Nützliche Redewendungen findest du in der *wordbank*
   auf Seite 168.
▸ Übe deinen Vortrag vor dem Spiegel, vor Freunden oder
   vor deiner Familie.

So sieht ein gelungenes Vortragsposter aus

▸ *ansprechende Überschrift*
▸ *interessante Informationen*
▸ *verständliche Sätze, aber nicht zu viel Text*
▸ *große Bilder und Schrift: Jeder im Raum muss sie sehen und lesen können.*
▸ *saubere Schrift*
▸ *Bilder mit Bildunterschriften*

2. Während du präsentierst

▸ Sprich langsam und deutlich.
▸ Sieh deine Zuhörerinnen und Zuhörer an, wenn du sprichst. Achte zum Beispiel bei einer
   Computerpräsentation darauf, nicht ständig auf den Bildschirm zu schauen.
▸ Versuche, frei zu sprechen. Du kannst die wichtigsten Punkte von deinen Karteikarten
   oder deinem Poster ablesen.

3. So wird dein Vortrag spannend und lebendig

▸ Musik, Videoclips, interessante Bilder oder Zitate machen deinen Vortrag abwechslungsreich.
▸ Achte darauf, dass dein Vortrag nicht klingt, als würdest du einen Text ablesen.
▸ Zeige deinen Zuhörerinnen und Zuhörern auf deinem Poster oder auf den Seiten deiner
   Computerpräsentation, worüber du gerade sprichst.

Tipp: Schau dir Tutorials an (media worksheet 4)

· Zum Präsentieren gibt es viele Tutorials im Internet. Schau dir einige an und überlege,
  was bei dir schon gut klappt und was du noch verbessern könntest.
· Zum Thema Computerpräsentationen kannst du dir ein passendes Arbeitsblatt herunterladen
  und dir Tutorials anschauen. Gehe dazu auf www.westermann.de/webcode und gib den
  Webcode WES-128206-001 ein.

10 PERFORMING A SCENE
Eine Szene vorspielen

Szenische Lesungen, Rollenspiele und Theaterstücke sind eine gute Methode, um Englisch zu trainieren. Denke immer daran, laut und deutlich und nicht zu schnell zu sprechen, damit man dich gut verstehen kann.

1. Szenische Lesung
▷ Für ein *dramatic reading* musst du deinen Text nicht auswendig lernen. Du solltest ihn aber so gut kennen, dass du auf deine Aussprache, Lautstärke, Betonung und Mimik achten kannst, ohne den Faden zu verlieren.
▷ Achte darauf, dass Aussprache, Lautstärke, Betonung und Mimik zu dem passen, was du liest.

2. Rollenspiele
▷ Halte beim Sprechen Augenkontakt zu deinem Gegenüber.
▷ Versetze dich in die Person hinein, die du darstellst. Denke beim Sprechen an die passende Mimik und Gestik.
▷ Wechselt auch mal die Rollen und übt mit anderen Partnern. So lernt ihr, spontan zu reagieren.
▷ Wenn ihr *cue cards* verwendet, denkt daran, nur Stichworte zu notieren, keine ganzen Sätze!

3. Theaterstücke
▷ Bei Theaterstücken geht es noch mehr als bei Rollenspielen um das Schauspielern. Du solltest deinen Text gut auswendig lernen, damit du dich besser auf das Spielen konzentrieren kannst. Mit der Methode *read – look up – speak* kannst du deine Rolle auswendig lernen: Du liest deinen Satz still, siehst dann auf und sprichst ihn.
▷ Versetze dich in die Person hinein, die du darstellst. Denke beim Sprechen an die passende Mimik und Gestik.
▷ Mit Requisiten *(props)* und Kostümen fällt es leichter, in eine Rolle hineinzuschlüpfen.

4. Präsentieren
▷ Mit Rollenspielen, kleinen Szenen, Sketchen und Theaterstücken könnt ihr zeigen, wie viel Englisch ihr schon könnt. Bei einem Schulfest oder an einem Tag der offenen Tür könnt ihr Eltern oder andere Klassen zu einer Vorführung einladen.

▓▒ 🔲 **Tipp: Schaut euch selbst zu** (media worksheet 2)

· Rollenspiele könnt ihr aufnehmen und so gemeinsam überprüfen, ob es noch etwas zu verbessern gibt.

Eating and eating out

I have never eaten octopus.
But I would like to try it.

My family's traditional dish
is Sunday roast.

I tried sushi but I didn't
like it.

On special occasions we go out
for a meal. We often go to a
traditional British restaurant.

My favourite food is mashed
potatoes with bacon and chips.

Food can be …

savoury · sweet · tasty · yummy · perfect · delicious · vegetarian · nice ·
spicy · good · bad · special · disgusting · fried · healthy ·
fresh · traditional · vegan · hot · grilled · overcooked

Preparing a meal

* *Heat the oil / butter /…*

* *Chop the tomatoes / vegetables /…*

* *Slice the onion / cucumber /…*

* *Cut the potatoes / carrots /… in half.*

* *Put the vegetables in the pot /…*

* *Add a teaspoon of salt / sugar /…*

* *Boil for 10 minutes / half an hour /…*

* *Stir in the flour / the milk /…*

* *Add a cup of yoghurt /…*

* *Cover the pot /…*

* *Bake for 20 minutes / one hour /…*

Ingredients

a bag of potatoes · some tomatoes ·
many carrots · a lot of peppers ·
a few onions · some cabbage ·
one cup of chickpeas · some garlic

a little water · some couscous ·
a bit of bread · a cup of rice

a bottle of milk · a little yoghurt ·
a piece of cheese

some cumin · a little coriander ·
pepper · a teaspoon of paprika ·
cayenne pepper · cinnamon ·
not too much salt

At a restaurant

On a menu you can find …

starters · main courses · desserts ·
drinks · sides · soups · salads

Restaurants can be …

expensive · good · bad · nice ·
cosy · cheap · delicious · vegetarian ·
traditional · perfect · vegan

A restaurant review

My favourite restaurant is …
The service was quick / good / bad / …
I had the …
The food was tasty / healthy / cheap /
* disgusting / spicy / overcooked / burnt / …*
I had the best / worst … I have ever eaten.
The atmosphere was friendly / cosy /
* relaxed / busy / …*
It is not as … as other restaurants.
It is … / more … than other restaurants.

Keeping fit

 My favourite sport is swimming. I'm really strong and I like being on my own. I like being indoors and outdoors, so I go swimming at the swimming pool but also in the sea.

 I love dancing! I don't like being outdoors, so climbing, cycling and going hiking are not my favourite sports. I prefer indoor sports. Dancing is perfect for me because I like music, too.

 I enjoy diving because I like being in the water and watching fish. I love outdoor sports. I just can't be indoors all the time. Being outside makes me happy and I feel less stressed.

Sports

> rowing · climbing · swimming ·
> weight training · running · riding · dancing ·
> diving · marathon · triathlon

> **play:** cricket · football · ball sports ·
> rugby · games · golf · chess ·
> tennis · baseball

> **do:** yoga · karate

Sports can be …

> fun · exciting · exhausting · difficult · easy ·
> good for you · dangerous · fast

 I don't really know what sport I would like.

You should play / go / do …

 I'm always stressed.

I think doing yoga would be a good idea because it is so relaxing.

My sports idol

My favourite sports idol is … because he / she is fast / good at … / …
He / She respects other players and is friendly / funny / …
He / She trains hard and gives a lot of money to charity.

 I have never tried playing football.

I think you would be good at it because you can run very fast.

Health

To stay healthy, it is important to ...

do sport regularly · get enough sleep · eat healthily · spend time outdoors · drink enough water ·
don't eat too many sweets · make sure you are not too stressed · do things that make you happy ·
relax · eat enough fruit and vegetables

At the doctor's

What's the matter?

Where does it hurt?

When did you fall?

Does your toe hurt?

Have you got a headache?

How long have you had a headache for?

You should rest until you feel better.

You will have to stay at home for a week.

There is something wrong with my leg.

It is swollen and it hurts.

My knee is bleeding.

I hurt my ankle.

What do I have to do?

How soon will I feel better?

When will I be able to do sports again?

You can have ...

a sore throat · a fever · a cough · a cold ·
a headache · an infection ·
a toothache · a broken arm · an injury ·
a sprained ankle · a stomach ache

You can feel ...

ill · sick · dizzy · tired · well again

You need ...

a plaster · a cast · some medicine ·
an ambulance · to go to the dentist's ·
to rest · to see a doctor · an X-ray ·
to make an appointment for a check-up ·
to keep your leg up

How are you feeling?   I'm a bit bored.

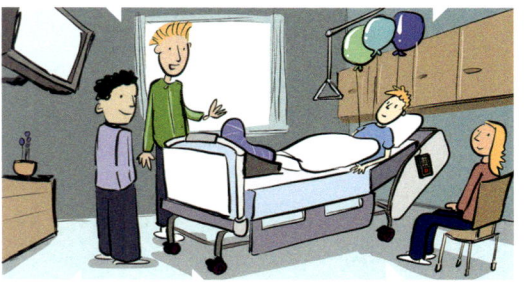

Don't worry,   Get well   It doesn't
you will feel   soon!   hurt too
better soon.   much.

What's on?

What shall we do in London this weekend?
Where could we go?

My favourite event is the Notting Hill Carnival.
I would like to see the costumes and listen to
the music. Do you want to go there?

Portobello Market is not really quiet.
What about going to the cinema?

There is a summer festival in
St James's Park. What about that?

Why don't we go to Portobello Market? You can
buy lots of different things there, try food from
all over the world and meet interesting people.

That's always so loud and there are so many
people. I really don't want to go there.
I would prefer something more quiet.

It's so warm and sunny, why don't we do
something outside?

That sounds good. Let's do that!
I've never been to an outdoor festival before.

When is it?

> this weekend · next month · on 3 July · Sunday morning ·
> Monday afternoon · in the evening · at twelve o'clock

Buying and selling

Can I help you?   Excuse me, I'm looking for a pair of jeans.

Why don't you try it on?

I can give it to you
for £25.50.

Do you have any
dark blue ones?

Anything else?

How much does
this pair cost?

That'll be £30.80.

How much are these?

Here's your change.

> Für die Schreibung von
> Geldbeträgen wird im
> Englischen zuerst das
> Währungssymbol geschrieben,
> dann – ohne Leerzeichen –
> der Betrag in Ziffern. Es wird
> ein Punkt und kein Komma
> verwendet! Zum Beispiel:
> £4.50 / €3.45

Advertising things

For just £2.50 you can get a …

It's ideal for …

This is the perfect … for you!   Are you looking for a …?

Events

When you go to a music festival, you can listen to lots of different bands.

You can watch many different actors perform at a theatre festival.

When you take part in a charity run, you can do something good while you're having fun.

At a flea market you can sell things you don't need anymore and buy things that other people don't need anymore.

If you like going to the cinema, a film festival is the event for you!

At the Notting Hill Carnival you can watch a brilliant parade.

Events can be …

loud · crowded · free · exciting · fun · for children · world-famous · interesting

For or against big events?

I think big events are great. You can meet new people and have new experiences. Sometimes you can learn something new.

I don't like big events because there are so many people. It gets very crowded and loud.

It is good that there are more customers in the shops.

Many visitors come by car and they leave their rubbish everywhere. That's bad for the environment.

Events are good for the people who work at them – for example musicians and actors who perform there.

Sometimes they are even free.

Those events are only about making money. The entrance fee can be really expensive.

Expressing opinions

In my opinion, …

I think that …

If you ask me, …

I agree that …

On the one hand, …

On the other hand, …

I would say that …

Family history

I am originally from Brighton. I moved when I was 19 and went to university in Leeds.

My parents met in London when they were studying there.

My mother spent her childhood in Edinburgh. When she was a teenager, her family moved to Wales.

My brother was born in London. My family moved to Brighton when he was three.

Two years later my parents got married.

My great-grandfather grew up in Trinidad. He started working when he was 16 years old and he met my great-grandmother when he was 18.

They had four children and emigrated to Great Britain in the 1950s.

When did it happen?

in the 1990s · in 2005 · around 2010 · on 22nd October 1999 · in the early 1930s · in the late 1960s · in March 1981

Family

mother · father · son · daughter · child · brother · sister · uncle · aunt · cousin · wife · husband · partner · grandmother · grandfather

Home

For me, home is where my family is.
I don't feel at home without friends and family.
I feel at home when I know everyone in my neighbourhood.
My home is in London / …
I used to live in a small village in the countryside but I like big cities more, so now I live in London.

Talking about pictures

In the picture there is … / are …

The picture shows two children. The girl is sitting on a couch on the left and the boy is sitting on a chair on the right.

There is a table between them. On the table I can see a vase with flowers.

I think it's a very old picture.
It's black and white.

The girl could be older than the boy. She looks a bit afraid.
The boy doesn't look very happy.

They might be listening to the radio.

Maybe the children are brother and sister.

Feelings

I am feeling ...

angry

afraid

worried

... **excited** because I'm going to a music festival at the weekend.

... **lonely** because all my friends are on holiday.

... **upset** about an argument with my mum.

... **stressed** because I have a problem at school.

... **proud** because I was very good at my maths test.

... **shy** because I have to start a new school.

... **scared** because there's a big black spider in my room.

... **nervous** about my next English test.

happy

bored

sad

Seeking and giving advice

I have a problem with my parents.
They are so strict. Do you have any tips?
What do you think I should do? Can you help?
How shall I deal with them?
I don't know what to do.
I need some advice.
Can you help me / give me some advice, please?

What's the problem?

What happened?
Why are you feeling so sad?

I'm sorry to hear that. Why don't you try to talk to them again?

How about you ask your brothers for help?

I think you should wait for a while and then try again.

Why do you think you can't talk to them?

Have you tried asking your grandma for advice?
Maybe you could speak to her.

Inventions

I proudly present my latest invention. It will solve a lot of problems.

You can save a lot of time and money with this machine.

It can improve people's lives because it helps them with different tasks.

It can work for hours without electricity.

It can be used anywhere.

My invention is very useful if you haven't got enough time.

You only have to switch it on.

It was invented in 1982. · It was invented by James Watt. · It can be used to pull heavy objects. · It can be seen all over the world. · It is used by many people every day. · It was built in 1895. · First versions of this invention appeared in 1723. · It was invented to help people.

Presenting something

Hello and welcome to my presentation about …
First I would like to introduce the topic of …
In the second part of my presentation, I will …
After that I will talk about …
Finally, I will look at …
I will first give some information on …
Here is an example of …
On this slide you can see …
This is a photo of …
This picture shows that …
It is also important to mention that …
The last aspect is …
Thanks for listening. Are there any questions?

Giving feedback

I enjoyed your presentation because you talked about all aspects of the topic.

There was a good summary at the end.

My favourite part of your presentation was when you talked about …

The best part were the pictures on the third slide.

I think it was a good / fantastic / well-researched / … presentation.

Well done for giving a good presentation!

You could improve by speaking more loudly / more clearly / more slowly / …

You need to research more facts / …

Next time you should have more pictures / less … / a handout / …

The presentation was a little hard to understand.

Communication

How do you communicate with your friends and family?

How often do you text your best friend?

What is the best way to communicate with your grandparents?

Have you ever been on a video chat?

I write text messages to my friends.

I send letters or emails to my grandparents.

I send postcards when I am on holiday.

I often call my best friend.

I react with a heart or a smiley to comment on my friend's post.

Dear Mr Kogan,
Dear Mrs Norris,
Dear Grandma,
Hi Ava,

How are you? I'm ...

Olivia Norris
Lexham Gardens 2A
London W8 5JL
UK

Yours sincerely, ...
Lots of love, ... / Love, ...
I look forward to hearing from you.
Please write to me soon!

Going online

I'm online for about two hours every day. I chat with my friends, watch videos or play games.

I don't post anything that I don't want to go on the Internet.

My password is strong. Nobody knows it but me and my parents.

I don't share things with people I don't know.

I always ask people for their permission before I take pictures of them.

I delete photos when the person in them asks me to.

Classroom phrases

Wenn man ankommt oder geht

Good morning.	Guten Morgen.
What's for homework?	Was haben wir als Hausaufgabe auf?
See you tomorrow.	Bis morgen.
Bye.	Tschüs.

Wenn es ein Problem gibt

Sorry I'm late.	Tut mir leid, dass ich zu spät bin.
Sorry, I haven't got my exercise book with me.	Tut mir leid, ich habe mein Heft nicht dabei.
Sorry, I haven't got my homework with me.	Tut mir leid, ich habe meine Hausaufgaben nicht dabei.
What's the matter?	Was ist los?
I'm fine.	Mir geht's gut.
I feel sick.	Mir ist schlecht.
I've got a headache.	Ich habe Kopfschmerzen.
Can I open the window, please?	Kann ich bitte das Fenster öffnen?
Can I go to the toilet, please?	Kann ich bitte zur Toilette gehen?

Wenn man Hilfe braucht

Can you help me, please?	Können Sie / Kannst du mir bitte helfen?
I've got a question.	Ich habe eine Frage.
I don't understand this.	Ich verstehe das hier nicht.
How can I do this exercise?	Wie kann ich diese Aufgabe machen?
What's ... in English / German?	Was heißt ... auf Englisch / Deutsch?
What does ... mean?	Was bedeutet ...?
Is that correct?	Ist das richtig?
Can you write that on the board, please?	Können Sie das bitte an die Tafel schreiben?
Can you spell that, please?	Können Sie das bitte buchstabieren?
Can you say that again, please?	Können Sie / Kannst du das bitte noch einmal sagen?
Can we listen to the audio track again, please?	Können wir den Audiotrack bitte noch einmal hören?
Sorry, I don't know.	Tut mir leid, das weiß ich nicht.
What page, please?	Auf welcher Seite bitte?

Wenn man zusammen arbeitet oder spielt

Whose turn is it?	Wer ist dran?
Do you want to work with me?	Möchtest du mit mir arbeiten?
Let's check ...	Lass uns ... überprüfen.
Let's compare ...	Lass uns ... vergleichen.
Let's talk about ...	Lass uns über ... sprechen.

Wenn man mit dem Computer arbeitet

What's your email address?	Wie ist deine E-Mail-Adresse?
You can click on this link.	Du kannst auf diesen Link klicken.
Can I print that out?	Kann ich das ausdrucken?
Can I download it?	Kann ich es herunterladen?
I saved the links to name the sources.	Ich habe die Links gespeichert, um die Quellen anzugeben.
I did research online. I used a search engine.	Ich habe online recherchiert. Ich habe eine Suchmaschine benutzt.

Was die Lehrerin oder der Lehrer sagt

Open your books at page …	Öffnet eure Bücher auf Seite …
Turn to page …	Blättert zu Seite …
Look at line …	Seht euch Zeile … an.
Look at the next paragraph.	Seht euch den nächsten Absatz an.
Read the text on page …	Lies / Lest den Text auf Seite …
Work in pairs / in groups of four.	Arbeitet zu zweit / zu viert.
Listen to the audio track.	Hör dir / Hört euch den Audiotrack an.
Listen to audio track number …	Hör dir / Hört euch Audiotrack Nummer … an.
Write about …	Schreibe / Schreibt über …
Talk about …	Sprich / Sprecht über …
Ask questions about …	Stelle / Stellt Fragen zu …
Answer the question, please.	Beantworte / Beantwortet bitte die Frage.
Match the sentences.	Ordne / Ordnet die Sätze zu.
Who wants to read out the text?	Wer möchte den Text vorlesen?
Write down the answers.	Schreibt die Antworten auf.
Act out the dialogue.	Spielt den Dialog vor.
Change roles.	Tauscht die Rollen.
Make your own dialogue / conversation.	Entwirf / Entwerft selbst einen Dialog / ein Gespräch.
Take a card.	Nimm / Nehmt eine Karte.
Come to the board, please.	Komm / Kommt bitte zur Tafel.
Do this exercise at home, please.	Mache / Macht diese Aufgabe bitte zu Hause.
Be quiet, please.	Sei / Seid bitte ruhig.
Sit down, please.	Setz dich bitte. / Setzt euch bitte.
Please speak up.	Sprich / Sprecht bitte lauter.
You can do better.	Das kannst du / könnt ihr besser.
Try again.	Versuch / Versucht es noch einmal.
Well done.	Gut gemacht.

1 THE PRESENT PERFECT: STATEMENTS (REVISION)
Das Perfekt: Aussagen *(revision)*

Das *present perfect* verwendest du, wenn etwas irgendwann in einem Zeitraum von der Vergangenheit bis zur Gegenwart passiert ist.

Du verwendest es auch, wenn ein Vorgang in der Vergangenheit noch Auswirkungen auf die Gegenwart hat.

> I have already finished my homework. Can I go out now?

a) Bejahte Aussagesätze im *present perfect*

DIGITAL+ video 17

Das *present perfect* bildest du mit *have / has* + Partizip Perfekt *(past participle)*. Statt *have* bzw. *has* kannst du auch die entsprechende Kurzform benutzen.

I **have cleaned** the kitchen.
I**'ve cleaned** the kitchen.   Ich **habe** die Küche **sauber gemacht**.

He **has finished** his dinner.
He**'s finished** his dinner.   Er **hat** sein Essen **beendet**.

Bei regelmäßigen Verben bildest du das Partizip Perfekt, indem du an die Grundform des Verbs die Endung *-ed* anhängst. Beachte auch die Besonderheiten bei der Schreibung, die auf Seite 184 im Grammatik-Kapitel 13 erläutert werden.

Grundform	*simple past*	*past participle*
clean	cleaned	clean**ed**
help	helped	help**ed**
play	played	play**ed**
tidy	tidied	tid**ied**
visit	visited	visit**ed**

Die Formen der unregelmäßigen Verben musst du wie Vokabeln auswendig lernen. Auf den Seiten 245–247 findest du eine Liste dieser Verben. Auf Seite 247 gibt es einen Tipp, wie du die unregelmäßigen Formen gruppieren kannst, um sie dir leichter einzuprägen.

Grundform	*simple past*	*past participle*
be	was / were	**been**
do	did	**done**
have	had	**had**
buy	bought	**bought**

b) Verneinte Aussagesätze im *present perfect*

Die Verneinung bildest du mit *have not / has not* + Partizip Perfekt bzw. mit den Kurzformen *haven't / hasn't* + Partizip Perfekt.

I **have not cleaned** the kitchen yet.
I **haven't cleaned** the kitchen yet.   Ich **habe** die Küche noch **nicht sauber gemacht**.

He **has not finished** his dinner.
He **hasn't finished** his dinner.   Er **hat** sein Essen **nicht beendet**.

2 THE PRESENT PERFECT: QUESTIONS (REVISION)
Das Perfekt: Fragen *(revision)*

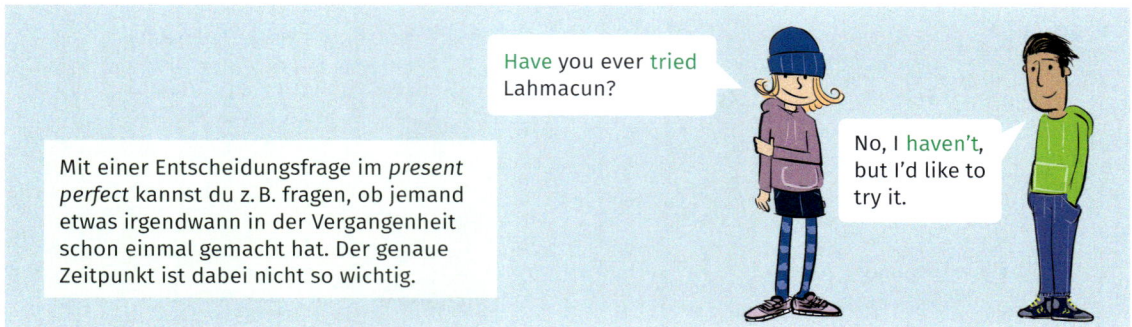

> Have you ever tried Lahmacun?

> No, I haven't, but I'd like to try it.

Mit einer Entscheidungsfrage im *present perfect* kannst du z. B. fragen, ob jemand etwas irgendwann in der Vergangenheit schon einmal gemacht hat. Der genaue Zeitpunkt ist dabei nicht so wichtig.

a) Fragen und Kurzantworten im *present perfect*

Entscheidungsfragen im *present perfect* bildest du, indem du *have* bzw. *has* an den Satzanfang stellst.

DIGITAL+ video 17

Entscheidungsfrage	Kurzantwort	Kurzantwort
Have you ever been to a Chinese restaurant?	Yes, I have.	No, I haven't.
Has Ava ever eaten a Sunday roast?	Yes, she has.	No, she hasn't.
Have the children finished their dinner?	Yes, they have.	No, they haven't.

b) Fragen mit Fragewort im *present perfect*

Bei Fragen mit Fragewort steht das Fragewort am Satzanfang.

***What** have you done?*
***Where** have you been?*
***Why** hasn't she called yet?*

c) Adverbien der unbestimmten Zeit

Beim *present perfect* ist es nicht wichtig, wann genau in der Vergangenheit etwas passiert ist. Daher werden bei Fragen und Aussagen im *present perfect* häufig Adverbien der unbestimmten Zeit verwendet, z. B. *ever* (= jemals), *never* (= nie), *already* (= schon), *just* (= gerade) und *not yet* (= noch nicht).

Die meisten Adverbien stehen dann direkt vor dem Partizip Perfekt.

*Have you **ever** been to London? – No, I've **never** been there.*
*Bist du **jemals** in London gewesen? – Nein, ich bin **(noch) nie** dort gewesen.*

*Has Ava **already** taken Ollie for a walk? – Yes, she has **just** come back.*
*Hat Ava Ollie **schon** Gassi geführt? – Ja, sie ist **gerade** zurückgekommen.*

Beachte die Ausnahme: *yet* steht am Satzende.

*Have you been to the new restaurant? – No, I have**n't** been there **yet**.*
*Bist du im neuen Restaurant gewesen? – Nein, ich bin **noch nicht** dort gewesen.*

3 QUANTIFIERS (REVISION)
Mengenangaben *(revision)*

There aren't many onions. But there are a lot of carrots and peppers and there's some cabbage. There isn't much cheese …

Some und *any* sind Mengenangaben. Sie bedeuten „einige", „ein paar" oder „etwas". Auch *much*, *many* und *a lot* of („viel, viele") sind Mengenangaben.

a) Die Mengenangaben *some* und *any*

DIGITAL+ video 18

In bejahten Aussagesätzen benutzt du *some*.

*There are **some** apples in the kitchen.*	*In der Küche sind **ein paar** Äpfel.*
*I need **some** milk for my cornflakes.*	*Ich brauche **etwas** Milch für meine Cornflakes.*

In verneinten Aussagesätzen und in den meisten Fragen verwendest du *any*.
Das Wort wird oft nicht übersetzt. Die Mengenangabe *not … any* bedeutet „kein" oder „keine".

*Are there **any** apples? Sind da Äpfel?*	*We haven**'t** got **any** apples. Wir haben **keine** Äpfel.*
*Have you got **any** milk? Hast du Milch?*	*There is**n't** any milk. Es gibt **keine** Milch.*

Achtung: Wenn du höflich um etwas bittest oder etwas anbietest, benutzt du auch in Fragen *some*:

*Can I have **some** milk, please?*	*Kann ich bitte **etwas** Milch haben?*
*Would you like **some** tea?*	*Möchtest du Tee?*

b) Die Mengenangaben *much, many* und *a lot of*

Much (auf Deutsch „viel") wird mit Nomen verwendet, die nicht zählbar sind, zum Beispiel *water, milk, juice, time, money*. Die Nomen stehen daher in der Einzahl.

*We haven't got **much** milk.*	*Wir haben nicht **viel** Milch.*
*How **much** cheese have we got?*	*Wie **viel** Käse haben wir?*

Many (auf Deutsch „viele") wird dagegen mit Nomen verwendet, die zählbar sind, zum Beispiel *apples, eggs, tomatoes*. Die Nomen stehen in der Mehrzahl.

*We haven't got **many** apples.*	*Wir haben nicht **viele** Äpfel.*
*How **many** tomatoes have we got?*	*Wie **viele** Tomaten haben wir?*

Much und *many* werden vor allem in Fragen und verneinten Aussagesätzen verwendet.
In bejahten Aussagesätzen verwendet man eher *a lot of* oder *lots of*. Hier unterscheidet man nicht zwischen zählbaren und nicht zählbaren Nomen.

*We need **lots of** juice and **lots of** snacks for the party.*	
*Wir brauchen **viel** Saft und **viele** Snacks für die Party.*	

4 THE COMPARISON OF ADJECTIVES (REVISION)
Die Steigerung von Adjektiven *(revision)*

Wenn du Personen oder Dinge näher beschreiben möchtest, verwendest du Adjektive. Wenn du Personen oder Dinge miteinander vergleichen möchtest, kannst du diese Adjektive steigern. Die erste Steigerungsform heißt Komparativ, die zweite Steigerungsform heißt Superlativ.

This is a very nice restaurant, don't you think?

Yes, much nicer than the other one. I think it's the nicest restaurant in Notting Hill.

a) Steigerung von Adjektiven mit *-er* und *-est*

Einsilbige Adjektive (z.B. *cheap* und *old*) werden durch das Anhängen von *-er* und *-est* gesteigert.

Bei manchen Adjektiven ändert sich die Schreibweise, *bigger* z.B. schreibt man mit zwei *g*, ein stummes *e* wie bei *nice* fällt weg.

Auch einige zweisilbige Adjektive können mit *-er* und *-est* gesteigert werden, z.B. Adjektive, die auf *-er, -le, -ow* und *-y* enden. Bei Adjektiven auf *-y* wird aus dem *-y* ein *-i*.

Einige Adjektive haben unregelmäßige Steigerungsformen. Diese Formen musst du wie Vokabeln lernen.

DIGITAL+ video 19

	Komparativ	Superlativ
cheap	cheap**er**	(the) cheap**est**
old	old**er**	(the) old**est**
big	big**ger**	(the) big**gest**
nice	nic**er**	(the) nic**est**
clever	clever**er**	(the) clever**est**
easy	eas**ier**	(the) eas**iest**
good	**better**	(the) **best**
bad	**worse**	(the) **worst**

b) Steigerung von Adjektiven mit *more* und *most*

Mehrsilbige Adjektive werden mit *more* und *most* gesteigert. Das Adjektiv bleibt unverändert.

	Komparativ	Superlativ
useful	**more** useful	(the) **most** useful
beautiful	**more** beautiful	(the) **most** beautiful
interesting	**more** interesting	(the) **most** interesting

c) Vergleichssätze

Willst du Personen oder Dinge miteinander vergleichen, dann benutzt du den Komparativ mit *than*.

*Noah is older **than** Ava. Noah ist älter **als** Ava.*
*The jacket is more expensive **than** the T-shirt. Die Jacke ist teurer **als** das T-Shirt.*

Sind die Eigenschaften gleich, benutzt du *as … as.*

*Lily is **as** old **as** Harry. Lily ist **so** alt **wie** Harry.*
*The jeans are **as** expensive **as** the jacket. Die Jeans sind **so** teuer **wie** die Jacke.*

5 THE PRESENT PROGRESSIVE (REVISION)
Die Verlaufsform der Gegenwart *(revision)*

Mit dem *present progressive* kannst du beschreiben, was gerade passiert oder was auf einem Bild zu sehen ist. Du kannst es auch verwenden, um über Pläne für die (nähere) Zukunft zu sprechen.

The man is waiting for his food.

a) Bejahte Aussagesätze im *present progressive*

🟩 DIGITAL+ video 20

So bildest du das *present progressive*:

Form von *be (am, is, are)* + Grundform des Verbs + Endung **-ing**.

The waiter **is** show**ing** the Kogans to their table.	Der Kellner **führt** die Kogans zu ihrem Tisch.
The Kogans **are** order**ing** their food.	Die Kogans **bestellen** ihr Essen.

Beachte: Endet das Verb auf einem stummen *-e*, dann fällt das *-e* in der *ing*-Form weg.

writ**e** → writ**ing**   danc**e** → danc**ing**   tak**e** → tak**ing**

Endet das Verb auf einem kurzen betonten Vokal + Konsonant, wird der Konsonant verdoppelt.

put → pu**tt**ing   run → ru**nn**ing   get → ge**tt**ing

b) Verneinte Aussagesätze im *present progressive*

Für die Verneinung fügst du *not* hinter der Form von *be* ein. Oft wird die Kurzform verwendet:

Harry **is not** danc**ing**.	Harry **isn't** danc**ing**.	Harry **tanzt (gerade) nicht**.
They **are not** watch**ing** TV.	They **aren't** watch**ing** TV.	Sie **gucken (gerade)** nicht Fernsehen.

c) Fragen im *present progressive*

Bei Entscheidungsfragen stellst du die Form von *be* (also *am, is* oder *are*) an den Satzanfang. In den Kurzantworten wird die Form von *be* aufgegriffen.

Is Ava enjoy**ing** her food?	**Genießt** Ava *(gerade)* ihr Essen?
Yes, she **is**. / No, she **isn't**.	
Are the Kogans eat**ing** at home?	**Essen** die Kogans *(gerade)* zu Hause?
Yes, they **are**. / No, they **aren't**.	

Bei Fragen mit Fragewort steht das Fragewort am Satzanfang:

What are you hav**ing** for dinner?	Was **isst** du *(gerade)* zum Abendessen?

6 THE GERUND
Das Gerundium

> I love playing football!
> Playing football is my favourite activity.

Wird ein Verb wie ein Nomen verwendet, nennt man die Form Gerundium *(gerund)*. Im Englischen benutzt man dafür die *ing*-Form des Verbs.

a) Das Gerundium als Subjekt

Wie die *ing*-Form eines Verbs gebildet wird, hast du schon auf Seite 176 gesehen. Eine solche Form kann Subjekt eines Satzes sein.

DIGITAL+ video 21

***Swimming** keeps you fit.* **(Das) Schwimmen** *hält einen fit.*
***Cycling** is fun.* **Radfahren** *macht Spaß.*
***Playing** the guitar is my favourite hobby.* *Gitarre**spielen** ist mein Lieblingshobby.*

b) Das Gerundium nach bestimmten Verben

Das Gerundium folgt oft nach bestimmten Verben, z. B. *like, love, hate, enjoy, suggest, try* und *prefer*.

*I **like being** outdoors.* *Ich **bin gerne** draußen.*
*I don't **like being** alone.* *Ich **bin nicht gerne** allein.*
*We **enjoy playing** games.* *Wir **genießen** es, Spiele zu **spielen**.*
*Do you **prefer running** or **swimming**?* ***Bevorzugst** du **Laufen** oder **Schwimmen**?*

c) Das Gerundium nach bestimmten Präpositionen

Auch bei verschiedenen Ausdrücken mit Präpositionen wird das Gerundium verwendet, z. B. *be good at, be interested in, care about* und *look forward to*.

*Are you **good at playing** basketball?*
*Bist du **gut darin**, Basketball **zu spielen**?*

*I'm **interested in playing** hockey.*
*Ich **habe Interesse daran**, Hockey **zu spielen**.*

*I don't really **care about winning** or **losing**.*
***Es ist mir wirklich egal**, ob ich **gewinne** oder **verliere**.*

*We're **looking forward to going** to the football match.*
*Wir **freuen uns darauf**, zum Fußballspiel zu **gehen**.*

7 CONDITIONAL CLAUSES 1
Bedingungssätze 1

If your knee doesn't get better soon, we'll see a doctor.

Mit Bedingungssätzen kannst du sagen, was unter bestimmten Bedingungen passieren wird bzw. passieren kann.

Ein Bedingungssatz besteht aus einem *if*-Satz und einem Hauptsatz. Der *if*-Satz nennt eine Bedingung. Der Hauptsatz drückt aus, was passiert, wenn die Bedingung erfüllt ist.
Im *if*-Satz steht das *simple present*, im Hauptsatz meist das *will-future*.

DIGITAL+ video 22

if-Satz (Bedingung: **Wenn** …)	Hauptsatz (Folge: … **dann** …)
If you **miss** the bus, **Wenn** du den Bus **verpasst**,	you **will be** late. **wirst** du zu spät **kommen**.
If it **rains**, **Wenn** es **regnet**,	the children **won't go** outside. **werden** die Kinder **nicht** nach draußen **gehen**.

Bedingungssätze können entweder mit dem *if*-Satz oder mit dem Hauptsatz beginnen.
Wenn sie mit dem *if*-Satz beginnen, werden sie mit einem Komma getrennt.
Wenn sie mit dem Hauptsatz beginnen, verwendest du im Englischen kein Komma.

If you go to the cinema, I'll come with you.   ***Wenn** du ins Kino gehst, komme ich mit dir.*
*I'll come with you **if** you go to the cinema.*   *Ich komme mit dir, **wenn** du ins Kino gehst.*

Im Hauptsatz kannst du auch Modalverben (z. B. *can, must*) oder den Imperativ verwenden.

*If you feel sick, you **can stay** at home.*
*Wenn du dich krank fühlst, **kannst** du zu Hause **bleiben**.*

*If you have broken your leg, you **must get** an X-ray.*
*Wenn du dir das Bein gebrochen hast, **musst** du dich röntgen **lassen**.*

*If you need help, **ask** your mum or dad.*
*Wenn du Hilfe brauchst, **frag** deine Mama oder deinen Papa.*

8 MODAL VERBS (REVISION)
Modalverben *(revision)*

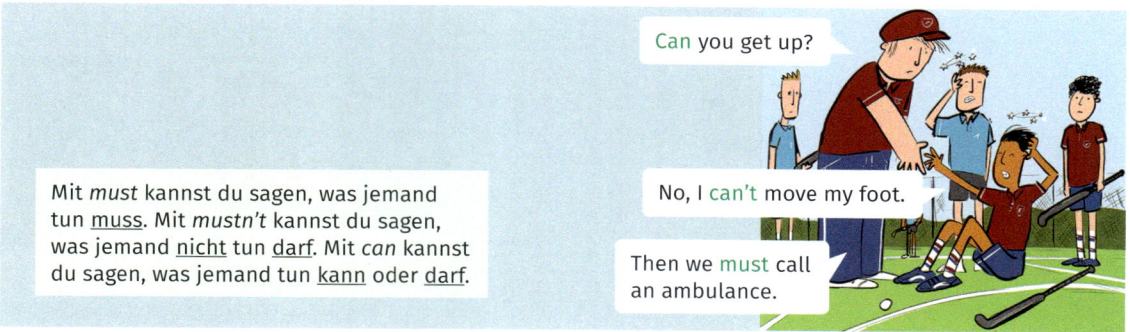

Mit *must* kannst du sagen, was jemand tun <u>muss</u>. Mit *mustn't* kannst du sagen, was jemand <u>nicht</u> tun <u>darf</u>. Mit *can* kannst du sagen, was jemand tun <u>kann</u> oder <u>darf</u>.

Can you get up?

No, I can't move my foot.

Then we must call an ambulance.

a) *Must / have to*

Must bedeutet „müssen". Die Form ist bei allen Personen gleich. Hinter *must* steht die Grundform des Hauptverbs. Du kannst *must* auch durch *have to* bzw. *has to* ersetzen.

*Demir **must** take his medicine. = Demir **has to** take his medicine.*
*Demir **muss** seine Medizin nehmen.*

Die Form *must* gibt es nur im *simple present*. Um z. B. auszudrücken, was jemand in der Vergangenheit tun musste oder in Zukunft wird tun müssen, brauchst du eine Form von *have to*.

*Last week, Demir **had to** go to hospital.*   *Letzte Woche **musste** Demir ins Krankenhaus gehen.*
*Tarek **will have to** stay at home for two days.*   *Tarek **wird** zwei Tage zu Hause bleiben **müssen**.*

b) *Mustn't / not be allowed to*

Mustn't bedeutet „nicht dürfen". Die Form ist bei allen Personen gleich. Hinter *mustn't* steht die Grundform des Hauptverbs. Du kannst *mustn't* auch durch *not be allowed to* ersetzen.

*Tarek **mustn't** do sports at the moment. = Tarek **isn't allowed to** do sports at the moment.*

Mustn't gibt es nur im *simple present*. In den anderen Zeitformen benutzt du *not be allowed to*.

*Tarek **wasn't allowed to** play video games yesterday.*
*Tarek **won't be allowed to** do sports for three weeks.*

c) *Can / be able to / be allowed to*

Can bedeutet „können" oder „dürfen". Die Form ist bei allen Personen gleich. Hinter *can* steht die Grundform des Hauptverbs.

Die Ersatzform für *can* mit der Bedeutung „können" ist *could* im *simple past* oder *be able to*.

*John **could** play tennis yesterday. = John **was able to** play tennis yesterday. Then he broke his arm.*
*John **will be able to** play tennis again in a few months, but he **won't be able to** play next week.*

Die Ersatzform für *can* mit der Bedeutung „dürfen" ist *be allowed to*.

*Tarek **couldn't** play video games yesterday. = Tarek **wasn't allowed to** play video games yesterday.*
*Tarek **will be allowed to** play video games while he is ill.*

9 RELATIVE CLAUSES
Relativsätze

> We could go to Portobello Road Market at the weekend.

> Mit Relativsätzen kannst du Personen oder Dinge näher beschreiben.

> Maybe that guy who sells those really funny T-shirts is still there.

Relativsätze sind Nebensätze, die Personen oder Dinge näher beschreiben. Ein Relativsatz beginnt meist mit einem Relativpronomen, also z.B. mit *who*, *which* oder *that*.

DIGITAL+ video 23

Dabei verwendest du *who* für Personen und *which* für Dinge. *That* kannst du sowohl für Dinge als auch für Personen benutzen.

	Relativsatz
There is a <u>man</u> Dort ist ein Mann,	**who** sells old cameras. **der** alte Kameras verkauft.
There is a <u>car boot sale</u> Dort ist ein Flohmarkt,	**which** takes place on Sunday. **der** am Sonntag stattfindet.

	Relativsatz
Tarek bought some <u>books</u> Tarek kaufte einige Bücher,	**that** were really cheap. **die** wirklich billig waren.
There are many <u>people</u> Es gibt viele Menschen,	**that** sell things at the car boot sale. **die** auf Flohmärkten Dinge verkaufen.

Relativsätze können auch in der Mitte eines Satzes stehen:
*The man **who is selling old cameras** is funny.*
*Der Mann, **der alte Kameras verkauft**, ist lustig.*

10 THE PROP WORDS ONE AND ONES
Die Stützwörter *one* und *ones*

I'm also looking for a teapot.

Wenn du ein Nomen ersetzen willst, das direkt vorher schon genannt wurde, benutzt du stattdessen *one* bzw. *ones*.

How do you like this one?

Wenn du ein Nomen ersetzen willst, das direkt vorher genannt wurde,
benutzt du stattdessen *one* bzw. *ones*. Du musst das Nomen nicht mehr wiederholen.
Im Deutschen kannst du es sogar einfach weglassen. Im Englischen ist das nicht möglich.

Du benutzt *one*, um ein Nomen im Singular zu ersetzen.

Englisch	Deutsch
Which <u>T-shirt</u> do you like? The red **one** or the blue **one**?	Welches T-Shirt magst du? Das rote oder das blaue?

Du benutzt *ones*, um ein Nomen im Plural zu ersetzen.

Englisch	Deutsch
Tarek bought some new <u>books</u> and now he has to get rid of some old **ones**.	Tarek hat ein paar neue Bücher gekauft und nun muss er ein paar alte loswerden.

11 THE PAST PROGRESSIVE: STATEMENTS
Die Verlaufsform der Vergangenheit: Aussagen

Mit dem *past progressive* kannst du ausdrücken, was zu einem bestimmten Zeitpunkt in der Vergangenheit gerade passierte.

5pm

At 5pm, two Vikings were fighting.

a) Bejahte Aussagesätze im *past progressive*

Auch für die Vergangenheit gibt es eine *progressive form*,
das *past progressive*. Es drückt aus,

 **DIGITAL+** video 24

- was jemand zu einem bestimmten Zeitpunkt in der Vergangenheit gerade tat oder was gerade passierte.
- was gerade vor sich ging, als plötzlich etwas anderes geschah.

Das *past progressive* wird ganz ähnlich gebildet wie das *present progressive*,
nur dass die Form von *be* im *simple past* steht.

Simple past-Form von *be (was / were)* + Grundform des Verbs + Endung *-ing*.

*Andy **was watching** a show.*   *Andy **schaute (gerade)** eine Show an.*
*The people **were eating**.*   *Die Leute **aßen (gerade)**.*

Wenn du beschreiben möchtest, was gerade vor sich ging, als etwas anderes geschah,
kannst du das so tun:

past progressive	simple past
The people **were** already **eating** Die Leute **aßen gerade**,	when Andy **came** in. als Andy **hereinkam**.
While Andy **was looking** at a stall, Während **sich** Andy **gerade** einen Stand **anschaute**,	it **started** to rain. **fing** es zu regnen **an**.

was gerade passierte:
past progressive

neues Ereignis:
simple past

b) Verneinte Aussagesätze im *past progressive*

Für die Verneinung fügst du einfach ***not*** hinter die Form von *be* (***was*** bzw. ***were***) ein:

*Andy **wasn't** danc**ing**.*   *Andy tanzte (gerade) **nicht**.*
*Some people **weren't** listen**ing** to the stories.*   *Einige Leute hörten sich **nicht** die Geschichten an.*

12 THE PAST PROGRESSIVE: QUESTIONS
Die Verlaufsform der Vergangenheit: Fragen

7pm

Bei einer Entscheidungsfrage im *past progressive* steht *was* bzw. *were* am Satzanfang. Bei einer Frage mit Fragewort steht das Fragewort am Satzanfang.

What was Andy doing yesterday at 7pm?

a) Entscheidungsfragen und Kurzantworten im *past progressive*

Entscheidungsfragen im past progressive bildest du, indem du *was* bzw. *were* an den Satzanfang stellst. In der Kurzantwort wird *was* bzw. *were* aufgegriffen:

Was Andy **having** dinner at 7pm? – Yes, he **was**. / No, he **wasn't**.
Aß Andy um 7 Uhr abends **gerade** Abendessen? – Ja. / Nein.

Were the people **dancing**? – Yes, they **were**. / No, they **weren't**.
Tanzten die Menschen **(gerade)**? – Ja. / Nein.

DIGITAL+ video 24

b) Fragen mit Fragewort im *past progressive*

Bei Fragen mit Fragewörtern stellst du das Fragewort an den Satzanfang:

What were you **doing** yesterday at 7pm?
What was Andy **doing**?
Why were the people **laughing**?
Who was taking pictures?

13 THE SIMPLE PAST: STATEMENTS (REVISION)
Die einfache Vergangenheit: Aussagen *(revision)*

> In the holidays, I went to Poland with my family. We visited my grandma. It was great!

> We didn't go abroad, we stayed in the UK. The weather wasn't bad, so we went outside a lot.

Das *simple past* verwendet man, wenn man über etwas spricht, das in der Vergangenheit liegt und abgeschlossen ist.

a) Formen und bejahte Aussagesätze im *simple past*

DIGITAL+ video 25, 26

Bei den regelmäßigen Verben hängst du -ed an die Grundform an:

stay + **ed** → stay**ed**   look + **ed** → look**ed**   visit + **ed** → visit**ed**

Achte auf die Rechtschreibung: Endet die Grundform des Verbs auf -e, dann wird nur -d angehängt.

arriv**e** → arriv**ed**

Endet das Verb auf einem kurzen betonten **Vokal + Konsonant**, dann wird der Konsonant verdoppelt.

sto**p** → sto**pped**

Endet das Verb auf **Konsonant + y**, dann wird aus dem -y ein -i und die Endung lautet -ied.

tid**y** → tid**ied**

Unregelmäßige Verben haben im *simple past* eine eigene Form (siehe Seite 245–247).

have → **had**	Tarek **had** a great holiday. Tarek **hatte** einen tollen Urlaub.
go → **went**	He **went** to Wales with his father. Er **fuhr** mit seinem Vater nach Wales.
do → **did**	They **did** lots of things together. Sie **machten** viele Sachen zusammen.

Das Verb *be* hat zwei Formen im *simple past*:
I / he / she / it **was**   –   you / we / they **were**
I **was** in London last week, but my friends **were** in Paris.

b) Verneinte Aussagesätze im *simple past*

Sätze im *simple past* verneinst du im Allgemeinen mit *didn't (= did not)*.
Didn't ist bei allen Personen gleich. Danach kommt dann das Verb in der Grundform.

I **didn't go** to Paris last week.   Letzte Woche **fuhr** ich **nicht** nach Paris.

Bei *was* und *were* hängst du nur *not* oder die Kurzform *n't* an.

I **wasn't** in Paris last week, and my friends **weren't** in London.
Ich **war** letzte Woche **nicht** in Paris, und meine Freunde **waren nicht** in London.

14 THE SIMPLE PAST: QUESTIONS (REVISION)
Die einfache Vergangenheit: Fragen *(revision)*

Fragen im *simple past* bildest du in den meisten Fällen mit *did*. Eine Ausnahme sind Sätze mit *was* oder *were*.

Did you go to Bristol in the holidays?

Yes, I did.

Was it good?

Yes, it was.

a) Entscheidungsfragen und Kurzantworten im *simple past*

Bei Entscheidungsfragen im *simple past* stellst du *did* an den Satzanfang. *Did* ist bei allen Personen gleich.
Achte auch hier darauf, das Verb danach in der Grundform zu verwenden.
In der Kurzantwort wird *did* wieder aufgegriffen.

DIGITAL+ video 25, 26

Entscheidungsfrage	Kurzantwort	Kurzantwort
Did you go on holiday?	Yes, I did.	No, I didn't.
Did Harry visit his grandparents?	Yes, he did.	No, he didn't.

Bei Fragen mit *was* und *were* benutzt du kein *did*.
Hier steht *was* oder *were* am Satzanfang.
In der Kurzantwort wird *was* bzw. *were* wieder aufgegriffen.

Entscheidungsfrage	Kurzantwort	Kurzantwort
Were your parents in Paris last year?	Yes, they were.	No, they weren't.
Was the weather good?	Yes, it was.	No, it wasn't.

b) Fragen mit Fragewort im *simple past*

Bei Sätzen mit Fragewort steht das Fragewort am Satzanfang. Es steht vor *did*.

What did you do in the holidays?
Where did you go?

Wenn *who* nach dem Subjekt fragt, benutzt du bei Fragen kein *did*:

Who went to Poland? – Ava went to Poland. *Wer fuhr nach Polen? – Ava fuhr nach Polen.*

Bei Fragen mit *was* oder *were* benutzt du kein *did*.

How was your holiday?
What were your favourite places?

15 REPORTED SPEECH 1
Indirekte Rede 1

Wenn du berichten willst, was jemand anderes sagt, benutzt du indirekte Rede.

My mum says that I have to go home now.

Indirekte Rede besteht aus einem Begleitsatz und der wiedergegebenen Aussage. Beide Satzteile können durch *that* verbunden werden.

DIGITAL+ video 27

Wenn der Begleitsatz in der Gegenwart steht, verändern sich die Zeiten in der wiedergegebenen Aussage nicht.

Wenn die Originalaussage Wörter enthält, die nur aus dem Zusammenhang richtig zu verstehen sind, musst du sie in der wiedergegebenen Aussage anpassen.

	Begleitsatz	wiedergegebene Aussage
James: "I will have **my** own party." James: „**Ich** werde **meine** eigene Party geben."	James says (that) James sagt, dass	**he** will have **his** own party. **er seine** eigene Party geben werde.
Emily: "**We** had an argument." Emily: „**Wir** hatten einen Streit."	Emily says (that) Emily sagt, dass	**they** had an argument. **sie** einen Streit gehabt hätten.
Emily: "Chloe is angry with **me**." Emily: „Chloe ist sauer auf **mich**."	Emily says (that) Emily sagt, dass	Chloe is angry with **her**. Chloe sauer auf **sie** sei.
Tom: "The dog is **here**." Tom: „Der Hund ist **hier**."	Tom says (that) Tom sagt, dass	the dog is **there**. der Hund **dort** sei.

16 THE PASSIVE
Das Passiv

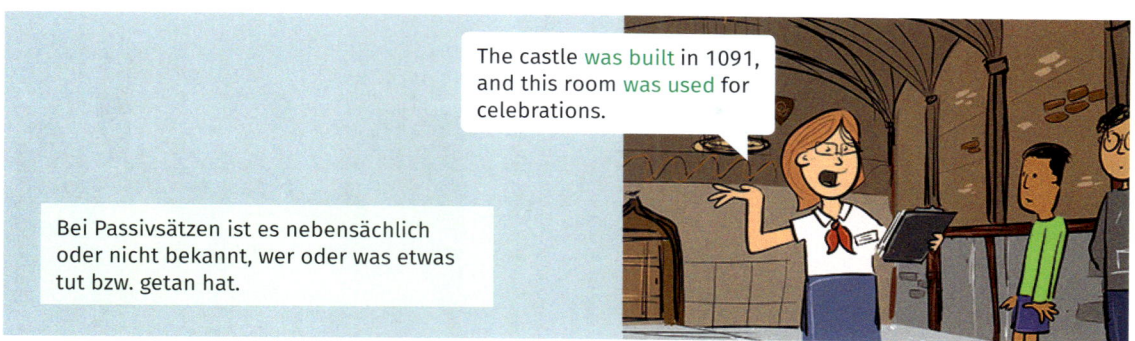

> The castle was built in 1091, and this room was used for celebrations.

> Bei Passivsätzen ist es nebensächlich oder nicht bekannt, wer oder was etwas tut bzw. getan hat.

Aktivsätze sagen uns, wer oder was handelt, hier z. B. *an author*:

DIGITAL+ video 28

*An author **wrote** the story in 2010.*
*Ein Schriftsteller/Eine Schriftstellerin **schrieb** 2010 die Geschichte.*

Wenn es aber nicht wichtig oder nicht bekannt ist, wer etwas tut oder getan hat, kannst du einen Passivsatz verwenden.

*The story **was written** in 2010. Die Geschichte **wurde** 2010 **geschrieben**.*

Das Objekt aus dem Aktivsatz, hier *the story*, wird zum Subjekt des Passivsatzes.

	Subjekt	Verb	Objekt	
Aktivsatz:	An author	wrote	the story	in 2010.
Passivsatz:	The story	was written		in 2010.

Das Passiv bildest du so:
Form von ***be*** + **Partizip Perfekt** *(past participle)*

Englisch	Deutsch
English **is spoken** all over the world.	Englisch **wird** überall auf der Welt **gesprochen**.
Matches **are used** to make fire.	Streichhölzer **werden** zum Feuermachen **benutzt**.
My computer **was made** in China.	Mein Computer **wurde** in China **hergestellt**.
These books **were written** in Germany.	Diese Bücher **wurden** in Deutschland **geschrieben**.

Wenn du in einem Passivsatz doch einmal die handelnde Person oder die Ursache für etwas nennen willst, hängst du sie mit ***by*** („von", „durch") an den Satz an:

*The story was written **by** an author in 2010.*
*The first car was invented **by** Karl Benz.*
*The house was destroyed **by** a fire.*

17 THE GOING TO-FUTURE: STATEMENTS (REVISION)
Das Futur mit *going to*: Aussagen *(revision)*

> I'm going to take part in a cool upcycling workshop next weekend. It's going to be fun!

Das Futur mit *going to* kannst du verwenden, um über Pläne für die Zukunft zu sprechen.
Man verwendet es auch bei Ereignissen, die wahrscheinlich passieren werden.

a) Bejahte Aussagesätze im *going to-future*

📀 **DIGITAL+** video 29

Im Deutschen gibt es keine Zeitform, die dem *going to-future* entspricht.
Du hast aber verschiedene Möglichkeiten, es im Deutschen wiederzugeben.

Englisch	Deutsch
I'm going to do a drama workshop.	Ich **werde** einen Theaterworkshop **machen**. Ich **möchte / will** einen Theaterworkshop **machen**. Ich **plane / habe vor**, einen Theaterworkshop **zu machen**.

Du bildest das Futur mit *going to* mit einer Form von *be + going to +* Grundform des Verbs.

	Langform	Kurzform			
Singular	I am	I'm			
	You are	You're			
	He/She is	He's/She's	going to	do	a drama workshop.
Plural	We are	We're			
	You are	You're			
	They are	They're			

b) Verneinte Aussagesätze im *going to-future*

Für die Verneinung stellst du *not* hinter die Form von *be*. Oft benutzt man Kurzformen.

	Langform	Kurzform			
Singular	I am not	I'm not			
	You are not	You aren't			
	He/She is not	He/She isn't	going to	do	a cooking workshop.
Plural	We are not	We aren't			
	You are not	You aren't			
	They are not	They aren't			

18

Das Futur mit *going to*: Fragen *(revision)*

Are you going to go to Poland in the holidays, Ava?

Mit einer Frage im *going to-future* kannst du z. B. danach fragen, was jemand für die Zukunft plant.

Yes, I am.

How long are you going to stay?

a) Entscheidungsfragen und Kurzantworten im *going to-future*

Bei Entscheidungsfragen rückt im *going to-future* die Form von *be (am, is, are)* an den Satzanfang.
In der Kurzantwort steht dann die entsprechende Form von *be*.

DIGITAL+ video 29

Entscheidungsfrage	Kurzantwort	Kurzantwort
Are you **going to do** a cooking workshop? **Wirst** du einen Koch-Workshop **machen**?	Yes, I am. Ja.	No, I'm not. Nein.
Is Ava **going to visit** her grandmother? **Wird** Ava ihre Großmutter **besuchen**?	Yes, she is. Ja.	No, she isn't. Nein.
Are the children **going to take part in** a workshop? **Werden** die Kinder an einem Workshop **teilnehmen**?	Yes, they are. Ja.	No, they aren't. Nein.

b) Fragen mit Fragewort im *going to-future*

Bei Fragen mit Fragewort steht das Fragewort an erster Stelle.

What are you going to do in the holidays?
When is the workshop going to start?
Where is the workshop going to take place?

Nach Vokabeln suchen

Alphabetische Wortliste (*Dictionary*): Du suchst nach der Bedeutung eines einzelnen englischen Wortes, das im Textbook vorgekommen ist? Dann nutze die alphabetische Wortliste ab Seite 213. Hier findest du auch die Wörter aus der *Story*, aus den Projekten, aus den *Wordbanks* und von den *Get together-* und *Challenge*-Seiten. Einige englische Wörter, die im Englischen und im Deutschen gleich sind, findest du auf Seite 192.

Wortlisten nach Kapiteln (*Vocabulary*): Du möchtest die Vokabeln zu einem ganzen Abschnitt im Buch lernen? Dann nutze die chronologische Wortliste ab Seite 193. Nach Kapiteln und Seitenzahlen sortiert findest du hier alle Wörter, die neu im Buch vorkommen.

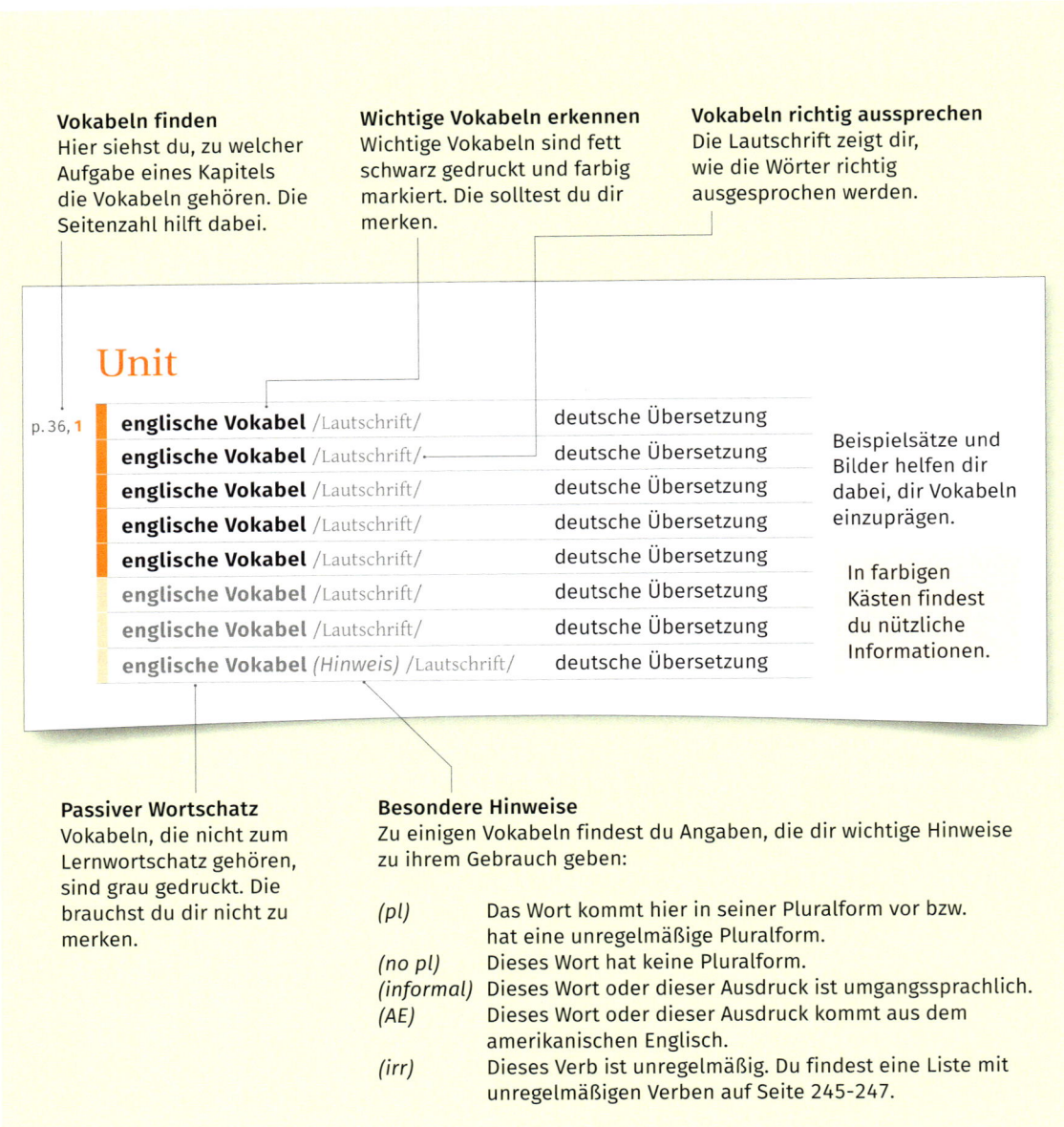

Vokabeln finden
Hier siehst du, zu welcher Aufgabe eines Kapitels die Vokabeln gehören. Die Seitenzahl hilft dabei.

Wichtige Vokabeln erkennen
Wichtige Vokabeln sind fett schwarz gedruckt und farbig markiert. Die solltest du dir merken.

Vokabeln richtig aussprechen
Die Lautschrift zeigt dir, wie die Wörter richtig ausgesprochen werden.

Unit

p. 36, **1**

englische Vokabel /Lautschrift/   deutsche Übersetzung
englische Vokabel /Lautschrift/   deutsche Übersetzung
englische Vokabel /Lautschrift/   deutsche Übersetzung
englische Vokabel /Lautschrift/   deutsche Übersetzung
englische Vokabel /Lautschrift/   deutsche Übersetzung
englische Vokabel /Lautschrift/   deutsche Übersetzung
englische Vokabel /Lautschrift/   deutsche Übersetzung
englische Vokabel *(Hinweis)* /Lautschrift/   deutsche Übersetzung

Beispielsätze und Bilder helfen dir dabei, dir Vokabeln einzuprägen.

In farbigen Kästen findest du nützliche Informationen.

Passiver Wortschatz
Vokabeln, die nicht zum Lernwortschatz gehören, sind grau gedruckt. Die brauchst du dir nicht zu merken.

Besondere Hinweise
Zu einigen Vokabeln findest du Angaben, die dir wichtige Hinweise zu ihrem Gebrauch geben:

(pl)   Das Wort kommt hier in seiner Pluralform vor bzw. hat eine unregelmäßige Pluralform.
(no pl)   Dieses Wort hat keine Pluralform.
(informal)   Dieses Wort oder dieser Ausdruck ist umgangssprachlich.
(AE)   Dieses Wort oder dieser Ausdruck kommt aus dem amerikanischen Englisch.
(irr)   Dieses Verb ist unregelmäßig. Du findest eine Liste mit unregelmäßigen Verben auf Seite 245-247.

Die richtige Aussprache

Im Englischen spricht man Wörter oft anders aus als man sie schreibt.
Die Aussprache der Wörter wird mithilfe der Lautschrift in jedem Wörterbuch angegeben.
Man kann so auch neue Wörter richtig aussprechen, ohne sie vorher gehört zu haben.
Die Lautschrift ist eine Schrift, deren Symbole jeden Laut genau bezeichnen.
Hier ist eine Liste mit den Symbolen dieser Lautschrift zusammen mit Beispielwörtern.

The English alphabet

a	/eɪ/
b	/biː/
c	/siː/
d	/diː/
e	/iː/
f	/ef/
g	/dʒiː/
h	/eɪtʃ/
i	/aɪ/
j	/dʒeɪ/
k	/keɪ/
l	/el/
m	/em/
n	/en/
o	/əʊ/
p	/piː/
q	/kjuː/
r	/ɑː/
s	/es/
t	/tiː/
u	/juː/
v	/viː/
w	/ˈdʌbljuː/
x	/eks/
y	/waɪ/
z	/zed/

English sounds

Vokale

/ɑː/	**arm**
/ʌ/	**but**
/e/	**desk**
/ə/	**a, an**
/ɜː/	**girl, bird**
/æ/	**apple**
/ɪ/	**in, it**
/i/	**happy**
/iː/	**easy, eat**
/ɒ/	**orange, sorry**
/ɔː/	**all, call**
/ʊ/	**look**
/u/	**January**
/uː/	**boot**

Doppellaute

/aɪ/	**eye, by, buy**
/aʊ/	**our**
/eə/	**air, there**
/eɪ/	**take, they**
/ɪə/	**here**
/ɔɪ/	**boy**
/əʊ/	**go, old**
/ʊə/	**tour**

Konsonanten

/b/	**bag, club**
/d/	**duck, card**
/f/	**fish, laugh**
/g/	**get, dog**
/h/	**hot**
/j/	**you**
/k/	**can, duck**
/l/	**lot, small**
/m/	**more, mum**
/n/	**now, sun**
/ŋ/	**song, long**
/p/	**present, top**
/r/	**red, around**
/s/	**sister, class** *(stimmlos)*
/z/	**nose, dogs** *(stimmhaft)*
/t/	**time, cat**
/ʒ/	**television**
/dʒ/	**sausage**
/ʃ/	**fresh**
/tʃ/	**child, cheese**
/ð/	**these, mother** *(stimmhaft)*
/θ/	**bathroom, think** *(stimmlos)*
/v/	**very, have**
/w/	**what, word**

Betonungszeichen für die folgende Silbe

/ˈ/	**Hauptbetonung**
/ˌ/	**Nebenbetonung**

Bekannte Wörter

Viele Wörter sind im Englischen und im Deutschen so gut wie gleich. Manche unterscheiden sich nur durch die Groß- bzw. Kleinschreibung – im Englischen werden die meisten Nomen kleingeschrieben. Viele dieser Wörter, die in deinem Buch vorkommen, findest du hier. Bei denen, die anders ausgesprochen werden als im Deutschen, ist die Lautschrift farbig hervorgehoben.

app /æp/
arm /ɑːm/
audio /ˈɔːdiəʊ/
baby /ˈbeɪbi/
ball /bɔːl/
band /bænd/
baseball /ˈbeɪsˌbɔːl/
basketball /ˈbɑːskɪtˌbɔːl/
beige /beɪʒ/
blind /blaɪnd/
blog /blɒg/
burger /ˈbɜːgə/
bus /bʌs/
butler /ˈbʌtlə/
butter /ˈbʌtə/
café /ˈkæfeɪ/
cafeteria /ˌkæfəˈtɪəriə/
cent /sent/
champion /ˈtʃæmpjən/
chance /tʃɑːns/
chat /tʃæt/
chicken nugget /ˌtʃɪkɪnˈnʌgɪt/
clip /klɪp/
cola /ˈkəʊlə/
collage /ˈkɒlɑːʒ/
computer /kəmˈpjuːtə/
cool /kuːl/
cornflakes /ˈkɔːnfleɪks/
couch /kaʊtʃ/
couscous /ˈkuːskuːs/
currywurst /ˈkʌriwɜːst/
darts /dɑːts/
definition /ˌdefəˈnɪʃn/
diesel /ˈdiːzl/
digital /ˈdɪdʒɪtl/
dip /dɪp/
display /dɪˈspleɪ/
dressing /ˈdresɪŋ/
element /ˈelɪmənt/
email /ˈiːmeɪl/
emoji /ɪˈməʊdʒi/
etc. (= etcetera) /etˈsetrə/
euro /ˈjʊərəʊ/
fair /feə/
fan /fæn/
fast food /ˌfɑːstˈfuːd/

film /fɪlm/
finger /ˈfɪŋgə/
fit /fɪt/
flyer /ˈflaɪə/
form /fɔːm/
format /ˈfɔːmæt/
front /frʌnt/
giraffe /dʒəˈrɑːf/
golden /ˈgəʊldn/
golf /gɒlf/
halfpipe /ˈhɑːfpaɪp/
hammer /ˈhæmə/
handout /ˈhændaʊt/
hieroglyph /ˈhaɪrəglɪf/
high-tech /ˌhaɪˈtek/
hobby /ˈhɒbi/
hockey /ˈhɒki/
home page /ˈhəʊm peɪdʒ/
hoodie /ˈhʊdi/
horde /hɔːd/
hot dog /ˌhɒtˈdɒg/
hotel /həʊˈtel/
ideal /aɪˈdɪəl/
idol /ˈaɪdl/
info /ˈɪnfəʊ/
instrument /ˈɪnstrʊmənt/
international /ˌɪntəˈnæʃnəl/
Internet /ˈɪntəˌnet/
interview /ˈɪntəˌvjuː/
jeans /dʒiːnz/
jury /ˈdʒʊəri/
karate /kəˈrɑːti/
ketchup /ˈketʃəp/
kilt /kɪlt/
laptop /ˈlæpˌtɒp/
limerick /ˈlɪmərɪk/
link /lɪŋk/
live /laɪv/
mango /ˈmæŋgəʊ/
marathon /ˈmærəθn/
material /məˈtɪəriəl/
meme /miːm/
mild /maɪld/
million /ˈmɪljən/
mini /ˈmɪni/
minute /ˈmɪnɪt/
mixer /ˈmɪksə/

modern /ˈmɒdən/
moment /ˈməʊmənt/
mozzarella /ˌmɒtsəˈrelə/
muffin /ˈmʌfɪn/
multimedia /ˌmʌltiˈmiːdiə/
museum /mjuːˈziːəm/
musical /ˈmjuːzɪkl/
name /neɪm/
national /ˈnæʃnəl/
OK (= okay) /əʊˈkeɪ/
olive /ˈɒlɪv/
online /ˈɒnlaɪn/
operation /ˌɒpəˈreɪʃn/
original /əˈrɪdʒnəl/
papyrus /pəˈpaɪrəs/
parade /pəˈreɪd/
paratriathlon /ˌpærətraɪˈæθlən/
park /pɑːk/
partner /ˈpɑːtnə/
party /ˈpɑːti/
patient /ˈpeɪʃnt/
penicillin /ˌpenəˈsɪlɪn/
person /ˈpɜːsn/
pilates /pɪˈlɑːtiːz/
pilot /ˈpaɪlət/
pizza /ˈpiːtsə/
plan /plæn/
planet /ˈplænɪt/
podcast /ˈpɒdˌkɑːst/
pool /puːl/
post /pəʊst/
poster /ˈpəʊstə/
problem /ˈprɒbləm/
quiz /kwɪz/
radio /ˈreɪdiəʊ/
rest /rest/
restaurant /ˈrestrɒnt/
ring /rɪŋ/
rucksack /ˈrʌkˌsæk/
rugby /ˈrʌgbi/
sand /sænd/
sandwich /ˈsænwɪdʒ/
science fiction /ˌsaɪəns ˈfɪkʃn/
service /ˈsɜːvɪs/
show /ʃəʊ/

situation /ˌsɪtʃuˈeɪʃn/
skateboard /ˈskeɪtbɔːd/
skateboarder /ˈskeɪtbɔːdə/
slogan /ˈsləʊgən/
smartphone /ˈsmɑːtˌfəʊn/
smiley /ˈsmaɪli/
snack /snæk/
so /səʊ/
softball /ˈsɒftˌbɔːl/
sorbet /ˈsɔːbeɪ/
spaghetti /spəˈgeti/
streaming /ˈstriːmɪŋ/
super /ˈsuːpə/
sushi /ˈsuːʃi/
T-shirt /ˈtiː ʃɜːt/
tablet /ˈtæblət/
team /tiːm/
teenager /ˈtiːnˌeɪdʒə/
tennis /ˈtenɪs/
test /test/
text /tekst/
ticket /ˈtɪkɪt/
toast /təʊst/
toaster /ˈtəʊstə/
tofu /ˈtəʊfuː/
touch-screen /ˈtʌtʃskriːn/
tour /tʊə/
tourist /ˈtʊərɪst/
training /ˈtreɪnɪŋ/
triathlon /traɪˈæθlən/
tunnel /ˈtʌnl/
tutorial /tjuːˈtɔːriəl/
upcycling /ˈʌpˌsaɪklɪŋ/
vase /vɑːz/
verb /vɜːb/
video /ˈvɪdiəʊ/
video clip /ˈvɪdiəʊ klɪp/
volleyball /ˈvɒlibɔːl/
warm /wɔːm/
webcode /ˈwebˌkəʊd/
website /ˈwebˌsaɪt/
winter /ˈwɪntə/
wok /wɒk/
workshop /ˈwɜːkˌʃɒp/
yoga /ˈjəʊgə/
yoghurt /ˈjɒgət/

p. 6	**grandma** *(informal)* /ˈɡrænˌmɑː/	(die) Oma	
	originally /əˈrɪdʒnəli/	ursprünglich	**originally** = at first
	Egypt /ˈiːdʒɪpt/	Ägypten	

Unit 1 | Part A Delicious dishes

p. 7	**dish** *(pl* **dishes***)* /dɪʃ, ˈdɪʃɪz/	(das) Gericht, (die) Speise	**Curry** is a traditional Indian **dish**.
p. 8, 1	**curry** /ˈkʌri/	(das) Curry(gericht)	
	pasta /ˈpæstə/	(die) Nudeln	
	sauce /sɔːs/	(die) Soße	
	yummy *(informal)* /ˈjʌmi/	lecker	
	mashed potatoes *(pl)* /ˌmæʃt pəˈteɪtəʊz/	(der) Kartoffelbrei	
	sausage /ˈsɒsɪdʒ/	(die) Wurst, (das) Würstchen	
p. 8, 2	(to) **order (in)** /ˈɔːdə, ˌɔːdərˈɪn/	bestellen	When you are **full**, you don't want to eat or drink anything.
	salad /ˈsæləd/	(der) Salat	
	full /fʊl/	satt	
	(to) **finish** /ˈfɪnɪʃ/	aufessen	
	absolutely /ˈæbsəluːtli/	absolut	
	potato *(pl* **potatoes***)* /pəˈteɪtəʊ, pəˈteɪtəʊz/	(die) Kartoffel	
	vegetarian /ˌvedʒəˈteəriən/	(der/die) Vegetarier/in; vegetarisch	A **vegetarian** doesn't eat fish or meat.
	savoury /ˈseɪvəri/	pikant, salzig	
	BFF (= best friends forever) *(informal)* /ˌbiː_efˈef, ˌbest ˌfrendz fərˈevə/	*allerbeste Freunde/Freundinnen*	
	greetings *(pl)* /ˈɡriːtɪŋz/	(die) Grüße	
	Greece /ɡriːs/	Griechenland	
	cucumber /ˈkjuːˌkʌmbə/	(die) Salatgurke	
	grilled /ɡrɪld/	gegrillt	
	octopus /ˈɒktəpəs/	(der) Tintenfisch	
	roast /rəʊst/	(der) Braten; gebraten, geröstet	
	gravy /ˈɡreɪvi/	(die) (Braten)soße	
	Yorkshire pudding /ˌjɔːkʃə ˈpʊdɪŋ/	*britische gebackene Beilage*	
p. 9, 2	**thin** /θɪn/	dünn	There is a **thin** slice of cheese in the burger.
	onion /ˈʌnjən/	(die) Zwiebel	
	spicy /ˈspaɪsi/	würzig, scharf	
	speciality /ˌspeʃiˈæləti/	(die) Spezialität	
	(to) **serve** /sɜːv/	servieren; reichen für	**disgusting** = not nice or yummy
	disgusting /dɪsˈɡʌstɪŋ/	widerlich	
	comfort food /ˈkʌmfət fuːd/	(das) Wohlfühlessen	
	Lahmacun /ˌlɑːməˈdʒuːn/	*traditionelles türkisches Gericht*	
	rolled /rəʊld/	gerollt	
	flatbread /ˈflætbred/	(der) Fladen	
	filled /fɪld/	gefüllt	
	minced meat /ˌmɪnst ˈmiːt/	(das) Hackfleisch	

Turkey /ˈtɜːki/	die Türkei	
Lebanon /ˈlebənən/	der Libanon	
Shakshuka /ʃəkˈʃuːkə/	*traditionelles israelisches und nordafrikanisches Gericht*	
North Africa /ˌnɔːθˈæfrɪkə/	Nordafrika	
garlic /ˈgɑːlɪk/	(der) Knoblauch	
(to) unscramble /ʌnˈskræmbl/	ordnen, in die richtige Reihenfolge bringen	

p. 11, 6	web page /ˈweb͜peɪdʒ/	(die) Webseite, (die) Internetseite
	from (all) around the world /frəm͜ˌɔːl͜ə,raʊnd ðə ˈwɜːld/	aus der (ganzen) Welt
	fried /fraɪd/	gebraten
	noodle /ˈnuːdl/	(die) Nudel
	(chicken) tikka masala, (chicken) tikka /ˌtʃɪkɪn ˌtiːkə məˈsɑːlə, ˌtʃɪkɪn ˈtiːkə/	*britisch-indisches (Hühnchen-)Gericht*
	India /ˈɪndiə/	Indien

The man is cooking food in a **pot**.

p. 12, 7	**pot** /pɒt/	(der) Topf
	quick /kwɪk/	schnell, kurz
	meat /miːt/	(das) Fleisch
	veggie *(informal)* /ˈvedʒi/	(das) Gemüse
	herb /hɜːb/	(das) (Gewürz)kraut
	spice /spaɪs/	(das) Gewürz
	fridge /frɪdʒ/	(der) Kühlschrank
	cupboard /ˈkʌbəd/	(der) Schrank
	pepper /ˈpepə/	(die) Paprika; (der) Pfeffer
	can /kæn/	(die) Dose, (die) Büchse
	left /left/	übrig
	recipe /ˈresəpi/	(das) Rezept
	(to) starve /stɑːv/	verhungern
	drawer /ˈdrɔːə/	(die) Schublade
	cabbage /ˈkæbɪdʒ/	(der) Kohl
	chickpea /ˈtʃɪk,piː/	(die) Kichererbse
	jar /dʒɑː/	(das) (Glas)gefäß
	crumb /krʌm/	(der) Krümel
	(to) bring to the boil *(irr)* /ˌbrɪŋ tə ðə ˈbɔɪl/	zum Kochen bringen
	Morocco /məˈrɒkəʊ/	Marokko
	cook-along video /ˈkʊk͜ə,lɒŋ ˌvɪdiəʊ/	*(das) Mitmach-Koch-Video*
p. 13, 7	bracket /ˈbrækɪt/	(die) Klammer
p. 13, 8	(to) **put in** *(irr)* /ˌpʊt͜ˈɪn/	hineintun, hinzufügen
	(to) **chop** /tʃɒp/	hacken
	(to) **heat** /hiːt/	erhitzen
	(to) **slice** /slaɪs/	in Scheiben schneiden
	(to) **stir in** /ˌstɜːr͜ˈɪn/	einrühren, unterrühren

There are lots of **spices** in a curry.

Everybody can learn to cook with the help of a **recipe**.

I**'m starving**! Ich habe einen Bärenhunger!, Ich habe riesigen Hunger!

to **slice** a cucumber

p. 14, 10	**vegan** /'vi:gən/	(der/die) Veganer/in; vegan
	by heart /ˌbaɪ 'hɑ:t/	auswendig
	(to) **kill** /kɪl/	töten
	season /'si:zn/	(die) Saison
	for no reason /fə ˌnəʊ 'ri:zn/	ohne Grund, grundlos
	foxhunting *(no pl)* /'fɒks ˌhʌntɪŋ/	(die) Fuchsjagd
p. 15, 11	**bread** /bred/	(das) Brot
	knight /naɪt/	(der) Ritter
p. 15, 12	**invented** /ɪn'ventɪd/	erfunden
	by accident /ˌbaɪ 'æksɪdnt/	zufällig, aus Versehen
p. 16, 14	cookbook /'kʊkˌbʊk/	(das) Kochbuch
p. 16, 15	odd one out /ˌɒd wʌn 'aʊt/	*(das) Wort, das nicht zu den anderen passt*
p. 16, 16	branch /brɑːntʃ/	(der) Zweig, (der) Ast
p. 17, 17	**original** /ə'rɪdʒnəl/	ursprünglich
	(to) **prepare** /prɪ'peə/	zubereiten
	starter /'stɑːtə/	(die) Vorspeise
	main (course) /'meɪn kɔːs/	(das) Hauptgericht
	dessert /dɪ'zɜːt/	(der) Nachtisch
	(to) **try out** /ˌtraɪ 'aʊt/	ausprobieren
	oil /ɔɪl/	(das) Öl
	teaspoon /'ti:ˌspuːn/	(der) Teelöffel
	vegetable /'vedʒtəbl/	(das) Gemüse
	soft /sɒft/	weich
	ingredient /ɪn'gri:diənt/	(die) Zutat
	paprika /'pæprɪkə/	(das) Paprikapulver
	coriander /ˌkɒri'ændə/	(der) Koriander
	cumin /'kjuːmɪn/	(der) Kreuzkümmel
	cinnamon /'sɪnəmən/	(der) Zimt
	cayenne pepper /ˌkeɪen 'pepə/	(der) Cayennepfeffer
	vegetable stock /'vedʒtəbl stɒk/	(die) Gemüsebrühe
	cooker /'kʊkə/	(der) Herd
	Enjoy! /ɪn'dʒɔɪ/	Guten Appetit!

Germany is famous for good **bread**.

by accident = not planned

They **are preparing** different meals in their restaurant.

teaspoon

soft ≠ hard

Paprika, coriander, cumin, cinnamon and cayenne pepper are spices.

Unit 1 | Part B At a restaurant

p. 18, 1	**takeaway** /'teɪkəˌweɪ/	(das) Essen zum Mitnehmen, (die) Imbissbude
	Italian /ɪ'tæljən/	(der/die) Italiener/in; italienisch
	Turkish /'tɜːkɪʃ/	türkisch
	Vietnamese /viˌetnə'mi:z/	(der/die) Vietnamese/Vietnamesin; vietnamesisch
	Thai /taɪ/	(der/die) Thailänder/in; thailändisch
p. 18, 2	**review** /rɪ'vjuː/	(die) Kritik, (die) Rezension
	(to) **skim** /skɪm/	überfliegen

A **takeaway** is a meal that you buy and take home to eat.

	cheap /tʃi:p/	billig
	quality /ˈkwɒləti/	(die) Qualität
	(to) **stay away from** /ˌsteɪ_əˈweɪ frɒm/	meiden; sich fernhalten von
	disappointing /ˌdɪsəˈpɔɪntɪŋ/	enttäuschend
	mine /maɪn/	meine(r, s)
	burnt /bɜ:nt/	verbrannt, angebrannt
p. 19, 2	**hot** /hɒt/	scharf
	atmosphere /ˈætməsˌfɪə/	(die) Atmosphäre
	north /nɔ:θ/	(der) Norden; Nord-
	side (dish) /ˈsaɪd_dɪʃ/	(die) Beilage
	pub /pʌb/	(die) Kneipe
	vindaloo /ˌvɪndəˈlu:/	*indisches Gericht*
	korma /ˈkɔ:mə/	*indisches Gericht*
	naan bread /ˈnɑ:n bred/	*indisches Fladenbrot*
	overcooked /ˌəʊvəˈkʊkt/	verkocht
	juicy /ˈdʒu:si/	saftig
	cosy /ˈkəʊzi/	gemütlich
p. 20, 3	**tasty** /ˈteɪsti/	lecker
	soup /su:p/	(die) Suppe
p. 20, 4	**syllable** /ˈsɪləbl/	(die) Silbe
p. 21, 5	(to) **be allergic to** *(irr)* /ˌbi_əˈlɜ:dʒɪk tʊ/	allergisch sein auf
	occasion /əˈkeɪʒn/	(die) Gelegenheit, (der) Anlass
	Indian /ˈɪndiən/	(der/die) Inder/in; indisch
	raw /rɔ:/	roh
p. 22, 6	**waiter/waitress** /ˈweɪtə, ˈweɪtrəs/	(der/die) Kellner/in
	reservation /ˌrezəˈveɪʃn/	(die) Reservierung
	certainly /ˈsɜ:tnli/	sicher, gerne
	this way /ˈðɪs weɪ/	hier entlang
	(to) **take a seat** *(irr)* /ˌteɪk_ə ˈsi:t/	sich setzen
	home-made /ˌhəʊmˈmeɪd/	hausgemacht
	(to) **take an order** *(irr)* /ˌteɪk_ənˈɔ:də/	eine Bestellung aufnehmen
	on the side /ˌɒn ðə ˈsaɪd/	als Beilage
	sir/Sir /sɜ:/	Sir; Herr *(Anrede vor Vornamen)*
	(to) **warn** /wɔ:n/	warnen
	extremely /ɪkˈstri:mli/	äußerst, höchst, außerordentlich
	palace /ˈpæləs/	(der) Palast
	(to) show to the table *(irr)* /ˌʃəʊ tə ðə ˈteɪbl/	zum Tisch führen
	salmon /ˈsæmən/	(der) Lachs
	lamb /læm/	(das) Lamm
	(to) **rewrite** *(irr)* /ˌri:ˈraɪt/	überarbeiten, umschreiben
p. 23, 7	**lemonade** /ˌleməˈneɪd/	(die) Limonade
	mineral water /ˈmɪnrəl ˌwɔ:tə/	(das) Mineralwasser

cheap ≠ expensive

hot ≠ mild

A **side dish** is food that you get at the same time as the main course.

There is a tablespoon in the **soup**.

They **have taken a seat** in a restaurant.

on the side = as a side dish

extremely = very

to rewrite = to make changes to a piece of writing

	lassi /ˈlæsi/	Joghurtgetränk	
	poppadom /ˈpɒpədəm/	dünnes indisches Brot	
	cracker /ˈkrækə/	(der) Kräcker	
	selection /sɪˈlekʃn/	(die) Auswahl	cooked /kʊkt/ gekocht
	bhaji /ˈbɑːdʒi/	indisches Gericht	mixed /mɪkst/ gemischt
	samosa /səˈməʊsə/	indische gefüllte Teigtasche	
	pastry /ˈpeɪstri/	(der) Brandteig, (der) Blätterteig	
	coconut cream /ˈkəʊkə,nʌt kriːm/	(die) Kokosmilch	
	ginger /ˈdʒɪndʒə/	(der) Ingwer	
	chilli (pl chillies) /ˈtʃɪli/	(der) Chili, (die) Peperoni	
	palak paneer /ˌpɑːlək pəˈnɪə/	indisches Gericht	
	spinach /ˈspɪnɪdʒ/	(der) Spinat	
	beef /biːf/	(das) Rindfleisch	
p. 24, 8	(to) **get** (irr) /get/	bringen	
	any more /ˌeni ˈmɔː/	noch mehr	The mother is not happy.
	not … either /ˌnɒt ˈaɪðə/	auch nicht	The father is **not** happy **either**.
	bill /bɪl/	(die) Rechnung	
	cash /kæʃ/	(das) Geld, (das) Bargeld	You can pay in **cash** or by credit card at a restaurant.
	(to) **bring over** (irr) /ˌbrɪŋˈəʊvə/	herbeibringen	
p. 25, 10	(to) **eat out** (irr) /ˌiːtˈaʊt/	auswärts essen; im Restaurant essen	to **eat out** = to not eat at home
	strawberry /ˈstrɔːbri/	(die) Erdbeere	
p. 25, 11	**lady** /ˈleɪdi/	(die) Frau, (die) Dame	
	both /bəʊθ/	beide	
p. 26, 12	(to) **go on** (irr) /ˌgəʊˈɒn/	passieren; weitergehen, weiterreden	
	caption /ˈkæpʃn/	(die) Bildunterschrift	
	OMG! (= Oh my God!) /ˌəʊ_em ˈdʒiː/	Oh mein Gott!	
	spider /ˈspaɪdə/	(die) Spinne	
p. 26, 13	**conversation** /ˌkɒnvəˈseɪʃn/	(das) Gespräch, (die) Unterhaltung	
	English-speaking /ˈɪŋglɪʃ_ˌspiːkɪŋ/	englischsprachig	There are usually lots of
p. 27, 14	**prop** /prɒp/	(die) Requisite	**props** on a theatre stage.

Unit 2 | Part A Keeping fit

p. 31	**living** /ˈlɪvɪŋ/	(der) Lebensstil	
	lifestyle /ˈlaɪf,staɪl/	(der) Lebensstil	Wenn man den Ort und nicht die Person meint,
	(to) **keep fit** (irr) /ˌkiːp ˈfɪt/	fit bleiben, (sich) fit halten	sagt man
	doctor /ˈdɒktə/	(der/die) Arzt/Ärztin	„at the doctor**'s**" –
p. 32, 1	(to) **prefer** /prɪˈfɜː/	vorziehen, bevorzugen	beim Arzt / bei der Ärztin.
	indoors /ˌɪnˈdɔːz/	drinnen, im Haus	
	outdoors /ˌaʊtˈdɔːz/	draußen, im Freien	**indoors ≠ outdoors**
	(to) **win** (irr) /wɪn/	gewinnen	
	(to) **lose** (irr) /luːz/	verlieren	to **win** ≠ to **lose**
	diving /ˈdaɪvɪŋ/	(das) Tauchen	
	loser /ˈluːzə/	(der/die) Verlierer/in	

	(to) care about /ˈkeər_əˌbaʊt/	sich etwas machen aus
	rowing /ˈrəʊɪŋ/	(das) Rudern
	weight training /ˈweɪtˌtreɪnɪŋ/	(das) Krafttraining
	climbing /ˈklaɪmɪŋ/	(das) Klettern
p. 33, 2	(to) scan /skæn/	absuchen, überfliegen
	profile /ˈprəʊfaɪl/	(das) Profil, (das) Porträt
	active /ˈæktɪv/	aktiv
	(to) sit (irr) /sɪt/	sitzen
	(to) train /treɪn/	trainieren
	(to) reach /riːtʃ/	erreichen
	skill /skɪl/	(die) Fähigkeit, (das) Geschick
	strength /streŋθ/	(die) Kraft, (die) Stärke
	in order to /ɪnˈɔːdə tʊ/	um zu
	outdoor /ˌaʊtˈdɔː/	Outdoor-, im Freien
	still /stɪl/	still, bewegungslos
	logical thinking /ˌlɒdʒɪkl ˈθɪŋkɪŋ/	(das) logische Denken
	puzzle /ˈpʌzl/	(das) Rätsel
p. 34, 4	exhausting /ɪgˈzɔːstɪŋ/	anstrengend
p. 35, 6	(to) look up /ˌlʊkˈʌp/	hochschauen; nachschlagen
	series /ˈsɪəriːz/	(die) Folge, (die) Serie
	prize /praɪz/	(der) Preis, (der) Gewinn
	physical /ˈfɪzɪkl/	körperlich
	(to) concentrate /ˈkɒnsnˌtreɪt/	sich konzentrieren
	chess /tʃes/	(das) Schach
	relaxing /rɪˈlæksɪŋ/	entspannend
	strategy /ˈstrætədʒi/	(die) Strategie
	tournament /ˈtʊənəmənt/	(das) Turnier
	competitive /kəmˈpetətɪv/	von Konkurrenzdenken geprägt
p. 36, 7	dance /dɑːns/	(der) Tanz
	(to) move /muːv/	(sich) bewegen
	wheelchair /ˈwiːltʃeə/	(der) Rollstuhl
	twice /twaɪs/	zweimal
	some day /ˈsʌmˌdeɪ/	eines Tages
	ourselves /aʊəˈselvz/	uns; wir selbst
	sleep /sliːp/	(der) Schlaf
	(to) stress /stres/	stressen
	(to) compete /kəmˈpiːt/	an einem Wettkampf teilnehmen; kämpfen
	indoor /ˌɪnˈdɔː/	Hallen-
	regularly /ˈreɡjʊləli/	regelmäßig
	flexible /ˈfleksəbl/	biegsam, gelenkig
	myself /maɪˈself/	mir/mich/ich (selbst)
	stressed /strest/	gestresst

They **are sitting** on the sofa.

Camping is an **outdoor** activity.

Training hard is very **exhausting**.

chess

dance

The girl has a good **sleep**.

The boy is very **flexible**.

	English	German	Example
	chance /tʃɑːns/	(die) Möglichkeit, (die) Gelegenheit	
	(to) exercise /ˈeksəsaɪz/	trainieren	
	workout /ˈwɜːkaʊt/	(das) Training	
	exhausted /ɪɡˈzɔːstɪd/	erschöpft	
p. 37, 7	(to) **get better** *(irr)* /ˌɡet ˈbetə/	besser werden; gesund werden	When you are ill, you hope to **get better** very soon.
	most of the time /ˈməʊst_əv ðə ˌtaɪm/	meistens	
	(to) **make somebody do something** *(irr)* /ˌmeɪk ˌsʌmbədi ˈduː ˌsʌmθɪŋ/	jemanden dazu bringen, etwas zu tun	My mum **made** me **do** my homework.
	sporty /ˈspɔːti/	sportlich	
	for some time /fə ˌsʌm ˈtaɪm/	eine Zeitlang	
p. 38, 8	**check** /tʃek/	(die) Überprüfung, (die) Kontrolle	
	dry suit /ˈdraɪsuːt/	(der) Taucheranzug	
	buddy *(informal)* /ˈbʌdi/	(der) Kumpel	
p. 39, 9	**advert (= ad)** /ˈædvɜːt, æd/	(die) Werbung, (die) Anzeige	
p. 39, 10	(to) **turn off** /ˌtɜːn ˈɒf/	ausschalten	
	helmet /ˈhelmɪt/	(der) Helm	**helmet**
	(to) **roll** /rəʊl/	rollen	
	(to) **shoot** *(irr)* /ʃuːt/	schießen	
	like that /ˌlaɪk ˈðæt/	so	
	rhyming word /ˈraɪmɪŋ wɜːd/	(das) Reimwort	Poems often have **rhyming words.**
	poet /ˈpəʊɪt/	(der/die) Dichter/in	
	soccer *(AE)* /ˈsɒkə/	(der) Fußball	**soccer** *(AE)* = football
	(to) grab /ɡræb/	sich schnappen, greifen	
	each and every /ˈiːtʃ_ən_ˌevri/	jede(r, s) einzelne	
	knee pad /ˈniː ˌpæd/	(der) Knieschützer	
	elbow pad /ˈelbəʊ ˌpæd/	(der) Ellenbogenschützer	
	Come on! /ˌkʌm ˈɒn/	Komm(t) schon!	
	(to) bounce /baʊns/	(auf)springen	
	all around /ˌɔːl_əˈraʊnd/	überall (in)	
	(to) pat /pæt/	einen Klaps geben	
	(to) head /hed/	köpfen	
	bat /bæt/	(der) Schläger	**bat**
	(to) biff *(informal)* /bɪf/	hauen, schlagen	
	(to) boot /buːt/	einen Tritt geben	
	(to) spin *(irr)* /spɪn/	drehen, einen Drall geben	
	(to) drop /drɒp/	fallen lassen	
p. 40, 11	(to) **belong** (to) /bɪˈlɒŋ/	gehören (zu)	When something **belongs to** you, it is yours.
p. 40, 12	(to) **be born** *(irr)* /ˌbiː ˈbɔːn/	geboren werden	
	skating /ˈskeɪtɪŋ/	*hier:* (das) Skateboardfahren	
	(to) look out for /ˌlʊk ˈaʊt fə/	*hier:* sich kümmern um	
p. 41, 13	**slide** /slaɪd/	(die) Folie	
	unit /ˈjuːnɪt/	(das) Kapitel	
	(to) **switch off** /ˌswɪtʃ ˈɒf/	ausschalten	It is dark when you **switch off** the light at night.
	leaflet /ˈliːflət/	(der) Prospekt, (die) Broschüre	

slide show /ˈslaɪd ʃəʊ/	(die) Bildschirmpräsentation
gallery walk /ˈgæləri wɔːk/	*(die) Gruppendiskussion in Stationsarbeit*
the most important ones /ðə ˌməʊst ɪmˈpɔːtnt wʌnz/	die wichtigsten

Unit 2 | Part B At the doctor's

p. 42, 1

What's the matter? /ˌwɒts ðə ˈmætə/	Was ist los?
toothache *(no pl)* /ˈtuːθeɪk/	(die) Zahnschmerzen
swollen /ˈswəʊlən/	geschwollen
wrist /rɪst/	(das) Handgelenk
cold /kəʊld/	(die) Erkältung
stomach ache *(no pl)* /ˈstʌmək ˌeɪk/	(die) Bauchschmerzen
wound /wuːnd/	(die) Wunde
shoulder /ˈʃəʊldə/	(die) Schulter
(to) **hurt** *(irr)* /hɜːt/	wehtun, schmerzen; verletzen
broken /ˈbrəʊkən/	gebrochen
(to) **take an X-ray** *(irr)* /ˌteɪk ən ˈeksreɪ/	eine Röntgenaufnahme machen
cast /kɑːst/	(der) Gips
tooth (*pl* **teeth**) /tuːθ, tiːθ/	(der) Zahn
appointment /əˈpɔɪntmənt/	(der) Termin
dentist /ˈdentɪst/	(der/die) Zahnarzt/Zahnärztin
practice /ˈpræktɪs/	(die) Praxis
This is … speaking. /ðɪs ɪz … ˈspiːkɪŋ/	Hier spricht …
(to) **catch a cold** *(irr)* /ˌkætʃ ə ˈkəʊld/	sich erkälten
headache /ˈhedeɪk/	(die) Kopfschmerzen
sore throat /ˌsɔː ˈθrəʊt/	(die) Halsschmerzen
fever /ˈfiːvə/	(das) Fieber
cough /kɒf/	(der) Husten
(to) **come in** *(irr)* /ˌkʌm ˈɪn/	hereinkommen
(to) **see** *(irr)* /siː/	empfangen, drannehmen
bad /bæd/	*hier:* stark
ow (= ouch) *(informal)* /aʊ, aʊtʃ/	aua, autsch
receptionist /rɪˈsepʃnɪst/	(die/der) Empfangsdame/Empfangschef

p. 43, 1

(to) **fall** *(irr)* /fɔːl/	fallen
(to) **bleed** *(irr)* /bliːd/	bluten
infection /ɪnˈfekʃn/	(die) Infektion
plaster /ˈplɑːstə/	(der) Gips, (das) Pflaster
soon /suːn/	bald
(to) **see a doctor** *(irr)* /ˌsiː ə ˈdɒktə/	einen Arzt/eine Ärztin aufsuchen
stomach /ˈstʌmək/	(der) Magen, (der) Bauch
medicine /ˈmedsn/	(die) Medizin, (die) Medikamente
health /helθ/	(die) Gesundheit

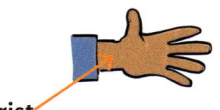

wrist

When you have a **stomach ache**, your stomach **hurts**.

Wenn man den Ort und nicht die Person meint, sagt man „at the dentist's" – „beim Zahnarzt / bei der Zahnärztin/ in der Zahnarztpraxis" oder „to the dentist's" – „zum Zahnarzt / zur Zahnärztin".

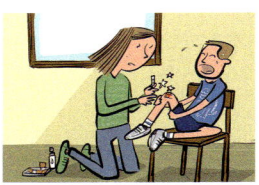

The **wound** on his knee **is bleeding**.

soon = in the near future

	dramatic /drəˈmætɪk/	dramatisch
	reading /ˈriːdɪŋ/	(die) Lesung
	oh dear *(informal)* /əʊ ˈdɪə/	oje
	painful /ˈpeɪnfl/	schmerzhaft
p. 44, 2	(to) **get well** *(irr)* /ˌget ˈwel/	gesund werden
p. 45, 4	**accident** /ˈæksɪdnt/	(der) Unfall
	coach /kəʊtʃ/	(der/die) Trainer/in
	hard /hɑːd/	fest, kräftig
	(to) **call an ambulance** /ˌkɔːl_ən_ˈæmbjʊləns/	einen Krankenwagen rufen
	emergency /ɪˈmɜːdʒnsi/	(der) Notfall
	(to) bang one's head /ˌbæŋ wʌnz ˈhed/	sich den Kopf anschlagen
	alright /ɔːlˈraɪt/	in Ordnung
	dizzy /ˈdɪzi/	schwindlig
	emergency services *(pl)* /ɪˈmɜːdʒnsi ˌsɜːvɪsɪz/	(der) Notdienst, (der) Rettungsdienst
	operator /ˈɒpəˌreɪtə/	(der/die) Telefonist/in
	playing field /ˈpleɪɪŋ ˌfiːld/	(der) Sportplatz
p. 46, 5	**meaning** /ˈmiːnɪŋ/	(die) Bedeutung
	injury /ˈɪndʒəri/	(die) Verletzung
	(to) **examine** /ɪgˈzæmɪn/	untersuchen
	sprained /spreɪnd/	verstaucht
	(to) **put on** *(irr)* /ˌpʊt_ˈɒn/	anlegen, auftragen
	bandage /ˈbændɪdʒ/	(der) Verband
	waiting room /ˈweɪtɪŋ ˌruːm/	(das) Wartezimmer
	yet /jet/	schon; noch
	(to) **calm down** /ˌkɑːm ˈdaʊn/	(sich) beruhigen
	(to) **sign** /saɪn/	unterschreiben
	news *(no pl)* /njuːz/	(die) Neuigkeit, (die) Nachrichten
	ankle /ˈæŋkl/	(der) (Fuß)knöchel
	(to) **rest** /rest/	ausruhen
	possible /ˈpɒsəbl/	möglich
	(to) **promise** /ˈprɒmɪs/	versprechen
	X-ray /ˈeksreɪ/	(das) Röntgenbild
	phew *(informal)* /fjuː/	puh
	doctor's practice /ˈdɒktəz ˌpræktɪs/	(die) Arztpraxis
	(to) keep up *(irr)* /ˌkiːp_ˈʌp/	*hier:* hochlegen
	No problem. /ˌnəʊ ˈprɒbləm/	*hier:* Keine Ursache.
	check-up /ˈtʃek_ʌp/	(die) Untersuchung
p. 47, 5	(to) **read out** *(irr)* /ˌriːd_ˈaʊt/	(laut) vorlesen
p. 47, 6	**properly** /ˈprɒpəli/	richtig
p. 48, 7	**Get well soon!** /ˌget ˌwel ˈsuːn/	Gute Besserung!
	(to) **cheer up** /ˌtʃɪər_ˈʌp/	aufmuntern, aufheitern
p. 48, 8	(to) **be wrong (with)** *(irr)* /ˌbiː ˈrɒŋ wɪθ/	nicht in Ordnung sein (mit)

In case of an **emergency**, you have to go to the hospital.

They are sitting in the **waiting room**.

When you **promise** something, you tell someone that you will definitely do something.

at the **doctor's practice** = at the doctor's

properly = correctly

p. 49, 10	(to) **help out** /ˌhelp ˈaʊt/	aushelfen
	exchange student /ɪksˈtʃeɪndʒ ˌstjuːdnt/	(der/die) Austauschschüler/in
p. 49, 11	**illness** /ˈɪlnəs/	(die) Krankheit
	(to) **mime** /maɪm/	mimen, pantomimisch darstellen
p. 50, 13	**emergency call** /ɪˈmɜːdʒnsi kɔːl/	(der) Notruf
p. 50, 14	(to) **mark** /mɑːk/	markieren, kennzeichnen
p. 51, 16	(to) **fall off** *(informal)* /ˌfɔːl ˈɒf/	(herunter)fallen
	medical /ˈmedɪkl/	medizinisch

An **exchange student** goes to school in another country for some time.

She is afraid of **falling off**.

Unit 3 | Part A At the car boot sale

p. 55	**car boot sale** /ˌkɑː ˈbuːt seɪl/	*(der) Kofferraum-Flohmarkt*
p. 56, 2	**stall** /stɔːl/	(der) Stand
	(to) **avoid** /əˈvɔɪd/	meiden, vermeiden
	crowd /kraʊd/	(die) Menschenmenge
	charity /ˈtʃærəti/	(die) Wohltätigkeitsorganisation
	run /rʌn/	(der) Lauf
	km (= kilometre) /ˈkɪləˌmiːtə/	(der) Kilometer
	at the same time /ˌæt ðə ˌseɪm ˈtaɪm/	gleichzeitig, zur gleichen Zeit
	second-hand /ˌsekənd ˈhænd/	gebraucht
	item /ˈaɪtəm/	(der) Gegenstand
	anywhere /ˈeniˌweə/	irgendwo
	fee /fiː/	(die) Gebühr, (das) Geld
	guide /gaɪd/	(der) Führer *(Buch)*
	arts and crafts /ˌɑːrts ən ˈkrɑːfts/	(das) Basteln, (die) Bastelarbeit
	charity run /ˈtʃærəti rʌn/	(der) Wohltätigkeitslauf
	registration fee /ˌredʒɪˈstreɪʃn fiː/	(die) Anmeldegebühr
	forever /fərˈevə/	ewig, für immer
p. 57, 3	**finally** /ˈfaɪnli/	schließlich, endlich
	neither /ˈnaɪðə, ˈniːðə/	auch nicht
	pocket money /ˈpɒkɪt ˌmʌni/	(das) Taschengeld
	(to) **keep doing something** *(irr)* /ˌkiːp ˈduːɪŋ sʌmθɪŋ/	etwas weiter tun
	flea market /ˈfliː ˌmɑːkɪt/	(der) Flohmarkt
	(to) **sell** *(irr)* /sel/	verkaufen
	nobody /ˈnəʊbədi/	niemand, keiner
	crowded /ˈkraʊdɪd/	überfüllt
	shall /ʃæl/	sollen; werden
	(to) **be up to something** *(irr)* /bi ˌʌp tə ˈsʌmθɪŋ/	etwas vorhaben
	for ages *(informal)* /fərˈeɪdʒɪz/	seit einer Ewigkeit
	(to) **have something left** *(irr)* /ˌhæv sʌmθɪŋ ˈleft/	etwas übrig haben
p. 58	**relative clause** /ˌrelətɪv ˈklɔːz/	(der) Relativsatz

Many people together are a **crowd**.

People sell **second-hand items** at a **car boot sale**.

Pocket money is money that children get from their parents every week or every month.

The concert was **crowded**.

p. 59, 7	hockey stick /ˈhɒki stɪk/	(der) Hockeyschläger
	bicycle bell /ˈbaɪsɪkl bel/	(die) Fahrradklingel
	singing /ˈsɪŋɪŋ/	singend
p. 60, 8	**bargain** /ˈbɑːgɪn/	(das) Schnäppchen
	above /əˈbʌv/	oben, oberhalb
	seller /ˈselə/	(der/die) Verkäufer/in
	taste /teɪst/	(der) Geschmack
	(to) **try on** /ˌtraɪ ˈɒn/	anprobieren
	much /mʌtʃ/	sehr
	price /praɪs/	(der) Preis (Kosten)
	…, doesn't it? /ˈdʌznt ɪt/	…, nicht wahr?
	curtain /ˈkɜːtn/	(der) Vorhang
	flowerpot /ˈflaʊəˌpɒt/	(der) Blumentopf
	lamp /læmp/	(die) Lampe
	coffee grinder /ˈkɒfi ˌgraɪndə/	(die) Kaffeemühle
	price tag /ˈpraɪs tæg/	(das) Preisschild
p. 61, 8	**successful** /səkˈsesfl/	erfolgreich
	(to) **get rid of** (irr) /ˌget ˈrɪd_əv/	loswerden
	charity shop /ˈtʃærəti ʃɒp/	(der) Laden, in dem gebrauchte Dinge zu Wohltätigkeitszwecken verkauft werden
p. 62, 10	**several** /ˈsevrəl/	einige, verschiedene
	elephant /ˈelɪfənt/	(der) Elefant
	travel guide /ˈtrævl gaɪd/	(der) Reiseführer (Buch)
p. 63, 11	(to) **contain** /kənˈteɪn/	enthalten
	chutney /ˈtʃʌtni/	indische Beilage
p. 63, 12	out and about /ˌaʊt_ən_əˈbaʊt/	unterwegs
	(to) upcycle /ˈʌpsaɪkl/	upcyceln
	odd /ɒd/	merkwürdig, seltsam
	(to) advertise /ˈædvətaɪz/	für etwas Werbung machen
p. 64, 13	**one** /wʌn/	eine(r, s)
	sock /sɒk/	(die) Socke
	broken /ˈbrəʊkən/	zerbrochen; kaputt
p. 65, 15	**part** /pɑːt/	(die) Rolle
	You're welcome. /jɔː ˈwelkəm/	Gern geschehen., Keine Ursache.

A **bargain** is something you can buy that costs much less than normal.

new ones /ˈnjuː wʌnz/
  neue
these ones /ˈðiːz wʌnz/
  diese
a nice one /ə ˈnaɪs wʌn/
  ein schöner/eine schöne/ein schönes
some old ones /səmˈˌəʊld wʌnz/ ein paar alte
a small one /ə ˈsmɔːl wʌn/
  ein kleiner/eine kleine/ein kleines

several = some, different

this one /ˈðɪs wʌn/
  diese(r, s) hier
the blue / red / green one /ðə ˈbluː / ˈred / ˈgriːn wʌn/
  der/die/das blaue / rote / grüne
the blue / brown / black ones /ðə ˈbluː / ˈbraʊn / ˈblæk wʌnz/ die blauen / braunen / schwarzen
a bigger one /ə ˈbɪgə wʌn/
  ein größerer/eine größere/ein größeres
another one /əˈnʌðə wʌn/
  noch ein/e; ein anderer/ein anderes/eine andere

Unit 3 | Part B Festivals

p. 66, 1	Viking /ˈvaɪkɪŋ/	(der/die) Wikinger/in; Wikinger-
p. 66, 2	**student** /ˈstjuːdnt/	(der/die) Student/in
	influence /ˈɪnfluəns/	(der) Einfluss
	(to) **check out** (informal) /ˌtʃek_ˈaʊt/	sich ansehen; ausprobieren
	fight /faɪt/	(der) Kampf, (der) Streit

	after that /ˌɑːftə ˈðæt/	danach	first → **after that**
	(to) conquer /ˈkɒŋkə/	erobern	
	combat arena /ˈkɒmbæt_əˌriːnə/	(die) Wettkampfarena	
	warrior /ˈwɒriə/	(der/die) Krieger/in	
	armour /ˈɑːmə/	(die) Rüstung	
	dining room /ˈdaɪnɪŋ ruːm/	hier: (der) Speisesaal	
p. 67, 2	**beard** /bɪəd/	(der) Bart	The man has a **beard**.
	anyone /ˈeniˌwʌn/	jede(r, s); (irgend)jemand	
	highlight /ˈhaɪˌlaɪt/	(der) Höhepunkt	**highlight** = the best part of an event
	battle /ˈbætl/	(der) Kampf	
	spectacular /spekˈtækjʊlə/	atemberaubend, spektakulär	
	content /ˈkɒntent/	(der) Inhalt	
	(to) **mention** /ˈmenʃn/	erwähnen	
	least /liːst/	am wenigsten	
	bird of prey /ˌbɜːd_əv ˈpreɪ/	(der) Raubvogel	
	breathtaking /ˈbreθˌteɪkɪŋ/	atemberaubend	
	firework display /ˈfaɪəˌwɜːk dɪˌspleɪ/	(das) Feuerwerk	**bird of prey**
	throughout /θruːˈaʊt/	während	
	coming soon /ˌkʌmɪŋ ˈsuːn/	in Kürze erscheinend	
p. 68, 3	(to) **prepare for** /prɪˈpeə fɔː/	sich vorbereiten auf	When you **have put on** clothes, you are wearing them.
	(to) **put on** (irr) /ˌpʊt_ˈɒn/	anziehen (Kleidung)	
	(to) style /staɪl/	frisieren	
p. 69, 5	(to) **run** (irr) /rʌn/	leiten, betreiben	
	(to) **steal** (irr) /rʌn/	stehlen	
	pocket /ˈpɒkɪt/	(die) Hosentasche	
	aspect /ˈæspekt/	(der) Aspekt, (der) Gesichtspunkt	
	on the one hand ... /ˌɒn ðə ˈwʌn hænd/	einerseits ...	
	on the other hand ... /ˌɒn ðiˌˈʌðə hænd/	andererseits ...	
	teddy bear /ˈtedi beə/	(der) Teddybär	**teddy bear**
	pickpocket /ˈpɪkˌpɒkɪt/	(der/die) Taschendieb/in	
p. 70, 6	**not anyone** /ˌnɒt_ˈeniwʌn/	niemand	
	itself /ɪtˈself/	selbst, sich selbst	
	world-famous /ˌwɜːld ˈfeɪməs/	weltberühmt	
	(to) **dive** /daɪv/	tauchen	
	impressive /ɪmˈpresɪv/	beeindruckend	
	colourful /ˈkʌləfl/	farbenfroh, bunt	The chair is **colourful**.
	cheerful /ˈtʃɪəfl/	fröhlich, vergnügt	
	serious /ˈsɪəriəs/	ernst	
	(to) **draw attention to** (irr) /ˌdrɔːˌəˈtenʃn tə/	Aufmerksamkeit lenken auf	An **immigrant** is someone who comes to live in a country from another country.
	immigrant /ˈɪmɪgrənt/	(der/die) Einwanderer/in, (der/die) Immigrant/in	
	lover /ˈlʌvə/	(der/die) Liebhaber/in	

	open-air /ˌəʊpən_ˈeə/	im Freien
	south-west /ˌsaʊθˈwest/	Südwest-
	tent /tent/	(das) Zelt
	muddy /ˈmʌdi/	matschig, schlammig
	camping site /ˈkæmpɪŋ ˌsaɪt/	(der) Campingplatz
	organizer /ˈɔːgəˌnaɪzə/	(der/die) Organisator/in
	Caribbean /ˌkærɪˈbiən/	karibisch
p. 71, 6	**multicultural** /ˌmʌltiˈkʌltʃərəl/	multikulturell
	such /sʌtʃ/	so, solch
	(to) **be worth** *(irr)* /ˌbiː ˈwɜːθ/	(sich) lohnen, wert sein
	(to) **lift** /lɪft/	(hoch)heben
	(to) **turn over** /ˌtɜːn_ˈəʊvə/	(sich) umdrehen
	(to) **land** /lænd/	landen
	steel drum /ˌstiːl ˈdrʌm/	Steeldrum
	spectacle /ˈspektəkl/	(das) Spektakel
	lad *(informal, Scottish)* /læd/	(der) Junge
	lass *(informal, Scottish)* /læs/	(das) Mädchen
	bagpipes *(pl)* /ˈbægˌpaɪps/	(der) Dudelsack
	tossing the caber /ˌtɒsɪŋ ðə ˈkeɪbə/	(das) Baumstammwerfen
	log /lɒg/	(der) Baumstamm
	(to) toss /tɒs/	werfen
p. 72, 8	**look** /lʊk/	(das) Aussehen, (der) Look
	(to) **dress** /dres/	sich anziehen, sich kleiden
	carnival /ˈkɑːnɪvl/	(das) Volksfest, (der) Karneval
p. 73, 9	(to) **attend** /əˈtend/	besuchen
	(to) **produce** /prəˈdjuːs/	produzieren
	waste /weɪst/	(der) Abfall
	green /griːn/	umweltfreundlich, ökologisch
	government /ˈgʌvənmənt/	(die) Regierung
	(to) **reduce** /rɪˈdjuːs/	reduzieren
	packaging /ˈpækɪdʒɪŋ/	(die) Verpackung
	made /meɪd/	hergestellt, gemacht
	use /juːs/	(die) Verwendung; (der) Einsatz
	no longer /ˌnəʊ ˈlɒŋgə/	nicht mehr
	site /saɪt/	(die) Stelle, (der) Platz
	(to) clear up /ˌklɪər_ˈʌp/	aufräumen
	ton /tʌn/	(die) Tonne
	straw /strɔː/	(der) Strohhalm
	across the country /əˌkrɒs ðə ˈkʌntri/	im ganzen Land
	zero waste /ˌzɪərəʊ ˈweɪst/	verpackungsfrei
p. 74, 12	(to) **set up** *(irr)* /ˌset_ˈʌp/	aufbauen

tent

A **multicultural** class is a class with pupils from many different cultures.

When you carry something, you often have to **lift** it first.

Tossing the caber is one of the events at the Highland Games.

We should **reduce** the amount of **waste** that we **produce**.

no longer = not anymore

The man **has set up** a stall.

Unit 4 | Part A Exploring roots

p. 79	**root** /ruːt/	(die) Wurzel	
	(to) **give a helping hand** *(irr)* /ˌɡɪv_ə ˌhelpɪŋ ˈhænd/	helfen	
p. 80, 1	**village** /ˈvɪlɪdʒ/	(das) Dorf	A **village** is much smaller than a town.
	thought /θɔːt/	(der) Gedanke	**memory** = something that you remember
p. 80, 2	**memory** /ˈmemri/	(die) Erinnerung	
	because of /bɪˈkɒz_əv/	wegen	
	accent /ˈæksnt/	(der) Akzent	
	Korean /kəˈriːən/	(der/die) Koreaner/in; koreanisch	
	riverside /ˈrɪvəˌsaɪd/	(das) Flussufer	
	Spain /speɪn/	Spanien	
	mountain biking /ˈmaʊntɪn ˌbaɪkɪŋ/	(das) Mountainbikefahren	
p. 81, 2	(to) **grow up** *(irr)* /ˌɡrəʊ_ˈʌp/	aufwachsen	When two people **get married**, there is usually a big party.
	university /ˌjuːnɪˈvɜːsəti/	(die) Universität	
	(to) **get married** *(irr)* /ˌɡet ˈmærid/	heiraten	
	strong /strɒŋ/	stark	
	community /kəˈmjuːnəti/	(die) Gemeinschaft, (die) Gemeinde	
	mixture /ˈmɪkstʃə/	(die) Mischung	
	the Science Museum /ðə ˈsaɪəns mjuːˌziːəm/	(das) Naturwissenschaftsmuseum	
	Sweden /ˈswiːdn/	Schweden	
	lively /ˈlaɪvli/	lebendig	
	West African /ˌwest_ˈæfrɪkən/	(der/die) Westafrikaner/in; westafrikanisch	
	Swedish /ˈswiːdɪʃ/	schwedisch	
p. 82, 4	(to) **study** /ˈstʌdi/	studieren; lernen	to **study** = to learn
	great-grandmother /ˌɡreɪt ˈɡrænˌmʌðə/	(die) Urgroßmutter	
p. 83, 5	**south** /saʊθ/	(der) Süden; Süd-	**population** = all the people who live in an area
	population /ˌpɒpjʊˈleɪʃn/	(die) Bevölkerung	
	South Asian /ˌsaʊθ_ˈeɪʒn/	südasiatisch	
	African /ˈæfrɪkən/	(der/die) Afrikaner/in; afrikanisch	
	Polish /ˈpəʊlɪʃ/	(das) Polnisch; polnisch	
p. 84, 6	(to) **connect** /kəˈnekt/	verbinden	to **connect** = to put things together
	grandpa *(informal)* /ˈɡrænˌpɑː/	(der) Opa	
	storytelling /ˈstɔːriˌtelɪŋ/	(das) Geschichtenerzählen	
p. 85, 7	**war** /wɔː/	(der) Krieg	When people **emigrate**, they leave their country to live in another country.
	(to) **emigrate** /ˈemɪɡreɪt/	auswandern	
	Great Britain /ˌɡreɪt ˈbrɪtn/	Großbritannien	
	(to) **marry** /ˈmæri/	heiraten	
	foreign /ˈfɒrɪn/	ausländisch, fremd	
	(to) **be homesick** *(irr)* /ˌbiː ˈhəʊmˌsɪk/	Heimweh haben	
	while /waɪl/	(die) Weile	

	great-grandfather /ˌɡreɪt ˈɡrænˌfɑːðə/	(der) Urgroßvater
	World War II /ˌwɜːld ˌwɔː ˈtuː/	der Zweite Weltkrieg
	The Royal Air Force /ðə ˌrɔɪəl ˈeə fɔːs/	(die) Königliche Luftwaffe
	air force /ˈeə fɔːs/	(die) Luftwaffe
p. 86, 8	**dress** /dres/	(das) Kleid, (die) Kleidung
	latest /ˈleɪtɪst/	neueste(r, s)
	mostly /ˈməʊstli/	meistens, größtenteils
	(to) be a shame *(irr)* /ˌbi_ə ˈʃeɪm/	schade sein
	grandad *(informal)* /ˈɡrænˌdæd/	(der) Opa
	still /stɪl/	nach wie vor, trotzdem
	(to) die /daɪ/	sterben
	cute /kjuːt/	süß, niedlich
	childhood /ˈtʃaɪldˌhʊd/	(die) Kindheit
p. 87, 8	**speech bubble** /ˈspiːtʃ ˌbʌbl/	(die) Sprechblase
	thought bubble /ˈθɔːt ˌbʌbl/	(die) Gedankenblase
	at that time /æt ˈðæt ˌtaɪm/	zu jener Zeit
	darling /ˈdɑːlɪŋ/	(der) Liebling, (der) Schatz
p. 87, 9	**timeline** /ˈtaɪmlaɪn/	(die) Zeitachse
p. 89, 13	**label** /ˈleɪbl/	(das) Etikett

dress

'…, wasn't he?' oder
'…, didn't he?' kannst
du mit 'oder? /
nicht wahr? / gell?'
übersetzen.

thought bubble

Unit 4 | Part B Giving a helping hand

p. 90, 2	**argument** /ˈɑːɡjʊmənt/	(der) Streit; (das) Argument
	herself /həˈself/	sich; (sie) selbst
p. 91, 2	**annoying** /əˈnɔɪɪŋ/	ärgerlich
	(to) join /dʒɔɪn/	sich zu jemandem gesellen
	(to) save /seɪv/	aufheben; sichern
	silly /ˈsɪli/	albern, dumm
	upset /ʌpˈset/	aufgebracht; aufgeregt
	(to) be up for something *(informal, irr)* /ˌbi_ˌʌp fɔː ˈsʌmθɪŋ/	Lust zu etwas haben
	(to) hang out *(informal, irr)* /ˌhæŋ ˈaʊt/	rumhängen, Zeit mit jemandem verbringen
	I'm in! *(informal)* /ˌaɪm ˈɪn/	Ich bin dabei!
	tuition /tjuːˈɪʃn/	*hier:* (die) Nachhilfe
	(to) skip /skɪp/	*hier:* ausfallen lassen
	D /diː/	*etwa:* Note 4, ausreichend
	What if …? /ˌwɒt ˈɪf/	Was wäre, wenn …?
	lame /leɪm/	lahm
p. 93, 5	**right now** /ˌraɪt ˈnaʊ/	jetzt, im Moment
	right /raɪt/	(das) Recht
	(to) delete /dɪˈliːt/	löschen
	guy /ɡaɪ/	(der) Kerl, (der) Typ
	chemistry club /ˈkemɪstri klʌb/	(die) Chemie-AG

How about …?
/ˈhaʊ_əˌbaʊt/
Wie wäre es mit …?,
Was ist mit …?
What's up? *(informal)*
/ˌwɒts_ˈʌp/ Was ist los?
What's wrong?
(informal) /ˌwɒts_ˈrɒŋ/
Was ist los?

to **skip** = to not do
something that you
normally do

How r u? /ˌhaʊ_ˈɑː jʊ/
Wie geht es dir / euch?
gr8 (= great) /ɡreɪt/
großartig
sec (= second) /sek,
ˈsekənd/ (die) Sekunde

	I'd (= I would) /aɪd, ˈaɪ wʊd/	ich würde
p. 94, 6	(to) **seek advice** *(irr)* /ˌsi:k_əd'vaɪs/	Rat suchen
	advice /əd'vaɪs/	(der) Rat, (der) Ratschlag
	(to) **stop** /stɒp/	stoppen
	(to) **agree** /ə'gri:/	zustimmen
	parent /ˈpeərənt/	(das) Elternteil
	All the best! /ˌɔ:l ðə ˈbest/	Alles Gute!
	Good luck! /ˌgʊd ˈlʌk/	Viel Glück!
	(to) **chat** /tʃæt/	plaudern; chatten
	unless /ən'les/	außer wenn
	headline /ˈhedˌlaɪn/	(die) Schlagzeile; *hier:* (die) Überschrift
	teen /ti:n/	Teenager
	anonymous(ly) /əˈnɒnɪməs, əˈnɒnɪməsli/	anonym
	(to) **be left out** *(irr)* /ˌbi: ˌleft_ˈaʊt/	ausgeschlossen werden
p. 95, 6	(to) **communicate** /kə'mju:nɪkeɪt/	kommunizieren, sprechen
	matter /ˈmætə/	(die) Angelegenheit
	(to) **prove** *(irr)* /pru:v/	beweisen
	official, officially /əˈfɪʃl, əˈfɪʃli/	offiziell
	(to) **wish** /wɪʃ/	wünschen
	shy /ʃaɪ/	schüchtern
	(to) **apologize (= apologise)** /əˈpɒlədʒaɪz/	sich entschuldigen
	(to) **tease** /ti:z/	hänseln, ärgern
	helpful /ˈhelpfl/	hilfreich, nützlich
	(to) keep a diary *(irr)* /ˌki:p_ə 'daɪəri/	Tagebuch führen
	screen time /ˈskri:n taɪm/	(die) Bildschirmzeit
p. 96, 8	school counsellor /ˌsku:l ˈkaʊnslə/	(der/die) Vertrauenslehrer/in
p. 96, 9	**call** /kɔ:l/	(der) Anruf, (das) Gespräch
	helpline /ˈhelpˌlaɪn/	*(der) telefonische Beratungsdienst*
p. 97, 10	(to) **deal with** *(irr)* /ˈdi:l wɪð/	sich befassen mit, umgehen mit
	word search /ˈwɜ:d sɜ:tʃ/	(die) Wortsuche
p. 97, 11	**company** /ˈkʌmpni/	(die) Firma, (das) Unternehmen
	office manager /ˈɒfɪs ˌmænɪdʒə/	(der/die) Sekretär/in
p. 98, 12	(to) **be wrong** *(irr)* /ˌbi: ˈrɒŋ/	im Unrecht sein
	hers /hɜ:z/	ihre(r, s)
	ours /ˈaʊəz/	unsere(r, s)
	neighbour /ˈneɪbə/	(der/die) Nachbar/in
	theirs /ðeəz/	ihre(r, s)
p. 98, 13	(to) **allow** /ə'laʊ/	erlauben
	(to) **stay up (late)** /ˌsteɪˌʌp ˈleɪt/	lange aufbleiben
	linking part /ˈlɪŋkɪŋ pɑ:t/	(das) Verbindungsteil
	linking word /ˈlɪŋkɪŋ wɜ:d/	(das) Verbindungswort
	rude /ru:d/	unhöflich; primitiv

stop ≠ start

Using your mobile is a good way to **communicate**.

Früher war die britische Schreibweise von Wörtern mit '-ise', 'isation' oder '-iser' eindeutig die mit 's', nur im amerikanischen Englisch wurden alle diese Wörter mit 'z' geschrieben. Mittlerweile werden kaum noch Unterschiede gemacht. Viele Briten schreiben 'organize, organizer, realize, ...'.
In vielen Wörterbüchern wird sogar die Schreibweise mit 'z' als die häufiger vorkommende gelistet.

An **office manager** is a person who works in an office.

mine /maɪn/ meine(r, s)
yours /jɔ:z/ deine(r, s); eure(r, s); Ihre(r, s)
his /hɪz/ seine(r, s)
hers /hɜ:z/ ihre(r, s)
ours /ˈaʊəz/ unsere(r, s)
theirs /ðeəz/ ihre(r, s)

p. 99, 15	(to) **give advice** *(irr)* /ˌgɪv_əd'vaɪs/	Rat geben	
	back /bæk/	(der) Rücken	
	pupil /'pjuːpl/	(der/die) Schüler/in	**pupil** = student
	complete /kəm'pliːt/	vollständig, komplett	
	fault /fɔːlt/	(die) Schuld, (der) Fehler	**fault** = mistake
	(to) **ask for advice** /ˌɑːsk fər_əd'vaɪs/	um Rat bitten	
	(to) panic /'pænɪk/	in Panik geraten	

Unit 5 | Part A Inventions

toothbrush

p. 103	**communication** /kəˌmjuːnɪ'keɪʃn/	(die) Verständigung, (die) Kommunikation	
p. 104, 1	**toothbrush** /'tuːθbrʌʃ/	(die) Zahnbürste	
	muscle /'mʌsl/	(der) Muskel	
	power /'paʊə/	(die) Kraft	
	author /'ɔːθə/	(der/die) Autor/in	
	electric /ɪ'lektrɪk/	elektrisch, Elektro-	
	cool /kuːl/	kühl; kalt	**cool** ≠ warm
p. 104, 2	steam locomotive /'stiːm ˌləʊkəˌməʊtɪv/	(die) Dampflokomotive, (die) Dampflok	
p. 105, 2	**basic** /'beɪsɪk/	grundlegend, wesentlich	
	steam engine /'stiːm_ˌendʒɪn/	(die) Dampfmaschine	
	(to) **pull** /pʊl/	ziehen	to **pull** ≠ to push
	passenger /'pæsɪndʒə/	(der/die) Passagier/in	
	most /məʊst/	die meisten; am meisten	
	engine /'endʒɪn/	(die) Maschine, (der) Motor	An **engine** is a machine.
	American /ə'merɪkən/	(der/die) Amerikaner/in; amerikanisch	
	television /'telɪˌvɪʒn/	(der) Fernseher, (das) Fernsehen	
	working /'wɜːkɪŋ/	funktionierend	was / were invented /ˌwɒz/ˌwɜːr_ɪn'ventɪd/ wurde/n erfunden
	inventor /ɪn'ventə/	(der/die) Erfinder/in	was made /ˌwɒz 'meɪd/ wurde gemacht
	named /neɪmd/	namens	are used /ˌɑː 'juːsd/ werden benutzt
	horsehair /'hɔːsˌheə/	(das) Rosshaar	was used /ˌwɒz 'juːzd/ wurde verwendet
	bone /bəʊn/	(der) Knochen	are pulled /ˌɑː 'pʊld/ werden gezogen
	high-pressure /ˌhaɪ 'preʃə/	Hochdruck-	was patented /ˌwɒz 'peɪtntɪd/ wurde patentiert
	locomotive /ˌləʊkə'məʊtɪv/	(die) Lokomotive	was presented /ˌwɒz prɪ'zentɪd/ wurde vorgestellt
	(to) patent /'peɪtnt/	sich patentieren lassen	was built /ˌwɒz 'bɪlt/ wurde gebaut
	phone call /'fəʊn kɔːl/	(der) Telefonanruf	was born /ˌwɒz 'bɔːn/ wurde geboren
	long-distance /ˌlɒŋ 'dɪstəns/	Fern-	
	transatlantic /ˌtrænzət'læntɪk/	transatlantisch	
p. 106, 3	railway company /'reɪlweɪ ˌkʌmpni/	(die) Eisenbahngesellschaft	
p. 106, 4	passive /'pæsɪv/	(das) Passiv	
	telescope /'telɪˌskəʊp/	(das) Teleskop	
p. 107, 5	**section** /'sekʃn/	(das) Teil, (das) Stück, (der) Abschnitt; (die) Abteilung	
	display /dɪ'spleɪ/	(die) Auslage, (die) Ausstellung	

	scientist /ˈsaɪəntɪst/	(der/die) Wissenschaftler/in
	space /speɪs/	(das) Weltall
p. 108, 6	**opening times** *(pl)* /ˈəʊpənɪŋ taɪmz/	(die) Öffnungszeiten
	(to) **be located** *(irr)* /ˌbiː ləˈkeɪtɪd/	gelegen sein
	in advance /ˌɪn ˌədˈvɑːns/	im Voraus
	picnic /ˈpɪknɪk/	(das) Picknick
	the Tube /ðə ˈtjuːb/	(die) (Londoner) U-Bahn
	(to) renovate /ˈrenəveɪt/	renovieren
p. 108, 7	(to) **save** /seɪv/	sparen; retten
	zip /zɪp/	(der) Reißverschluss
	(to) **count** /kaʊnt/	zählen
	(to) **appear** /əˈpɪə/	erscheinen, auftauchen
	industry /ˈɪndəstri/	(die) Industrie
	construction /kənˈstrʌkʃn/	(der) Bau
	(to) button /ˈbʌtən/	knöpfen
	onwards /ˈɒnwədz/	von ... an
p. 109, 7	**simple** /ˈsɪmpl/	einfach, simpel
	(to) **prevent** /prɪˈvent/	verhindern, vorbeugen
	comfortable /ˈkʌmftəbl/	bequem
	tin /tɪn/	(die) Büchse, (die) Dose
	tool /tuːl/	(das) Werkzeug
	accidentally /ˌæksɪˈdentli/	versehentlich, zufällig
	(to) **grow** *(irr)* /grəʊ/	wachsen
	discovery /dɪˈskʌvri/	(die) Entdeckung
	seat belt /ˈsiːt belt/	(der) Sicherheitsgurt
	strap /stræp/	(der) Riemen
	leather /ˈleðə/	(das) Leder
	(to) fasten /ˈfɑːsn/	schließen, zumachen
	belt /belt/	(der) Gürtel
	seat /siːt/	(der) Sitz
	tin opener /ˈtɪn ˌəʊpnə/	(der) Dosenöffner
	inside /ˈɪnˌsaɪd/	in ... hinein
	(to) store /stɔː/	lagern
	(to) become infected *(irr)* /bɪˌkʌm ɪnˈfektɪd/	sich infizieren
	bacteria *(pl)* /bækˈtɪəriə/	(die) Bakterien
	antibiotic /ˌæntibaɪˈɒtɪk/	(das) Antibiotikum
	(Petri) dish /ˈpiːtri ˌdɪʃ/	(die) Petrischale
	lab /læb/	(das) Labor
	mould /məʊld/	(der) Schimmel
	(to) be estimated *(irr)* /ˌbiː ˈestɪmeɪtəd/	geschätzt werden
p. 110, 8	(to) **rate** /reɪt/	einschätzen, bewerten
	rating /ˈreɪtɪŋ/	(die) Einschätzung, (die) Einstufung

opening times = the time of day when a shop or museum is open

zip

simple = easy to understand

to **grow** = to become taller

to **fasten** = to close

at the **lab**

p. 110, 9	**electricity** /ɪˌlek'trɪsəti/	(die) Elektrizität, (der) Strom
p. 111, 10	**brochure** /'brəʊʃə/	(die) Broschüre
p. 111, 11	**practical** /'præktɪkl/	praktisch
	baker /'beɪkə/	*hier: (die) Backmaschine*
	cleaning skates *(pl)* /'kliːnɪŋ ˌskeɪts/	*(die) Reinigungsskates*
	X-ray glasses *(pl)* /'eksreɪ ˌglɑːsɪz/	*(die) Röntgenbrille*
	toilet roll /baker 'beɪkə//	(die) Toilettenpapier-Rolle
p. 112, 12	**owner** /'əʊnə/	(der/die) Besitzer/in
	rich /rɪtʃ/	reich
	flour /'flaʊə/	(das) Mehl
p. 113, 15	(to) **agree on** /ə'griː_ɒn/	sich einigen auf

She is the proud **owner** of a new blue bike.

Unit 5 | Part B Communication

p. 114, 2	**development** /dɪ'veləpmənt/	(die) Entwicklung
	writing /'raɪtɪŋ/	(die) Schrift, (das) Schreiben
	result /rɪ'zʌlt/	(das) Ergebnis
	finding /'faɪndɪŋ/	(die) Entdeckung, (das) Ergebnis
	general /'dʒenrəl/	allgemein
	(to) **give a presentation** *(irr)* /ˌgɪv_ə ˌprezn'teɪʃn/	eine Präsentation halten
	low-tech /ˌləʊ 'tek/	technisch einfach
	on demand /ˌɒn dɪ'mɑːnd/	auf Anfrage
p. 115, 3	(to) **be interested in** *(irr)* /ˌbi_'ɪntrəstɪd_ɪn/	interessiert sein an
p. 116, 5	**planner** /'plænə/	(der) Kalender, (der) Planer
p. 117, 6	**network** /'netˌwɜːk/	(das) Netzwerk
	method /'meθəd/	(die) Methode
	(to) **research** /rɪ'sɜːtʃ/	recherchieren
	search engine /'sɜːtʃˌendʒɪn/	(die) Suchmaschine
	source /sɔːs/	(die) Quelle
	(to) **copy** /'kɒpi/	kopieren
	document /'dɒkjʊmənt/	(das) Dokument
	(to) be done with *(informal, irr)* /ˌbiː 'dʌn wɪð/	fertig sein mit
p. 118, 7	**rock** /rɒk/	(der) Stein, (der) Fels
	stone /stəʊn/	(der) Stein
	theory /'θɪəri/	(die) Theorie
	function /'fʌŋkʃn/	(die) Aufgabe, (die) Funktion
	BC (= before Christ) /ˌbiː 'siː, bɪˌfɔː 'kraɪst/	v. Chr. (= vor Christus)
	around /ə'raʊnd/	ungefähr
	AD (= Anno Domini) /ˌeɪ 'diː, ˌænəʊ 'dɒmɪnaɪ/	n. Chr. (= nach Christus)
	wide /waɪd/	weit

A letter is a piece of **writing**.

The boy **is interested in** buying a T-shirt.

A **method** is a way of doing something.

Wendungen wie 'isn't it?' oder 'aren't you?' nennt man Bestätigungsfragen (= *question tags*). Du kannst sie mit 'oder? / nicht wahr? / gell?' übersetzen und bildest sie, indem du die Verbform aus einem bejahten Aussagesatz verneinst.
You're connected to the Internet, **aren't** you?
She can speak Chinese, **can't** she?
Harry used a search engine, **didn't** he?
The friends like each other, **don't** they?

	tablet /ˈtæblət/	(der) Block, (die) Platte
	clay /kleɪ/	(der) Lehm, (der) Ton
	printing press /ˈprɪntɪŋ pres/	(die) Druckerpresse
p. 119, 7	**rise** /raɪz/	(der) Aufstieg
	(to) **keep in touch** *(irr)* /ˌkiːp ɪn ˈtʌtʃ/	Kontakt halten, in Verbindung bleiben
	thumb /θʌm/	(der) Daumen
	once more /ˌwʌns ˈmɔː/	noch einmal
	(to) message /ˈmesɪdʒ/	eine Nachricht schicken
	uncomplicated /ʌnˈkɒmplɪˌkeɪtɪd/	unkompliziert
p. 119, 8	**habit** /ˈhæbɪt/	(die) Gewohnheit, (die) Angewohnheit
p. 120, 9	challenge /ˈtʃæləndʒ/	*hier:* (die) Wette
p. 120, 10	console /kənˈsəʊl/	(die) Konsole
p. 121, 12	**dos and don'ts** /ˌduːz ˌən ˈdəʊnts/	was man tun und was man nicht tun sollte
	magazine /ˌmægəˈziːn/	(die) Zeitschrift
	password /ˈpɑːsˌwɜːd/	(das) Passwort
	(to) **download** /ˌdaʊnˈləʊd/	herunterladen
	(to) **click on** /ˈklɪk_ɒn/	anklicken
	(to) **trust** /trʌst/	vertrauen
	anybody /ˈenibɒdi/	irgendjemand; jede(r, s)
	(to) **treat** /triːt/	behandeln
	(to) befriend /bɪˈfrend/	sich anfreunden mit
	(to) bully /ˈbʊli/	mobben
	respectful /rɪˈspektfl/	respektvoll
p. 121, 13	**summary** /ˈsʌməri/	(die) Zusammenfassung
p. 122, 14	**happy** /ˈhæpi/	zufrieden
p. 122, 15	(to) be prepared *(irr)* /ˌbiː prɪˈpeəd/	vorbereitet sein
p. 123, 16	**talk** /tɔːk/	(das) Gespräch, (der) Vortrag

thumb

A vet **treats** animals.

talk = conversation

Hier findest du alphabetisch sortiert alle Wörter aus dem vorliegenden Buch mit der Angabe der Seite *(p.)*, auf der das Wort das erste Mal vorkommt oder auf der es zum Lernwort gemacht wird. Die Zahl hinter dem Komma bezeichnet die Aufgabe auf der Seite.

Lernwörter aus den vorigen Bänden sind mit „NHG 5" oder „NHG 6" markiert.

Die **fett** gedruckten Lernwörter solltest du dir merken.

(informal) bedeutet: Dieses Wort oder dieser Ausdruck ist umgangssprachlich.

Folgende Abkürzungen werden verwendet: *(pl)* = (unregelmäßige) Mehrzahlform, *(no pl)* = keine Mehrzahlform, *(irr)* = unregelmäßiges Verb, *(AE)* = amerikanisches Englisch, L&L = Land und Leute

A

a, an /ə/eɪ, ən/ ein(e) NHG 5

a /ə/ pro NHG 6

A /eɪ/ *etwa:* Note 1, sehr gut p. 101

abbey /ˈæbi/ Abtei(kirche) p. 78

(to) **be able to do something** *(irr)* /ˌbiˌeɪbl tə ˈduː ˌsʌmθɪŋ/ etwas tun können NHG 6

about /əˈbaʊt/ über; an NHG 5; ungefähr NHG 6

(to) **be about** *(irr)* /ˌbiˌəˈbaʊt/ gehen um; handeln von NHG 5

above /əˈbʌv/ über NHG 5; oben, oberhalb p. 60, 8

(to) **go abroad** *(irr)* /ˌgəʊ‿əˈbrɔːd/ ins Ausland gehen / fahren NHG 6

absolutely /ˈæbsəluːtli/ absolut p. 8, 2

accent /ˈæksnt/ Akzent p. 80, 2

accident /ˈæksɪdnt/ Unfall p. 45, 4

by accident /ˌbaɪ ˈæksɪdnt/ zufällig; aus Versehen p. 15, 12

accidentally /ˌæksɪˈdentli/ versehentlich; zufällig p. 109, 7

across the country /əˌkrɒs ðə ˈkʌntri/ im ganzen Land p. 73, 9

(to) **act** /ækt/ handeln; spielen NHG 6

(to) **act out** /ˌækt ˈaʊt/ nachspielen; vorspielen NHG 5

action /ˈækʃn/ Handlung NHG 5

(to) **activate** /ˈæktɪveɪt/ aktivieren p. 8, 2

active /ˈæktɪv/ aktiv p. 33, 2

activity /ækˈtɪvəti/ Aktivität NHG 5

actor/actress /ˈæktə, ˈæktrəs/ Schauspieler/in NHG 6

actually /ˈæktʃuəli/ eigentlich; tatsächlich NHG 6

AD (= Anno Domini) /ˌeɪ ˈdiː, ˌænəʊ ˈdɒmɪnaɪ/ n. Chr. (= nach Christus) p. 118, 7

(to) **add** /æd/ hinzufügen NHG 5

additional /əˈdɪʃnəl/ zusätzlich p. 132

address /əˈdres/ Adresse NHG 5

adjective /ˈædʒɪktɪv/ Adjektiv NHG 6

adult /ˈædʌlt/ Erwachsene/r NHG 6

in advance /ɪnˌədˈvɑːns/ im Voraus p. 108, 6

adventure /ədˈventʃə/ Abenteuer NHG 6

advert (= ad) /ˈædvɜːt, æd/ Werbung; Anzeige p. 39, 9

(to) advertise /ˈædvətaɪz/ für etwas Werbung machen p. 63, 12

advice /ədˈvaɪs/ Rat(schlag) p. 94, 6

(to) **give advice** *(irr)* /ˌgɪvˌədˈvaɪs/ Rat geben p. 99, 15

(to) **seek advice** *(irr)* /ˌsiːkˌədˈvaɪs/ Rat suchen p. 94, 6

(to) **be afraid of** *(irr)* /ˌbiˌəˈfreɪdˌəv/ Angst haben vor NHG 6

African /ˈæfrɪkən/ Afrikaner/in; afrikanisch p. 83, 5

after /ˈɑːftə/ nach NHG 5

after that /ˌɑːftə ˈðæt/ danach p. 66, 2

afternoon /ˌɑːftəˈnuːn/ Nachmittag NHG 5

afterwards /ˈɑːftəwədz/ anschließend; später NHG 6

again /əˈgen/ wieder; noch einmal NHG 5

against /əˈgenst/ gegen NHG 6

for ages *(informal)* /fərˈeɪdʒɪz/ seit einer Ewigkeit p. 57, 3

... ago /əˈgəʊ/ vor ... NHG 6

(to) **agree** /əˈgriː/ zustimmen p. 94, 6

(to) **agree on** /əˈgriː ɒn/ sich einigen auf p. 113, 15

air force /ˈeə fɔːs/ Luftwaffe p. 85, 7

airport /ˈeəpɔːt/ Flughafen NHG 6

all /ɔːl/ alle; alles; ganz; völlig NHG 5

all around /ˌɔːl‿əˈraʊnd/ überall (in) p. 39, 10

all kinds of /ˌɔːl ˈkaɪndz‿əv/ alle möglichen NHG 6

all over /ˌɔːl‿ˈəʊvə/ überall NHG 6

all over the world /ˌɔːl‿əʊvə ðə ˈwɜːld/ auf der ganzen Welt NHG 6

All the best! /ˌɔːl ðə ˈbest/ Alles Gute! p. 94, 6

all the time /ˌɔːl ðə ˈtaɪm/ die ganze Zeit NHG 6

(to) **be allergic to** *(irr)* /ˌbiˌəˈlɜːdʒɪk tʊ/ allergisch sein auf p. 21, 5

(to) **allow** /əˈlaʊ/ erlauben p. 98, 13

(to) **be allowed (to)** *(irr)* /ˌbiˌəˈlaʊdˌtə/ erlaubt sein, dürfen NHG 6

almost /ˈɔːlməʊst/ fast; beinahe NHG 6

alone /əˈləʊn/ allein NHG 5

along /əˈlɒŋ/ entlang NHG 6

already /ɔːlˈredi/ schon; bereits NHG 5

alright /ɔːlˈraɪt/ in Ordnung p. 45, 4

also /ˈɔːlsəʊ/ auch NHG 5

although /ɔːlˈðəʊ/ obwohl NHG 6

always /ˈɔːlweɪz/ immer NHG 5

am (= ante meridiem) /ˌeɪˈem, ˌænti məˈrɪdiəm/ morgens, vormittags *(hinter Uhrzeit zwischen Mitternacht und 12 Uhr mittags)* NHG 5

amazing *(informal)* /əˈmeɪzɪŋ/ toll NHG 6

ambulance /ˈæmbjʊləns/ Krankenwagen p. 163

(to) **call an ambulance** /ˌkɔːlˌənˌˈæmbjʊləns/ einen Krankenwagen rufen p. 45, 4

American /əˈmerɪkən/ Amerikaner/in; amerikanisch p. 105, 2

ancient /'eɪnʃnt/ alt; antik NHG 6

and /ænd/ und NHG 5

and so on /ænd 'səʊ_ɒn/ und so weiter NHG 6

angry /'æŋgri/ zornig, wütend NHG 6

animal /'ænɪml/ Tier NHG 5

ankle /'æŋkl/ (Fuß)knöchel p. 46, 5

(to) **announce** /ə'naʊns/ bekannt geben p. 53

announcement /ə'naʊnsmənt/ Mitteilung; Durchsage NHG 6

annoyed /ə'nɔɪd/ genervt NHG 6

annoying /ə'nɔɪɪŋ/ ärgerlich p. 91, 2

anonymous(ly) /ə'nɒnɪməs, ə'nɒnɪməsli/ anonym p. 94, 6

another /ə'nʌðə/ noch ein/e; ein anderer/ein anderes/eine andere NHG 5

answer /'ɑːnsə/ Antwort NHG 5

(to) **answer** /'ɑːnsə/ (be)antworten NHG 5

antibiotic /ˌæntibaɪ'ɒtɪk/ Antibiotikum p. 109, 7

any /'eni/ (irgend)ein(e) NHG 5

any more /ˌeni 'mɔː/ noch mehr p. 24, 8

anybody /'enibɒdi/ irgendjemand; jede(r, s) p. 121, 12

anyone /'eni,wʌn/ jede(r, s); (irgend)jemand p. 67, 2

anything /'eni,θɪŋ/ irgendetwas NHG 5

anyway /'eniweɪ/ jedenfalls NHG 6

anywhere /'eni,weə/ überall; irgendwo p. 56, 2

apart /ə'pɑːt/ auseinander NHG 6

(to) **apologize (= apologise)** /ə'pɒlədʒaɪz/ sich entschuldigen p. 95, 6

(to) **appear** /ə'pɪə/ erscheinen, auftauchen p. 108, 7

apple /'æpl/ Apfel NHG 5

(to) **apply** /ə'plaɪ/ anwenden p. 8, 2

appointment /ə'pɔɪntmənt/ Termin p. 42, 1

April /'eɪprəl/ April NHG 5

area /'eəriə/ Gebiet; Region NHG 5

arena /ə'riːnə/ Arena; Stadion p. 77

argument /'ɑːgjʊmənt/ Streit; Argument p. 90, 2

armour /'ɑːmə/ Rüstung p. 66, 2

around /ə'raʊnd/ um; herum; umher NHG 6; ungefähr p. 118, 7

from (all) around the world /frəm ˌɔːl_əˌraʊnd ðə 'wɜːld/ aus der (ganzen) Welt p. 11, 6

(to) **arrive** /ə'raɪv/ ankommen NHG 5

art /ɑːt/ Kunst NHG 5

article /'ɑːtɪkl/ Artikel NHG 5

arts and crafts /ˌɑːts_ən 'krɑːfts/ Basteln; Bastelarbeit p. 56, 2

as /əz/ als; wie; während NHG 5

as ... as /əz æz/ so ... wie NHG 6

as soon as /əz_'suːn_əz/ so bald wie p. 53

as well /ˌəz_'wel/ auch NHG 6

Asia /'eɪʒə/ Asien p. 30

(to) **ask** /ɑːsk/ fragen; bitten NHG 5

(to) **ask for advice** /ˌɑːsk fər_əd'vaɪs/ um Rat bitten p. 99, 15

(to) **ask questions** /ˌɑːsk 'kwestʃnz/ Fragen stellen NHG 5

aspect /'æspekt/ Aspekt; Gesichtspunkt p. 69, 5

assembly /ə'sembli/ (Schüler)versammlung NHG 5

at /æt/ an; in; bei; um NHG 5

at first /ˌæt 'fɜːst/ zuerst NHG 6

at home /ˌæt 'həʊm/ zu Hause NHG 5

at least /ˌæt 'liːst/ mindestens; wenigstens NHG 6

at that time /ˌæt_'ðæt_taɪm/ zu jener Zeit p. 87, 8

at the doctor's /ˌæt_ðə 'dɒktəz/ beim Arzt/bei der Ärztin p. 31

at the same time /ˌæt_ðə ˌseɪm 'taɪm/ gleichzeitig; zur gleichen Zeit p. 56, 2

at/in the back /ˌæt/ˌɪn ðə 'bæk/ hinten NHG 5

at/in the front /ˌæt/ˌɪn ðə 'frʌnt/ vorne NHG 6

athlete /'æθliːt/ Athlet/in p. 53

(to) **do athletics** (irr) /ˌduː_ˌæθ'letɪks/ Leichtathletik machen NHG 5

atmosphere /'ætməs,fɪə/ Atmosphäre p. 19, 2

(to) **attend** /ə'tend/ besuchen p. 73, 9

(to) **draw attention to** (irr) /ˌdrɔː_ə'tenʃn tə/ Aufmerksamkeit lenken auf p. 70, 6

(to) **pay attention (to)** (irr) /ˌpeɪ_ə'tenʃn tʊ/ aufpassen; achten auf NHG 6

attraction /ə'trækʃn/ Attraktion NHG 6

August /'ɔːgəst/ August NHG 5

aunt /ɑːnt/ Tante NHG 5

authentic /ɔː'θentɪk/ authentisch p. 76

author /'ɔːθə/ Autor/in p. 104, 1

autumn /'ɔːtəm/ Herbst NHG 6

(to) **avoid** /ə'vɔɪd/ meiden; vermeiden p. 56, 2

award ceremony /ə'wɔːd ˌserəməni/ Preisverleihung p. 53

away /ə'weɪ/ weg NHG 5

(to) **go away** (irr) /ˌgəʊ_ə'weɪ/ weggehen; verschwinden NHG 6

B

back /bæk/ zurück NHG 5; Rücken p. 99, 15

at/in the back /ˌæt/ˌɪn ðə 'bæk/ hinten NHG 5

background /'bæk,graʊnd/ Hintergrund NHG 6

bacon /'beɪkən/ Schinkenspeck p. 128

bacteria (pl) /bæk'tɪəriə/ Bakterien p. 109, 7

bad /bæd/ schlecht; schlimm NHG 5

bad /bæd/ hier: stark p. 42, 1

bag /bæg/ Tasche; Tüte NHG 5

bagpipes (pl) /'bæg,paɪps/ Dudelsack p. 71, 6

(to) **bake** /beɪk/ backen NHG 5

baker /'beɪkə/ Bäcker/in NHG 6

baker /'beɪkə/ hier: Backmaschine p. 111, 11

balloon /bə'luːn/ Luftballon NHG 5

banana /bə'nɑːnə/ Banane NHG 5

bandage /'bændɪdʒ/ Verband p. 46, 5

(to) **bang one's head** /ˌbæŋ wʌnz 'hed/ sich den Kopf anschlagen p. 45, 4

bangers and mash /ˌbæŋəz_ən 'mæʃ/ Würstchen mit Kartoffelbrei L&L 1

Bangladesh /ˌbæŋglə'deʃ/ Bangladesch p. 30

barely /'beəli/ kaum p. 77

bargain /'bɑːgɪn/ Schnäppchen p. 60, 8

basic /ˈbeɪsɪk/ grundlegend; wesentlich p. 105, 2

basil /ˈbæzl/ Basilikum p. 131

bat /bæt/ Schläger p. 39, 10; Fledermaus p. 127

bathroom /ˈbɑːθˌruːm/ Badezimmer NHG 5

battle /ˈbætl/ Kampf p. 67, 2

battlefield /ˈbætlˌfiːld/ Schlachtfeld p. 29

BC (= before Christ) /ˌbiː ˈsiː, bɪˌfɔːˈkraɪst/ v. Chr. (= vor Christus) p. 118, 7

(to) **be** (irr) /biː/ sein NHG 5

(to) **be a shame** (irr) /ˌbi ə ˈʃeɪm/ schade sein p. 86, 8

(to) **be able to do something** (irr) /biˌeɪbl tə ˈduː ˌsʌmθɪŋ/ etwas tun können NHG 6

(to) **be about** (irr) /ˌbi əˈbaʊt/ gehen um; handeln von NHG 5

(to) be about to do something (irr) /ˌbi əˌbaʊt tə ˈduː ˌsʌmθɪŋ/ im Begriff sein, etwas zu tun p. 52

(to) **be afraid of** (irr) /ˌbi əˈfreɪd əv/ Angst haben vor NHG 6

(to) be alive (irr) /ˌbi əˈlaɪv/ leben p. 102

(to) **be allergic to** (irr) /ˌbi əˈlɜːdʒɪk tʊ/ allergisch sein auf p. 21, 5

(to) **be allowed (to)** (irr) /ˌbi əˈlaʊd tə/ erlaubt sein, dürfen NHG 6

(to) **be born** (irr) /ˌbi ˈbɔːn/ geboren werden p. 40, 12

(to) be connected with (irr) /ˌbi kəˈnektɪd wɪð/ in Verbindung gebracht werden p. 78

(to) be done with (informal, irr) /ˌbi ˈdʌn wɪð/ fertig sein mit p. 117, 6

(to) be estimated (irr) /ˌbiˈestɪmeɪtəd/ geschätzt werden p. 109, 7

(to) **be good at doing something** (irr) /ˌbi ˈɡʊd ət ˈduːɪŋ ˌsʌmθɪŋ/ gut darin sein, etwas zu tun NHG 5

(to) **be good at something** (irr) /ˌbi ˈɡʊd æt ˌsʌmθɪŋ/ gut in etwas sein NHG 6

(to) **be (good/great) fun** (irr) /ˌbi ˌɡʊd/ˌɡreɪt ˈfʌn/ (viel/großen) Spaß machen NHG 5

(to) **be homesick** (irr) /ˌbi ˈhəʊmˌsɪk/ Heimweh haben p. 85, 7

(to) **be interested in** (irr) /ˌbiˈɪntrəstɪd ˌɪn/ interessiert sein an p. 115, 3

(to) be left out (irr) /ˌbi ˌleftˈaʊt/ ausgeschlossen werden p. 94, 6

(to) **be located** (irr) /ˌbi ləˈkeɪtɪd/ gelegen sein p. 108, 6

(to) be lost (irr) /ˌbi ˈlɒst/ sich verirrt haben p. 126

(to) be made up of (irr) /ˌbi ˌmeɪd ˈʌp əv/ zusammengesetzt sein aus p. 54

(to) be missing (irr) /ˌbi ˈmɪsɪŋ/ fehlen p. 124

(to) be off (informal, irr) /ˌbi ˈɒf/ hier: weg sein p. 52

(to) **be one's turn** (irr) /ˌbi wʌnz ˈtɜːn/ an der Reihe sein NHG 5

(to) be prepared (irr) /ˌbi prɪˈpeəd/ vorbereitet sein p. 122, 15

(to) **be right** (irr) /ˌbi ˈraɪt/ recht haben NHG 5

(to) be up for something (informal, irr) /ˌbiˌʌp fɔː ˈsʌmθɪŋ/ Lust zu etwas haben p. 91, 2

(to) be up to something (irr) /ˌbiˌʌp tə ˈsʌmθɪŋ/ etwas vorhaben p. 57, 3

(to) **be worth** (irr) /ˌbi ˈwɜːθ/ (sich) lohnen; wert sein p. 71, 6

(to) **be wrong** (irr) /ˌbi ˈrɒŋ/ im Unrecht sein p. 98, 12

(to) **be wrong (with)** (irr) /ˌbi ˈrɒŋ wɪθ/ nicht in Ordnung sein (mit) p. 48, 8

beach /biːtʃ/ Strand NHG 5

beak /biːk/ Schnabel p. 127

beak-like /ˈbiːkˌlaɪk/ schnabelähnlich p. 127

beard /bɪəd/ Bart p. 67, 2

beautiful /ˈbjuːtəfl/ schön NHG 5

because /bɪˈkɒz/ weil; da NHG 5

because of /bɪˈkɒz əv/ wegen p. 80, 2

(to) **become** (irr) /bɪˈkʌm/ werden NHG 6

(to) become infected (irr) /bɪˌkʌmˌɪnˈfektɪd/ sich infizieren p. 109, 7

bed /bed/ Bett NHG 5

bedroom /ˈbedruːm/ Schlafzimmer NHG 5

bee /biː/ Biene NHG 6

beef /biːf/ Rindfleisch p. 23, 7

before /bɪˈfɔː/ bevor; zuvor, vorher; vor NHG 5

(to) befriend /bɪˈfrend/ sich anfreunden mit p. 121, 12

(to) **begin** (irr) /bɪˈɡɪn/ anfangen; beginnen NHG 5

beginning /bɪˈɡɪnɪŋ/ Anfang; Beginn NHG 6

(to) **behave** /bɪˈheɪv/ sich verhalten, sich benehmen p. 28

behind /bɪˈhaɪnd/ hinter NHG 5

(to) **believe (in)** /bɪˈliːv ˌɪn/ glauben (an) NHG 6

bell /bel/ Glocke NHG 6

(to) **belong (to)** /bɪˈlɒŋ/ gehören (zu) p. 40, 11

below /bɪˈləʊ/ unten, unter NHG 6

belt /belt/ Gürtel p. 109, 7

best /best/ beste(r, s) NHG 5

All the best! /ˌɔːl ðə ˈbest/ Alles Gute! p. 94, 6

the best /ðə ˈbest/ der/die/das beste NHG 5; am besten NHG 6

(to) **like best** /ˌlaɪk ˈbest/ am liebsten mögen NHG 5

better /ˈbetə/ besser NHG 6

(to) **get better** (irr) /ˌɡet ˈbetə/ besser / gesund werden p. 37, 7

between /bɪˈtwiːn/ zwischen NHG 5

BFF (= best friends forever) (informal) /ˌbiˌefˈef, ˌbest ˌfrendz fərˈevə/ allerbeste Freunde/Freundinnen p. 8, 2

bhaji /ˈbɑːdʒi/ indisches Gericht p. 23, 7

bicycle bell /ˈbaɪsɪkl bel/ Fahrradklingel p. 59, 7

(to) biff (informal) /bɪf/ hauen, schlagen p. 39, 10

big /bɪɡ/ groß NHG 5

bike /baɪk/ Fahrrad NHG 6

(to) **ride a bike** (irr) /ˌraɪd ə ˈbaɪk/ Fahrrad fahren NHG 5

bill /bɪl/ Rechnung p. 24, 8

billion /ˈbɪljən/ Milliarde p. 147

bin /bɪn/ Abfalleimer NHG 5

bird /bɜːd/ Vogel NHG 6

bird of prey /ˌbɜːd əv ˈpreɪ/ Raubvogel p. 67, 2

birthday /'bɜːθdeɪ/ Geburtstag NHG 5

Happy birthday (to you)! /ˌhæpi 'bɜːθdeɪ tʊ juː/ Herzlichen Glückwunsch zum Geburtstag! NHG 5

birthplace /'bɜːθˌpleɪs/ Geburtsort p. 149

biscuit /'bɪskɪt/ Keks NHG 5

bit /bɪt/ Teil; Stück p. 125

a bit /ə 'bɪt/ ein bisschen NHG 5

black /blæk/ schwarz NHG 5

(to) **bleed** *(irr)* /bliːd/ bluten p. 43, 1

blood /blʌd/ Blut NHG 6

blue /bluː/ blau NHG 5

board /bɔːd/ Tafel; Brett NHG 5

board game /'bɔːd ɡeɪm/ Brettspiel NHG 6

boat /bəʊt/ Boot NHG 5

body /'bɒdi/ Körper NHG 5

(to) boil /bɔɪl/ kochen *(Flüssigkeit)* p. 160

(to) **bring to the boil** *(irr)* /ˌbrɪŋ tə ðə 'bɔɪl/ zum Kochen bringen p. 12, 7

bone /bəʊn/ Knochen p. 105, 2

book /bʊk/ Buch NHG 5

(to) **book** /bʊk/ buchen, reservieren NHG 6

bookshelf /'bʊkˌʃelf/ Bücherregal NHG 5

boot /buːt/ Kofferraum p. 76

(to) boot /buːt/ einen Tritt geben p. 39, 10

bored /bɔːd/ gelangweilt NHG 6

boring /'bɔːrɪŋ/ langweilig NHG 5

(to) **borrow** /'bɒrəʊ/ (aus)leihen NHG 5

both /bəʊθ/ beide p. 25, 11

(to) **bother** /'bɒðə/ sich Mühe geben p. 101

bottle /'bɒtl/ Flasche NHG 5

(to) **bounce** /baʊns/ (auf)springen p. 39, 10

bowl /bəʊl/ Schüssel; Schale NHG 6

box /bɒks/ Kasten; Kiste NHG 5

boy /bɔɪ/ Junge NHG 5

bracket /'brækɪt/ Klammer p. 13, 7

branch /brɑːntʃ/ Zweig; Ast p. 16, 16

bravely /breɪvli/ mutig p. 78

bread /bred/ Brot p. 15, 11

break /breɪk/ Pause NHG 5

(to) **break** *(irr)* /breɪk/ brechen, zerbrechen; kaputt machen NHG 6

breakfast /'brekfəst/ Frühstück NHG 5

breathtaking /'breθˌteɪkɪŋ/ atemberaubend p. 67, 2

bridge /brɪdʒ/ Brücke NHG 6

bright, brightly /braɪt,'braɪtli/ hell; strahlend NHG 6

brilliant /'brɪljənt/ genial, klasse NHG 5

(to) **bring** *(irr)* /brɪŋ/ mitbringen NHG 5

(to) **bring over** *(irr)* /ˌbrɪŋ_'əʊvə/ herbeibringen p. 24, 8

(to) bring to the boil *(irr)* /ˌbrɪŋ tə ðə 'bɔɪl/ zum Kochen bringen p. 12, 7

Britain /'brɪtn/ Großbritannien NHG 6

British /'brɪtɪʃ/ britisch NHG 6

brochure /'brəʊʃə/ Broschüre p. 111, 10

broken /'brəʊkən/ gebrochen p. 42, 1; zerbrochen; kaputt p. 64, 13

brother /'brʌðə/ Bruder NHG 5

brown /braʊn/ braun NHG 5

(to) **brush one's teeth** /ˌbrʌʃ wʌnz 'tiːθ/ sich die Zähne putzen NHG 5

bubble and squeak /ˌbʌbl_ən 'skwiːk/ *Resteessen aus gebratenem Kartoffelbrei und zerstampftem Gemüse* L&L 1

buddy *(informal)* /'bʌdi/ Kumpel p. 38, 8

(to) **build** *(irr)* /bɪld/ bauen NHG 5

building /'bɪldɪŋ/ Gebäude NHG 6

(to) **bully** /'bʊli/ mobben p. 121, 12

burdock /'bɜːdɒk/ Große Klette p. 127

burnt /bɜːnt/ verbrannt, angebrannt p. 18, 2

(to) **bury** /'beri/ begraben; vergraben p. 78

business /'bɪznəs/ Geschäft; Handel p. 89, 13

busy /'bɪzi/ beschäftigt NHG 5; bewegt, ereignisreich; belebt; verkehrsreich NHG 6

but /bʌt/ aber NHG 5; außer NHG 6

(to) button /'bʌtən/ knöpfen p. 108, 7

(to) **buy** *(irr)* /baɪ/ kaufen NHG 5

(to) **buzz** /bʌz/ summen, brummen p. 78

by /baɪ/ von; mit NHG 5; bei, an; *hier:* (spätestens) bis NHG 6

by *(+ Verbform mit -ing)* /baɪ/ indem NHG 6

by accident /ˌbaɪ_'æksɪdnt/ zufällig; aus Versehen p. 15, 12

by heart /ˌbaɪ 'hɑːt/ auswendig p. 14, 10

by ourselves /ˌbaɪ aʊə'selvz/ (wir) selbst p. 125

bye /baɪ/ tschüs(s) NHG 5

C

C /siː/ *etwa:* Note 3, befriedigend p. 101

cabbage /'kæbɪdʒ/ Kohl p. 12, 7

tossing the caber /ˌtɒsɪŋ ðə 'keɪbə/ Baumstammwerfen p. 71, 6

cage /keɪdʒ/ Käfig NHG 5

cake /keɪk/ Kuchen NHG 5

calculator /'kælkjʊˌleɪtə/ Taschenrechner NHG 5

calendar /'kælɪndə/ Kalender NHG 5

call /kɔːl/ Anruf; Gespräch p. 96, 9

(to) **call** /kɔːl/ anrufen NHG 6

(to) **call an ambulance** /ˌkɔːl_ən_'æmbjʊləns/ einen Krankenwagen rufen p. 45, 4

(to) be called /ˌbiː 'kɔːld/ heißen, genannt werden NHG 5

(to) **calm down** /ˌkɑːm 'daʊn/ (sich) beruhigen p. 46, 5

camera /'kæmrə/ Kamera; Fotoapparat NHG 6

camp /kæmp/ (Zelt)lager NHG 6

camping gear /'kæmpɪŋ ˌɡɪə/ Campingausrüstung p. 76

camping site /'kæmpɪŋ ˌsaɪt/ Campingplatz p. 70, 6

can /kæn/ können NHG 5; Dose; Büchse p. 12, 7

can't (= cannot) /kɑːnt, 'kænɒt/ nicht können NHG 5

candle /'kændl/ Kerze NHG 5

cap /kæp/ Mütze NHG 6

capital /'kæpɪtl/ Hauptstadt p. 147

caption /'kæpʃn/ Bildunterschrift p. 26, 12

car /kɑː/ Auto NHG 5

car boot sale /ˌka: ˈbu:t seɪl/ *Kofferraum-Flohmarkt* p. 55
carbohydrate /ˌka:bəʊˈhaɪdreɪt/ Kohlenhydrat p. 53
card /ka:d/ Karte NHG 5
cardamom /ˈka:dəməm/ Kardamom p. 30
(to) **take care (of)** *(irr)* /ˌteɪk ˈkeər ˌəv/ sich kümmern um NHG 6
(to) care about /ˈkeər ˌəˌbaʊt/ sich etwas machen aus p. 32, 1
careful /ˈkeəfl/ vorsichtig NHG 6
carefully /ˈkeəfli/ vorsichtig NHG 6
Caribbean /ˌkærɪˈbiən/ karibisch p. 70, 6
carnival /ˈka:nɪvl/ Volksfest, Karneval p. 72, 8
carrot /ˈkærət/ Möhre; Karotte NHG 5
(to) carry /ˈkæri/ tragen p. 130
case /keɪs/ Fall NHG 6
cash /kæʃ/ Geld; Bargeld p. 24, 8
cast /ka:st/ Gips p. 42, 1
castle /ˈka:sl/ Burg; Schloss NHG 6
cat /kæt/ Katze NHG 5
(to) **catch** *(irr)* /kætʃ/ fangen NHG 5
(to) **catch a cold** *(irr)* /ˌkætʃ ə ˈkəʊld/ sich erkälten p. 42, 1
(to) catch a plane *(irr)* /ˌkætʃ ə ˈpleɪn/ ein Flugzeug nehmen p. 102
category /ˈkætəgri/ Kategorie NHG 6
cathedral /kəˈθi:drəl/ Kathedrale p. 124
(to) cause /kɔ:z/ verursachen p. 127
charity /ˈtʃærəti/ Wohltätigkeitsorganisation p. 57, 3
cayenne pepper /ˌkeɪen ˈpepə/ Cayennepfeffer p. 17, 17
(to) **celebrate** /ˈseləˌbreɪt/ feiern NHG 6
celebration /ˌseləˈbreɪʃn/ Feier NHG 6
centre /ˈsentə/ Zentrum NHG 6
shopping centre /ˈʃɒpɪŋ ˌsentə/ Einkaufszentrum NHG 5
century /ˈsentʃəri/ Jahrhundert NHG 6
certainly /ˈsɜ:tnli/ sicher; gerne p. 22, 6
chain /tʃeɪn/ Kette NHG 6
chair /tʃeə/ Stuhl NHG 5

challenge /ˈtʃæləndʒ/ Herausforderung NHG 5
challenge /ˈtʃæləndʒ/ *hier:* Wette p. 120, 9
chance /tʃa:ns/ Möglichkeit; Gelegenheit p. 36, 7
change /tʃeɪndʒ/ Wechselgeld NHG 5
(to) **change** /tʃeɪndʒ/ (sich) ändern; verändern NHG 6
(to) **change lines** /ˌtʃeɪndʒ ˈlaɪnz/ umsteigen NHG 6
(to) **change one's mind** /ˌtʃeɪndʒ wʌnz ˈmaɪnd/ seine Meinung ändern NHG 6
character /ˈkærəktə/ Figur; Charakter NHG 6
charity /ˈtʃærəti/ Wohltätigkeitsorganisation p. 56, 2
charity run /ˈtʃærəti rʌn/ Wohltätigkeitslauf p. 56, 2
charity shop /ˈtʃærəti ʃɒp/ *Laden, in dem gebrauchte Dinge zu Wohltätigkeitszwecken verkauft werden* p. 61, 8
(to) **chat** /tʃæt/ plaudern; chatten p. 94, 6
cheap /tʃi:p/ billig p. 18, 2
check /tʃek/ Überprüfung; Kontrolle p. 38, 8
(to) **check** /tʃek/ überprüfen; kontrollieren NHG 5
(to) **check out** *(informal)* /ˌtʃek ˈaʊt/ sich ansehen; ausprobieren p. 66, 2
(to) check out /ˌtʃek ˈaʊt/ auschecken p. 27, 14
check-up /ˈtʃek ʌp/ Untersuchung p. 46, 5
(to) **cheer** /tʃɪə/ jubeln p. 53
(to) **cheer somebody on** /ˌtʃɪə ˌsʌmbədi ˈɒn/ jemanden anfeuern p. 52
(to) **cheer up** /ˌtʃɪər ˈʌp/ aufmuntern, aufheitern p. 48, 7
cheerful /ˈtʃɪəfl/ fröhlich, vergnügt p. 70, 6
cheese /tʃi:z/ Käse NHG 5
chemistry club /ˈkemɪstri klʌb/ Chemie-AG p. 93, 5
chess /tʃes/ Schach p. 35, 6
chicken /ˈtʃɪkɪn/ Huhn NHG 6

(chicken) tikka masala, (chicken) tikka /ˌtʃɪkɪn ˌti:kə məˈsa:lə, ˌtʃɪkɪn ˈti:kə/ *britisch-indisches (Hühnchen-)Gericht* p. 11, 6
chickpea /ˈtʃɪkˌpi:/ Kichererbse p. 12, 7
child *(pl* **children)** /tʃaɪld, ˈtʃɪldrən/ Kind NHG 5
childhood /ˈtʃaɪldˌhʊd/ Kindheit p. 86, 8
chilli *(pl* chillies) /ˈtʃɪli, ˈtʃɪliz/ Chili; Peperoni p. 23, 7
Chinese /tʃaɪˈni:z/ Chinese/ Chinesin; chinesisch NHG 6
chips *(pl)* /tʃɪps/ Pommes frites NHG 5
chocolate /ˈtʃɒklət/ Schokolade NHG 5
(to) **choose** *(irr)* /tʃu:z/ wählen; sich entscheiden NHG 5
(to) **chop** /tʃɒp/ hacken p. 13, 8
chore /tʃɔ:/ lästige Aufgabe; Hausarbeit NHG 5
Christian /ˈkrɪstʃən/ Christ/in; christlich NHG 6
Christmas /ˈkrɪsməs/ Weihnachten NHG 6
church /tʃɜ:tʃ/ Kirche NHG 6
chutney /ˈtʃʌtni/ *würzige indische Soße* p. 63, 11
cinema /ˈsɪnəmə/ Kino NHG 5
cinnamon /ˈsɪnəmən/ Zimt p. 17, 17
city /ˈsɪti/ Stadt; Innenstadt NHG 5
city centre /ˌsɪti ˈsentə/ Innenstadt p. 28
class /kla:s/ Klasse; Unterrichtsstunde NHG 5
classmate /ˈkla:sˌmeɪt/ Klassenkamerad/in; Mitschüler/in NHG 5
classroom /ˈkla:sˌru:m/ Klassenzimmer NHG 5
clay /kleɪ/ Lehm; Ton p. 118, 7
clean /kli:n/ sauber NHG 5
(to) **clean (up)** /kli:n, ˌkli:n ˈʌp/ sauber machen NHG 5
cleaning skates *(pl)* /ˈkli:nɪŋ ˌskeɪts/ *Reinigungsskates* p. 111, 11
clear /klɪə/ klar; deutlich NHG 6
(to) clear up /ˌklɪər ˈʌp/ aufräumen p. 73, 9
clearly /ˈklɪəli/ klar; deutlich NHG 6
clever /ˈklevə/ klug; schlau p. 126

(to) **click on** /'klɪk‿ɒn/ anklicken
   p. 121, 12

(to) **climb** /klaɪm/ auf etwas
   (hinauf)steigen; klettern NHG 5

climbing /'klaɪmɪŋ/ Klettern p. 32, 1

clock /klɒk/ Uhr NHG 5

(to) **close** /kləʊz/ zumachen;
   schließen NHG 5

closed /kləʊzd/ geschlossen
   NHG 6

clothes *(pl)* /kləʊðz/ Kleider;
   Kleidung NHG 5

clothing /'kləʊðɪŋ/ Kleidung p. 76

club /klʌb/ AG; Klub NHG 5

coach /kəʊtʃ/ Trainer/in p. 45, 4

coconut cream /'kəʊkə,nʌt kriːm/
   Kokosmilch p. 23, 7

coffee /'kɒfi/ Kaffee NHG 5

coffee grinder /'kɒfi ,graɪndə/
   Kaffeemühle p. 60, 8

cold /kəʊld/ kalt NHG 5; Erkältung
   p. 42, 1

(to) **catch a cold** *(irr)* /,kætʃ‿ə
   'kəʊld/ sich erkälten p. 42, 1

(to) **collect** /kə'lekt/ sammeln NHG 5

collection /kə'lekʃn/ Sammlung
   NHG 6

colony /'kɒləni/ Kolonie p. 30

colour /'kʌlə/ Farbe NHG 5

colourful /'kʌləfl/ farbenfroh; bunt
   p. 70, 6

combat arena /'kɒmbæt‿ə,riːnə/
   Wettkampfarena p. 66, 2

combination /,kɒmbɪ'neɪʃn/
   Kombination; Mischung NHG 6

(to) **come** *(irr)* /kʌm/ kommen
   NHG 5

(to) **come back** *(irr)* /,kʌm 'bæk/
   zurückkommen NHG 5

(to) come by *(irr)* /,kʌm 'baɪ/
   vorbeikommen p. 77

(to) **come in** *(irr)* /,kʌm‿'ɪn/
   hereinkommen p. 42, 1

Come on! /,kʌm‿'ɒn/ Komm(t)
   schon! p. 39, 10

(to) come together *(irr)* /,kʌm
   tə'geðə/ zusammenkommen p. 54

comfort food /'kʌmfət fuːd/
   Wohlfühlessen p. 9, 2

comfortable /'kʌmftəbl/ bequem
   p. 109, 7

coming soon /,kʌmɪŋ 'suːn/ in Kürze
   erscheinend p. 67, 2

command /kə'mɑːnd/ Befehl NHG 5

(to) **comment on** /'kɒment‿ɒn/
   kommentieren NHG 6

commercial /kə'mɜːʃl/ kommerziell,
   profitorientiert NHG 6

(to) **have in common** *(irr)* /,hæv‿ɪn
   'kɒmən/ gemeinsam haben NHG 6

(to) **communicate** /kə'mjuːnɪkeɪt/
   kommunizieren, sprechen p. 95, 6

communication /kə,mjuːnɪ'keɪʃn/
   Verständigung; Kommunikation
   p. 103

community /kə'mjuːnəti/ Gemein-
   schaft, Gemeinde p. 81, 2

company /'kʌmpni/ Firma; Unter-
   nehmen p. 97, 11

(to) **compare** /kəm'peə/ vergleichen
   NHG 6

comparison /kəm'pærɪsn/ Vergleich
   NHG 6

(to) **compete** /kəm'piːt/ an einem
   Wettkampf teilnehmen; kämpfen
   p. 36, 7

(to) compete in /kəm'piːt‿ɪn/ teilnehmen an p. 53

competition /,kɒmpə'tɪʃn/ Wettbewerb NHG 5

competitive /kəm'petətɪv/ *von
   Konkurrenzdenken geprägt*
   p. 35, 6

complete /kəm'pliːt/ vollständig,
   komplett p. 99, 15

(to) **complete** /kəm'pliːt/
   vervollständigen NHG 5

completely /kəm'pliːtli/ völlig,
   absolut NHG 6

compromise /'kɒmprəmaɪz/
   Kompromiss NHG 6

con /kɒn/ Nachteil; Kontra NHG 6

(to) **concentrate** /'kɒnsn,treɪt/ sich
   konzentrieren p. 35, 6

concept /'kɒnsept/ Entwurf;
   Konzept NHG 6

concert /'kɒnsət/ Konzert NHG 6

conditional (clause) /kən'dɪʃnəl klɔːz/
   Konditional(satz) p. 44

conflict /'kɒnflɪkt/ Konflikt NHG 6

(to) **connect** /kə'nekt/ verbinden
   p. 84, 6

connection /kə'nekʃn/ Verbindung
   p. 146

(to) **conquer** /'kɒŋkə/ erobern p. 66, 2

(to) **consist of** /kən'sɪst‿əv/
   bestehen aus p. 54

console /kən'səʊl/ Konsole p. 76

construction /kən'strʌkʃn/ Bau
   p. 108, 7

(to) **contact** /'kɒntækt/ sich in
   Verbindung setzen mit NHG 6

(to) **contain** /kən'teɪn/ enthalten
   p. 63, 11

container /kən'teɪnə/ Behälter
   p. 136

content /'kɒntent/ Inhalt p. 67, 2

(to) **continue to do** /kən,tɪnjuː tə
   'duː/ weiter(hin) tun, nach wie vor
   tun p. 125

(to) control /kən'trəʊl/ kontrollieren;
   steuern p. 30

conversation /,kɒnvə'seɪʃn/
   Gespräch; Unterhaltung p. 26, 13

(to) **cook** /kʊk/ kochen NHG 5;
   braten, backen NHG 6

cook-along video /'kʊk‿ə,lɒŋ ,vɪdiəʊ/
   Mitmach-Koch-Video p. 12, 7

cookbook /'kʊk,bʊk/ Kochbuch
   p. 16, 14

cooked /kʊkt/ gekocht p. 23, 7

cooker /'kʊkə/ Herd p. 17, 17

cooking /'kʊkɪŋ/ Kochen; Koch-
   NHG 5

(to) **do the cooking** *(irr)* /,duː ðə
   'kʊkɪŋ/ kochen NHG 5

cool /kuːl/ kühl; kalt p. 104, 1

(to) **copy** /'kɒpi/ abschreiben NHG 5;
   kopieren p. 117, 6

coriander /,kɒri'ændə/ Koriander
   p. 17, 17

corner /'kɔːnə/ Ecke NHG 6

correct /kə'rekt/ richtig, korrekt;
   korrigieren NHG 5

(to) **cost** *(irr)* /kɒst/ kosten NHG 5

costume /'kɒstjuːm/ Kostüm NHG 6

cosy /'kəʊzi/ gemütlich p. 19, 2

cotton /'kɒtn/ Baumwolle;
   Baumwoll- p. 125

cough /kɒf/ Husten p. 42, 1

could /kʊd/ könnte(st, n, t) NHG 5;
   Vergangenheitsform von can
   NHG 6

counsellor /ˈkaʊnslə/ Berater/in p. 78

(to) **count** /kaʊnt/ zählen p. 108, 7

country /ˈkʌntri/ Land NHG 6

across the country /əˌkrɒs ðə ˈkʌntri/ im ganzen Land p. 73, 9

countryside /ˈkʌntriˌsaɪd/ Land; Landschaft NHG 6

a couple of /ə ˈkʌpl̩ əv/ einige, ein paar NHG 6

course /kɔːs/ Kurs NHG 6

course /kɔːs/ Gang p. 28

court /kɔːt/ Platz NHG 5

cousin /ˈkʌzn̩/ Cousin/e NHG 5

(to) **cover** /ˈkʌvə/ bedecken NHG 6

cow /kaʊ/ Kuh NHG 6

cracker /ˈkrækə/ Kräcker p. 23, 7

arts and crafts /ˌɑːts ən ˈkrɑːfts/ Basteln; Bastelarbeit p. 56, 2

(to) crash into /ˈkræʃˌɪntʊ/ zusammenstoßen mit p. 125

cream /kriːm/ Sahne p. 16, 14

coconut cream /ˈkəʊkəˌnʌt kriːm/ Kokosmilch p. 23, 7

(to) **create** /kriˈeɪt/ erschaffen; erzeugen NHG 5

creative /kriˈeɪtɪv/ kreativ NHG 5

cricket /ˈkrɪkɪt/ Kricket p. 162

(to) **cross** /krɒs/ überqueren NHG 6

crowd /kraʊd/ Menschenmenge p. 56, 2

crowded /ˈkraʊdɪd/ überfüllt p. 57, 3

crumb /krʌm/ Krümel p. 12, 7

(to) **cry** /kraɪ/ weinen; schreien NHG 6

cucumber /ˈkjuːˌkʌmbə/ Salatgurke p. 8, 2

cue card /ˈkjuː kɑːd/ *Stichwortkarte* NHG 6

culture /ˈkʌltʃə/ Kultur NHG 6

cumin /ˈkjuːmɪn/ Kreuzkümmel p. 17, 17

cup /kʌp/ Tasse NHG 5

cupboard /ˈkʌbəd/ Schrank p. 12, 7

curious /ˈkjʊəriəs/ neugierig p. 30

curry /ˈkʌri/ Curry(gericht) p. 8, 1

curtain /ˈkɜːtn̩/ Vorhang p. 60, 8

customer /ˈkʌstəmə/ Kunde/ Kundin NHG 6

(to) **cut** *(irr)* /kʌt/ schneiden NHG 6

(to) cut off *(irr)* /ˌkʌt ˈɒf/ abschneiden p. 77

cute /kjuːt/ süß; niedlich p. 86, 8

(to) **cycle** /ˈsaɪkl̩/ Rad fahren, radeln NHG 6

(to) **go cycling** *(irr)* /ˌgəʊ ˈsaɪklɪŋ/ Rad fahren gehen NHG 6

D

D /diː/ *etwa:* Note 4, ausreichend p. 91, 2

dad /dæd/ Papa; Vati NHG 5

daily /ˈdeɪli/ täglich NHG 5

dance /dɑːns/ Tanz p. 36, 7

(to) **dance** /dɑːns/ tanzen NHG 5

dancer /ˈdɑːnsə/ Tänzer/in NHG 6

dancing /ˈdɑːnsɪŋ/ Tanzen NHG 5

danger /ˈdeɪndʒə/ Gefahr NHG 6

dangerous /ˈdeɪndʒərəs/ gefährlich NHG 6

dark /dɑːk/ dunkel; Dunkelheit NHG 6

darkness /ˈdɑːknəs/ Dunkelheit NHG 6

darling /ˈdɑːlɪŋ/ Liebling; Schatz p. 52

date /deɪt/ Datum NHG 5

(to) set a date /ˌset ə ˈdeɪt/ sich verabreden p. 101

daughter /ˈdɔːtə/ Tochter NHG 5

day /deɪ/ Tag NHG 5

some day /ˈsʌmˌdeɪ/ eines Tages p. 36, 7

day out /ˌdeɪ ˈaʊt/ *Ausflugstag* NHG 6

(to) **deal with** *(irr)* /ˈdiːl wɪð/ sich befassen mit, umgehen mit p. 97, 10

dear /dɪə/ liebe/r *(Anrede)* NHG 5

dear /dɪə/ Liebes *(Anrede)* p. 29

December /dɪˈsembə/ Dezember NHG 5

(to) **decide** /dɪˈsaɪd/ entscheiden; sich entscheiden NHG 5

(to) **decorate** /ˈdekəreɪt/ schmücken; dekorieren NHG 5

decoration /ˌdekəˈreɪʃn̩/ Dekoration; Schmuck NHG 6

decorative /ˈdekrətɪv/ dekorativ p. 63, 12

definitely /ˈdefnətli/ eindeutig, definitiv NHG 6

(to) **delete** /dɪˈliːt/ löschen p. 93, 5

delicious /dɪˈlɪʃəs/ köstlich, lecker NHG 6

on demand /ˌɒn dɪˈmɑːnd/ auf Anfrage p. 114, 2

dentist /ˈdentɪst/ Zahnarzt/ Zahnärztin p. 42, 1

to the dentist's /ˌtʊ ðə ˈdentɪsts/ in die Zahnarztpraxis p. 163

(to) **depend on** /dɪˈpend ɒn/ abhängen von NHG 6

(to) **describe** /dɪˈskraɪb/ beschreiben NHG 5

description /dɪˈskrɪpʃn̩/ Beschreibung NHG 6

design /dɪˈzaɪn/ Entwurf; Design NHG 6

(to) **design** /dɪˈzaɪn/ entwerfen NHG 5

desk /desk/ Schreibtisch NHG 5

dessert /dɪˈzɜːt/ Nachtisch p. 17, 17

(to) **destroy** /dɪˈstrɔɪ/ zerstören NHG 6

detail /ˈdiːteɪl/ Detail; Einzelheit NHG 5

(to) develop /dɪˈveləp/ erarbeiten; (sich) entwickeln p. 8, 2

development /dɪˈveləpmənt/ Entwicklung p. 114, 2

dialogue /ˈdaɪəˌlɒg/ Gespräch; Dialog NHG 5

diary /ˈdaɪəri/ Tagebuch NHG 6

diary entry /ˈdaɪəriˌentri/ Tagebucheintrag NHG 6

(to) keep a diary *(irr)* /ˌkiːp ə ˈdaɪəri/ Tagebuch führen p. 95, 6

dictionary /ˈdɪkʃənri/ Lexikon; Wörterbuch NHG 6

(to) **die** /daɪ/ sterben p. 86, 8

different /ˈdɪfrənt/ anders; andere(r, s); verschiedene(r, s) NHG 5

difficult /ˈdɪfɪklt/ schwierig; schwer NHG 6

dining room /ˈdaɪnɪŋ ruːm/ *hier:* Speisesaal p. 66, 2

dinner /ˈdɪnə/ Abendessen NHG 5

(to) direct /daɪˈrekt/ leiten, führen p. 54

directions *(pl)* /daɪˈrekʃnz/ *hier:* Wegbeschreibungen NHG 6

(to) **give directions** *(irr)* /ˌgɪv daɪˈrekʃnz/ den Weg beschreiben NHG 6

dirty /ˈdɜːti/ dreckig; schmutzig
NHG 5

disability /ˌdɪsəˈbɪləti/ Behinderung;
Einschränkung p. 54

(to) **disappear** /ˌdɪsəˈpɪə/
verschwinden NHG 6

disappointed /ˌdɪsəˈpɔɪntɪd/
enttäuscht NHG 6

disappointing /ˌdɪsəˈpɔɪntɪŋ/
enttäuschend p. 18, 2

disaster /dɪˈzɑːstə/ Katastrophe p. 28

discipline /ˈdɪsəplɪn/ Disziplin p. 52

(to) **discover** /dɪˈskʌvə/ entdecken
NHG 6

discovery /dɪˈskʌvri/ Entdeckung
p. 109, 7

discus /ˈdɪskəs/ Diskus(werfen) p. 53

(to) **discuss** /dɪˈskʌs/ besprechen;
diskutieren NHG 6

discussion /dɪˈskʌʃn/ Diskussion
NHG 6

disgusting /dɪsˈɡʌstɪŋ/ widerlich
p. 9, 2

dish (pl **dishes**) /dɪʃ, ˈdɪʃɪz/ Gericht;
Speise p. 7

(Petri) **dish** /ˈpiːtri ˌdɪʃ/ Petrischale
p. 109, 7

dishwasher /ˈdɪʃˌwɒʃə/ Spül-
maschine NHG 5

display /dɪˈspleɪ/ Auslage;
Ausstellung p. 107, 5

(to) **display** /dɪˈspleɪ/ aushängen;
zeigen NHG 5

(to) **put on display** (irr) /ˌpʊt ɒn
dɪˈspleɪ/ ausstellen NHG 6

firework display /ˈfaɪəˌwɜːk dɪˌspleɪ/
Feuerwerk p. 67, 2

distance /ˈdɪstəns/ Ferne;
Entfernung p. 136

(to) **dive** /daɪv/ tauchen p. 70, 6

diving /ˈdaɪvɪŋ/ Tauchen p. 32, 1

Diwali /dɪˈwɑːli/ hinduistisches Fest
p. 146

dizzy /ˈdɪzi/ schwindlig p. 45, 4

(to) **do** (irr) /duː/ tun; machen NHG 5

(to) **do athletics** (irr) /ˌduː ˌæθˈletɪks/
Leichtathletik machen NHG 5

(to) **do gymnastics** (irr) /ˌduː
dʒɪmˈnæstɪks/ turnen NHG 5

(to) **do research** (irr) /ˌduː rɪˈsɜːtʃ/
recherchieren NHG 5

(to) **do sports** (irr) /ˌduː ˈspɔːts/
Sport treiben NHG 6

(to) **do the cooking** (irr) /ˌduː ðə
ˈkʊkɪŋ/ kochen NHG 5

(to) **do the shopping** (irr) /ˌduː ðə
ˈʃɒpɪŋ/ einkaufen NHG 5

doctor /ˈdɒktə/ Arzt/Ärztin p. 31

doctor's practice /ˈdɒktəz ˌpræktɪs/
Arztpraxis p. 46, 5

at the doctor's /ˌæt ðə ˈdɒktəz/
beim Arzt/bei der Ärztin p. 31

(to) **see a doctor** (irr) /siː ə ˈdɒktə/
einen Arzt/eine Ärztin aufsuchen
p. 43, 1

document /ˈdɒkjʊmənt/ Dokument
p. 117, 6

dog /dɒɡ/ Hund NHG 5

door /dɔː/ Tür NHG 6

dos and don'ts /ˌduːz ən ˈdəʊnts/
was man tun und was man nicht
tun sollte p. 121, 12

double /ˈdʌbl/ doppelt, Doppel-
NHG 5

down /daʊn/ hinunter; (nach)
unten NHG 6

(to) **download** /ˌdaʊnˈləʊd/
herunterladen p. 121, 12

Dr (= Doctor) /ˈdɒktə/
Dr. (= Doktor) NHG 6

draft /drɑːft/ Entwurf NHG 6

dragon /ˈdræɡən/ Drache NHG 6

drama /ˈdrɑːmə/ Theater-;
Schauspiel- NHG 6

dramatic /drəˈmætɪk/ dramatisch
p. 43, 1

(to) **draw** (irr) /drɔː/ zeichnen NHG 5

(to) **draw attention to** (irr)
/ˌdrɔː əˈtenʃn tə/ Aufmerksamkeit
lenken auf p. 70, 6

drawer /ˈdrɔːə/ Schublade p. 12, 7

drawing /ˈdrɔːɪŋ/ Zeichnung NHG 6

dream /driːm/ Traum NHG 5

dress /dres/ Kleid; Kleidung p. 86, 8

(to) **dress** /dres/ sich anziehen;
sich kleiden p. 72, 8

drink /drɪŋk/ Trinken; Getränk NHG 5

(to) **drink** (irr) /drɪŋk/ trinken NHG 5

(to) **drive** (irr) /draɪv/ fahren NHG 6

drone /drəʊn/ Drohne p. 124

(to) **drop** /drɒp/ fallen lassen
p. 39, 10

dry /draɪ/ trocken NHG 6

dry suit /ˈdraɪsuːt/ Taucheranzug
p. 38, 8

during /ˈdjʊərɪŋ/ während NHG 6

E

each /iːtʃ/ jede(r, s) NHG 5

each and every /ˈiːtʃ ən ˌevri/
jede(r, s) einzelne p. 39, 10

each other /ˌiːtʃ ˈʌðə/ einander
NHG 5

ear /ɪə/ Ohr NHG 5

earlier /ˈɜːliə/ vorhin, früher NHG 6

early /ˈɜːli/ früh NHG 6

(to) **earn** /ɜːn/ verdienen NHG 6

earth /ɜːθ/ Erde NHG 6

Easter /ˈiːstə/ Ostern NHG 6

easy /ˈiːzi/ leicht; einfach NHG 5

(to) **eat** (irr) /iːt/ essen NHG 5

(to) **eat out** (irr) /ˌiːt ˈaʊt/ auswärts
essen; im Restaurant essen
p. 25, 10

eating habit /ˈiːtɪŋ ˌhæbɪt/
Essgewohnheit p. 30

(to) **echo** /ˈekəʊ/ (wider)hallen p. 127

(to) **edit** /ˈedɪt/ bearbeiten NHG 5

egg /eɡ/ Ei NHG 5

Egypt /ˈiːdʒɪpt/ Ägypten p. 6

not ... either /ˌnɒt ˈaɪðə/ auch nicht
p. 24, 8

either ... or ... /ˌaɪðə ˈɔː/ entweder ...
oder ... NHG 6

elbow pad /ˈelbəʊ ˌpæd/ Ellenbogen-
schützer p. 39, 10

electric /ɪˈlektrɪk/ elektrisch;
Elektro- p. 104, 1

electrical /ɪˈlektrɪkl/ elektrisch p. 142

electricity /ɪˌlekˈtrɪsəti/ Elektrizität;
Strom p. 110, 9

elephant /ˈelɪfənt/ Elefant p. 62, 10

else /els/ anders; sonst NHG 5

emergency /ɪˈmɜːdʒnsi/ Notfall p. 45, 4

emergency call /ɪˈmɜːdʒnsi kɔːl/
Notruf p. 50, 13

emergency services (pl) /ɪˈmɜːdʒnsi
ˌsɜːvɪsɪz/ Notdienst, Rettungs-
dienst p. 45, 4

(to) **emigrate** /ˈemɪɡreɪt/
auswandern p. 85, 7

(to) **empty** /ˈempti/ ausleeren;
ausräumen NHG 5

end /end/ Ende; Schluss NHG 5

(to) **end** /end/ enden; beenden NHG 6

in the end /ˌɪn ðiˈend/ am Ende, schließlich NHG 6

ending /ˈendɪŋ/ Ende; Schluss NHG 6

energy /ˈenədʒi/ Energie; Kraft p. 133

engine /ˈendʒɪn/ Maschine; Motor p. 105, 2

engineer /ˌendʒɪˈnɪə/ Ingenieur/in NHG 6

English /ˈɪŋglɪʃ/ Englisch; englisch NHG 5

English-speaking /ˈɪŋglɪʃˌspiːkɪŋ/ englischsprachig p. 26, 13

(to) **enjoy** /ɪnˈdʒɔɪ/ genießen NHG 5

Enjoy! /ɪnˈdʒɔɪ/ Guten Appetit! p. 17, 17

enough /ɪˈnʌf/ genug NHG 5

(to) **enter** /ˈentə/ eingeben; betreten NHG 6

entertainment /ˌentəˈteɪnmənt/ Unterhaltung NHG 6

entrance /ˈentrəns/ Eingang; Eintritt NHG 6

entry /ˈentri/ Eintritt NHG 6

entry /ˈentri/ Zutritt p. 125

diary entry /ˈdaɪəriˌentri/ Tagebucheintrag NHG 6

environment /ɪnˈvaɪrənmənt/ Umwelt; Umgebung NHG 6

equipment /ɪˈkwɪpmənt/ Ausrüstung; Ausstattung NHG 5

eraser /ɪˈreɪzə/ Radiergummi NHG 5

(to) **escape** /ɪˈskeɪp/ fliehen; entkommen NHG 5

especially /ɪˈspeʃli/ besonders; vor allem NHG 6

(to) **be estimated** *(irr)* /ˌbiˈestɪmeɪtəd/ geschätzt werden p. 109, 7

Europe /ˈjʊərəp/ Europa NHG 6

(to) **evaporate** /ɪˈvæpəreɪt/ verdampfen, verdunsten p. 139

even /ˈiːvn/ selbst; sogar NHG 5

evening /ˈiːvnɪŋ/ Abend NHG 5

event /ɪˈvent/ Ereignis; Veranstaltung NHG 5

ever /ˈevə/ jemals NHG 6

ever since /ˌevə ˈsɪns/ seitdem p. 101

every /ˈevri/ jede(r, s) NHG 5

each and every /ˈiːtʃ_ənˌevri/ jede(r, s) einzelne p. 39, 10

everybody /ˈevriˌbɒdi/ alle; jeder NHG 5

everyday /ˈevriˌdeɪ/ alltäglich, Alltags- NHG 6

everyone /ˈevriwʌn/ alle; jeder NHG 5

everything /ˈevriθɪŋ/ alles NHG 5

everywhere /ˈevriweə/ überall NHG 5

exactly /ɪgˈzækli/ genau NHG 6

exam /ɪgˈzæm/ Prüfung p. 100

(to) **examine** /ɪgˈzæmɪn/ untersuchen p. 46, 5

example /ɪgˈzɑːmpl/ Beispiel NHG 5

for example /fərˌɪgˈzɑːmpl/ zum Beispiel NHG 5

excellent /ˈeksələnt/ ausgezeichnet NHG 5

except /ɪkˈsept/ außer NHG 6

exchange student /ɪksˈtʃeɪndʒ ˌstjuːdnt/ Austauschschüler/in p. 49, 10

excited /ɪkˈsaɪtɪd/ aufgeregt NHG 6

exciting /ɪkˈsaɪtɪŋ/ aufregend NHG 5

Excuse me! /ɪkˈskjuːz ˌmi/ Entschuldigung! NHG 5

exercise /ˈeksəsaɪz/ Übung NHG 6

exercise /ˈeksəsaɪz/ Bewegung p. 124

(to) **exercise** /ˈeksəsaɪz/ trainieren p. 36, 7

exercise book /ˈeksəsaɪzˌbʊk/ Heft NHG 5

exhausted /ɪgˈzɔːstɪd/ erschöpft p. 36, 7

exhausting /ɪgˈzɔːstɪŋ/ anstrengend p. 34, 4

exhibition /ˌeksɪˈbɪʃn/ Ausstellung NHG 6

(to) **exist** /ɪgˈzɪst/ existieren NHG 6

(to) **expect** /ɪkˈspekt/ erwarten NHG 6

expensive /ɪkˈspensɪv/ teuer NHG 6

experience /ɪkˈspɪəriəns/ Erfahrung NHG 5

experiment /ɪkˈsperɪmənt/ Experiment; Versuch NHG 5

expert /ˈekspɜːt/ Experte/Expertin NHG 6

(to) **explain** /ɪkˈspleɪn/ erklären NHG 5

(to) **explore** /ɪkˈsplɔː/ erforschen; untersuchen NHG 6

(to) **express** /ɪkˈspres/ ausdrücken NHG 6

extra /ˈekstrə/ zusätzlich NHG 5

extremely /ɪkˈstriːmli/ äußerst, höchst; außerordentlich p. 22, 6

eye /aɪ/ Auge NHG 5

eyeball /ˈaɪˌbɔːl/ Augapfel p. 125

F

face /feɪs/ Gesicht NHG 5

fact /fækt/ Tatsache; Fakt NHG 5

fact file /ˈfækt faɪl/ Steckbrief NHG 5

(to) **fall** *(irr)* /fɔːl/ fallen p. 43, 1

(to) **fall off** *(irr)* /ˌfɔːlˈɒf/ (herunter)fallen p. 51, 16

false /fɔːls/ falsch NHG 5

family /ˈfæmli/ Familie NHG 5

famous /ˈfeɪməs/ berühmt NHG 5

fancy /ˈfænsi/ nobel p. 28

fantastic /fænˈtæstɪk/ fantastisch; super NHG 5

far /fɑː/ weit NHG 5

far /fɑː/ *hier:* weit weg p. 102

farm /fɑːm/ Bauernhof NHG 6

fashion /ˈfæʃn/ Mode NHG 6

fast /fɑːst/ schnell NHG 5

(to) fasten /ˈfɑːsn/ schließen; zumachen p. 109, 7

father /ˈfɑːðə/ Vater NHG 5

fault /fɔːlt/ Schuld; Fehler p. 99, 15

favourite /ˈfeɪvrət/ Liebling; Lieblings- NHG 5

February /ˈfebruəri/ Februar NHG 5

fee /fiː/ Gebühr; Geld p. 56, 2

registration fee /ˌredʒɪˈstreɪʃn fiː/ Anmeldegebühr p. 56, 2

(to) **feed** *(irr)* /fiːd/ füttern NHG 6

feedback /ˈfiːdbæk/ Feedback; Rückmeldung NHG 5

(to) **feel** *(irr)* /fiːl/ (sich) fühlen NHG 6

feeling /ˈfiːlɪŋ/ Gefühl NHG 6

felt-tip /ˈfeltˌtɪp/ Filzstift NHG 5

festival /ˈfestɪvl/ Fest; Festival NHG 6

fever /ˈfiːvə/ Fieber p. 42, 1

a few /ə ˈfjuː/ einige; wenige NHG 6

field /fiːld/ Feld NHG 5

playing field /ˈpleɪɪŋ ˌfiːld/ Sportplatz p. 45, 4

field trip /ˈfiːld ˌtrɪp/ Exkursion p. 124

fight /faɪt/ Kampf; Streit p. 66, 2

(to) **fight** *(irr)* /faɪt/ bekämpfen; ankämpfen gegen NHG 6

(to) **fill** /fɪl/ füllen NHG 6

(to) **fill in** /ˌfɪl ˈɪn/ eintragen, ausfüllen NHG 5

filled /fɪld/ gefüllt p. 9, 2

(to) **film** /fɪlm/ drehen, filmen NHG 6

final /ˈfaɪnl/ letzte(r, s); endgültig NHG 5

finally /ˈfaɪnli/ schließlich; endlich p. 57, 3

(to) **find** *(irr)* /faɪnd/ finden NHG 5

(to) **find out** *(irr)* /ˌfaɪnd ˈaʊt/ herausfinden NHG 5

finding /ˈfaɪndɪŋ/ Entdeckung; Ergebnis p. 114, 2

fine /faɪn/ in Ordnung, gut NHG 5

(to) **finish** /ˈfɪnɪʃ/ beenden; enden; fertigstellen NHG 6; aufessen p. 8, 2

finished /ˈfɪnɪʃt/ fertig p. 53

finishing line /ˈfɪnɪʃɪŋ ˌlaɪn/ Ziellinie p. 52

fire /ˈfaɪə/ Feuer NHG 6

firefighter /ˈfaɪəˌfaɪtə/ Feuerwehrmann/-frau NHG 6

firework display /ˈfaɪəˌwɜːk dɪˌspleɪ/ Feuerwerk p. 67, 2

fireworks *(pl)* /ˈfaɪəˌwɜːks/ Feuerwerk NHG 6

first /fɜːst/ erste(r, s); zuerst NHG 5

at first /ˌæt ˈfɜːst/ zuerst NHG 6

fish *(pl* **fish** *or* **fishes)** /fɪʃ, fɪʃ, fɪʃɪz/ Fisch NHG 5

fish and chips /ˌfɪʃ ən ˈtʃɪps/ *Fisch mit Pommes* L&L 1

(to) **fit** /fɪt/ passen NHG 5

(to) **keep fit** *(irr)* /ˌkiːp ˈfɪt/ fit bleiben, (sich) fit halten p. 31

flag /flæg/ Fahne; Flagge p. 52

flat /flæt/ Wohnung NHG 6

flatbread /ˈflætbred/ Fladen p. 9, 2

flea market /ˈfliː ˌmɑːkɪt/ Flohmarkt p. 57, 3

flexible /ˈfleksəbl/ biegsam, gelenkig p. 36, 7

floor /flɔː/ Fußboden NHG 5

flour /ˈflaʊə/ Mehl p. 112, 12

flower /ˈflaʊə/ Blume NHG 6

flowerpot /ˈflaʊəˌpɒt/ Blumentopf p. 60, 8

(to) **fly** *(irr)* /flaɪ/ fliegen NHG 6

(to) **focus on** /ˈfəʊkəs ˌɒn/ sich konzentrieren auf NHG 5

folder /ˈfəʊldə/ Mappe; Ordner NHG 5

(to) **follow** /ˈfɒləʊ/ folgen; verfolgen NHG 6

following /ˈfɒləʊɪŋ/ folgende(r, s) NHG 6

food /fuːd/ Essen NHG 5

foot *(pl* **feet)** /fʊt, fiːt/ Fuß NHG 5

football /ˈfʊtbɔːl/ Fußball NHG 5

football 5-a-side /ˌfʊtbɔːl ˌfaɪv ə ˈsaɪd/ 5er-Fußball p. 54

for /fɔː/ für NHG 5

for *(+ Zeitraum)* /fɔː/ ... lang NHG 6

for ages *(informal)* /fər ˈeɪdʒɪz/ seit einer Ewigkeit p. 57, 3

for example /fər ɪɡˈzɑːmpl/ zum Beispiel NHG 5

for free /fə ˈfriː/ gratis NHG 6

for some time /fə ˌsʌm ˈtaɪm/ eine Zeitlang p. 37, 7

for the first time /fə ðə ˈfɜːst ˌtaɪm/ zum ersten Mal NHG 6

(to) **force** /fɔːs/ (er)zwingen p. 76

foreign /ˈfɒrɪn/ ausländisch; fremd p. 85, 7

forest /ˈfɒrɪst/ Wald NHG 6

forever /fərˈevə/ ewig, für immer p. 56, 2

(to) **forget** *(irr)* /fəˈɡet/ vergessen NHG 5

fork /fɔːk/ Gabel NHG 5

form /fɔːm/ Klasse NHG 5

foxhunting *(no pl)* /ˈfɒks ˌhʌntɪŋ/ Fuchsjagd p. 14, 10

France /frɑːns/ Frankreich NHG 5

free /friː/ frei; kostenlos NHG 6

for free /fə ˈfriː/ gratis NHG 6

free time /friː ˈtaɪm/ Freizeit NHG 5

French /frentʃ/ Französisch NHG 5

fresh /freʃ/ frisch; neu NHG 6

Friday /ˈfraɪdeɪ/ Freitag NHG 5

(on) Fridays /ˈfraɪdeɪz/ freitags NHG 5

fridge /frɪdʒ/ Kühlschrank p. 12, 7

fried /fraɪd/ gebraten p. 11, 6

fried egg /ˌfraɪd ˈeɡ/ Spiegelei p. 52

friend /frend/ Freund/in NHG 5

friendly /ˈfrendli/ freundlich NHG 6

(to) **make friends (with)** *(irr)* /ˌmeɪk ˈfrendz/ sich anfreunden (mit) NHG 6

friendship /ˈfrendʃɪp/ Freundschaft NHG 6

from /frɒm/ von; aus NHG 5

from (all) around the world /frəm ˌɔːl əˌraʊnd ðə ˈwɜːld/ aus der (ganzen) Welt p. 11, 6

from all over the world /frəm ˌɔːl ˌəʊvə ðə ˈwɜːld/ aus der ganzen Welt NHG 5

at/in the front /ˌæt/ˌɪn ðə ˈfrʌnt/ vorne NHG 5

in front of /ɪn ˈfrʌnt əv/ vor NHG 5

fruit /fruːt/ Frucht; Obst NHG 5

frustrated /frʌˈstreɪtɪd/ frustriert NHG 6

full /fʊl/ voll, vollständig NHG 6; satt p. 8, 2

full of /ˈfʊl əv/ voller p. 76

fun /fʌn/ Spaß NHG 5; lustig; witzig NHG 6

(to) **be (good/great) fun** *(irr)* /ˌbiː ˌɡʊd/ˌɡreɪt ˈfʌn/ (viel/großen) Spaß machen NHG 5

(to) **have (a lot of) fun** *(irr)* /ˌhæv ə ˌlɒt əv ˈfʌn/ (viel) Spaß haben NHG 6

function /ˈfʌŋkʃn/ Aufgabe; Funktion p. 118, 7

funny /ˈfʌni/ lustig; komisch NHG 5

furniture /ˈfɜːnɪtʃə/ Möbel(stück) NHG 5

future /ˈfjuːtʃə/ Zukunft NHG 6

G

gallery walk /ˈɡæləri wɔːk/ *Gruppendiskussion in Stationsarbeit* p. 41, 13

(to) **gallop** /ˈɡæləp/ galoppieren p. 77

game /ɡeɪm/ Spiel NHG 5

board game /ˈbɔːd ɡeɪm/ Brettspiel NHG 6

gap /ɡæp/ Lücke NHG 5

garden /ˈɡɑːdn/ Garten NHG 5

garlic /ˈɡɑːlɪk/ Knoblauch p. 9, 2

gate /ɡeɪt/ Tor NHG 6

general /ˈdʒenrəl/ allgemein p. 114, 2

geography /dʒiˈɒɡrəfi/ Erdkunde NHG 5

German /ˈdʒɜːmən/ Deutsch; deutsch NHG 5

Germany /ˈdʒɜːməni/ Deutschland NHG 5

gerund /ˈdʒerənd/ Gerundium p. 34

(to) **get** *(irr)* /get/ bekommen; holen; kaufen NHG 5; kommen; gelangen; werden NHG 6; bringen p. 24, 8

(to) get *(irr)* /get/ *hier:* gehen p. 77; verstehen p. 126

(to) **get along** *(irr)* /ˌget_əˈlɒŋ/ sich verstehen NHG 6

(to) **get away** *(irr)* /ˌget_əˈweɪ/ wegkommen, flüchten p. 102

(to) **get better** *(irr)* /ˌget ˈbetə/ besser werden, gesund werden p. 37, 7

(to) get dressed *(irr)* /ˌget_ˈdrest/ sich anziehen p. 76

(to) get killed *(irr)* /ˌget ˈkɪld/ umgebracht werden p. 76

(to) get lost *(irr)* /ˌget ˈlɒst/ verloren gehen, sich verirren p. 124

(to) **get married** *(irr)* /ˌget ˈmærid/ heiraten p. 81, 2

(to) **get rid of** *(irr)* /ˌget ˈrɪd_əv/ loswerden p. 61, 8

(to) get stuck *(irr)* /ˌget ˈstʌk/ festsitzen p. 102

(to) **get together** *(irr)* /ˌget_təˈgeðə/ zusammenkommen NHG 5

(to) **get up** *(irr)* /ˌget_ˈʌp/ aufstehen NHG 6

(to) **get well** *(irr)* /ˌget ˈwel/ gesund werden p. 44, 2

Get well soon! /ˌget ˌwel ˈsuːn/ Gute Besserung! p. 48, 7

ghost /gəʊst/ Geist; Gespenst NHG 6

ginger /ˈdʒɪndʒə/ Ingwer p. 23, 7

girl /gɜːl/ Mädchen NHG 5

(to) **give** *(irr)* /gɪv/ geben NHG 5; angeben, mitteilen NHG 6

(to) give a helping hand *(irr)* /ˌgɪv_ə ˌhelpɪŋ ˈhænd/ helfen p. 79

(to) **give a presentation** *(irr)* /ˌgɪv_ə ˌpreznˈteɪʃn/ eine Präsentation halten p. 114, 2

(to) give a try *(irr)* /ˌgɪv_ə ˈtraɪ/ ausprobieren p. 100

(to) **give advice** *(irr)* /ˌgɪv_ədˈvaɪs/ Rat geben p. 99, 15

(to) **give directions** *(irr)* /ˌgɪv daɪˈrekʃnz/ den Weg beschreiben NHG 6

(to) **give off** *(irr)* /ˌgɪv_ˈɒf/ abgeben p. 127

glad /glæd/ glücklich, froh p. 52

glass /glɑːs/ Glas NHG 6

VR glasses *(pl)* /ˌviːˈɑː ˌglɑːsɪz/ VR-Brille p. 125

X-ray glasses *(pl)* /ˈeksreɪ ˌglɑːsɪz/ *Röntgenbrille* p. 111, 11

glue /gluː/ Klebstoff NHG 5

(to) **go** *(irr)* /gəʊ/ gehen; fahren NHG 5

(to) **go abroad** *(irr)* /ˌgəʊ_əˈbrɔːd/ ins Ausland gehen / fahren NHG 6

(to) **go away** *(irr)* /ˌgəʊ_əˈweɪ/ weggehen; verschwinden NHG 6

(to) **go cycling** *(irr)* /ˌgəʊ ˈsaɪklɪŋ/ Rad fahren gehen NHG 6

(to) go for the top *(irr)* /ˌgəʊ fə ðə ˈtɒp/ sich um Höchstleistungen bemühen p. 52

(to) **go hiking** *(irr)* /ˌgəʊ ˈhaɪkɪŋ/ wandern gehen NHG 6

(to) **go off** *(irr)* /ˌgəʊ_ˈɒf/ weggehen p. 77

(to) **go on** *(irr)* /ˌgəʊ_ˈɒn/ passieren; weitergehen, weiterreden p. 26, 12

(to) **go out** *(irr)* /ˌgəʊ_ˈaʊt/ (hinaus) gehen; ausgehen NHG 6

(to) **go riding** *(irr)* /ˌgəʊ ˈraɪdɪŋ/ reiten gehen NHG 6

(to) **go shopping** *(irr)* /ˌgəʊ ˈʃɒpɪŋ/ einkaufen gehen NHG 6

(to) **go swimming** *(irr)* /ˌgəʊ ˈswɪmɪŋ/ schwimmen gehen NHG 6

(to) **go with** *(irr)* /ˌgəʊ ˈwɪθ/ gehören zu; passen zu NHG 6

in one go /ˌɪn wʌn ˈgəʊ/ auf einmal p. 136

goal /gəʊl/ Tor NHG 5

goalkeeper /ˈgəʊlˌkiːpə/ Tormann/ Torfrau p. 54

(to) be going to *(irr)* /ˌbiː ˈgəʊɪŋ tʊ/ werden NHG 6

gone /gɒn/ weg NHG 6

good /gʊd/ gut NHG 5

(to) **be good at something** *(irr)* /ˌbiː ˈgʊd_æt ˌsʌmθɪŋ/ gut in etwas sein NHG 6

I'm good, thanks. /aɪm ˈgʊd ˌθæŋks/ Es geht mir gut, danke. NHG 5

Good luck! /ˌgʊd ˈlʌk/ Viel Glück! p. 94, 6

Good morning! /ˌgʊd ˈmɔːnɪŋ/ Guten Morgen! NHG 5

goodbye /ˌgʊdˈbaɪ/ auf Wiedersehen NHG 5

goods *(pl)* /gʊdz/ Waren p. 30

gotta (= have got to) *(informal)* /ˈgɒtə/ müssen p. 102

government /ˈgʌvənmənt/ Regierung p. 73, 9

(to) **grab** /græb/ sich schnappen; greifen p. 39, 10

grammar /ˈgræmə/ Grammatik p. 10

grandad *(informal)* /ˈgrænˌdæd/ Opa p. 86, 8

grandchild (pl grandchildren) /ˈgrænˌtʃaɪld, ˈgrænˌtʃɪldrən/ Enkelkind p. 89, 13

grandfather /ˈgrænˌfɑːðə/ Großvater NHG 5

grandma *(informal)* /ˈgrænˌmɑː/ Oma p. 6

grandmother /ˈgrænˌmʌðə/ Großmutter NHG 5

grandpa *(informal)* /ˈgrænˌpɑː/ Opa p. 84, 6

grandparents *(pl)* /ˈgrænˌpeərənts/ Großeltern NHG 6

grape /greɪp/ (Wein)traube NHG 6

grass /grɑːs/ Gras NHG 6

gravy /ˈgreɪvi/ (Braten)soße p. 8, 2

great /greɪt/ groß; großartig NHG 5

Great Britain /ˌgreɪt ˈbrɪtn/ Großbritannien p. 85, 7

great-grandchild (pl great-grandchildren) /ˌgreɪt ˈgrænˌtʃaɪld, ˌgreɪt ˈgrænˌtʃɪldrən/ Urenkelkind p. 89, 13

great-grandfather /ˌgreɪt ˈgrænˌfɑːðə/ Urgroßvater p. 85, 7

great-grandmother /ˌgreɪt ˈgrænˌmʌðə/ Urgroßmutter p. 82, 4

Greece /griːs/ Griechenland p. 8, 2

Greek /gri:k/ Grieche/Griechin; griechisch p. 18, 1

green /gri:n/ grün NHG 5; umweltfreundlich, ökologisch p. 73, 9

greetings *(pl)* /'gri:tɪŋz/ Grüße p. 8, 2

grey /greɪ/ grau NHG 5

(to) **grieve** /gri:v/ traurig sein, trauern p. 102

grilled /grɪld/ gegrillt p. 8, 2

ground /graʊnd/ Boden NHG 6

group /gru:p/ Gruppe NHG 5

(to) **grow** *(irr)* /grəʊ/ anbauen NHG 6; wachsen p. 109, 7

(to) **grow up** *(irr)* /ˌgrəʊ_'ʌp/ erwachsen sein / werden NHG 6; aufwachsen p. 81, 2

gruel /'gru:əl/ Haferschleim; Grütze p. 76

(to) **guess** /ges/ (er)raten NHG 5

guest /gest/ Gast NHG 5

guide /gaɪd/ Führer/in p. 54; Führer *(Buch)* p. 56, 2

guided /'gaɪdɪd/ geführt p. 124

guitar /gɪ'tɑ:/ Gitarre NHG 5

guy /gaɪ/ Kerl; Typ p. 76

(you) guys *(pl, informal)* /gaɪz/ Leute *(umgangssprachl.)* NHG 6

gym (= gymnasium) /dʒɪm, dʒɪm'neɪziəm/ Turnhalle NHG 5

(to) **do gymnastics** *(irr)* /ˌdu: dʒɪm'næstɪks/ turnen NHG 5

H

habit /'hæbɪt/ Gewohnheit, Angewohnheit p. 119, 8

hair /heə/ Haar; Haare NHG 5

hairdresser /'heəˌdresə/ Friseur/in NHG 6

half /hɑ:f/ halb NHG 5

half *(pl **halves**)* /hɑ:f, hɑ:vz/ Hälfte NHG 6

hall /hɔ:l/ Halle p. 125

ham /hæm/ Schinken p. 131

(to) hand /hænd/ übergeben p. 53

on the one hand, … /ˌɒn ðə 'wʌn hænd/ einerseits … p. 69, 5

on the other hand, … /ˌɒn ðiˌ'ʌðə hænd/ andererseits … p. 69, 5

(to) give a helping hand *(irr)* /ˌgɪv_ə ˌhelpɪŋ 'hænd/ helfen p. 79

(to) **hand in** /ˌhænd_'ɪn/ einreichen; abgeben NHG 6

(to) hang on *(irr)* /ˌhæŋ_'ɒn/ sich festhalten p. 77

(to) hang out *(informal, irr)* /ˌhæŋ_'aʊt/ rumhängen; Zeit mit jemandem verbringen p. 91, 2

(to) **hang (up)** *(irr)* /ˌhæŋ_'ʌp/ hängen, aufhängen NHG 6

(to) **happen** /'hæpən/ geschehen; passieren NHG 5

happy /'hæpi/ glücklich NHG 5; zufrieden p. 122, 14

Happy birthday (to you)! /ˌhæpi 'bɜ:θdeɪ tʊ ju:/ Herzlichen Glückwunsch zum Geburtstag! NHG 5

hard /hɑ:d/ hart, schwierig NHG 6; fest; kräftig p. 45, 4

hardly /'hɑ:dli/ kaum p. 127

(to) **hate** /heɪt/ hassen; nicht ausstehen können NHG 5

(to) **have** *(irr)* /hæv/ haben; essen; trinken NHG 5

(to) **have a look at** *(irr)* /ˌhæv_ə 'lʊk_ət/ sich ansehen NHG 6

(to) **have (a lot of) fun** *(irr)* /ˌhæv_ə ˌlɒt_əv_'fʌn/ (viel) Spaß haben NHG 6

(to) **have got** *(irr)* /ˌhæv 'gɒt/ haben NHG 5

(to) **have in common** *(irr)* /ˌhæv_ɪn 'kɒmən/ gemeinsam haben NHG 6

(to) **have to** *(irr)* /'hæv tə/ müssen NHG 5

he /hi:/ er NHG 5

head /hed/ Kopf NHG 6

(to) bang one's head /ˌbæŋ wʌnz 'hed/ sich den Kopf anschlagen p. 45, 4

(to) head /hed/ köpfen p. 39, 10

headache /'hedeɪk/ Kopfschmerzen p. 42, 1

heading /'hedɪŋ/ Überschrift; Titel NHG 6

headline /'hedˌlaɪn/ Schlagzeile; *hier:* Überschrift p. 94, 6

headteacher /ˌhed'ti:tʃə/ Schulleiter/in; Rektor/in p. 53

health /helθ/ Gesundheit p. 43, 1

healthy /'helθi/ gesund NHG 6

(to) **hear** *(irr)* /hɪə/ hören NHG 5

heart /hɑ:t/ Herz NHG 6

by heart /ˌbaɪ 'hɑ:t/ auswendig p. 14, 10

(to) **heat** /hi:t/ erhitzen p. 13, 8

heavy /'hevi/ schwer NHG 5

hedgehog /'hedʒˌhɒg/ Igel NHG 6

height /haɪt/ Höhe NHG 6

hello /hə'ləʊ/ hallo NHG 5

helmet /'helmɪt/ Helm p. 39, 10

help /help/ Hilfe NHG 5

(to) **help** /help/ helfen NHG 5

(to) **help out** /ˌhelp_'aʊt/ aushelfen p. 49, 10

helpful /'helpfl/ hilfreich; nützlich p. 95, 6

(to) **give a helping hand** *(irr)* /ˌgɪv_ə ˌhelpɪŋ 'hænd/ helfen p. 79

helpline /'helpˌlaɪn/ *telefonischer Beratungsdienst* p. 130

her /hɜ:/ ihr/ihre; sie NHG 5

herb /hɜ:b/ (Gewürz)kraut p. 12, 7

here /hɪə/ hier; hierher NHG 5

Here you are! /ˌhɪə ju_'ɑ:/ Hier, bitte! NHG 5

hers /hɜ:z/ ihre(r, s) p. 98, 12

herself /hə'self/ sich; (sie) selbst p. 90, 2

(to) **hide** *(irr)* /haɪd/ verstecken, sich verstecken NHG 6

high /haɪ/ hoch NHG 5

high jump /'haɪ dʒʌmp/ Hochsprung p. 53

high-pressure /ˌhaɪ 'preʃə/ Hochdruck- p. 105, 2

high-speed train /ˌhaɪspi:d 'treɪn/ Hochgeschwindigkeitszug p. 127

highlight /'haɪˌlaɪt/ Höhepunkt p. 67, 2

(to) take a hike *(AE, informal, irr)* /ˌteɪk_ə 'haɪk/ abhauen p. 102

(to) **go hiking** *(irr)* /ˌgəʊ 'haɪkɪŋ/ wandern gehen NHG 6

hill /hɪl/ Hügel NHG 6

him /hɪm/ ihm, ihn NHG 5

himself /hɪm'self/ selbst; sich (selbst) NHG 6

Hinduism /'hɪnduˌɪzm/ Hinduismus NHG 6

(to) **hire** /'haɪə/ mieten NHG 6

his /hɪz/ sein; seine(r, s) NHG 5

historical /hɪ'stɒrɪkl/ geschichtlich; historisch p. 146

history /ˈhɪstri/ Geschichte NHG 5

(to) **hit** *(irr)* /hɪt/ schlagen NHG 5

(to) hit *(irr)* /hɪt/ treffen; stoßen gegen p. 127

hockey stick /ˈhɒki stɪk/ Hockeyschläger p. 59, 7

(to) **hold** *(irr)* /həʊld/ (fest)halten NHG 5

hole /həʊl/ Loch NHG 5

Holi /ˈhɒli/ *hinduistisches Fest der Farben* p. 146

holiday /ˈhɒlɪdeɪ/ Feiertag NHG 6

holiday(s) /ˈhɒlɪdeɪ(z)/ Ferien; Urlaub NHG 5

home /həʊm/ nach Hause; zu Hause; daheim NHG 5; Zuhause; Haus NHG 6

at home /ˌæt ˈhəʊm/ zu Hause NHG 5

home town /ˈhəʊm ˌtaʊn/ Heimatstadt NHG 5

home-made /ˌhəʊmˈmeɪd/ hausgemacht, selbst gemacht p. 22, 6

(to) **be homesick** *(irr)* /ˌbiː ˈhəʊmˌsɪk/ Heimweh haben p. 85, 7

homework /ˈhəʊmwɜːk/ Hausaufgaben NHG 5

honest /ˈɒnɪst/ ehrlich NHG 6

honey /ˈhʌni/ Honig p. 137

hook /hʊk/ Haken p. 127

hook-and-loop fastener /ˌhʊkˌən ˈluːp ˌfɑːsnə/ *Klettverschluss* p. 127

(to) **hope** /həʊp/ hoffen NHG 5

horrible /ˈhɒrəbl/ schrecklich; gemein NHG 6

horse /hɔːs/ Pferd NHG 6

(to) **ride a horse** *(irr)* /ˌraɪd_ə ˈhɔːs/ reiten NHG 5

horse riding /ˈhɔːs ˌraɪdɪŋ/ Reiten p. 76

horsehair /ˈhɔːsˌheə/ Rosshaar p. 105, 2

hospital /ˈhɒspɪtl/ Krankenhaus NHG 6

hot /hɒt/ heiß NHG 6; scharf p. 19, 2

hour /ˈaʊə/ Stunde NHG 5

house /haʊs/ Haus NHG 5

how /haʊ/ wie NHG 5

How about ...? /ˈhaʊˌəˌbaʊt/ Wie wäre es mit ...?, Was ist mit ...? p. 90, 1

How are you? /ˌhaʊˈɑː jʊ/ Wie geht es dir / euch / Ihnen? NHG 5

How much is it? /ˌhaʊ mʌtʃˈɪzˌɪt/ Wie viel kostet es? NHG 5

however /haʊˈevə/ aber; wie auch immer p. 78

huge /hjuːdʒ/ riesig NHG 6

hundred /ˈhʌndrəd/ Hundert NHG 6

hungry /ˈhʌŋgri/ hungrig NHG 5

hurdle /ˈhɜːdl/ Hürdenlauf; Hürde p. 52

(to) **hurry (up)** /ˌhʌriˈʌp/ sich beeilen NHG 5

(to) **hurt** *(irr)* /hɜːt/ wehtun, schmerzen; verletzen p. 42, 1

husband /ˈhʌzbənd/ Ehemann NHG 5

hysterical /hɪˈsterɪkl/ hysterisch p. 125

I

I /aɪ/ ich NHG 5

I don't know. /aɪ ˌdəʊnt ˈnəʊ/ Ich weiß es nicht. NHG 5

I don't like ... /aɪ ˈdəʊnt laɪk/ Ich mag ... nicht. NHG 5

I'd (= I would) /aɪd, ˈaɪ wʊd/ ich würde p. 93, 5

I'd love to ... /aɪd ˈlʌv tə/ Ich würde sehr gern ... NHG 5

I'm (= I am) /aɪm, ˈaɪ æm/ ich bin, ich heiße NHG 5

I'm good, thanks. /aɪm ˈgʊd ˌθæŋks/ Es geht mir gut, danke. NHG 5

ice /aɪs/ Eis NHG 6

ice cream /ˈaɪs ˌkriːm/ Eis NHG 5

ice hockey /ˈaɪs ˌhɒki/ Eishockey p. 129

(to) **ice-skate** /ˈaɪsˌskeɪt/ Schlittschuh laufen NHG 5

ICT (= Information and Communication Technology) /ˌaɪˌsiːˈtiː, ɪnfəˈmeɪʃn_ən kəˌmjuːnɪˈkeɪʃn tekˌnɒlədʒi/ Informatik *(Schulfach)* NHG 5

idea /aɪˈdɪə/ Idee; Vorstellung NHG 5

if /ɪf/ wenn; falls; ob NHG 5

ill /ɪl/ krank NHG 6

illness /ˈɪlnəs/ Krankheit p. 49, 11

image /ˈɪmɪdʒ/ Bild p. 101

(to) **imagine** /ɪˈmædʒɪn/ sich etwas vorstellen NHG 5

immediately /ɪˈmiːdiətli/ sofort p. 53

immigrant /ˈɪmɪgrənt/ Einwanderer/in; Immigrant/in p. 70, 6

important /ɪmˈpɔːtnt/ wichtig NHG 5

impossible /ɪmˈpɒsəbl/ unmöglich NHG 6

impression /ɪmˈpreʃn/ Eindruck p. 100

impressive /ɪmˈpresɪv/ beeindruckend p. 70, 6

(to) **improve** /ɪmˈpruːv/ verbessern; besser werden NHG 6

in /ɪn/ in; auf NHG 5

in advance /ˌɪn_ədˈvɑːns/ im Voraus p. 108, 6

in front of /ˌɪn ˈfrʌnt_əv/ vor NHG 5

in general /ɪn ˈdʒenrəl/ im Allgemeinen p. 30

in my opinion /ɪn ˈmaɪ_əˌpɪnjən/ meiner Meinung nach NHG 6

in one go /ˌɪn wʌn ˈgəʊ/ auf einmal p. 130

in order to /ˌɪnˈɔːdə tʊ/ um zu p. 33, 2

in the end /ˌɪn ðiˈend/ am Ende, schließlich NHG 6

I'm in! *(informal)* /ˌaɪmˈɪn/ Ich bin dabei! p. 91, 2

(to) **include** /ɪnˈkluːd/ beinhalten; einbeziehen NHG 6

including /ɪnˈkluːdɪŋ/ einschließlich p. 54

independent /ˌɪndɪˈpendənt/ unabhängig p. 30

India /ˈɪndiə/ Indien p. 11, 6

Indian /ˈɪndiən/ Inder/in; indisch p. 21, 5

indoor /ˌɪnˈdɔː/ Hallen- p. 36, 7

indoors /ˌɪnˈdɔːz/ drinnen, im Haus p. 32, 1

industry /ˈɪndəstri/ Industrie p. 108, 7

(to) become infected *(irr)* /bɪˌkʌm_ɪnˈfektɪd/ sich infizieren p. 109, 7

infection /ɪnˈfekʃn/ Infektion p. 43, 1

influence /ˈɪnfluəns/ Einfluss p. 66, 2

(to) **inform** /ɪnˈfɔːm/ informieren NHG 6

information *(no pl)* /ˌɪnfəˈmeɪʃn/ Informationen NHG 5

ingredient /ɪnˈgriːdiənt/ Zutat p. 17, 17

injury /ˈɪndʒəri/ Verletzung p. 46, 5

inline skating /ˌɪnlaɪn ˈskeɪtɪŋ/ Inlinerfahren p. 138

inside /ɪnˌsaɪd/ innerhalb NHG 5; innen; drinnen; hinein NHG 6

inside /ɪnˌsaɪd/ in … hinein p. 109, 7

(to) inspire /ɪnˈspaɪə/ inspirieren p. 127

inspired /ɪnˈspaɪəd/ inspiriert p. 127

instruction /ɪnˈstrʌkʃn/ Anweisung; Instruktion NHG 6

interested /ˈɪntrəstɪd/ interessiert NHG 6

(to) **be interested in** (irr) /ˌbiˈɪntrəstɪd‿ɪn/ interessiert sein an p. 115, 3

interesting /ˈɪntrəstɪŋ/ interessant NHG 5

(to) interrupt /ˌɪntəˈrʌpt/ unterbrechen p. 101

(to) **interview** /ˈɪntəˌvjuː/ interviewen, befragen NHG 5

into /ˈɪntuː/ in NHG 5

(to) **introduce** /ˌɪntrəˈdjuːs/ einführen; vorstellen NHG 5

introduction /ˌɪntrəˈdʌkʃn/ Einleitung NHG 5

(to) **invent** /ɪnˈvent/ erfinden NHG 6

invented /ɪnˈventɪd/ erfunden p. 15, 12

invention /ɪnˈvenʃn/ Erfindung NHG 6

inventor /ɪnˈventə/ Erfinder/in p. 105, 2

invitation /ˌɪnvɪˈteɪʃn/ Einladung NHG 5

(to) **invite** /ɪnˈvaɪt/ einladen NHG 5

Ireland /ˈaɪələnd/ Irland NHG 6

island /ˈaɪlənd/ Insel p. 78

it /ɪt/ es NHG 5

Italian /ɪˈtæljən/ Italiener/in; italienisch p. 18, 1

Italy /ˈɪtəli/ Italien NHG 5

item /ˈaɪtəm/ Gegenstand p. 56, 2

its /ɪts/ sein(e), ihr(e) (sächlich) NHG 5

itself /ɪtˈself/ (sich) selbst p. 70, 6

J

jacket /ˈdʒækɪt/ Jacke NHG 6

January /ˈdʒænjuəri/ Januar NHG 5

Japanese /ˌdʒæpəˈniːz/ Japaner/in; japanisch p. 127

jar /dʒɑː/ (Glas)gefäß p. 12, 7

javelin /ˈdʒævlɪn/ Speerwerfen p. 52

jewellery (no pl) /ˈdʒuːəlri/ Schmuck NHG 6

Jewish /ˈdʒuːɪʃ/ jüdisch NHG 6

job /dʒɒb/ Aufgabe; Beruf NHG 6

(to) **join** /dʒɔɪn/ mitmachen (bei) NHG 5; sich zu jemandem gesellen p. 91, 2

(to) **join in** /ˌdʒɔɪn‿ˈɪn/ sich beteiligen an; mitmachen bei NHG 6

journey /ˈdʒɜːni/ Reise; Fahrt NHG 6

juice /dʒuːs/ Saft NHG 5

juicy /ˈdʒuːsi/ saftig p. 19, 2

July /dʒuˈlaɪ/ Juli NHG 5

jump /dʒʌmp/ Sprung p. 52

(to) **jump** /dʒʌmp/ springen NHG 5

June /dʒuːn/ Juni NHG 5

just /dʒʌst/ nur; bloß NHG 5; einfach; wirklich; gerade NHG 6

K

(to) **keep** (irr) /kiːp/ halten; behalten; aufbewahren NHG 5

(to) keep a diary (irr) /ˌkiːp‿ə ˈdaɪəri/ Tagebuch führen p. 95, 6

(to) **keep doing something** (irr) /ˌkiːp ˈduːɪŋ sʌmθɪŋ/ etwas weiter tun p. 57, 3

(to) **keep fit** (irr) /ˌkiːp ˈfɪt/ fit bleiben, (sich) fit halten p. 31

(to) **keep in touch** (irr) /ˌkiːp‿ɪn ˈtʌtʃ/ Kontakt halten; in Verbindung bleiben p. 119, 7

(to) keep up (irr) /ˌkiːp‿ˈʌp/ hier: hochlegen p. 46, 5

kg (= kilogram) /ˈkɪləˌgræm/ Kilogramm NHG 6

(to) **kick** /kɪk/ treten NHG 5

kid /kɪd/ Kind NHG 5

(to) **kill** /kɪl/ töten p. 14, 10

kind /kaɪnd/ Art; Sorte NHG 5

kindly /ˈkaɪndli/ freundlich p. 78

all kinds of /ˌɔːl ˈkaɪndz‿əv/ alle möglichen NHG 6

king /kɪŋ/ König NHG 6

kingdom /ˈkɪŋdəm/ Königreich p. 78

kingfisher /ˈkɪŋˌfɪʃə/ Eisvogel p. 127

kitchen /ˈkɪtʃən/ Küche NHG 5

km (= kilometre) /ˈkɪləˌmiːtə/ Kilometer p. 56, 2

km/h (= kilometres per hour) /ˌkeɪˌemˈeɪtʃ/ Kilometer pro Stunde p. 127

knee /niː/ Knie NHG 6

knee pad /ˈniː ˌpæd/ Knieschützer p. 39, 10

knife (pl knives) /naɪf, naɪvz/ Messer NHG 5

knight /naɪt/ Ritter p. 15, 11

(to) **knock** /nɒk/ klopfen NHG 6

(to) knock over /ˌnɒk‿ˈəʊvə/ umstoßen p. 52

(to) **know** (irr) /nəʊ/ wissen; kennen NHG 5

I don't know. /ˌaɪ ˌdəʊnt ˈnəʊ/ Ich weiß es nicht. NHG 5

Korean /kəˈriːən/ Koreaner/in; koreanisch p. 80, 2

korma /ˈkɔːmə/ indisches Gericht p. 19, 2

L

lab /læb/ Labor p. 109, 7

label /ˈleɪbl/ Etikett p. 89, 13

(to) **label** /ˈleɪbl/ beschriften NHG 5

lad (informal, Scottish) /læd/ Junge p. 71, 6

lady /ˈleɪdi/ Frau; Dame p. 25, 11

Lahmacun /ˌlɑːməˈdʒuːn/ traditionelles türkisches Gericht p. 9, 2

lake /leɪk/ See NHG 5

lamb /læm/ Lamm p. 22, 6

lame /leɪm/ lahm p. 91, 2

lamp /læmp/ Lampe p. 60, 8

(to) **land** /lænd/ landen p. 71, 6

language /ˈlæŋgwɪdʒ/ Sprache NHG 5

lantern /ˈlæntən/ Laterne NHG 6

large /lɑːdʒ/ groß NHG 6

lass (informal, Scottish) /læs/ Mädchen p. 71, 6

lassi /ˈlæsi/ Joghurtgetränk p. 23, 7

last /lɑːst/ letzte(r, s) NHG 5; (an)dauern NHG 6

last /lɑːst/ als Letzte(r, s) p. 53

late /leɪt/ (zu) spät NHG 5

(to) **stay up (late)** /ˌsteɪ‿ˌʌp ˈleɪt/ lange aufbleiben p. 98, 13

later /ˈleɪtə/ später NHG 5

latest /ˈleɪtɪst/ neueste(r, s) p. 86, 8

(to) **laugh** /lɑ:f/ lachen NHG 6

lazy /ˈleɪzi/ faul NHG 6

lead /li:d/ Leine NHG 6

leader /ˈli:də/ Leiter/in NHG 6

leaf (pl **leaves**) /li:f, li:vz/ Blatt NHG 6

leaflet /ˈli:flət/ Prospekt; Broschüre p. 41, 13

(to) **learn** (irr) /lɜ:n/ lernen NHG 6

least /li:st/ am wenigsten p. 67, 2

leather /ˈleðə/ Leder p. 109, 7

(to) **leave** (irr) /li:v/ weggehen NHG 5; verlassen, abfahren; (übrig) lassen; zurücklassen; hinterlassen NHG 6

(to) leave behind (irr) /ˌli:v bɪˈhaɪnd/ zurücklassen p. 102

Lebanon /ˈlebənən/ der Libanon p. 9, 2

left /left/ links, nach links NHG 6; übrig p. 12, 7

on the left /ˌɒn ðə ˈleft/ links, auf der linken Seite NHG 5

(to) be left out (irr) /ˌbi: ˌleft ˈaʊt/ ausgeschlossen werden p. 94, 6

(to) have something left (irr) /ˌhæv sʌmθɪŋ ˈleft/ etwas übrig haben p. 57, 3

leg /leg/ Bein NHG 6

legend /ˈledʒnd/ Legende p. 78

lemon /ˈlemən/ Zitrone NHG 5

lemonade /ˌleməˈneɪd/ Limonade p. 23, 7

less /les/ weniger NHG 6

lesson /ˈlesn/ Stunde; Unterricht NHG 5

(to) **let** (irr) /let/ lassen NHG 5

(to) let in (irr) /ˌlet ˈɪn/ hereinlassen p. 28

let's ... /lets/ lass(t) uns ... NHG 5

letter /ˈletə/ Buchstabe NHG 5; Brief NHG 6

level /ˈlevl/ Stufe; Level NHG 5

library /ˈlaɪbrəri/ Bücherei NHG 5

(to) lick /lɪk/ (ab)lecken p. 29

life (pl **lives**) /laɪf, laɪvz/ Leben NHG 5

lifestyle /ˈlaɪfstaɪl/ Lebensstil p. 31

(to) **lift** /lɪft/ (hoch)heben p. 71, 6

light /laɪt/ Licht NHG 5

(to) **light** (irr) /laɪt/ anzünden NHG 6

like /laɪk/ wie; mögen NHG 5

I would like ... (= I'd like ...) /aɪ ˌwʊd ˈlaɪk, aɪd ˈlaɪk/ Ich würde gern ... / Ich hätte gern ... NHG 5

(to) **like best** /ˌlaɪk ˈbest/ am liebsten mögen NHG 5

(to) **like doing something** /laɪk ˈdu:ɪŋ ˌsʌmθɪŋ/ etwas gern tun NHG 6

like that /ˌlaɪk ˈðæt/ so p. 39, 10

line /laɪn/ Linie; Zeile NHG 5

linking part /ˈlɪŋkɪŋ pɑ:t/ Verbindungsteil p. 98, 13

linking word /ˈlɪŋkɪŋ wɜ:d/ Verbindungswort p. 98, 13

The Lion King /ðə ˈlaɪən ˌkɪŋ/ Der König der Löwen (Musical) p. 56, 2

list /lɪst/ Liste NHG 5

(to) **list** /lɪst/ auflisten NHG 5

(to) **listen (to)** /ˈlɪsn/ zuhören, anhören NHG 5

listening /ˈlɪsnɪŋ/ Hören p. 11, 6

literature /ˈlɪtrətʃə/ Literatur p. 100

little /ˈlɪtl/ klein NHG 5

a little /ə ˈlɪtl/ ein bisschen NHG 6

(to) **live** /lɪv/ leben; wohnen NHG 5

lively /ˈlaɪvli/ lebendig p. 81, 2

living /ˈlɪvɪŋ/ Lebensstil p. 31

living /ˈlɪvɪŋ/ lebend p. 76

living room /ˈlɪvɪŋ ˌru:m/ Wohnzimmer NHG 5

'll (= will) /l, wɪl/ werden NHG 6

(to) **load** /ləʊd/ laden NHG 5

loads of /ˈləʊdz əv/ jede Menge p. 76

locomotive /ˌləʊkəˈməʊtɪv/ Lokomotive p. 105, 2

log /lɒg/ Baumstamm p. 71, 6

logical thinking /ˌlɒdʒɪkl ˈθɪŋkɪŋ/ logische Denken p. 33, 2

lonely /ˈləʊnli/ einsam NHG 6

long /lɒŋ/ lang NHG 5

long jump /ˈlɒŋ dʒʌmp/ Weitsprung p. 52

long-distance /ˌlɒŋ ˈdɪstəns/ Fern- p. 105, 2

look /lʊk/ Aussehen; Look p. 72, 8

(to) **look** /lʊk/ aussehen NHG 5

(to) **have a look at** (irr) /ˌhæv ə ˈlʊk ət/ sich ansehen NHG 6

(to) **look after** /ˌlʊk ˈɑ:ftə/ sich kümmern um; aufpassen auf NHG 5

(to) **look (at)** /ˈlʊk ət/ (an)sehen, (an)schauen NHG 5

(to) **look for** /ˈlʊk fə/ suchen nach NHG 5

(to) **look forward to** /ˌlʊk ˈfɔ:wəd tʊ/ sich freuen auf NHG 6

(to) look out for /ˌlʊk ˈaʊt fə/ hier: sich kümmern um p. 40, 12

(to) **look up** /ˌlʊk ˈʌp/ hochschauen; nachschlagen p. 35, 6

-looking /ˈlʊkɪŋ/ aussehend p. 28

(to) **lose** (irr) /lu:z/ verlieren p. 32, 1

loser /ˈlu:zə/ Verlierer/in p. 32, 1

a lot /ə ˈlɒt/ viel, sehr NHG 5

a lot (of) /ə ˈlɒt/ viel(e), jede Menge NHG 5

thanks a lot /ˌθæŋks ə ˈlɒt/ vielen Dank NHG 5

lots of /ˈlɒts əv/ viel(e) NHG 5

loud /laʊd/ laut NHG 5

love /lʌv/ viele Grüße; alles Liebe (in Briefen) NHG 6

(to) **love** /lʌv/ lieben, sehr mögen NHG 5

(to) **love doing something** /lʌv ˈdu:ɪŋ ˌsʌmθɪŋ/ etwas sehr gern tun NHG 5

lovely /ˈlʌvli/ schön p. 29

lover /ˈlʌvə/ Liebhaber/in p. 70, 6

low-tech /ˌləʊ ˈtek/ technisch einfach p. 114, 2

lower /ˈləʊə/ niedriger p. 54

loyal /ˈlɔɪəl/ treu; loyal p. 78

Good luck! /ˌgʊd ˈlʌk/ Viel Glück! p. 94, 6

(good) luck /lʌk/ Glück NHG 6

luckily /ˈlʌkɪli/ zum Glück; glücklicherweise p. 53

lunch /lʌntʃ/ Mittagessen NHG 5

lunch break /ˈlʌntʃ breɪk/ Mittagspause p. 53

lychee /ˈlaɪtʃi/ Litschi p. 140

M

machine /məˈʃi:n/ Maschine; Apparat NHG 6

made /meɪd/ hergestellt, gemacht p. 73, 9

magazine /ˌmægəˈzi:n/ Zeitschrift p. 117, 6

main /meɪn/ Haupt- NHG 5

main (course) /ˈmeɪn kɔːs/ Hauptgericht p. 17, 17

main entrance /ˌmeɪn ˈentrəns/ Haupteingang p. 125

(to) **make (irr)** /meɪk/ machen NHG 5

(to) **make friends (with) (irr)** /ˌmeɪk ˈfrendz/ sich anfreunden (mit) NHG 6

(to) make money (irr) /ˌmeɪk ˈmʌni/ Geld verdienen p. 165

(to) **make notes (irr)** /ˌmeɪk ˈnəʊts/ sich Notizen machen NHG 5

(to) **make somebody do something (irr)** /ˌmeɪk ˌsʌmbədi ˈduː ˌsʌmθɪŋ/ jemanden dazu bringen, etwas zu tun p. 37, 7

(to) **make sure (irr)** /ˌmeɪk ˈʃɔː/ darauf achten, dass … NHG 6

(to) make sure (irr) /ˌmeɪk ˈʃɔː/ sich versichern; achten auf p. 124

(to) **make up (irr)** /ˌmeɪk ˈʌp/ erfinden, sich ausdenken NHG 6

man (pl men) /mæn, men/ Mann NHG 5

(to) **manage** /ˈmænɪdʒ/ zurecht-kommen, es schaffen p. 29

many /ˈmeni/ viele NHG 5

map /mæp/ Karte NHG 5

March /mɑːtʃ/ März NHG 5

mark /mɑːk/ Note; Zensur NHG 6

(to) **mark** /mɑːk/ markieren, kennzeichnen p. 50, 14

market /ˈmɑːkɪt/ Markt NHG 5

(to) **be married (irr)** /ˌbi ˈmærid/ verheiratet sein NHG 6

(to) **get married (irr)** /ˌget ˈmærid/ heiraten p. 81, 2

(to) **marry** /ˈmæri/ heiraten p. 85, 7

masala /məˈsɑːlə/ *Gewürzmischung* L&L 1

mashed potatoes (pl) /ˌmæʃt pəˈteɪtəʊz/ Kartoffelbrei p. 8, 1

match /mætʃ/ Spiel NHG 5

(to) **match** /mætʃ/ passen zu NHG 6

(to) **match (with/to)** /mætʃ/ zuordnen NHG 5

maths (informal) /mæθ/ Mathe (Schulfach) NHG 5

matter /ˈmætə/ Angelegenheit p. 95, 6

What's the matter? /ˌwɒts ðə ˈmætə/ Was ist los? p. 42, 1

May /meɪ/ Mai NHG 5

may /meɪ/ können; dürfen NHG 6

maybe /ˈmeɪbi/ vielleicht NHG 5

me, to me /miː/ mir; mich; ich NHG 5

meal /miːl/ Mahlzeit; Essen NHG 5

(to) **mean (irr)** /miːn/ meinen; bedeuten NHG 6

meaning /ˈmiːnɪŋ/ Bedeutung p. 46, 5

meanwhile /ˈmiːnˌwaɪl/ inzwischen; unterdessen p. 77

meat /miːt/ Fleisch p. 12, 7

mechanic /mɪˈkænɪk/ Mechaniker / Mechanikerin NHG 6

the media /ðə ˈmiːdiə/ die Medien p. 14, 9

mediation /ˌmiːdiˈeɪʃn/ Sprach-mittlung; Mediation p. 15, 12

medical /ˈmedɪkl/ medizinisch p. 51, 16

medicine /ˈmedsn/ Medizin; Medikamente p. 43, 1

medieval /ˌmediˈiːvl/ mittelalterlich p. 76

(to) **meet (irr)** /miːt/ treffen; sich treffen NHG 5; kennenlernen NHG 6

Nice to meet you. /ˌnaɪs tə ˈmiːt jə/ Schön, dich / euch / Sie zu treffen. NHG 5

meeting /ˈmiːtɪŋ/ Versammlung; Treffen NHG 6

meeting point /ˈmiːtɪŋ pɔɪnt/ Treffpunkt p. 125

member /ˈmembə/ Mitglied NHG 5

memory /ˈmemri/ Erinnerung p. 80, 2

(to) **mention** /ˈmenʃn/ erwähnen p. 67, 2

menu /ˈmenjuː/ Speisekarte; Menü NHG 5

mess /mes/ Unordnung p. 29

message /ˈmesɪdʒ/ Nachricht; Botschaft NHG 5

(to) message /ˈmesɪdʒ/ eine Nachricht schicken p. 119, 7

method /ˈmeθəd/ Methode p. 117, 6

metre /ˈmiːtə/ Meter NHG 6

middle /ˈmɪdl/ Mitte NHG 5

the Middle Ages (pl) /ðə ˌmɪdl ˈeɪdʒɪz/ Mittelalter p. 77

might /maɪt/ könnte(st, n, t) NHG 6

mile /maɪl/ Meile NHG 6

milk /mɪlk/ Milch NHG 5

milkshake /ˈmɪlkˌʃeɪk/ Milchshake p. 52

(to) **mime** /maɪm/ mimen, panto-mimisch darstellen p. 49, 11

minced meat /ˌmɪnst ˈmiːt/ Hackfleisch p. 9, 2

mind /maɪnd/ Geist; Verstand p. 102

(to) **change one's mind** /ˌtʃeɪndʒ wʌnz ˈmaɪnd/ seine Meinung ändern NHG 6

mine /maɪn/ meine(r, s) p. 18, 2

mineral water /ˈmɪnrəl ˌwɔːtə/ Mineralwasser p. 23, 7

mischief /ˈmɪstʃɪf/ Unfug p. 76

(to) **miss** /mɪs/ vermissen; verpassen NHG 5

missing /ˈmɪsɪŋ/ fehlend NHG 5

(to) **be missing (irr)** /ˌbi ˈmɪsɪŋ/ fehlen p. 124

mistake /mɪˈsteɪk/ Fehler p. 147

mix /mɪks/ Mischung p. 30

(to) **mix** /mɪks/ sich (ver)mischen NHG 6

mixed /mɪkst/ gemischt p. 23, 7

mixture /ˈmɪkstʃə/ Mischung p. 81, 2

mobile (phone) /ˈməʊbaɪl/ Handy NHG 6

modal verb /ˈməʊdl vɜːb/ Modalverb p. 47, 6

model /ˈmɒdl/ Modell NHG 6

Monday /ˈmʌndeɪ/ Montag NHG 5

(on) Mondays /ˈmʌndeɪz/ montags NHG 5

money /ˈmʌni/ Geld NHG 5

(to) make money (irr) /ˌmeɪk ˈmʌni/ Geld verdienen p. 165

pocket money /ˈpɒkɪt ˌmʌni/ Taschengeld p. 57, 3

month /mʌnθ/ Monat NHG 5

mood /muːd/ Laune; Stimmung NHG 6

moon /muːn/ Mond NHG 5

more /mɔː/ mehr; weitere NHG 5

morning /ˈmɔːnɪŋ/ Morgen NHG 5

Morocco /məˈrɒkəʊ/ Marokko p. 12, 7

mosque /mɒsk/ Moschee NHG 6

most /məʊst/ die meisten; am meisten p. 105, 2

most of the time /ˌməʊst_əv ðə ˌtaɪm/ meistens p. 37, 7

mostly /ˈməʊstli/ meistens, größtenteils p. 86, 8

mother /ˈmʌðə/ Mutter NHG 5

mould /məʊld/ Schimmel p. 109, 7

mountain /ˈmaʊntɪn/ Berg NHG 5

mountain biking /ˈmaʊntɪn ˌbaɪkɪŋ/ Mountainbikefahren p. 80, 2

move /muːv/ Bewegung NHG 5

on the move /ˌɒn ðə ˈmuːv/ unterwegs p. 102

(to) **move** /muːv/ umziehen NHG 6; (sich) bewegen p. 36, 7

(to) move out /ˌmuːv_ˈaʊt/ ausziehen p. 139

(to) **move something** /ˈmuːv ˌsʌmθɪŋ/ etwas wegräumen, etwas woanders hinstellen NHG 6

moving /ˈmuːvɪŋ/ beweglich NHG 6

Mr /ˈmɪstə/ Herr *(Anrede)* NHG 5

Mrs /ˈmɪsɪz/ Frau *(Anrede)* NHG 5

Ms /mɪz/ Fr. (= Frau) *(Anrede)* p. 53

much /mʌtʃ/ viel NHG 5; sehr p. 60, 8

mud /mʌd/ Schlamm p. 72, 8

muddy /ˈmʌdi/ matschig; schlammig p. 70, 6

multicultural /ˌmʌltiˈkʌltʃərəl/ multikulturell p. 71, 6

mum /mʌm/ Mama; Mutti NHG 5

muscle /ˈmʌsl/ Muskel p. 104, 1

mushroom /ˈmʌʃruːm/ Pilz p. 128

music /ˈmjuːzɪk/ Musik NHG 5

musician /mjʊˈzɪʃn/ Musiker/in NHG 6

Muslim /ˈmʊzləm/ Muslim/in; muslimisch NHG 6

must /mʌst/ müssen NHG 6

mustn't (= must not) /ˈmʌsnt, mʌst ˈnɒt/ nicht dürfen NHG 6

my /maɪ/ mein(e) NHG 5

myself /maɪˈself/ mir/mich/ich (selbst) p. 36, 7

mythical /ˈmɪθɪkl/ sagenumwoben p. 78

N

naan bread /ˈnɑːn bred/ *indisches Fladenbrot* p. 19, 2

(to) **name** /neɪm/ (be)nennen NHG 5

named /neɪmd/ namens p. 105, 2

national park /ˌnæʃnl ˈpɑːk/ Nationalpark NHG 6

nature /ˈneɪtʃə/ Natur NHG 5

near /nɪə/ nahe, in der Nähe von NHG 5

nearly /ˈnɪəli/ fast; beinahe p. 77

necessary /ˈnesəsri/ notwendig, erforderlich NHG 5

(to) **need** /niːd/ brauchen NHG 5

(to) **need to** /ˈniːd_tʊ/ müssen NHG 5

negative /ˈnegətɪv/ negativ NHG 6

neighbour /ˈneɪbə/ Nachbar/in p. 98, 12

neighbourhood /ˈneɪbəˌhʊd/ Viertel; Nachbarschaft NHG 5

neither /ˈnaɪðə, ˈniːðə/ auch nicht p. 57, 3

nervous /ˈnɜːvəs/ nervös NHG 5

net /net/ Netz NHG 5

network /ˈnetˌwɜːk/ Netzwerk p. 117, 6

never /ˈnevə/ nie, niemals NHG 5

new /njuː/ neu NHG 5

New Year /ˌnjuː ˈjɪə/ Neujahr NHG 6

news *(no pl)* /njuːz/ Neuigkeit; Nachrichten p. 46, 5

newspaper /ˈnjuːzˌpeɪpə/ Zeitung NHG 6

next /nekst/ nächste(r, s) NHG 5; dann, als Nächstes NHG 6

next to /ˈnekst_tə/ neben NHG 5

nice /naɪs/ schön; nett NHG 5

Nice to meet you. /ˌnaɪs tə ˈmiːt jə/ Schön, dich / euch / Sie zu treffen. NHG 5

night /naɪt/ Nacht; Abend NHG 6

no /nəʊ/ kein(e); nein NHG 5

no longer /nəʊ ˈlɒŋgə/ nicht mehr p. 73, 9

no one /ˈnəʊ wʌn/ keiner NHG 6

nobody /ˈnəʊbədi/ niemand; keiner p. 57, 3

noise /nɔɪz/ Geräusch; Lärm NHG 6

noodle /ˈnuːdl/ Nudel p. 11, 6

north /nɔːθ/ Norden; Nord- p. 19, 2

North Africa /ˌnɔːθ_ˈæfrɪkə/ Nordafrika p. 9, 2

northern /ˈnɔːðən/ nördlich, Nord- NHG 6

nose /nəʊz/ Nase NHG 5

not /nɒt/ nicht NHG 5

not … either /ˌnɒt_ˈaɪðə/ auch nicht p. 24, 8

not any /ˌnɒt_ˈeni/ kein(e) NHG 5

not anymore /ˌnɒt_ˌeni ˈmɔː/ nicht mehr NHG 6

not anyone /ˌnɒt_ˈeniwʌn/ niemand p. 70, 6

not anything /ˌnɒt_ˈeniˌθɪŋ/ nichts NHG 6

not anywhere /ˌnɒt_ˈeniˌweə/ nirgendwo NHG 6

not at all /ˌnɒt_ət_ˈɔːl/ überhaupt nicht p. 124

not yet /ˌnɒt ˈjet/ noch nicht NHG 6

note /nəʊt/ Nachricht; Notiz NHG 5

(to) **note** /nəʊt/ beachten, zur Kenntnis nehmen NHG 6

notepad /ˈnəʊtˌpæd/ Notizblock NHG 5

(to) **make notes** *(irr)* /ˌmeɪk ˈnəʊts/ sich Notizen machen NHG 5

nothing /ˈnʌθɪŋ/ nichts NHG 6

(to) **notice** /ˈnəʊtɪs/ bemerken; wahrnehmen NHG 6

noticeboard /ˈnəʊtɪsˌbɔːd/ Schwarzes Brett NHG 5

noun /naʊn/ Hauptwort; Substantiv; Nomen NHG 5

November /nəʊˈvembə/ November NHG 5

now /naʊ/ jetzt NHG 5

nowhere /ˈnəʊweə/ nirgends; nirgendwo p. 53

number /ˈnʌmbə/ Zahl; Nummer; Anzahl NHG 5

phone number /ˈfəʊn ˌnʌmbə/ Telefonnummer NHG 5

nurse /nɜːs/ Krankenschwester; Krankenpfleger NHG 6

O

o'clock /əˈklɒk/ Uhr *(bei Nennung einer Uhrzeit)* NHG 5

object /ˈɒbdʒekt/ Gegenstand NHG 6

occasion /əˈkeɪʒn/ Gelegenheit; Anlass p. 21, 5

October /ɒkˈtəʊbə/ Oktober NHG 5

octopus /ˈɒktəpəs/ Tintenfisch p. 8, 2

odd /ɒd/ merkwürdig, seltsam
p. 63, 12

odd one out /ɒd wʌn ˈaʊt/ *Wort,
das nicht zu den anderen passt*
p. 16, 15

of /əv/ von; aus NHG 5

Of course! /əv ˈkɔːs/ Natürlich! NHG 5

off /ɒf/ von; hinunter, herunter NHG 6

offer /ˈɒfə/ Angebot p. 128

(to) offer /ˈɒfə/ anbieten NHG 6

office /ˈɒfɪs/ Büro NHG 5

office manager /ˈɒfɪs ˌmænɪdʒə/
Sekretär/in p. 97, 11

official, officially /əˈfɪʃl, əˈfɪʃli/
offiziell p. 95, 6

often /ˈɒfn/ oft; häufig NHG 5

oh dear *(informal)* /əʊ ˈdɪə/ oje p. 43,1

oil /ɔɪl/ Öl p. 17, 17

old /əʊld/ alt NHG 5

the Olympics *(pl)* /ðiː əˈlɪmpɪks/
Olympische Spiele p. 54

OMG! (= Oh my God!) /ˌəʊ em ˈdʒiː/
Oh mein Gott! p. 26, 12

on /ɒn/ auf; an; in NHG 5

on /ɒn/ *hier:* über p. 124

on demand /ˌɒn dɪˈmɑːnd/ auf
Anfrage p. 114, 2

on one's own /ˌɒn ˌwʌnz ˈəʊn/
allein NHG 5

on the left /ˌɒn ðə ˈleft/ links, auf
der linken Seite NHG 5

on the move /ˌɒn ðə ˈmuːv/
unterwegs p. 102

on the one hand, ... /ˌɒn ðə ˈwʌn
hænd/ einerseits ... p. 69, 5

on the other hand, ... /ˌɒn ðiˈ ʌðə
hænd/ andererseits ... p. 69, 5

on the right /ˌɒn ðə ˈraɪt/ rechts,
auf der rechten Seite NHG 5

on time /ˌɒn ˈtaɪm/ pünktlich NHG 5

once /wʌns/ früher p. 146

once again /ˌwʌns əˈgen/ abermals
p. 53

once more /ˌwʌns ˈmɔː/ noch einmal
p. 119, 7

once upon a time /ˌwʌns əˌpɒn ə
ˈtaɪm/ es war einmal p. 78

one /wʌn/ ein(e); eins NHG 5;
eine(r, s) p. 64, 13

this one /ˈðɪs wʌn/ diese(r, s) hier
p. 63, 11

these ones /ˈðiːz wʌnz/ diese p. 60, 8

onion /ˈʌnjən/ Zwiebel p. 9, 2

only /ˈəʊnli/ nur, bloß; erst;
einzige(r, s) NHG 5

onto /ˈɒntə/ auf, in NHG 6

onwards /ˈɒnwədz/ von ... an p. 108, 7

open /ˈəʊpən/ offen; geöffnet NHG 5

(to) open /ˈəʊpən/ öffnen;
aufmachen NHG 5; sich öffnen,
aufgehen; eröffnen NHG 6

open-air /ˌəʊpən ˈeə/ im Freien p.70,6

tin opener /ˈtɪn ˌəʊpnə/ Dosenöffner p. 109, 7

opening times *(pl)* /ˈəʊpənɪŋ taɪmz/
Öffnungszeiten NHG 5

operator /ˈɒpəˌreɪtə/ Telefonist/in
p. 45, 4

opinion /əˈpɪnjən/ Meinung; Ansicht
NHG 6

in my opinion /ɪn ˈmaɪ əˌpɪnjən/
meiner Meinung nach NHG 6

opposite /ˈɒpəzɪt/ Gegenteil NHG 5

or /ɔː/ oder NHG 5

orange /ˈɒrɪndʒ/ Orange; Apfelsine;
orange NHG 5

order /ˈɔːdə/ Reihenfolge; Ordnung
NHG 6

order /ˈɔːdə/ Befehl p. 125

in order to /ˌɪn ˈɔːdə tʊ/ um zu p. 33, 2

(to) take an order *(irr)*
/ˌteɪk ən ˈɔːdə/ eine Bestellung
aufnehmen p. 22, 6

(to) order (in) /ˈɔːdə, ˌɔːdər ˈɪn/
bestellen p. 8, 2

(to) organize (= organise)
/ˈɔːgənaɪz/ organisieren NHG 6

organizer /ˈɔːgəˌnaɪzə/ Organisator/
Organisatorin p. 70, 6

original /əˈrɪdʒnəl/ ursprünglich,
p. 17, 17

originally /əˈrɪdʒnəli/ ursprünglich
p. 6

other /ˈʌðə/ andere(r, s) NHG 5

otherwise /ˈʌðəˌwaɪz/ sonst, im
Übrigen p. 101

our /aʊə/ unser(e) NHG 5

ours /aʊəz/ unsere(r, s) p. 98, 12

ourselves /aʊəˈselvz/ uns;
wir selbst p. 36, 7

out /aʊt/ heraus, hinaus; aus NHG 5;
draußen NHG 6

out and about /ˌaʊt ən əˈbaʊt/
unterwegs p. 63, 12

out of /ˈaʊt əv/ aus NHG 6

out of breath /ˌaʊt əv ˈbreθ/ außer
Atem p. 77

outdoor /ˌaʊtˈdɔː/ Outdoor-, im
Freien p. 33, 2

outdoors /ˌaʊtˈdɔːz/ draußen; im
Freien p. 32, 1

outside /ˌaʊtˈsaɪd/ außen; (nach)
draußen NHG 5

over /ˈəʊvə/ über, hinüber; vorbei
NHG 5

all over the world /ˌɔːl ˌəʊvə ðə
ˈwɜːld/ auf der ganzen Welt NHG 6

over there /ˌəʊvə ˈðeə/ dort
(drüben) NHG 5

overcooked /ˌəʊvəˈkʊkt/ verkocht
p. 19, 2

ow (= ouch) *(informal)* /aʊ, aʊtʃ/
aua, autsch p. 42, 1

own /əʊn/ eigene(r, s) NHG 5

on one's own /ˌɒn ˌwʌnz ˈəʊn/
allein NHG 5

owner /ˈəʊnə/ Besitzer/in p. 112, 12

P
---

p (= penny, *pl* pence) /piː, ˈpeni,
pens/ Penny *(brit. Währung)* NHG 5

p. (= page) /peɪdʒ/ Seite p. 9, 2

(to) pack /pæk/ packen NHG 5

packaging /ˈpækɪdʒɪŋ/ Verpackung
p. 73, 9

packed /pækt/ voll p. 132

packet /ˈpækɪt/ Packung NHG 5

page /peɪdʒ/ Seite NHG 5

pain /peɪn/ Schmerz p. 102

painful /ˈpeɪnfl/ schmerzhaft p. 43, 1

(to) paint /peɪnt/ (an)malen NHG 5

painting /ˈpeɪntɪŋ/ Bild; Gemälde
NHG 5

pair /peə/ Paar NHG 6

(a pair of) trousers /ə ˌpeər əv
ˈtraʊzəz/ Hose NHG 5

palace /ˈpæləs/ Palast NHG 6

palak paneer /ˌpɑːlək pəˈnɪə/
indisches Gericht p. 23, 7

pancake /ˈpænˌkeɪk/ Pfannkuchen
p. 29

(to) panic /ˈpænɪk/ in Panik geraten
p. 77

paper /ˈpeɪpə/ Papier NHG 6

paper /ˈpeɪpə/ *hier:* Klausur p. 101

paprika /ˈpæprɪkə/ Paprikapulver p. 17, 17

paragraph /ˈpærəˌgraːf/ Absatz; Abschnitt NHG 6

Paralympic /ˌpærəˈlɪmpɪk/ paralympisch p. 54

the Paralympic Games *(pl)* /ðə ˌpærəˈlɪmpɪk ˈgeɪmz/ Paralympische Spiele p. 54

the Paralympics *(pl)* /ðə ˌpærəˈlɪmpɪks/ *Olympische Spiele für Menschen mit Behinderungen* p. 54

parent /ˈpeərənt/ Elternteil p. 94, 6

parents *(pl)* /ˈpeərənts/ Eltern NHG 5

(to) park /paːk/ parken p. 76

parliament /ˈpɑːləmənt/ Parlament NHG 6

part /pɑːt/ Teil NHG 5; Rolle p. 65, 15

(to) **pass** /pɑːs/ geben, herüberreichen NHG 5

passenger /ˈpæsɪndʒə/ Passagier/in p. 105, 2

passive /ˈpæsɪv/ Passiv p. 106

password /ˈpɑːsˌwɜːd/ Passwort p. 121, 12

past /pɑːst/ nach; Vergangenheit NHG 5; vorbei; vorüber NHG 6

past progressive /ˌpɑːst prəʊˈgresɪv/ Verlaufsform der Vergangenheit p. 68

pasta /ˈpæstə/ Nudeln p. 8, 1

pastry /ˈpeɪstri/ Brandteig; Blätterteig p. 23, 7

(to) **pat** /pæt/ einen Klaps geben p. 39, 10

(to) patent /ˈpeɪtnt/ sich patentieren lassen p. 105, 2

path /pɑːθ/ Weg; Pfad NHG 6

(to) **pay** *(irr)* /peɪ/ (be)zahlen NHG 5

(to) **pay attention (to)** *(irr)* /ˌpeɪ əˈtenʃn tʊ/ aufpassen; achten auf NHG 6

payment /ˈpeɪmənt/ Bezahlung NHG 6

PE (= Physical Education) /ˌpiːˈiː, ˌfɪzɪklˌedjʊˈkeɪʃn/ Sport *(Schulfach)* NHG 5

(to) peel /piːl/ schälen p. 29

pen /pen/ Stift NHG 5

pencil /ˈpensl/ Bleistift NHG 5

pencil case /ˈpensl ˌkeɪs/ Federmäppchen NHG 5

pencil sharpener /ˈpensl ˌʃɑːpnə/ Bleistiftspitzer NHG 5

people /ˈpiːpl/ Leute; Menschen NHG 5

pepper /ˈpepə/ Paprika; Pfeffer p. 12, 7

per /pɜː/ pro NHG 5

perfect /ˈpɜːfɪkt/ perfekt NHG 5

(to) **perform** /pəˈfɔːm/ aufführen; durchführen NHG 6

performance /pəˈfɔːməns/ Aufführung; Leistung NHG 6

permission /pəˈmɪʃn/ Erlaubnis; Genehmigung NHG 6

personal /ˈpɜːsnəl/ persönlich NHG 5

pet /pet/ Haustier NHG 5

(Petri) dish /ˈpiːtri ˌdɪʃ/ Petrischale p. 109, 7

phew *(informal)* /fjuː/ puh p. 46, 5

phone /fəʊn/ Telefon NHG 5

phone call /ˈfəʊn kɔːl/ Telefonanruf p. 105, 2

phone number /ˈfəʊn ˌnʌmbə/ Telefonnummer NHG 5

photo /ˈfəʊtəʊ/ Foto NHG 5

(to) **take a photo** *(irr)* /ˌteɪk ə ˈfəʊtəʊ/ ein Foto machen NHG 5

photograph /ˈfəʊtəˌgraːf/ Fotografie; Foto NHG 6

photographer /fəˈtɒgrəfə/ Fotograf/in NHG 6

phrase /freɪz/ Satz; Ausdruck NHG 5

physical /ˈfɪzɪkl/ körperlich p. 35, 6

piano /piˈænəʊ/ Klavier NHG 5

(to) **pick up** /ˌpɪkˈʌp/ aufheben; abholen NHG 5

pickpocket /ˈpɪkˌpɒkɪt/ Taschendieb/in p. 69, 5

picnic /ˈpɪknɪk/ Picknick p. 108, 6

picture /ˈpɪktʃə/ Bild NHG 5

(to) **take a picture** *(irr)* /ˌteɪk ə ˈpɪktʃə/ ein Foto machen NHG 5

piece /piːs/ Stück; Teil NHG 6

piece of art /ˌpiːs əvˈɑːt/ Kunstwerk p. 126

pile /paɪl/ Stapel; Haufen p. 101

place /pleɪs/ Ort; Platz; Haus, Zuhause NHG 5

(to) **place** /pleɪs/ platzieren; stellen NHG 5

(to) **take place** *(irr)* /ˌteɪk ˈpleɪs/ stattfinden NHG 6

(to) **plan** /plæn/ planen NHG 5

plane /pleɪn/ Flugzeug NHG 6

(to) catch a plane *(irr)* /ˌkætʃ ə ˈpleɪn/ ein Flugzeug nehmen p. 102

planner /ˈplænə/ Kalender; Planer p. 116, 5

plant /plɑːnt/ Pflanze NHG 6

plaster /ˈplɑːstə/ Gips; Pflaster p. 43, 1

plastic /ˈplæstɪk/ Plastik NHG 6

plate /pleɪt/ Teller NHG 5

platform /ˈplætˌfɔːm/ Bahnsteig; Plattform NHG 6

play /pleɪ/ Spiel; (Theater)stück NHG 6

(to) **play** /pleɪ/ spielen NHG 5

player /ˈpleɪə/ Spieler/in NHG 5

playground /ˈpleɪˌgraʊnd/ Spielplatz NHG 5

playing /ˈpleɪɪŋ/ Spielen NHG 5

playing field /ˈpleɪɪŋ ˌfiːld/ Sportplatz p. 45, 4

please /pliːz/ bitte NHG 5

pleased /pliːzd/ erfreut; zufrieden p. 53

pm (= post meridiem) /ˌpiːˈem, ˌpəʊst məˈrɪdiəm/ nachmittags; abends *(hinter Uhrzeit zwischen 12 Uhr mittags und Mitternacht)* NHG 5

pocket /ˈpɒkɪt/ (Hosen)tasche p. 69, 5

pocket money /ˈpɒkɪt ˌmʌni/ Taschengeld p. 57, 3

poem /ˈpəʊɪm/ Gedicht NHG 5

poet /ˈpəʊɪt/ Dichter/in p. 39, 10

point /pɔɪnt/ Punkt NHG 5

(to) **point (at/to)** /pɔɪnt/ deuten (auf); zeigen (auf) NHG 5

Poland /ˈpəʊlənd/ Polen NHG 5

police /pəˈliːs/ Polizei p. 125

police officer /pəˈliːsˌɒfɪsə/ Polizeibeamter/Polizeibeamtin NHG 6

Polish /ˈpəʊlɪʃ/ Polnisch; polnisch p. 83, 5

polite /pə'laɪt/ höflich NHG 6

poor /pɔː/ arm NHG 6

poppadom /'pɒpədəm/ *dünnes indisches Brot* p. 23, 7

popular /'pɒpjʊlə/ beliebt NHG 6

population /ˌpɒpjʊ'leɪʃn/ Bevölkerung p. 83, 5

pork /pɔːk/ Schweinefleisch p. 140

porridge /'pɒrɪdʒ/ Haferbrei p. 52

positive /'pɒzətɪv/ positiv NHG 6

possibility /ˌpɒsə'bɪləti/ Möglichkeit NHG 6

possible /'pɒsəbl/ möglich p. 46, 5

(to) **post** /pəʊst/ posten; bekannt geben NHG 6

postcard /'pəʊstˌkɑːd/ Postkarte; Ansichtskarte NHG 5

pot /pɒt/ Topf p. 12, 7

potato (*pl* **potatoes**) /pə'teɪtəʊ, pə'teɪtəʊz/ Kartoffel p. 8, 2

pound (= £) /paʊnd/ Pfund *(britische Währung)* NHG 5

powder /'paʊdə/ Pulver p. 30

power /'paʊə/ Kraft p. 104, 1

practical /'præktɪkl/ praktisch p. 111, 11

practice /'præktɪs/ Übung; Training NHG 6; Praxis p. 42, 1

doctor's practice /'dɒktəz ˌpræktɪs/ Arztpraxis p. 46, 5

(to) **practise** /'præktɪs/ üben; trainieren NHG 5

prayer /preə/ Gebet NHG 6

(to) **prefer** /prɪ'fɜː/ vorziehen; bevorzugen p. 32, 1

(to) **prepare** /prɪ'peə/ vorbereiten NHG 5; zubereiten p. 17, 17

(to) **prepare for** /prɪ'peə fɔː/ sich vorbereiten auf p. 68, 3

(to) be prepared *(irr)* /ˌbi: prɪ'peəd/ vorbereitet sein p. 122, 15

present /'preznt/ Geschenk NHG 5; Gegenwart NHG 6

present perfect /ˌpreznt 'pɜːfɪkt/ Perfekt p. 10

present progressive /ˌpreznt prəʊ'gresɪv/ Verlaufsform der Gegenwart p. 22, 6

(to) **present (to)** /prɪ'zent/ präsentieren, vorstellen NHG 5

presentation /ˌprezn'teɪʃn/ Präsentation; Vortrag NHG 5

(to) **give a presentation** *(irr)* /ˌgɪv_ə ˌprezn'teɪʃn/ eine Präsentation halten p. 114, 2

pretty /'prɪti/ ziemlich NHG 5

(to) **prevent** /prɪ'vent/ verhindern, vorbeugen p. 109, 7

price /praɪs/ Preis *(Kosten)* p. 60, 8

price tag /'praɪs tæg/ Preisschild p. 60, 8

printing press /'prɪntɪŋ pres/ Druckerpresse p. 118, 7

prize /praɪz/ Preis; Gewinn p. 35, 6

pro /prəʊ/ Vorteil; Pro NHG 6

probably /'prɒbəbli/ wahrscheinlich NHG 6

No problem. /ˌnəʊ 'prɒbləm/ *hier:* Keine Ursache. p. 46, 5

(to) **produce** /prə'djuːs/ herstellen NHG 6; produzieren p. 73, 9

product /'prɒdʌkt/ Produkt p. 147

profile /'prəʊfaɪl/ Profil; Porträt p. 33, 2

programme /'prəʊgræm/ Programm NHG 6

project /'prɒdʒekt/ Projekt NHG 6

(to) **promise** /'prɒmɪs/ versprechen p. 46, 5

(to) **pronounce** /prə'naʊns/ aussprechen NHG 6

prop /prɒp/ Requisite p. 27, 14

prop word /'prɒp wɜːd/ Stützwort p. 64, 13

properly /'prɒpəli/ richtig p. 47, 6

(to) **protect** /prə'tekt/ beschützen NHG 6

proud(ly) /'praʊd(li)/ stolz NHG 6

(to) **prove** *(irr)* /pruːv/ beweisen p. 95, 6

pub /pʌb/ Kneipe p. 19, 2

public /'pʌblɪk/ öffentlich NHG 6

the public /ðə 'pʌblɪk/ die Öffentlichkeit NHG 6

(to) **publish** /'pʌblɪʃ/ veröffentlichen; herausgeben NHG 6

pudding /'pʊdɪŋ/ Nachspeise L&L 1

(to) **pull** /pʊl/ ziehen p. 105, 2

pumpkin /'pʌmpkɪn/ Kürbis NHG 6

pupil /'pjuːpl/ Schüler/in p. 99, 15

purple /'pɜːpl/ violett; lila NHG 5

(to) **push** /pʊʃ/ schieben; stoßen NHG 6

(to) **put** *(irr)* /pʊt/ setzen; stellen; legen NHG 5

(to) **put in** *(irr)* /ˌpʊt_'ɪn/ hineintun, hinzufügen p. 13, 8

(to) **put on** *(irr)* /ˌpʊt_'ɒn/ anlegen; auftragen p. 46, 5; anziehen *(Kleidung)* p. 68, 3

(to) **put on display** *(irr)* /ˌpʊt_ɒn dɪ'spleɪ/ ausstellen NHG 6

(to) **put together** *(irr)* /ˌpʊt_tə'geðə/ zusammenstellen; zusammensetzen NHG 6

(to) **put up** *(irr)* /ˌpʊt_'ʌp/ aufhängen; aufstellen NHG 6

puzzle /'pʌzl/ Rätsel p. 33, 2

Q

quality /'kwɒləti/ Qualität p. 18, 2

quantifier /'kwɒntɪˌfaɪə/ *hier:* Mengenangabe p. 16, 13

quarter /'kwɔːtə/ Viertel NHG 5

queen /kwiːn/ Königin NHG 6

question /'kwestʃn/ Frage NHG 5

queue /kjuː/ Schlange; Reihe p. 100

quick /kwɪk/ schnell, kurz p. 12, 7

quickly /'kwɪkli/ schnell NHG 6

quiet /'kwaɪət/ leise; ruhig NHG 5

quite /kwaɪt/ ziemlich NHG 6

quotation /kwəʊ'teɪʃn/ Zitat p. 148

R

rabbit /'ræbɪt/ Kaninchen NHG 5

race /reɪs/ Rennen p. 52

railway company /'reɪlweɪ ˌkʌmpni/ Eisenbahngesellschaft p. 106, 3

rain /reɪn/ Regen NHG 6

(to) **rain** /reɪn/ regnen NHG 5

rainy /'reɪni/ regnerisch NHG 5

(to) **raise** /reɪz/ aufziehen, großziehen p. 78

(to) **rate** /reɪt/ einschätzen; bewerten p. 110, 8

rather /'rɑːðə/ eher, lieber NHG 6

rather than /'rɑːðə ðæn/ anstatt NHG 6

rating /'reɪtɪŋ/ Einschätzung; Einstufung p. 110, 8

raw /rɔː/ roh p. 21, 5

RE (= Religious Education) /ˌɑːrˈiː, reˌlɪdʒəsˌedjʊˈkeɪʃn/ Religion *(Schulfach)* NHG 5

(to) **reach** /riːtʃ/ erreichen p. 33, 2

(to) **react (to)** /riˈækt/ reagieren (auf) NHG 6

reaction /riˈækʃn/ Reaktion NHG 6

(to) **read** *(irr)* /riːd/ lesen NHG 5

(to) **read along** *(irr)* /ˌriːd_əˈlɒŋ/ mitlesen NHG 5

(to) read out *(irr)* /ˌriːd_ˈaʊt/ (laut) vorlesen p. 47, 5

reading /ˈriːdɪŋ/ Lesen NHG 5; Lesung p. 43, 1

ready /ˈredi/ fertig, bereit NHG 5

real /rɪəl/ wirklich; echt NHG 6

(to) **realize (= realise)** /ˈrɪəlaɪz/ sich bewusst sein, erkennen NHG 6

really /ˈrɪəli/ wirklich NHG 5

reason /ˈriːzn/ Grund NHG 6

for no reason /fə ˌnəʊ ˈriːzn/ ohne Grund, grundlos p. 14, 10

(to) receive /rɪˈsiːv/ erhalten; empfangen p. 127

receptionist /rɪˈsepʃnɪst/ Empfangs-dame/Empfangschef p. 42, 1

recipe /ˈresəpi/ Rezept p. 12, 7

(to) recognize (= recognise) /ˈrekəgnaɪz/ erkennen p. 78

(to) **recommend** /ˌrekəˈmend/ empfehlen NHG 6

record /ˈrekɔːd/ Rekord p. 53

(to) **record** /riˈkɔːd/ aufnehmen NHG 5

recording /riˈkɔːdɪŋ/ Aufnahme NHG 5

red /red/ rot NHG 5

(to) **reduce** /rɪˈdjuːs/ reduzieren p. 73, 9

(to) register /ˈredʒɪstə/ registrieren, anmelden p. 76

registration /ˌredʒɪˈstreɪʃn/ *Über-prüfung der Anwesenheit* NHG 5

registration fee /ˌredʒɪˈstreɪʃn fiː/ Anmeldegebühr p. 56, 2

regular /ˈregjʊlə/ üblich, normal NHG 6

regularly /ˈregjʊləli/ regelmäßig p. 36, 7

relative /ˈrelətɪv/ Verwandte/r NHG 6

relative clause /ˌrelətɪv ˈklɔːz/ Relativsatz p. 58

(to) **relax** /rɪˈlæks/ entspannen NHG 5

relaxed /rɪˈlækst/ entspannt NHG 6

relaxing /rɪˈlæksɪŋ/ entspannend p. 35, 6

relay /ˈriːleɪ/ Staffellauf p. 53

religious /rəˈlɪdʒəs/ religiöse(r, s) NHG 6

(to) **remember** /rɪˈmembə/ sich erinnern an NHG 5

(to) **remove** /rɪˈmuːv/ entfernen NHG 6

(to) renovate /ˈrenəveɪt/ renovieren p. 108, 6

(to) **repair** /rɪˈpeə/ reparieren NHG 6

(to) **repeat** /riˈpiːt/ wiederholen NHG 5

(to) **reply** /rɪˈplaɪ/ antworten; erwidern NHG 6

(to) **report** /rɪˈpɔːt/ sich melden NHG 6

(to) report /rɪˈpɔːt/ berichten; melden p. 30

reported speech /ˌrɪ pɔːtɪd ˈspiːtʃ/ indirekte Rede p. 92

(to) **research** /rɪˈsɜːtʃ/ recherchieren p. 117, 6

(to) **do research** *(irr)* /duː rɪˈsɜːtʃ/ recherchieren NHG 5

reservation /ˌrezəˈveɪʃn/ Reservierung p. 22, 6

respect /rɪˈspekt/ Respekt; respektieren NHG 6

respectful /rɪˈspektfl/ respektvoll p. 121, 12

(to) **rest** /rest/ ausruhen p. 46, 5

result /rɪˈzʌlt/ Ergebnis p. 114, 2

(to) **return** /rɪˈtɜːn/ zurückgeben NHG 6

review /rɪˈvjuː/ Kritik; Rezension p. 18, 2

(to) **rewrite** *(irr)* /ˌriːˈraɪt/ über-arbeiten, umschreiben p. 22, 6

rhyming word /ˈraɪmɪŋ wɜːd/ Reimwort p. 39, 10

rice /raɪs/ Reis NHG 5

rich /rɪtʃ/ reich p. 112, 12

(to) **get rid of** *(irr)* /ˌget ˈrɪd_əv/ loswerden p. 61, 8

(to) **ride** *(irr)* /raɪd/ fahren; reiten NHG 5

(to) **ride a bike** *(irr)* /ˌraɪd_ə ˈbaɪk/ Fahrrad fahren NHG 5

(to) **ride a horse** *(irr)* /ˌraɪd_ə ˈhɔːs/ reiten NHG 5

riding /ˈraɪdɪŋ/ Reiten p. 34

(to) **go riding** *(irr)* /ˌgəʊ ˈraɪdɪŋ/ reiten gehen NHG 6

right /raɪt/ richtig NHG 5; rechts, nach rechts; genau; direkt NHG 6; Recht p. 93, 5

(to) **be right** *(irr)* /ˌbiː ˈraɪt/ recht haben NHG 5

on the right /ˌɒn ðə ˈraɪt/ rechts, auf der rechten Seite NHG 5

right now /raɪt ˈnaʊ/ jetzt; im Moment p. 93, 5

rightful /ˈraɪtfl/ rechtmäßig p. 78

ripple /ˈrɪpl/ leichte Welle p. 127

rise /raɪz/ Aufstieg p. 119, 7

river /ˈrɪvə/ Fluss NHG 6

riverside /ˈrɪvəˌsaɪd/ Flussufer p. 80, 2

road /rəʊd/ Straße NHG 5

roast /rəʊst/ Braten; gebraten, geröstet p. 8, 2

robot /ˈrəʊbɒt/ Roboter p. 125

rock /rɒk/ Stein; Fels p. 118, 7

role /rəʊl/ Rolle NHG 6

role play /ˈrəʊl pleɪ/ Rollenspiel NHG 6

(to) **roll** /rəʊl/ rollen p. 39, 10

rolled /rəʊld/ gerollt p. 9, 2

Roman /ˈrəʊmən/ Römer/in; römisch NHG 6

room /ruːm/ Platz; Raum; Zimmer NHG 5

waiting room /ˈweɪtɪŋ ˌruːm/ Wartezimmer p. 46, 5

root /ruːt/ Wurzel p. 79

round /raʊnd/ rund NHG 5; (um …) herum NHG 6

rowing /ˈrəʊɪŋ/ Rudern p. 32, 1

royal /ˈrɔɪəl/ königlich NHG 6

The Royal Air Force /ðə ˌrɔɪəl_ˈeə fɔːs/ Königliche Luftwaffe p. 85, 7

rubbish /ˈrʌbɪʃ/ Müll NHG 5

rude /ruːd/ unhöflich; primitiv p. 98, 13

ruin /ˈruːɪn/ Ruine p. 78

rule /ruːl/ Regel NHG 5

(to) **rule** /ruːl/ herrschen, regieren NHG 6

ruler /'ruːlə/ Lineal NHG 5

run /rʌn/ Lauf p. 56, 2

(to) **run** *(irr)* /rʌn/ laufen; rennen NHG 6; leiten, betreiben p. 69, 5

runner /'rʌnə/ Läufer/in NHG 6

running race /'rʌnɪŋ reɪs/ Wettrennen p. 54

rural /'rʊərəl/ ländlich p. 145

(to) **rush** /rʌʃ/ eilen p. 78

S

sad /sæd/ traurig NHG 6

safe /seɪf/ sicher; ungefährlich NHG 6

safety /'seɪfti/ Sicherheit NHG 6

salad /'sæləd/ Salat p. 8, 2

salmon /'sæmən/ Lachs p. 22, 6

salt /sɔːlt/ Salz NHG 5

the same /ðə 'seɪm/ der/die/das Gleiche; derselbe/dieselbe/ dasselbe NHG 5

at the same time /æt ˌðə ˌseɪm 'taɪm/ gleichzeitig; zur gleichen Zeit p. 56, 2

samosa /sə'məʊsə/ *indische gefüllte Teigtasche* p. 23, 7

Saturday /'sætədeɪ/ Samstag NHG 5

(on) Saturdays /'sætədeɪz/ samstags NHG 5

sauce /sɔːs/ Soße p. 8, 1

sausage /'sɒsɪdʒ/ Wurst; Würstchen p. 8, 1

(to) **save** /seɪv/ aufheben; sichern p. 91, 2; sparen; retten p. 108, 7

savoury /'seɪvəri/ pikant; salzig p. 8, 2

(to) **say** *(irr)* /seɪ/ sagen NHG 5

(to) **scan** /skæn/ absuchen, überfliegen p. 33, 2

scared /skeəd/ verängstigt, ängstlich NHG 6

(to) be scared (of) /ˌbiː 'skeəd ˌəv/ Angst haben (vor) NHG 5

scary /'skeəri/ Furcht erregend NHG 6

scene /siːn/ Szene NHG 5

school /skuːl/ Schule NHG 5

school counsellor /ˌskuːl 'kaʊnslə/ Vertrauenslehrer/in p. 96, 8

school grounds *(pl)* /'skuːl ˌgraʊndz/ Schulgelände NHG 6

schoolbag /'skuːl,bæg/ Schultasche NHG 5

science /'saɪəns/ Naturwissenschaft NHG 5

the Science Museum /ðə 'saɪəns mjuːˌziːəm/ Naturwissenschafts-museum p. 81, 2

scientist /'saɪəntɪst/ Wissen-schaftler/in p. 107, 5

(a pair of) scissors /'sɪzəz/ Schere NHG 5

score /skɔː/ Punktestand p. 76

Scotland /'skɒtlənd/ Schottland NHG 5

screen /skriːn/ Bildschirm NHG 6

screen time /'skriːn taɪm/ Bild-schirmzeit p. 95, 6

script /skrɪpt/ Drehbuch; Skript NHG 6

search /sɜːtʃ/ Suche NHG 5

(to) **search** /sɜːtʃ/ suchen NHG 5

search engine /'sɜːtʃ ˌendʒɪn/ Suchmaschine p. 117, 6

(to) **search the Internet** /ˌsɜːtʃ ðiˌ'ɪntənet/ im Internet suchen NHG 5

seaside /'siːˌsaɪd/ (Meeres)küste; Meer NHG 6

season /'siːzn/ Saison p. 14, 10

seat /siːt/ Sitz p. 109, 7

(to) **take a seat** *(irr)* /ˌteɪk ə 'siːt/ sich setzen p. 22, 6

seat belt /'siːt belt/ Sicherheitsgurt p. 109, 7

second /'sekənd/ Sekunde; zweite(r, s) NHG 5

second-hand /ˌsekənd 'hænd/ gebraucht p. 56, 2

secret /'siːkrət/ geheim p. 126

section /'sekʃn/ Teil, Stück, Abschnitt; Abteilung p. 107, 5

(to) **see** *(irr)* /siː/ sehen NHG 5; *hier:* empfangen, drannehmen p. 42, 1

(to) **see a doctor** *(irr)* /ˌsiː ə 'dɒktə/ einen Arzt/eine Ärztin aufsuchen p. 43, 1

See you (soon)! /ˌsiː juː 'suːn/ Bis bald! NHG 6

seed /siːd/ Samen p. 127

(to) **seek advice** *(irr)* /ˌsiːk əd'vaɪs/ Rat suchen p. 94, 6

(to) **seem** /siːm/ scheinen p. 100

selection /sɪ'lekʃn/ Auswahl p. 23, 7

(to) **sell** *(irr)* /sel/ verkaufen p. 57, 3

seller /'selə/ Verkäufer/in p. 60, 8

(to) **send** *(irr)* /send/ schicken NHG 5

sentence /'sentəns/ Satz NHG 5

September /sep'tembə/ September NHG 5

series /'sɪəriːz/ Folge; Serie p. 35, 6

serious /'sɪəriəs/ ernst p. 70, 6

(to) **serve** /sɜːv/ servieren; reichen für p. 9, 2

session /'seʃn/ Stunde; Session NHG 5

set /set/ *hier:* Einstellung p. 113, 15

(to) set a date /ˌset ə 'deɪt/ sich verabreden p. 101

(to) **set the table** /ˌset ðə 'teɪbl/ den Tisch decken NHG 5

(to) **set up** *(irr)* /ˌsetˌ'ʌp/ aufbauen p. 74, 12

several /'sevrəl/ einige; verschie-dene p. 62, 10

Shakshuka /ʃək'ʃuːkə/ *traditionelles israelisches und nordafrikani-sches Gericht* p. 9, 2

shall /ʃæl/ sollen; werden p. 57, 3

(to) **be a shame** *(irr)* /ˌbiˌə 'ʃeɪm/ schade sein p. 86, 8

(to) **share** /ʃeə/ teilen NHG 5

she /ʃiː/ sie NHG 5

sheet /ʃiːt/ Blatt; Bogen NHG 6

shelf *(pl* **shelves)** /ʃelf, ʃelvz/ Regal NHG 5

(to) shine *(irr)* /ʃaɪn/ scheinen p. 52

ship /ʃɪp/ Schiff p. 102

shirt /ʃɜːt/ Hemd NHG 5

shoe /ʃuː/ Schuh NHG 6

(to) **shoot** *(irr)* /ʃuːt/ schießen p. 39, 10

shop /ʃɒp/ Geschäft; Laden NHG 5

shop assistant /'ʃɒp əˌsɪstnt/ Verkäufer/in NHG 6

shopping /'ʃɒpɪŋ/ Einkaufen; Einkaufs- NHG 5

(to) **do the shopping** *(irr)* /ˌduː ðə 'ʃɒpɪŋ/ einkaufen NHG 5 (to) **go shopping** *(irr)* /ˌgəʊ ˈʃɒpɪŋ/ einkaufen gehen NHG 6

shopping centre /ˈʃɒpɪŋ ˌsentə/ Einkaufszentrum NHG 5

short /ʃɔːt/ kurz NHG 5

should /ʃʊd/ sollte(st, n, t) NHG 6

shoulder /ˈʃəʊldə/ Schulter p. 51, 16

(to) shout /ʃaʊt/ rufen; schreien p. 77

(to) **shout at somebody** /ˈʃaʊt ət ˌsʌmbədi/ jemanden anschreien NHG 6

(to) **show** *(irr)* /ʃəʊ/ zeigen NHG 5

(to) show somebody around *(irr)* /ˈʃəʊ ˌsʌmbədi əˈraʊnd/ jemanden herumführen p. 124

(to) show to the table *(irr)* /ˈʃəʊ tə ðə ˈteɪbl/ zum Tisch führen p. 22, 6

shy /ʃaɪ/ schüchtern p. 95, 6

sick /sɪk/ krank NHG 6

side /saɪd/ Seite NHG 6

side (dish) /ˈsaɪd dɪʃ/ Beilage p. 19, 2

on the side /ˌɒn ðə ˈsaɪd/ als Beilage p. 22, 6

sight /saɪt/ Sehenswürdigkeit NHG 5

sighted /ˈsaɪtɪd/ sehend p. 54

sign /saɪn/ Zeichen; Schild NHG 6

(to) **sign** /saɪn/ unterschreiben p. 46, 5

(to) sign up (for) /ˌsaɪn ˈʌp/ sich anmelden p. 52

silly /ˈsɪli/ albern; dumm p. 91, 2

similar /ˈsɪmɪlə/ ähnlich NHG 6

simple /ˈsɪmpl/ einfach; simpel p. 109, 7

simple past /ˌsɪmpl ˈpɑːst/ einfache Vergangenheit p. 82

simply /ˈsɪmpli/ einfach NHG 6

since /sɪns/ seit NHG 6

since /sɪns/ da; weil p. 52

(to) **sing** *(irr)* /sɪŋ/ singen NHG 5

(to) **sing along** *(irr)* /ˌsɪŋ əˈlɒŋ/ mitsingen NHG 5

singer /ˈsɪŋə/ Sänger/in NHG 6

singing /ˈsɪŋɪŋ/ singend p. 59, 7

single /ˈsɪŋgl/ einzelne(r, s) NHG 6

sir/Sir /sɜː/ Sir; Herr *(Anrede vor Vornamen)* p. 22, 6

sister /ˈsɪstə/ Schwester NHG 5

(to) **sit** *(irr)* /sɪt/ sitzen p. 33, 2

(to) **sit down** *(irr)* /ˌsɪt ˈdaʊn/ sich hinsetzen NHG 5

site /saɪt/ Stelle; Platz p. 73, 9

size /saɪz/ Größe NHG 5

skateboarding /ˈskeɪtbɔːdɪŋ/ Skateboardfahren NHG 5

cleaning skates *(pl)* /ˈkliːnɪŋ ˌskeɪts/ *Reinigungsskates* p. 111, 11

skating /ˈskeɪtɪŋ/ *hier:* Skateboardfahren p. 40, 12

skill /skɪl/ Fähigkeit; Geschick p. 33, 2

skill /skɪl/ Fertigkeit; Kompetenz p. 9, 2

(to) **skim** /skɪm/ überfliegen p. 18, 2

(to) skip /skɪp/ *hier:* ausfallen lassen p. 91, 2

skirt /skɜːt/ Rock NHG 5

sleep /sliːp/ Schlaf p. 36, 7

(to) **sleep** *(irr)* /sliːp/ schlafen NHG 5

(to) sleep in *(irr)* /ˌsliːp ˈɪn/ ausschlafen p. 129

(to) **slice** /slaɪs/ in Scheiben schneiden p. 13, 8

slide /slaɪd/ Folie p. 41, 13

slide show /ˈslaɪd ʃəʊ/ Bildschirmpräsentation p. 41, 13

slow, slowly /sləʊ, ˈsləʊli/ langsam NHG 6

small /smɔːl/ klein NHG 5

smart /smɑːt/ schlau, clever NHG 6

(to) **smile** /smaɪl/ lächeln NHG 6

so /səʊ/ also; deshalb; daher NHG 5

so far /ˈsəʊ fɑː/ bisher NHG 6

so that /ˈsəʊ ðæt/ damit NHG 6

soccer *(AE)* /ˈsɒkə/ Fußball p. 39, 10

sock /sɒk/ Socke p. 64, 13

soft /sɒft/ weich p. 17, 17

solution /səˈluːʃn/ Lösung NHG 6

(to) **solve** /sɒlv/ lösen NHG 6

some /sʌm/ einige, ein paar; etwas NHG 5

some day /ˈsʌm ˌdeɪ/ eines Tages p. 36, 7

somebody /ˈsʌmbədi/ jemand; irgendwer NHG 6

someone /ˈsʌmwʌn/ jemand; irgendwer NHG 5

something /ˈsʌmθɪŋ/ etwas NHG 5

sometimes /ˈsʌmtaɪmz/ manchmal NHG 5

somewhere /ˈsʌmweə/ irgendwo NHG 6

son /sʌn/ Sohn NHG 5

song /sɒŋ/ Lied NHG 5

soon /suːn/ bald p. 43, 1

See you (soon)! /ˌsiː ju ˈsuːn/ Bis bald! NHG 6

coming soon /ˌkʌmɪŋ ˈsuːn/ in Kürze erscheinend p. 67, 2

sore throat /ˌsɔː ˈθrəʊt/ Halsschmerzen p. 42, 1

sorry /ˈsɒri/ es tut mir leid, Entschuldigung NHG 5

sort /sɔːt/ Sorte; Art NHG 6

(to) **sort** /sɔːt/ sortieren NHG 5

sound /saʊnd/ Geräusch; Klang NHG 6

(to) **sound** /saʊnd/ klingen, sich anhören NHG 5

sound wave /ˈsaʊnd weɪv/ Schallwelle p. 127

soup /suːp/ Suppe p. 20, 3

sour /ˈsaʊə/ sauer p. 140

source /sɔːs/ Quelle p. 117, 6

south /saʊθ/ Süden; Süd- p. 83, 5

South Asian /ˌsaʊθ ˈeɪʒn/ südasiatisch p. 83, 5

South India /ˌsaʊθ ˈɪndiə/ Südindien p. 30

south-west /ˌsaʊθˈwest/ Südwest- p. 70, 6

soy /sɔɪ/ Soja p. 143

space /speɪs/ Raum; Platz NHG 6; Weltall p. 107, 5

Spain /speɪn/ Spanien p. 80, 2

(to) **speak** *(irr)* /spiːk/ sprechen; reden NHG 5

This is … speaking. /ðɪs ɪz … ˈspiːkɪŋ/ Hier spricht … p. 42, 1

special /ˈspeʃl/ besondere(r, s); besonders NHG 5

speciality /ˌspeʃiˈæləti/ Spezialität p. 9, 2

species *(pl* **species***)* /ˈspiːʃiːz, ˈspiːʃiːz/ Art; Spezies NHG 6

spectacle /ˈspektəkl/ Spektakel p. 71, 6

spectacular /spekˈtækjʊlə/ atemberaubend; spektakulär p. 67, 2

speech bubble /'spi:tʃ ˌbʌbl/ Sprechblase p. 87, 8

(to) **spell** *(irr)* /spel/ buchstabieren NHG 5

spelling /'spelɪŋ/ Buchstabieren; Rechtschreibung NHG 6

(to) **spend** *(irr)* /spend/ verbringen *(Zeit)*; ausgeben *(Geld)* NHG 6

spice /spaɪs/ Gewürz p. 12, 7

spicy /'spaɪsi/ würzig; scharf p. 9, 2

spider /'spaɪdə/ Spinne p. 26, 12

(to) **spin** *(irr)* /spɪn/ drehen, einen Drall geben p. 39, 10; spinnen p. 77

spinach /'spɪnɪdʒ/ Spinat p. 23, 7

Spinning Jenny /ˌspɪnɪŋ 'dʒeni/ *Feinspinnmaschine* p. 125

spinning wheel /'spɪnɪŋ ˌwiːl/ Spinnrad p. 76

spirit /'spɪrɪt/ Geist; Stimmung p. 53

spoken /'spəʊkən/ gesprochen p. 30

spoon /spuːn/ Löffel NHG 5

sport /spɔːt/ Sport; Sportart NHG 5

sports day /'spɔːts deɪ/ *Sportfest* p. 52

sporty /'spɔːti/ sportlich p. 37, 7

sprained /spreɪnd/ verstaucht p. 46, 5

spring /sprɪŋ/ Frühling NHG 6

spring roll /'sprɪŋ rəʊl/ Frühlingsrolle p. 137

stage /steɪdʒ/ Bühne NHG 6

stair /steə/ Stufe NHG 6

stairs *(pl)* /steəz/ Treppe NHG 6

stall /stɔːl/ Stand p. 56, 2

(to) **stand** *(irr)* /stænd/ stehen NHG 6

(to) **stand for** *(irr)* /'stænd fɔː/ stehen für NHG 6

star /stɑː/ Stern NHG 5

(to) **stare at** /'steər ˌæt/ anstarren p. 28

start /stɑːt/ Anfang; Beginn NHG 5

(to) **start** /stɑːt/ anfangen; beginnen NHG 5

starter /'stɑːtə/ Vorspeise p. 17, 17

(to) **starve** /stɑːv/ verhungern p. 12, 7

statement /'steɪtmənt/ Äußerung, Aussage NHG 5

station /'steɪʃn/ U-Bahn-Station; Bahnhof NHG 5

station /'steɪʃn/ *hier:* Station p. 125

(to) **stay** /steɪ/ bleiben; wohnen NHG 5

(to) **stay away from** /ˌsteɪ ə'weɪ frɒm/ meiden; sich fernhalten von p. 18, 2

(to) **stay up (late)** /ˌsteɪ ˌʌp 'leɪt/ lange aufbleiben p. 98, 13

(to) **steal** *(irr)* /stiːl/ stehlen p. 69, 5

steam engine /'stiːm ˌendʒɪn/ Dampfmaschine p. 105, 2

steam locomotive /'stiːm ˌləʊkəˌməʊtɪv/ Dampflokomotive; Dampflok p. 105, 2

steam machine /'stiːm məˈʃiːn/ Dampfmaschine p. 126

steel drum /ˌstiːl 'drʌm/ *Steeldrum* p. 71, 6

step /step/ Stufe; Schritt NHG 5

(to) **step** /step/ treten; steigen NHG 6

stick /stɪk/ Stock p. 127

(to) **stick** *(irr)* /stɪk/ festhängen p. 76

(to) **stick to** *(irr)* /'stɪk tʊ/ kleben; *hier:* sich halten an p. 127

still /stɪl/ (immer) noch NHG 5; nach wie vor, trotzdem p. 86, 8

still /stɪl/ still; bewegungslos p. 33, 2

(to) **stir in** /ˌstɜːr 'ɪn/ einrühren; unterrühren p. 13, 8

vegetable stock /'vedʒtəbl stɒk/ Gemüsebrühe p. 17, 17

stomach /'stʌmək/ Magen; Bauch p. 43, 1

stomach ache *(no pl)* /'stʌmək ˌeɪk/ Bauchschmerzen p. 42, 1

stone /stəʊn/ Stein p. 118, 7

(to) **stop** /stɒp/ stehen bleiben; anhalten NHG 5; aufhören NHG 6; stoppen p. 94, 6

(to) **store** /stɔː/ lagern p. 109, 7

story /'stɔːri/ Geschichte, Erzählung NHG 5

storytelling /'stɔːriˌtelɪŋ/ Geschichtenerzählen p. 84, 6

straight on /ˌstreɪt 'ɒn/ geradeaus NHG 6

strange /streɪndʒ/ sonderbar; merkwürdig NHG 6

strap /stræp/ Riemen p. 109, 7

strategy /'strætədʒi/ Strategie p. 35, 6

straw /strɔː/ Strohhalm p. 73, 9

strawberry /'strɔːbri/ Erdbeere p. 25, 10

streamer /'striːmə/ Wimpel; Fähnchen p. 52

street /striːt/ Straße NHG 5

strength /streŋθ/ Kraft; Stärke p. 33, 2

stress /stres/ Betonung NHG 6

(to) **stress** /stres/ stressen p. 36, 7

stressed /strest/ gestresst p. 36, 7

strict /strɪkt/ streng NHG 6

string /strɪŋ/ Schnur; Kordel NHG 6

strong /strɒŋ/ stark p. 81, 2

student /'stjuːdnt/ Schüler/in NHG 5; Student/in p. 66, 2

(to) **study** /'stʌdi/ studieren; lernen p. 82, 4

stuff *(informal)* /stʌf/ Zeug NHG 6

stupid /'stjuːpɪd/ dumm, blöd NHG 6

(to) **stutter** /'stʌtə/ stottern p. 78

style /staɪl/ Stil NHG 6

(to) **style** /staɪl/ frisieren p. 68, 3

subject /'sʌbdʒɪkt/ Schulfach NHG 5; Thema; Betreff *(in Emails)* NHG 6

(to) **succeed** /sək'siːd/ Erfolg haben p. 78

success /sək'ses/ Erfolg p. 53

successful /sək'sesfl/ erfolgreich p. 61, 8

such /sʌtʃ/ so; solch p. 71, 6

such as /'sʌtʃ ˌæz/ wie p. 30

suddenly /'sʌdnli/ plötzlich NHG 6

sugar /'ʃʊgə/ Zucker NHG 6

(to) **suggest** /sə'dʒest/ vorschlagen NHG 6

suggestion /sə'dʒestʃn/ Vorschlag NHG 6

summary /'sʌməri/ Zusammenfassung p. 121, 13

summer /'sʌmə/ Sommer NHG 5

sun /sʌn/ Sonne NHG 5

Sunday /'sʌndeɪ/ Sonntag NHG 5

(on) Sundays /'sʌndeɪz/ sonntags NHG 5

sunny /'sʌni/ sonnig NHG 5

sunshine /'sʌnʃaɪn/ Sonnenschein NHG 5

sure /ʃɔː/ sicher NHG 5

(to) **make sure** *(irr)* /ˌmeɪk 'ʃɔː/ darauf achten, dass … NHG 6

surprise /sə'praɪz/ Überraschung
p. 29

surprised /sə'praɪzd/ überrascht;
erstaunt NHG 6

surprising /sə'praɪzɪŋ/ über-
raschend NHG 6

(to) sweat /swet/ schwitzen p. 52

Sweden /'swiːdn/ Schweden p. 81, 2

Swedish /'swiːdɪʃ/ schwedisch p. 81, 2

sweet /swiːt/ süß NHG 5; Süßigkeit
NHG 6

(to) **swim** *(irr)* /swɪm/ schwimmen
NHG 5

swimming /'swɪmɪŋ/ Schwimmen
NHG 5

(to) **go swimming** *(irr)* /ˌgəʊ
'swɪmɪŋ/ schwimmen gehen NHG 6

swimming pool /'swɪmɪŋ puːl/
Schwimmbad NHG 5

(to) **switch off** /ˌswɪtʃ_'ɒf/
ausschalten p. 41, 13

(to) **switch on** /ˌswɪtʃ_'ɒn/
einschalten NHG 5

swollen /'swəʊlən/ geschwollen
p. 42, 1

sword /sɔːd/ Schwert p. 76

syllable /'sɪləbl/ Silbe p. 20, 4

T

table /'teɪbl/ Tisch NHG 5; Tabelle
NHG 6

(to) **set the table** /ˌset ðə 'teɪbl/ den
Tisch decken NHG 5

table tennis /'teɪbl ˌtenɪs/ Tisch-
tennis NHG 5

tablet /'tæblət/ Block; Platte p. 118, 7

(to) **take** *(irr)* /teɪk/ nehmen;
bringen; benötigen; brauchen
NHG 5; dauern NHG 6

(to) take a hike *(AE, informal, irr)*
/ˌteɪk_ə 'haɪk/ abhauen p. 102

(to) **take a photo** *(irr)* /ˌteɪk_ə
'fəʊtəʊ/ ein Foto machen NHG 5

(to) **take a picture** *(irr)* /ˌteɪk_ə
'pɪktʃə/ ein Foto machen NHG 5

(to) **take a seat** *(irr)* /ˌteɪk_ə 'siːt/
sich setzen p. 22, 6

(to) **take an order** *(irr)*
/ˌteɪk_ən_'ɔːdə/ eine Bestellung
aufnehmen p. 22, 6

(to) **take an X-ray** *(irr)* /ˌteɪk_ən
'eksreɪ/ eine Röntgenaufnahme
machen p. 42, 1

(to) **take away** *(irr)* /ˌteɪk_ə'weɪ/
wegnehmen; mitnehmen NHG 6

(to) **take care (of)** *(irr)*
/ˌteɪk_'keər_əv/ sich kümmern um
NHG 6

(to) take in *(irr)* /ˌteɪk_'ɪn/
aufnehmen p. 78

(to) **take notes (on)** *(irr)* /ˌteɪk
'nəʊts/ sich Notizen machen (zu)
NHG 5

(to) **take out** *(irr)* /ˌteɪk_'aʊt/
hinausbringen NHG 5

(to) **take out** *(irr)* /ˌteɪk_'aʊt/
herausnehmen p. 29

(to) **take part in** *(irr)* /ˌteɪk 'paːt_ɪn/
teilnehmen an NHG 6

(to) **take place** *(irr)* /ˌteɪk 'pleɪs/
stattfinden NHG 6

(to) **take turns** *(irr)* /ˌteɪk 'tɜːnz/
sich abwechseln NHG 6

(to) take up time *(irr)* /ˌteɪk_ʌp 'taɪm/
Zeit beanspruchen p. 136

takeaway /'teɪkəˌweɪ/ Essen zum
Mitnehmen; Imbissbude p. 18, 1

talented /'tæləntɪd/ talentiert
p. 125

talk /tɔːk/ Gespräch; Vortrag
p. 123, 16

(to) **talk about** /'tɔːk_əˌbaʊt/
sprechen über NHG 5

(to) **talk (to)** /tɔːk/ sprechen (mit);
reden (mit) NHG 5

tall /tɔːl/ groß NHG 6

target task /'taːgɪt ˌtaːsk/
Zielaufgabe p. 17, 17

task /taːsk/ Aufgabe NHG 5

taste /teɪst/ Geschmack p. 60, 8

(to) **taste** /teɪst/ schmecken NHG 6

tasty /'teɪsti/ lecker p. 20, 3

tea /tiː/ Tee NHG 5

(to) **teach** *(irr)* /tiːtʃ/ unterrichten
NHG 5

teacher /'tiːtʃə/ Lehrer/in NHG 5

(to) **tease** /tiːz/ hänseln, ärgern
p. 95, 6

teaspoon /'tiːˌspuːn/ Teelöffel
p. 17, 17

technique /tek'niːk/ Technik p. 52

technology /tek'nɒlədʒi/
Technologie; Technik NHG 6

teddy bear /'tedi beə/ Teddybär
p. 69, 5

teen /tiːn/ Teenager p. 94, 6

(to) **brush one's teeth** /ˌbrʌʃ wʌnz
'tiːθ/ sich die Zähne putzen NHG 5

telephone /'telɪˌfəʊn/ Telefon NHG 6

telescope /'telɪˌskəʊp/ Teleskop
p. 106, 4

television /'telɪˌvɪʒn/ Fernseher;
Fernsehen p. 105, 2

(to) **tell** *(irr)* /tel/ erzählen NHG 5

temp (= temperature) /'temprɪtʃə/
Temperatur p. 113, 15

tender /'tendə/ zart p. 143

tent /tent/ Zelt p. 70, 6

term /tɜːm/ Trimester; Begriff NHG 5

terrible /'terəbl/ schrecklich NHG 5

(to) **text** /tekst/ eine Textnachricht
schreiben NHG 5

text (message) /'tekst ˌmesɪdʒ/
Textnachricht NHG 5

Textiles Gallery /'tekstaɪlz ˌgæləri/
*Bereich im Museum, in dem es
um Stoffe geht* p. 125

Thai /taɪ/ Thailänder/in;
thailändisch p. 18, 1

than /ðæn/ als *(bei Vergleich)*
NHG 6

thank you /'θæŋk ju/ danke NHG 5

thanks /θæŋks/ danke NHG 5

thanks a lot /ˌθæŋks_ə 'lɒt/
vielen Dank NHG 5

I'm good, thanks. /aɪm 'gʊd ˌθæŋks/
Es geht mir gut, danke. NHG 5

that /ðæt/ das; der/die/das (dort);
dass NHG 5; so NHG 6

that's (= that is) /ðæts, 'ðæt_ɪz/
hier: das kostet NHG 5

the /ðə/ der/die/das NHG 5

theatre /'θɪətə/ Theater NHG 6

their /ðeə/ ihr(e) NHG 5

theirs /ðeəz/ ihre(r, s) p. 98, 12

them /ðem/ sie; ihnen NHG 5

theme /θiːm/ Thema NHG 6

themselves /ðəm'selvz/ sich; selbst
p. 126

then /ðen/ dann NHG 5

theory /'θɪəri/ Theorie p. 118, 7

there /ðeə/ dort; dahin NHG 5

there are /ðeər_'ɑː/ dort sind; es gibt NHG 5

there's (= there is) /ðeəz, ðeər_'ɪz/ dort ist; es gibt NHG 5

these (*pl of* **this**) /ði:z/ diese; das NHG 5

they /ðeɪ/ sie NHG 5

thin /θɪn/ dünn p. 9, 2

thing /θɪŋ/ Ding; Gegenstand NHG 5

(to) **think** *(irr)* /θɪŋk/ denken; glauben NHG 5

(to) **think about** *(irr)* /'θɪŋk_ə,baʊt/ denken an, nachdenken über NHG 5

(to) **think of** *(irr)* /'θɪŋk_əv/ denken an, sich ausdenken NHG 5

logical thinking /ˌlɒdʒɪkl 'θɪŋkɪŋ/ logisches Denken p. 33, 2

third /θɜːd/ dritte(r, s) NHG 5

this /ðɪs/ diese(r, s) NHG 5

This is … speaking. /ðɪs_ɪz … 'spiːkɪŋ/ Hier spricht … p. 42, 1

this way /'ðɪs weɪ/ hier entlang p. 22, 6

those (*pl of* **that**) /ðəʊz/ diese, jene NHG 5

thought /θɔːt/ Gedanke p. 80, 1

thought bubble /'θɔːt ˌbʌbl/ Gedankenblase p. 87, 8

thousand /'θaʊznd/ tausend NHG 6

sore throat /ˌsɔː 'θrəʊt/ Halsschmerzen p. 42, 1

throne /θrəʊn/ Thron p. 78

through /θruː/ durch NHG 6

throughout /θruː'aʊt/ während p. 67, 2

throw /θrəʊ/ Wurf p. 53

(to) **throw** *(irr)* /θrəʊ/ werfen NHG 5

(to) **throw away** *(irr)* /ˌθrəʊ_ə'weɪ/ wegwerfen NHG 6

throwing /'θrəʊɪŋ/ Weitwurf p. 53

thumb /θʌm/ Daumen p. 119, 7

Thursday /'θɜːzdeɪ/ Donnerstag NHG 5

(on) Thursdays /'θɜːzdeɪz/ donnerstags NHG 5

tidy /'taɪdi/ ordentlich; aufgeräumt NHG 5

(to) **tidy (up)** /'taɪdi, ˌtaɪdi_'ʌp/ aufräumen NHG 5

tie /taɪ/ Krawatte NHG 5

till /tɪl/ bis NHG 5

time /taɪm/ Zeit; Mal NHG 5

all the time /ˌɔːl ðə 'taɪm/ die ganze Zeit NHG 6

at that time /ˌæt_'ðæt_taɪm/ zu jener Zeit p. 87, 8

at the same time /ˌæt_ðə ˌseɪm 'taɪm/ gleichzeitig; zur gleichen Zeit p. 56, 2

for some time /fə ˌsʌm 'taɪm/ eine Zeitlang p. 37, 7

for the first time /fə ðə 'fɜːst_taɪm/ zum ersten Mal NHG 6

most of the time /'məʊst_əv ðə ˌtaɪm/ meistens p. 37, 7

on time /ˌɒn 'taɪm/ pünktlich NHG 5

What time is it? / What's the time, please? /wɒt_'taɪm_ɪz_ɪt, ˌwɒts ðə 'taɪm pliːz/ Wie spät ist es (bitte)? NHG 5

(to) take up time *(irr)* /ˌteɪk_ʌp 'taɪm/ Zeit beanspruchen p. 136

time travelling /'taɪm ˌtrævlɪŋ/ Zeitreisen p. 126

timeline /'taɪmlaɪn/ Zeitachse p. 87, 9

timetable /'taɪmteɪbl/ Stundenplan NHG 5; Fahrplan NHG 6

tin /tɪn/ Büchse; Dose p. 109, 7

tin opener /'tɪn_ˌəʊpnə/ Dosenöffner p. 109, 7

tip /tɪp/ Tipp NHG 6

tired /'taɪəd/ müde NHG 6

title /'taɪtl/ Titel; Überschrift NHG 6

to /tʊ/ (um) zu; in; nach; zu; an; bis; vor NHG 5

toad in the hole /ˌtəʊd_ɪn ðə 'həʊl/ *Bratwürste in einem Yorkshire Pudding* L&L 1

today /tə'deɪ/ heute NHG 5; heutzutage NHG 6

toe /təʊ/ Zeh NHG 5

together /tə'geðə/ zusammen NHG 5

toilet /'tɔɪlət/ Toilette NHG 5

toilet roll /'tɔɪlət rəʊl/ Toilettenpapier-Rolle p. 111, 11

Tokyo /'təʊkiəʊ/ Tokio p. 54

tomato (*pl* **tomatoes**) /tə'mɑːtəʊ, tə'mɑːtəʊz/ Tomate NHG 5

tomorrow /tə'mɒrəʊ/ morgen NHG 5

ton /tʌn/ Tonne p. 73, 9

tonight /tə'naɪt/ heute Abend p. 28

too /tuː/ auch; zu NHG 5

tool /tuːl/ Werkzeug p. 109, 7

tooth (*pl* **teeth**) /tuːθ, tiːθ/ Zahn p. 42, 1

toothache (*no pl*) /'tuːθeɪk/ Zahnschmerzen p. 42, 1

toothbrush /'tuːθbrʌʃ/ Zahnbürste p. 104, 2

top /tɒp/ beste(r, s) NHG 5; oberes Ende; Spitze NHG 6

(to) **go for the top** *(irr)* /ˌgəʊ fə ðə 'tɒp/ sich um Höchstleistungen bemühen p. 52

topic /'tɒpɪk/ Thema NHG 5

tor /tɔː/ Felsturm p. 78

torch /tɔːtʃ/ Taschenlampe NHG 6

(to) **toss** /tɒs/ werfen p. 71, 6

tossing the caber /ˌtɒsɪŋ ðə 'keɪbə/ Baumstammwerfen p. 71, 6

(to) **touch** /tʌtʃ/ berühren NHG 5

(to) **keep in touch** *(irr)* /ˌkiːp_ɪn 'tʌtʃ/ Kontakt halten; in Verbindung bleiben p. 119, 7

tournament /'tʊənəmənt/ Turnier p. 35, 6

towards /tə'wɔːdz/ in Richtung, zu; gegenüber NHG 6

tower /'taʊə/ Turm NHG 6

town /taʊn/ Stadt NHG 5

toy /tɔɪ/ Spielzeug NHG 5

track /træk/ *hier:* Bahn p. 53

trade /treɪd/ Handel p. 30

(to) trade /treɪd/ Geschäfte machen; handeln p. 30

traditional /trə'dɪʃnəl/ traditionell NHG 6

train /treɪn/ Zug NHG 5

(to) **train** /treɪn/ trainieren p. 33, 2

transatlantic /ˌtrænzət'læntɪk/ transatlantisch p. 105, 2

(to) **translate** /træns'leɪt/ übersetzen p. 15, 11

transport /'trænspɔːt/ Transport; Verkehrsmittel NHG 6

(to) transport /træns'pɔːt/ transportieren p. 130

travel /'trævl/ Reise NHG 6

(to) **travel** /'trævl/ reisen; fahren NHG 5

travel guide /ˈtrævl ɡaɪd/
Reiseführer *(Buch)* p. 62, 10

travelling /ˈtrævlɪŋ/ Reisen
NHG 6

(to) **treat** /triːt/ behandeln p. 121, 12

tree /triː/ Baum NHG 5

trick /trɪk/ Trick; Kunststück NHG 5

trip /trɪp/ Ausflug; Fahrt NHG 6

triple jump /ˈtrɪpl dʒʌmp/ Drei-
sprung p. 53

trophy /ˈtrəʊfi/ Trophäe p. 53

trouble /ˈtrʌbl/ Ärger; Schwierig-
keiten NHG 6

(a pair of) trousers /ə ˌpeər ˌəv
ˈtraʊzəz/ Hose NHG 5

truck /trʌk/ Lastwagen p. 102

true /truː/ wahr NHG 5

(to) **trust** /trʌst/ vertrauen p. 121, 12

(to) **try** /traɪ/ (aus)probieren;
versuchen NHG 5

(to) give a try *(irr)* /ˌɡɪv ə ˈtraɪ/
ausprobieren p. 100

(to) **try on** /ˌtraɪ ˈɒn/ anprobieren
p. 60, 8

(to) **try out** /ˌtraɪ ˈaʊt/ ausprobieren p. 17, 17

the Tube /ðə ˈtjuːb/ (Londoner)
U-Bahn p. 108, 6

Tuesday /ˈtjuːzdeɪ/ Dienstag NHG 5

(on) Tuesdays /ˈtjuːzdeɪz/
dienstags NHG 5

tuition /tjuˈɪʃn/ *hier:* Nachhilfe p. 91, 2

tunic /ˈtjuːnɪk/ Tunika p. 76

Turkey /ˈtɜːki/ die Türkei p. 9, 2

Turkish /ˈtɜːkɪʃ/ türkisch p. 18, 1

turmeric /ˈtɜːmərɪk/ Kurkuma p. 30

(to) **turn** /tɜːn/ abbiegen NHG 6

(to) turn around /ˌtɜːn ə'raʊnd/ sich
umdrehen p. 77

(to) **turn off** /ˌtɜːn ˈɒf/ ausschalten
p. 39, 10

(to) **turn over** /ˌtɜːn ˈəʊvə/ (sich)
umdrehen p. 71, 6

(to) turn to /ˈtɜːn tʊ/ (sich) wenden
an p. 127

(to) **be one's turn** *(irr)* /ˌbiː wʌnz
ˈtɜːn/ an der Reihe sein NHG 5

(to) **take turns** *(irr)* /ˌteɪk ˈtɜːnz/
sich abwechseln NHG 6

TV (= television) /ˌtiː ˈviː, ˈtelɪˌvɪʒn/
Fernsehen; Fernseher NHG 6

(to) **watch TV** /ˌwɒtʃ tiː ˈviː/
Fernsehen gucken NHG 5

twice /twaɪs/ zweimal p. 36, 7

twin /twɪn/ Zwilling; Zwillings- NHG 5

type /taɪp/ Art NHG 6

typical /ˈtɪpɪkl/ typisch NHG 5

U

ugly /ˈʌɡli/ hässlich NHG 6

the UK (= United Kingdom) /ðə ˌjuː
ˈkeɪ, juːˌnaɪtɪd ˈkɪŋdəm/ Vereinigtes
Königreich NHG 6

umbrella /ʌmˈbrelə/ Regenschirm
p. 126

uncle /ˈʌŋkl/ Onkel NHG 5

uncomplicated /ʌnˈkɒmplɪˌkeɪtɪd/
unkompliziert p. 119, 7

under /ˈʌndə/ unter NHG 5

underground /ˈʌndəˌɡraʊnd/
U-Bahn NHG 6

(to) **understand** *(irr)* /ˌʌndəˈstænd/
verstehen NHG 5

unfortunately /ʌnˈfɔːtʃnətli/
unglücklicherweise NHG 6

unit /ˈjuːnɪt/ Kapitel p. 41, 13

university /ˌjuːnɪˈvɜːsəti/ Universität
p. 81, 2

unless /ənˈles/ außer wenn p. 94, 6

(to) unscramble /ʌnˈskræmbl/
ordnen, in die richtige
Reihenfolge bringen p. 9, 2

until /ənˈtɪl/ bis NHG 6

unusual /ʌnˈjuːʒuəl/ ungewöhnlich
NHG 5

up /ʌp/ nach oben; hinauf; oben
NHG 5

What's up? *(informal)* /ˌwɒts ˈʌp/
Was ist los? p. 90, 2

(to) be up for something *(informal,
irr)* /ˌbi ˌʌp fɔː ˈsʌmθɪŋ/ Lust zu
etwas haben p. 91, 2

(to) be up to something *(irr)* /ˌbi ˌʌp
tə ˈsʌmθɪŋ/ etwas vorhaben p. 57, 3

(to) upcycle /ˈʌpsaɪkl/ upcyceln
p. 63, 12

upset /ʌpˈset/ aufgebracht;
aufgeregt p. 91, 2

upstairs /ʌpˈsteəz/ (nach) oben
p. 100

us /ʌs/ uns NHG 5

**the USA (= United States
of America)** /ðə ˌjuː_esˌˈeɪ, juːˌnaɪtɪd
ˌsteɪts ˌəv əˈmerɪkə/ USA; Vereinigte
Staaten von Amerika NHG 6

use /juːs/ Verwendung; Einsatz
p. 73, 9

(to) **use** /juːz/ benutzen NHG 5

used to + *infinitive* /ˈjuːst ˌtuː/
früher + *Vergangenheitsform*
NHG 6

useful /ˈjuːsfl/ nützlich NHG 5

user /ˈjuːzə/ Benutzer/in p. 127

usual /ˈjuːʒuəl/ gewöhnlich, üblich
p. 29

usually /ˈjuːʒuəli/ gewöhnlich;
normalerweise NHG 5

V

(to) **vacuum** /ˈvækjuəm/
staubsaugen NHG 5

vegan /ˈviːɡən/ Veganer/in; vegan
p. 14, 10

vegetable /ˈvedʒtəbl/ Gemüse
p. 17, 17

vegetable stock /ˈvedʒtəbl stɒk/
Gemüsebrühe p. 17, 17

vegetarian /ˌvedʒəˈteəriən/
Vegetarier/in; vegetarisch p. 8, 2

veggie *(informal)* /ˈvedʒi, ˈvedʒtəbl/
Gemüse p. 12, 7

Velcro® /ˈvelkrəʊ/ *Klettverschluss*
p. 127

verse /vɜːs/ Strophe; Vers NHG 6

version /ˈvɜːʃn/ Version, Fassung
NHG 6

very /ˈveri/ sehr NHG 5

the very first /ðə ˌveri ˈfɜːst/ der/die/
das allererste p. 101

very much /ˌveri ˈmʌtʃ/ sehr NHG 6

vet /vet/ Tierarzt/-ärztin NHG 6

victory /ˈvɪktri/ Sieg NHG 6

Vietnamese /ˌviˌetnəˈmiːz/
Vietnamese/Vietnamesin;
vietnamesisch p. 18, 1

view /vjuː/ (Aus)sicht NHG 6

Viking /ˈvaɪkɪŋ/ Wikinger/in;
Wikinger- p. 66, 1

village /ˈvɪlɪdʒ/ Dorf p. 81, 2

vindaloo /ˌvɪndəˈluː/ *indisches
Gericht* p. 19, 2

visit /ˈvɪzɪt/ Besuch NHG 5

(to) **visit** /ˈvɪzɪt/ besuchen NHG 6

visitor /ˈvɪzɪtə/ Besucher/in
NHG 6

voice /vɔɪs/ Stimme NHG 6

VR glasses *(pl)* /ˌviˌˈɑː ˌɡlɑːsɪz/
VR-Brille p. 125

W

(to) **wait** /weɪt/ warten, erwarten
NHG 5

waiter/waitress /ˈweɪtə, ˈweɪtrəs/
Kellner/in p. 22, 6

waiting room /ˈweɪtɪŋ ˌruːm/
Wartezimmer p. 46, 5

(to) **wake up** *(irr)* /ˌweɪkˈʌp/
aufwachen NHG 6

(to) wake up *(irr)* /ˌweɪkˈʌp/
aufwecken p. 76

walk /wɔːk/ Spaziergang

(to) **walk** /wɔːk/ gehen NHG 5

walking stick /ˈwɔːkɪŋ stɪk/
Spazierstock; Krückstock p. 127

wall /wɔːl/ Wand NHG 6

(to) wander around
/ˌwɒndərˌəˈraʊnd/ umherstreifen
p. 125

(to) **want (to)** /wɒnt/ wollen
NHG 5

war /wɔː/ Krieg p. 85, 7

World War II /ˌwɜːld ˌwɔː ˈtuː/ Zweiter
Weltkrieg p. 85, 7

(to) **warn** /wɔːn/ warnen p. 22, 6

warrior /ˈwɒriə/ Krieger/in p. 66, 2

(to) **wash** /wɒʃ/ waschen; sich
waschen NHG 5

waste /weɪst/ Abfall p. 73, 9

watch /wɒtʃ/ (Armband)uhr NHG 6

(to) **watch** /wɒtʃ/ beobachten;
ansehen NHG 5

(to) **watch TV** /ˌwɒtʃ tiː ˈviː/
Fernsehen gucken NHG 5

water /ˈwɔːtə/ Wasser NHG 5

way /weɪ/ Weg; Art NHG 5

this way /ˈðɪs weɪ/ hier entlang
p. 22, 6

we /wiː/ wir NHG 5

(to) **wear** *(irr)* /weə/ tragen
(Kleidung) NHG 5

weather /ˈweðə/ Wetter NHG 5

web page /ˈweb ˌpeɪdʒ/ Webseite;
Internetseite p. 11, 6

Wednesday /ˈwenzdeɪ/ Mittwoch
NHG 5

(on) Wednesdays /ˈwenzdeɪz/
mittwochs NHG 5

week /wiːk/ Woche NHG 5

weekend /ˌwiːkˈend/ Wochenende
NHG 5

weight /weɪt/ Gewicht p. 133

weight training /ˈweɪtˌtreɪnɪŋ/
Krafttraining p. 32, 1

welcome (to) /ˈwelkəm tʊ/
willkommen (in) NHG 5

You're welcome. /jɔː ˈwelkəm/ Gern
geschehen.; Keine Ursache.
p. 65, 15

well /wel/ nun NHG 5; gut NHG 6

(to) **get well** *(irr)* /ˌget ˈwel/ gesund
werden p. 44, 2

well done /ˌwel ˈdʌn/ gut gemacht
NHG 6

well-known /ˌwelˈnəʊn/ bekannt;
berühmt p. 78

West African /ˌwestˈæfrɪkən/ West-
afrikaner/in; westafrikanisch
p. 81, 2

Western /ˈwestən/ West-, westlich
p. 30

wet /wet/ nass NHG 6

what /wɒt/ was; welche(r, s) NHG 5

What about …? /ˌwɒt əˌbaʊt ˈ…/ Was
ist mit …? / Wie wäre es mit …?
NHG 5

What if …? /ˌwɒt ˈɪf/ Was wäre,
wenn …? p. 91, 2

What time is it? /wɒt ˈtaɪm ɪz ɪt/
Wie spät ist es? NHG 5

What … would you like? /ˌwɒt …
wəd jə ˈlaɪk/ Was für ein / eine …
hättest du / hättet ihr / hätten
Sie gern? NHG 5

What's on? *(informal)* /ˌwɒtsˈɒn/
Was ist los? NHG 6

What's the matter? /ˌwɒtsˌðə
ˈmætə/ Was ist los? p. 42, 1

What's the time, please? /ˌwɒts ðə
ˈtaɪm pliːz/ Wie spät ist es, bitte?
NHG 5

What's up? *(informal)* /ˌwɒtsˈʌp/
Was ist los? p. 90, 2

What's wrong? *(informal)*
/ˌwɒtsˈrɒŋ/ Was ist los? p. 90, 2

whatever /wɒtˈevə/ was (auch
immer) NHG 6

wheel /wiːl/ Rad NHG 6

wheelchair /ˈwiːltʃeə/ Rollstuhl
p. 36, 7

when /wen/ wann; wenn; als NHG 5

whenever /wenˈevə/ wann auch
immer p. 63, 12

where /weə/ wo; wohin NHG 5

which /wɪtʃ/ welche(r, s); was NHG 5

while /waɪl/ während NHG 6; Weile
p. 85, 7

(to) **whip cream** /ˌwɪp ˈkriːm/ Sahne
schlagen p. 29

white /waɪt/ weiß NHG 5

who /huː/ wer; der/die/das NHG 5

whole /həʊl/ ganz, gesamt NHG 6

whose /huːz/ wessen NHG 5

why /waɪ/ warum NHG 5

wide /waɪd/ weit p. 118, 7

wife *(pl* **wives)** /waɪf, waɪvz/
Ehefrau NHG 5

WiFi /ˈwaɪ faɪ/ WLAN p. 113, 15

wildlife /ˈwaɪldlaɪf/ Tier- und
Pflanzenwelt; Flora und Fauna
NHG 6

will /wɪl/ werden NHG 6

(to) **win** *(irr)* /wɪn/ gewinnen p. 32, 1

window /ˈwɪndəʊ/ Fenster NHG 5

winner /ˈwɪnə/ Gewinner/in p. 53

(to) **wish** /wɪʃ/ wünschen p. 95, 6

with /wɪð/ mit; bei NHG 5

without /wɪðˈaʊt/ ohne NHG 5

wizard /ˈwɪzəd/ Zauberer p. 78

woman *(pl* **women)** /ˈwʊmən,
ˈwɪmɪn/ Frau NHG 5

won't /wəʊnt/ nicht werden NHG 6

(to) **wonder** /ˈwʌndə/ sich fragen
NHG 6

wonderful /ˈwʌndəfl/ wunderbar,
wundervoll NHG 6

wood /wʊd/ Holz NHG 6

wooden /ˈwʊdn/ Holz-, hölzern
p. 76

word /wɜːd/ Wort NHG 5

word search /ˈwɜːd sɜːtʃ/ Wortsuche
p. 97, 10

word web /ˈwɜːd web/ Wortnetz
NHG 5

wordbank /ˈwɜːdbæŋk/
Wortsammlung NHG 5

work /wɜːk/ Arbeit; Werk NHG 5

(to) **work** /wɜːk/ arbeiten NHG 5; funktionieren NHG 6

(to) **work out** /ˌwɜːk ˈaʊt/ ausarbeiten p. 100; *hier:* aufgehen p. 101

workbook /ˈwɜːkbʊk/ Arbeitsheft p. 8, 1

working /ˈwɜːkɪŋ/ funktionierend p. 105, 2

workout /ˈwɜːkaʊt/ Training p. 36, 7

worksheet /ˈwɜːkʃiːt/ Arbeitsblatt p. 14, 9

world /wɜːld/ Welt NHG 5

all over the world /ˌɔːl ˌəʊvə ðə ˈwɜːld/ auf der ganzen Welt NHG 6

from all over the world /frəm ˌɔːl ˌəʊvə ðə ˈwɜːld/ aus der ganzen Welt NHG 5

from (all) around the world /frəm ˌɔːl əˌraʊnd ðə ˈwɜːld/ aus der (ganzen) Welt p. 11, 6

World War II /ˌwɜːld ˌwɔː ˈtuː/ Zweiter Weltkrieg p. 85, 7

world-famous /ˌwɜːld ˈfeɪməs/ weltberühmt p. 70, 6

worried /ˈwʌrid/ beunruhigt; besorgt NHG 6

(to) **worry** /ˈwʌri/ sich Sorgen machen NHG 5

worse /wɜːs/ schlechter, schlimmer NHG 6

the worst /ðə ˈwɜːst/ der/die/das schlechteste/schlimmste; am schlechtesten/schlimmsten NHG 6

would /wʊd/ würde(st, n, t) NHG 5

I would like ... (= I'd like ...) /aɪ ˌwʊd ˈlaɪk, aɪd ˈlaɪk/ Ich würde gern ... / Ich hätte gern ... NHG 5

Would you like ...? /ˌwʊd ju ˈlaɪk/ Hättest du / Hättet ihr / Hätten Sie gern ...? NHG 5

wound /wuːnd/ Wunde p. 42, 1

wrist /rɪst/ Handgelenk p. 42, 1

(to) **write** *(irr)* /raɪt/ schreiben NHG 5

(to) **write down** *(irr)* /ˌraɪt ˈdaʊn/ aufschreiben NHG 5

writing /ˈraɪtɪŋ/ Schrift; Schreiben p. 114, 2

written /ˈrɪtn/ schriftlich NHG 6

wrong /rɒŋ/ falsch NHG 6

(to) **be wrong** *(irr)* /ˌbiː ˈrɒŋ/ im Unrecht sein p. 98, 12

(to) **be wrong (with)** *(irr)* /ˌbiː ˈrɒŋ wɪθ/ nicht in Ordnung sein (mit) p. 48, 8

What's wrong? *(informal)* /ˌwɒts ˈrɒŋ/ Was ist los? p. 90, 2

X

X-ray /ˈeksreɪ/ Röntgenbild p. 46, 5

(to) **take an X-ray** *(irr)* /ˌteɪk ən ˈeksreɪ/ eine Röntgenaufnahme machen p. 42, 1

X-ray glasses *(pl)* /ˈeksreɪ ˌglɑːsɪz/ *Röntgenbrille* p. 111, 11

Y

year /jɪə/ Jahr NHG 5; Schuljahr; Klasse NHG 6

yellow /ˈjeləʊ/ gelb NHG 5

yes /jes/ ja NHG 5

yesterday /ˈjestədeɪ/ gestern NHG 6

yet /jet/ schon; noch p. 46, 5

Yorkshire pudding /ˌjɔːkʃə ˈpʊdɪŋ/ *britische gebackene Beilage* p. 8, 2

you /juː/ du; dich; dir; man; ihr; euch; Sie; Ihnen NHG 5

young /jʌŋ/ jung NHG 6

your /jɔː/ dein(e); euer/eure; Ihr(e) NHG 5

yours /jɔːz/ deine(r, s); eure(r, s); Ihre(r, s) NHG 6

yours sincerely /ˌjɔːz sɪnˈsɪəli/ mit freundlichen Grüßen *(am Ende eines formellen Briefes)* NHG 6

yourself /jɔːˈself/ dir, dich; sich NHG 5

youth club /ˈjuːθ ˌklʌb/ Jugendklub NHG 6

yummy *(informal)* /ˈjʌmi/ lecker p. 8, 1

Z

zero waste /ˌzɪərəʊ ˈweɪst/ verpackungsfrei p. 73, 9

zip /zɪp/ Reißverschluss p. 108, 7

Names

First names

Agata *(f.)* /əˈgɑːtə/
Alex *(m., f.)* /ˈæliks/
Alexander *(m.)*
  /ˌælɪɡˈzɑːndə/
Amira *(f.)* /əˈmiːrə/
Andy *(m., f.)* /ˈændi/
Anna *(f.)* /ˈænə/
Arthur *(m.)* /ˈɑːθə/
Ava *(f.)* /ˈeɪvə/
Ayaz *(m.)* /ˈaɪəz/
Becky *(f.)* /ˈbeki/
Ben *(m.)* /ben/
Benjamin *(m.)*
  /ˈbendʒəmɪn/
Billie *(m., f.)* /ˈbɪli/
Bob *(m., f.)* /bɒb/
Cathy *(f.)* /ˈkæθi/
Chloe *(f.)* /ˈkləʊi/
Chris *(m., f.)* /krɪs/
Claire *(f.)* /kleə/
Dan *(m.)* /dæn/
Daniel *(m.)* /ˈdænjəl/
Delia *(f.)* /ˈdiːliə/
Demir *(m.)* /deˈmɪə/
Ector *(m.)* /ˈektə/
Edward *(m.)* /ˈedwəd/
Edyta *(f.)* /əˈdiːtə/
Ellie *(f.)* /ˈeli/
Emily *(f.)* /ˈeməli/
Emma *(f.)* /ˈemə/
Eric *(m.)* /ˈerɪk/
Erika *(f.)* /ˈerɪkə/
Faisal *(m.)* /ˈfaɪsl/
Filip *(m.)* /ˈfɪlɪp/
Fiona *(f.)* /fiˈəʊnə/
Gemma *(f.)* /ˈdʒemə/
George *(m.)* /dʒɔːdʒ/
Harry *(m., f.)* /ˈhæri/
Harvey *(m.)* /ˈhɑːvi/
Jack *(m.)* /dʒæk/
Jacob *(m.)* /ˈdʒeɪkəb/
Jada *(f.)* /ˈdʒeɪdə/
James *(m.)* /dʒeɪmz/
Jamie *(m.)* /ˈdʒeɪmi/
Jan *(m., f.)* /dʒæn, jæn, jɑːn/
Jason *(m.)* /ˈdʒeɪsn/
Jemima *(f.)* /dʒɪˈmaɪmə/

Jenna *(f.)* /ˈdʒenə/
Jill *(f.)* /dʒɪl/
Joe *(m., f.)* /dʒəʊ/
John *(m.)* /dʒɒn/
Joshua *(m.)* /ˈdʒɒʃjuə/
Juan *(m.)* /wɑːn/
Karim *(m.)* /kəˈriːm/
Katie *(f.)* /ˈkeɪti/
Kay *(m., f.)* /keɪ/
Kristin *(f.)* /krɪˈstiːn/
Laura *(f.)* /ˈlɔːrə/
Leon *(m.)* /ˈliːən/
Leona *(f.)* /liˈəʊnə/
Levi *(m.)* /ˈliːvaɪ/
Lily *(f.)* /ˈlɪli/
Linda *(f.)* /ˈlɪndə/
Logie *(m.)* /ˈləʊgi/
Louise *(f.)* /luˈiːz/
Lucy *(f.)* /ˈluːsi/
Makena *(f.)* /məˈkiːnə/
Margo *(f.)* /ˈmɑːgəʊ/
Marianne *(f.)* /ˌmæriˈæn/
Martin *(m.)* /ˈmɑːtɪn/
Matilda *(f.)* /məˈtɪldə/
Matt *(m.)* /mæt/
Matthew *(m.)* /ˈmæθjuː/
Merlin *(m.)* /ˈmɜːlɪn/
Mia *(f.)* /ˈmiːə/
Michael *(m.)* /ˈmaɪkl/
Michelle *(f.)* /miːˈʃel/
Mira *(f.)* /ˈmaɪrə/
Nils *(m.)* /nɪlz/
Noah *(m.)* /ˈnəʊə/
Oliver *(m.)* /ˈɒlɪvə/
Olivia *(f.)* /əˈlɪviə/
Ollie *(m.)* /ˈɒli/
Paolo *(m.)* /pəˈəʊləʊ/
Paul *(m.)* /pɔːl/
Pavel *(m.)* /ˈpɑːvl/
Peter *(m.)* /ˈpiːtə/
Phil *(m.)* /fɪl/
Radek *(m.)* /ˈrɑːdek/
Raymond *(m.)* /ˈreɪmənd/
Richard *(m.)* /ˈrɪtʃəd/
Robert *(m.)* /ˈrɒbət/
Ryan *(m.)* /ˈraɪən/
Sally *(f.)* /ˈsæli/
Sam *(m., f.)* /sæm/
Sami *(m.)* /ˈsæmi/

Sarah *(f.)* /ˈseərə/
Sebastian *(m.)*
  /səˈbæstiən/
Sheree *(f.)* /ʃəˈriː/
Sophie *(f.)* /ˈsəʊfi/
Stephen *(m.)* /ˈstiːvn/
Steven *(m.)* /ˈstiːvn/
Suzy *(f.)* /ˈsuːzi/
Tarek *(m.)* /ˈtærɪk/
Thomas *(m.)* /ˈtɒməs/
Tim *(m.)* /tɪm/
Toby *(m.)* /ˈtəʊbi/
Tom *(m.)* /tɒm/
Tony *(m., f.)* /ˈtəʊni/
Uther *(m.)* /ˈjuːθə/
William *(m.)* /ˈwɪljəm/
Zara *(f.)* /ˈzɑːrə/

Families

Addis /ˈædɪs/
Adil /əˈdiːl/
Baird /beəd/
Barlow /ˈbɑːləʊ/
Bell /bel/
Bohlin /ˈbəːlɪn/
Carter /ˈkɑːtə/
Cooper /ˈkuːpə/
Dill /dɪl/
Dunkerley /ˈdʌŋkərli/
Durand /ˈdʌrənd/
Eilish /ˈaɪlɪʃ/
Fisher /ˈfɪʃə/
Fleming /ˈflemɪŋ/
Graham /ˈgreɪəm/
Hamilton /ˈhæmltən/
Hawk /hɔːk/
Hawking /ˈhɔːkɪŋ/
Hill /hɪl/
Kellog /ˈkelɒg/
Kershaw /ˈkɜːʃɔː/
Kogan /ˈkəʊgən/
Miller /ˈmɪlə/
Norris /ˈnɒrɪs/
Patel /pəˈtel/
Peters /ˈpiːtəz/
Rogers /ˈrɒdʒəz/
Rosen /ˈrəʊzn/
Spratt /spræt/

Stephenson /ˈstiːvnsən/
Strauss /straʊs/
Thomas /ˈtɒməs/
Tomlinson /ˈtɒmlɪnsən/
Trevithick /ˈtrevɪθɪk/
Watson /ˈwɒtsn/
Watt /wɒt/
Weston /ˈwestən/
Zephaniah /ˌzefəˈnaɪə/

Other names

Adventuring Andy
  /ədˌventʃərɪŋˈændi/
American football
  /əˌmerɪkən ˈfʊtˌbɔːl/
Arundel Castle
  /ˈærəndl kɑːsl/
Ayaz London /ˌaɪəzˈlʌndən/
bangers and mash
  /ˌbæŋəz_ən ˈmæʃ/
Barbican /ˈbɑːbɪkən/
Barley Hall /ˌbɑːli ˈhɔːl/
bhaji /ˈbɑːdʒi/
The Black Horse
  /ðə ˌblæk ˈhɔːs/
bubble and squeak
  /ˌbʌbl_ən ˈskwiːk/
burdock /ˈbɜːdɒk/
(chicken) tikka (masala),
  (chicken) tikka
  /ˌtʃɪkɪn ˌtiːkə məˈsɑːlə,
  ˌtʃɪkɪn ˈtiːkə/
Dim Sum /ˌdɪm ˈsʌm/
Diwali /dɪˈwɑːli/
Double /ˈdʌbl/
East India Company
  /ˌiːstˌɪndiə ˈkʌmpni/
Farmhouse
  /ˈfɑːmˌhaʊs/
Feastival /ˈfiːstɪvl/
Foodlover /ˈfuːdˌlʌvə/
Glastonbury Abbey
  /ˌglæstənbəriˈæbi/
Glastonbury Tor
  /ˌglæstənbəri ˈtɔː/
The Highland Games
  /ðə ˈhaɪlənd geɪmz/
Hindi /ˈhɪndi/

hippo roller /'hɪpəʊ ˌrəʊlə/
Holi /'hɒli/
Holland Park /ˌhɒlənd 'pɑːk/
Hyde Park /ˌhaɪd 'pɑːk/
Isabel3589 /ˌɪzəbel ˌθriː
 faɪv_eɪt 'naɪn/
Jorvik /'jɔː vɪk/
kari /'kɑːri/
kebab /kɪ'bæb/
The King's Head /ðə ˌkɪŋz
 'hed/
kingfisher /'kɪŋˌfɪʃə/
korma /'kɔːmə/
Lahmacun /ˌlɑːmə'dʒuːn/
lassi /'læsi/
The London Eye
 /ðə ˌlʌndən_'aɪ/
Lonelygirl /'ləʊnliˈgɜːl/
Lyceum Theatre /laɪˌsiːəm
 'θɪətə/
Manchester Cathedral
 /ˌmæntʃɪstə kə'θiːdrəl/
Margherita /ˌmɑːgə'riːtə/
masala /mə'sɑːlə/
The Museum of London
 /ðə mjuːˌziːəm_əv 'lʌndən/
naan /nɑːn/
Nazi /'nɑːtsi/
Notting Hill /ˌnɒtɪŋ 'hɪl/
Notting Hill Carnival
 /ˌnɒtɪŋ hɪl 'kɑːnɪvl/
The Olympics (pl)
 /ðɪ_ə'lɪmpɪks/
one-pot pasta
 /ˌwʌnˌpɒt 'pæstə/
The Palace of India
 /ðə ˌpæləs_əv_'ɪndiə/
palak paneer
 /ˌpɑːlək pə'nɪə/
The Paralympic
 Games (pl)
 /ðə ˌpærəlɪmpɪkˈgeɪmz/
The Paralympics (pl)
 /ðə ˌpærə'lɪmpɪks/
Pizza Extra /ˌpiːtsə_'ekstrə/
poppadom /'pɒpədəm/
Portobello Market
 /ˌpɔːtəˌbeləʊ 'mɑːkɪt/
Portobello Road
 /ˌpɔːtəˌbeləʊ 'rəʊd/
Preppy Rappy
 /ˌprepi 'ræpi/

reggae /'regeɪ/
The Royal Air Force
 /ðə ˌrɔɪəl_'eə fɔːs/
samosa /sə'məʊsə/
The Science and Industry
 Museum
 / ðə ˌsaɪəns_ən_'ɪndəstri
 mjuːˌziːəm/
The Science Museum
 /ðə 'saɪəns mjuːˌziːəm/
Shakshuka /ʃək'ʃuːkə/
sitting volleyball
 /ˌsɪtɪŋ 'vɒlibɔːl/
Skatepark Project
 /'skeɪtpɑːk ˌprɒdʒekt/
spaghetti bolognese
 /spəˌgeti 'bɒləˌneɪz/
Spinning Jenny
 /ˌspɪnɪŋ 'dʒeni/
St James /sənt 'dʒeɪmz/
Sunnyday /ˌsʌni'deɪ/
Sushi Blue /ˌsuːʃi 'bluː/
The Taj Mahal
 /ðə ˌtɑːdʒ mə'hɑːl/
Tamil /'tæməl/
Textiles Gallery
 /'tekstaɪlz ˌgæləri/
Tiramisu /ˌtɪrəmi'suː/
toad in the hole
 /ˌtəʊd_ɪn ðə 'həʊl/
Tokyo /'təʊkiəʊ/
Trouble /'trʌbl/
Uther Pendragon
 /ˌjuːθə pen'drægən/
Velcro® /'velkrəʊ/
Viking Lodge
 /'vaɪkɪŋ lɒdʒ/
vindaloo /ˌvɪndə'luː/
Wonton /ˌwɒn'tɒn/
Yorkshire pudding
 /jɔːkʃə 'pʊdɪŋ/

Geographical Names

Asia /'eɪʒə/
Avalon /'ævəlɒn/
Bangladesh /ˌbæŋglə'deʃ/
Battersea /'bætəsi/
Bayswater /'beɪzˌwɔːtə/
Berlin /bɜː'lɪn/
Braemar /ˌbreɪ'mɑː/
Brighton /'braɪtn/

Bristol /'brɪstl/
Britain /'brɪtn/
Brixton /'brɪkstən/
China /'tʃaɪnə/
Chinatown /'tʃaɪnəˌtaʊn/
the Cotswolds
 /ðə 'kɒtswəʊldz/
Edinburgh /'edɪnbərə/
Egypt /'iːdʒɪpt/
Elephant & Castle
 /ˌelɪfənt_ən 'kɑːsl/
England /'ɪŋglənd/
Exeter /'eksɪtə/
Exhibition Road
 /ˌeksɪ'bɪʃn rəʊd/
Finsbury Park
 /'fɪnzbəri pɑːk/
Germany /'dʒɜːməni/
Ghana /'gɑːnə/
Glastonbury
 /'glæstənbəri/
Golders Green /ˌgəʊldəz
 'griːn/
Great Britain /ˌgreɪt 'brɪtn/
Greece /griːs/
Hammersmith
 /'hæməsmɪθ/
Highland /'haɪlənd/
India /'ɪndiə/
Isle of Wight /ˌaɪl_əv 'waɪt/
Israel /'ɪzreɪl/
Italy /'ɪtəli/
Japan /dʒə'pæn/
Korea /kə'rɪə/
Lebanon /'lebənən/
Leeds /liːdz/
Liverpool /'lɪvəpuːl/
London /'lʌndən/
Los Angeles
 /lɒs_'ændʒəliːz/
Manchester /'mæntʃɪstə/
Mars /mɑːz/
Merton /'mɜːtn/
Morocco /mə'rɒkəʊ/
New Delhi /ˌnjuː 'deli/
North Africa /ˌnɔːθ_'æfrɪkə/
Pakistan /ˌpɑːkɪ'stɑːn/
Poland /'pəʊlənd/
Scotland /'skɒtlənd/
South India /ˌsaʊθ_'ɪndiə/
South Kensington
 /ˌsaʊθ 'kenzɪŋtən/

Southall /'saʊθɔːl/
Spain /speɪn/
Stoke-on-Trent
 /ˌstəʊk_ɒn 'trent/
Sweden /'swiːdn/
Trinidad /'trɪnɪdæd/
Turkey /'tɜːki/
the UK (= United
 Kingdom) /ðə ˌjuː 'keɪ,
 juːˌnaɪtɪd 'kɪŋdəm/
the USA (= United States
 of America)
 /ðə ˌjuː es_'eɪ, juːˌnaɪtɪd
 ˌsteɪts_əv_ə'merɪkə/
Wales /weɪlz/
York /jɔːk/

Numbers

0	oh, zero, nil /əʊ, ˈzɪərəʊ, nɪl/		1st	**first** /fɜːst/
1	one /wʌn/		2nd	**second** /ˈsekənd/
2	two /tuː/		3rd	**third** /θɜːd/
3	three /θriː/		4th	fourth /fɔːθ/
4	four /fɔː/		5th	**fif**th /fɪfθ/
5	five /faɪv/		6th	sixth /sɪksθ/
6	six /sɪks/		7th	seventh /sevnθ/
7	seven /sevn/		8th	**eigh**th /eɪtθ/
8	eight /eɪt/		9th	**nin**th /naɪnθ/
9	nine /naɪn/		10th	tenth /tenθ/
10	ten /ten/		11th	eleventh /ɪˈlevnθ/
11	eleven /ɪˈlevn/		12th	**twelf**th /twelfθ/
12	twelve /twelv/		13th	thirteenth /ˌθɜːˈtiːnθ/
13	**thir**teen /ˌθɜːˈtiːn/		19th	nineteenth /ˌnaɪnˈtiːnθ/
14	fourteen /ˌfɔːˈtiːn		20th	twent**ie**th /ˈtwentiəθ/
15	**fif**teen /ˌfɪfˈtiːn/			
16	sixteen /ˌsɪksˈtiːn/		21st	twenty-first /ˌtwentiˈfɜːst/
17	seventeen /ˌsevnˈtiːn/		22nd	twenty-second /ˌtwentiˈsekənd/
18	**eigh**teen /eɪˈtiːn/		23rd	twenty-third /ˌtwentiˈθɜːd/
19	nineteen /ˌnaɪnˈtiːn/			
20	**twen**ty /ˈtwenti/		30th	thirt**ie**th /ˈθɜːtiəθ/
			40th	fort**ie**th /ˈfɔːtiəθ/
21	twenty-one /ˌtwentiˈwʌn/		50th	fift**ie**th /ˈfɪftiəθ/
30	**thir**ty /ˈθɜːti/		60th	sixt**ie**th /ˈsɪkstiəθ/
33	thirty-three /ˌθɜːtiˈθriː/		70th	sevent**ie**th /ˈsevntiəθ/
40	**for**ty /ˈfɔːti/		80th	eight**ie**th /ˈeɪtiəθ/
45	forty-five /ˌfɔːtiˈfaɪv/		90th	ninet**ie**th /ˈnaɪntiəθ/
50	**fif**ty /ˈfɪfti/		100th	hundredth /ˈhʌndrədθ/
56	fifty-six /ˌfɪftiˈsɪks/			
60	sixty /ˈsɪksti/			
67	sixty-seven /ˌsɪkstiˈsevn/			
70	seventy /ˈsevnti/			
78	seventy-eight /ˌsevntiˈeɪt/			
80	**eigh**ty /ˈeɪti/			
89	eighty-nine /ˌeɪtiˈnaɪn/			
90	ninety /ˈnaɪnti/			

> Daten schreibst du im britischen
>   Englisch so:
>   1 August, 2 January, 5 November
>   oder so: 1st / 1ˢᵗ August,
>   2nd / 2ⁿᵈ January, 5th / 5ᵗʰ November

100	a/one hundred /ə/wʌn ˈhʌndrəd/
101	one hundred and one /wʌn ˌhʌndrəd ən ˈwʌn/
200	two hundred /tuː ˈhʌndrəd/
1,000	one thousand /ə/wʌn ˈθaʊznd/
2,000	two thousand /tuː ˈθaʊznd/

> Jahreszahlen sprichst du so aus:
> 1939 nineteen thirty-nine
> 1951 nineteen fifty-one
> 2010 two thousand and ten

> Bei Zahlen mit vier oder mehr Ziffern
>   werden, falls erforderlich, im
>   Englischen Kommata verwendet,
>   keine Punkte!

$\frac{1}{2}$	a / one half /ə/wʌn ˈhaːf/
$\frac{1}{3}$	a / one third /ə/wʌn ˈθɜːd/
$\frac{1}{4}$	a / one quarter /ə/wʌn ˈkwɔːtə/
$\frac{1}{8}$	a / one eighth /ə/wʌn ˈeɪtθ/
$\frac{3}{4}$	three quarters /θriː ˈkwɔːtəz/

Irregular verbs

infinitive	simple past	past participle	German
(to) be /biː/	was/were /wɒz/wɜː/	been /biːn/	sein
(to) become /bɪˈkʌm/	became /bɪˈkeɪm/	become /bɪˈkʌm/	werden
(to) begin /bɪˈgɪn/	began /bɪˈgæn/	begun /bɪˈgʌn/	anfangen; beginnen
(to) bleed /bliːd/	bled /bled/	bled /bled/	bluten
(to) break /breɪk/	broke /brəʊk/	broken /ˈbrəʊkən/	(zer)brechen; kaputt machen
(to) bring /brɪŋ/	brought /brɔːt/	brought /brɔːt/	mitbringen
(to) build /bɪld/	built /bɪlt/	built /bɪlt/	bauen
(to) buy /baɪ/	bought /bɔːt/	bought /bɔːt/	kaufen
(to) catch /kætʃ/	caught /kɔːt/	caught /kɔːt/	fangen
(to) choose /tʃuːz/	chose /tʃəʊz/	chosen /ˈtʃəʊzn/	wählen; sich entscheiden
(to) come /kʌm/	came /keɪm/	come /kʌm/	kommen
(to) cost /kɒst/	cost /kɒst/	cost /kɒst/	kosten
(to) cut /kʌt/	cut /kʌt/	cut /kʌt/	schneiden
(to) deal with /ˈdiːl wɪð/	dealt with /ˈdelt wɪð/	dealt with /ˈdelt wɪð/	sich befassen mit, umgehen mit
(to) do /duː/	did /dɪd/	done /dʌn/	machen; tun
(to) draw /drɔː/	drew /druː/	drawn /drɔːn/	zeichnen
(to) drink /drɪŋk/	drank /dræŋk/	drunk /drʌŋk/	trinken
(to) drive /draɪv/	drove /drəʊv/	driven /ˈdrɪvn/	fahren
(to) eat /iːt/	ate /et/eɪt/	eaten /ˈiːtn/	essen
(to) fall /fɔːl/	fell /fel/	fallen /ˈfɔːlən/	fallen
(to) feed /fiːd/	fed /fed/	fed /fed/	füttern
(to) feel /fiːl/	felt /felt/	felt /felt/	(sich) fühlen
(to) fight /faɪt/	fought /fɔːt/	fought /fɔːt/	bekämpfen; ankämpfen gegen
(to) find /faɪnd/	found /faʊnd/	found /faʊnd/	finden
(to) fly /flaɪ/	flew /fluː/	flown /fləʊn/	fliegen
(to) forget /fəˈget/	forgot /fəˈgɒt/	forgotten /fəˈgɒtən/	vergessen
(to) get /get/	got /gɒt/	got /gɒt/	bekommen; holen; kaufen; kommen, gelangen; werden; bringen
(to) give /gɪv/	gave /geɪv/	given /ˈgɪvn/	geben; angeben, mitteilen
(to) go /gəʊ/	went /went/	gone /gɒn/	gehen; fahren
(to) grow /grəʊ/	grew /gruː/	grown /grəʊn/	wachsen; anbauen
(to) hang (up) /ˌhæŋˈʌp/	hung (up) /ˌhʌŋˈʌp/	hung (up) /ˌhʌŋˈʌp/	hängen, aufhängen
(to) have /hæv/	had /hæd/	had /hæd/	haben; essen; trinken
(to) hear /hɪə/	heard /hɜːd/	heard /hɜːd/	hören
(to) hide /haɪd/	hid /hɪd/	hidden /ˈhɪdn/	(sich) verstecken
(to) hit /hɪt/	hit /hɪt/	hit /hɪt/	schlagen; stoßen gegen
(to) hold /həʊld/	held /held/	held /held/	(fest)halten
(to) hurt /hɜːt/	hurt /hɜːt/	hurt /hɜːt/	wehtun, schmerzen; verletzen

Irregular verbs

infinitive	simple past	past participle	German
(to) keep /kiːp/	kept /kept/	kept /kept/	aufbewahren; (be)halten
(to) know /nəʊ/	knew /njuː/	known /nəʊn/	wissen; kennen
(to) learn /lɜːn/	learnt/learned /lɜːnt/lɜːnd/	learnt/learned /lɜːnt/lɜːnd/	lernen
(to) leave /liːv/	left /left/	left /left/	weggehen; verlassen, abfahren; (übrig) lassen; zurücklassen; hinterlassen
(to) let /let/	let /let/	let /let/	lassen
(to) light /laɪt/	lit /lɪt/	lit /lɪt/	anzünden
(to) lose /luːz/	lost /lɒst/	lost /lɒst/	verlieren
(to) make /meɪk/	made /meɪd/	made /meɪd/	machen
(to) mean /miːn/	meant /ment/	meant /ment/	meinen; bedeuten
(to) meet /miːt/	met /met/	met /met/	(sich) treffen; kennenlernen
(to) pay /peɪ/	paid /peɪd/	paid /peɪd/	(be)zahlen
(to) prove /pruːv/	proved /pruːvd/	proved/proven /pruːvd/ˈpruːvn/	beweisen
(to) put /pʊt/	put /pʊt/	put /pʊt/	setzen; stellen; legen
(to) read /riːd/	read /red/	read /red/	lesen
(to) rewrite /ˌriːˈraɪt/	rewrote /ˌriːˈrəʊt/	rewritten /ˌriːˈrɪtn/	überarbeiten, umschreiben
(to) ride /raɪd/	rode /rəʊd/	ridden /ˈrɪdn/	fahren; reiten
(to) run /rʌn/	ran /ræn/	run /rʌn/	laufen; rennen; leiten, betreiben
(to) say /seɪ/	said /sed/	said /sed/	sagen
(to) see /siː/	saw /sɔː/	seen /siːn/	sehen; empfangen, drannehmen
(to) sell /sel/	sold /səʊld/	sold /səʊld/	verkaufen
(to) send /send/	sent /sent/	sent /sent/	schicken
(to) shine /ʃaɪn/	shone /ʃɒn/	shone /ʃɒn/	scheinen
(to) shoot /ʃuːt/	shot /ʃɒt/	shot /ʃɒt/	schießen
(to) show /ʃəʊ/	showed /ʃəʊd/	shown /ʃəʊn/	zeigen
(to) sing /sɪŋ/	sang /sæŋ/	sung /sʌŋ/	singen
(to) sit /sɪt/	sat /sæt/	sat /sæt/	sitzen
(to) sit down /ˌsɪtˈdaʊn/	sat down /ˌsætˈdaʊn/	sat down /ˌsætˈdaʊn/	sich hinsetzen
(to) sleep /sliːp/	slept /slept/	slept /slept/	schlafen
(to) speak /spiːk/	spoke /spəʊk/	spoken /ˈspəʊkən/	reden; sprechen
(to) spell /spel/	spelt/spelled /spelt/speld/	spelt/spelled /spelt/speld/	buchstabieren
(to) spend /spend/	spent /spent/	spent /spent/	ausgeben (Geld); verbringen (Zeit)
(to) spin /spɪn/	spun/span /spʌn/spæn/	spun /spʌn/	spinnen; drehen
(to) stand /stænd/	stood /stʊd/	stood /stʊd/	stehen
(to) steal /stiːl/	stole /stəʊl/	stolen /ˈstəʊlən/	stehlen
(to) stick /stɪk/	stuck /stʌk/	stuck /stʌk/	festhängen
(to) swim /swɪm/	swam /swæm/	swum /swʌm/	schwimmen

Irregular verbs

infinitive	simple past	past participle	German
(to) take /teɪk/	took /tʊk/	taken /'teɪkən/	nehmen; bringen; benötigen; brauchen; dauern
(to) teach /tiːtʃ/	taught /tɔːt/	taught /tɔːt/	unterrichten
(to) tell /tel/	told /təʊld/	told /təʊld/	erzählen
(to) think /θɪŋk/	thought /θɔːt/	thought /θɔːt/	denken; glauben
(to) throw /θrəʊ/	threw /θruː/	thrown /θrəʊn/	werfen
(to) understand /ˌʌndəˈstænd/	understood /ˌʌndəˈstʊd/	understood /ˌʌndəˈstʊd/	verstehen
(to) wake up /ˌweɪkˈʌp/	woke up /ˌwəʊkˈʌp/	woken up /ˌwəʊkənˈʌp/	aufwachen; aufwecken
(to) wear /weə/	wore /wɔː/	worn /wɔːn/	tragen (Kleidung)
(to) win /wɪn/	won /wʌn/	won /wʌn/	gewinnen
(to) write /raɪt/	wrote /rəʊt/	written /'rɪtn/	schreiben

Tipp:

Einige Verben bilden das **simple past** und das **past participle** nach einem ähnlichen Muster. Wenn du sie dir in Gruppen sortierst, kannst du dir die Formen vielleicht besser merken.
Findest du weitere Beispiele für diese Gruppen oder andere Gruppen?

bring	brought	brought	mitbringen
buy	bought	bought	kaufen
catch	caught	caught	fangen
fight	fought	fought	bekämpfen
think	thought	thought	denken; glauben
sing	sang	sung	singen
swim	swam	swum	schwimmen
draw	drew	drawn	zeichnen
fly	flew	flown	fliegen
grow	grew	grown	wachsen
know	knew	known	kennen; wissen
throw	threw	thrown	werfen
cost	cost	cost	kosten
cut	cut	cut	schneiden
hit	hit	hit	schlagen
let	let	let	lassen
put	put	put	legen, setzen, stellen

Bildquellen

|Alamy Stock Photo, Abingdon/Oxfordshire: agefotostock 71.2; Allsorts Stock Photo 108.1; Alternative Occasions 67.5; Ammentorp Photography 80.1; Art Directors & TRIP 92.3; Baker, Darren 80.2; Baldesare, Paul 79.2; Ballard, Laura Clay 62.5; Barton, William 83.2; BasPhoto 103.1; Cavan Images 67.3; Chilvers, Clive 70.2; Classic Picture Library 109.1; Dack, Simon 155.1; Daemmrich, Bob 54.1, 54.2, 54.3; Dale, Veryan 79.4; David R. Frazier Photolibrary, Inc. 59.1; Doering, Olaf 119.6; Doyle, Paul 71.1; E.J.Westmacott 55.2; Farrell, Wayne 70.1; Fernandez, Antonio Guillem 79.1; Gilbert, Jeff 55.3; Gustafsson, Jeppe 63.1; Hoare, Jeremy 83.4; Hrda, Lucia 72.5; Huang, I-Wei 59.5; Image Source 92.2; Imagebroker 65.1; imageBROKER 65.2; Janine Wiedel Photolibrary 79.3; John Freeman 111.1; Karki, Hari 19.3; Liasi, Theodore 38.1; Lloyd 78.1; Lordprice Collection 108.2; Lyons, David 72.3; MBI 31.2; Muller, Cora 59.2; Noir, Nathaniel 19.1; PA Images 66.1, 67.2, 67.6; Pearson, David 73.1; Pound, Philip 72.1; PURPLE MARBLES YORK 1 66.2; Reinholds, Aigars 62.1; Richardson, Jason 72.4; Rivera M, Carlos J 18.1; robertharding 30.4; Roger Cracknell 01/classic 72.2; Saxena, Ashok 83.1; Spitzbart, Wolfgang 75.2; Tack, Jochen 75.1; Torontonian 15.2; True Images 119.1; Vorobiev, Mikhail 62.4; Walmsley, Alan 67.1, 67.4; WENN Rights Ltd 83.3; Whitefoot, Tracey 78.2; Yarvin World Journeys 62.2; YAY Media AS 59.7. |Alamy Stock Photo (RMB), Abingdon/Oxfordshire: anther Media GmbH 62.3; Art Directors & TRIP 7.3; Camandona, Fabio 31.1; Finizio, Roberto 149.1; MacDonald, Dennis 35.1; Picture Partners 127.5; Studioshots 169.2; World History Archive 106.1; © Mike Booth 104.10. |Amortegui, Miguel, Brighton: 15.1, 25.1, 38.2, 48.6, 62.6, 96.1, 110.2. |Arrandale, Denise, Neumünster: 49.2. |Courtesy of Kopernik, kopernik.info: 130.1, 133.1, 136.1. |Fast, Lisa, Hannover: 13.1, 59.3, 120.1, 166.1. |fotolia.com, New York: davidevison 146.1; denis_vermenko 7.5; ExQuisine 20.1; fergregory 78.3; Gennadiy Poznyakov 148.2; Gorilla 34.2; RRF 104.8; Shaiith 20.2; Steiner, C. 20.4; Stocksnapper 127.2. |Getty Images, München: AFP 66.3; Stringer 40.1; Wheeler, Nik 55.1. |Getty Images (RF), München: fstop123 92.1; Mcbride, Joe 39.1. |Hardy, Helen, Braunschweig: 120.3. |Interfoto, München: Delimont, Danita/Merrill, John & Lisa 36.1. |iStockphoto.com, Calgary: aggiebilly Titel; Arnese, Claudio 59.4; Circle Creative Studio 81.1; coffeekai 31.3; Daisy-Daisy 31.4; dejankrsmanovic 65.3; Elizaquibel, Jorge 81.2; HAYKIRDI 33.1; Iaroshenko, Maryna 9.2; kissesfromholland 104.7; mgstudyo 92.4; Okea 112.1; perrygerenday 63.3; Philary 18.2; Ridofranz 31.5; serikbaib 59.9; SolStock 7.1; undefined undefined 103.3; visual7 147.1; Wirestock 168.2; Yobro10 36.2; © travellinglight 14.1, 30.3. |mauritius images GmbH, Mittenwald: Westend61 /Fischinger, Mareen 7.4. |Nordzieke, Paula: 89.1, 89.2, 89.3, 89.4, 89.5, 89.6. |OKAPIA KG - Michael Grzimek & Co., Frankfurt/M.: BIOS/Labat, Jean-Michel 118.1; Groß 127.4; imagebroker/Robiller, Franz Christoph 127.3; Vock, Karl Gottfried 127.1. |PantherMedia GmbH (panthermedia.net), München: Popov, Andriy 49.1, 49.3; Schmid, Christophe 154.1. |Picture-Alliance GmbH, Frankfurt a.M.: Bildagentur-online 8.2; Schönherr, Maximilian 104.9; ZB/Thieme, Wolfgang 110.1. |Science Museum Group © The Board of Trustees of the Science Museum: Boer War rations, gravy soup. 1965-239/6/2/5Science Museum Group Collection Online. Accessed September 20, 2023. https , Lizenz Creative Commons Zero 109.2. |Shutterstock.com, New York: Agarianna76 139.1, 142.1, 145.1; AJR_photo 33.3; auremar 169.1; chrisdorney 84.1; DenPhotos 103.4; Es sarawuth 103.2; Esin, Deniz 9.1; Gingell, Ben 36.3; gkrphoto 19.2; Kumar Barui, Tutun 59.8; Marius GODOI 63.2; Monkey Business Images 7.2; muzsy 34.1; Rehorst, Bernd 59.6; yackers1 8.3. |stock.adobe.com, Dublin: Alvaro 8.1; Aphotostudio 148.3; asife 37.1; cougarsan 48.5; denisgorelkin 119.2, 119.3, 119.4, 119.5; guteksk7 120.2; Iakov Kalinin 82.1; mdurson 33.2; nikolaydonetsk 8.4; peregrinus 48.3; Richardt, Dagmar 118.2; Schwier, Christian 168.1; sergojpg 148.1; sinhyu 109.3; somegirl 30.1; Sughra 48.1, 48.2; UJac 20.3; valvectors 48.4; victoria p. 30.2. |Todd, Gary, Henan: Anyang-Museum 118.3. |Visuelle Lebensfreude - Bodem + Sötebier GbR, Hannover: 11.1, 11.2, 11.3, 11.4, 11.5, 104.1, 104.2, 104.3, 104.4, 104.5, 104.6.

Textquellen

14 „Vegan Steven" Benjamin Zephaniah, „The little book of vegan poems – Explicit vegan lyrics", AK Press, Edinburgh, 2002.
39 „Choose your sports", Martin Dejnicki, Toronto, Canada. 25.7.2022: https://wordswan.com/author/martin-dejnicki/sports-poems
39 „Skateboarding", Margo L. Dill, St. Louis, Missouri, USA. 26.7.2022: https://www.scrapbook.com/poems/cat/38.html
39 „What Can You Do With a Football?", James Carter, „Journey to The Centre Of My Brain", London, Macmillan Children's Books. 2012.
114 „On the Move Again", „On the Move: Poems About Migration" by Michael Rosen with drawings by Quentin Blake, Walker Books Ltd., London, 2020.

North Sea

Shetland
Islands

Orkney
Islands

Aberdeen

Balmoral

Tweed

Scotland

▲ Ben Nevis
  1344 m

Edinburgh

Lewis

Glasgow

Skye

Outer
Hebrides

Atlantic Ocean